IARIA Congress 2025

The 2025 IARIA Annual Congress on Frontiers in Science, Technology, Services, and Applications

July 6th– 10th, 2025

Venice, Italy

IARIA Congress 2025 Editors

Constantine Kotropoulos, Aristotle University of Thessaloniki, Greece

Matthias Harter, Hochschule RheinMain - University of Applied Sciences, Germany

Andre Schneider de Oliveira, UTFPR, Brazil

Printed from e-media with permission by:

Curran Associates, Inc.
57 Morehouse Lane
Red Hook, NY 12571

Some format issues inherent in the e-media version may also appear in this print version.

International Academy, Research, and Industry Association (IARIA)
412 Derby Way
Wilmington, DE 19810

Phone: (408) 893-6407
Fax: (408) 527-6351

petre@iaria.org

Additional copies of this publication are available from:

Curran Associates, Inc.
57 Morehouse Lane
Red Hook, NY 12571 USA
Phone: 845-758-0400
Fax: 845-758-2633
Email: curran@proceedings.com
Web: www.proceedings.com

IARIA Congress 2025

Forward

The 2025 IARIA Annual Congress on Frontiers in Science, Technology, Services, and Applications (IARIA Congress 2025), held between July 6th, 2025, and July 10th, 2025, in Venice, Italy, continued a series of international events keeping pace with the achievements and challenges our society is facing in science, technologies, services, and applications.

The annual event was a multidomain assembly of scientists, specialists, and decision makers from all economical, educational, and governmental entities, on Social Systems, Software, Data Science Analytics, Communications, Technology, and Networked Services. Apart from classical topics, the congress targeted frontier achievements on Knowledge Science, Data Science, Artificial Intelligence/Machine Learning (AI/ML)-based systems, Self-managing systems, Human-centric technologies, Advanced robotics, Virtual Worlds, Mobility, Sensing, Energy, Electric Vehicles, Green Energy, etc.

The IARIA Congress had a special scientific format where outstanding former IARIA scientists delivered dedicated speeches (Keynote speeches, Tutorial lectures) along with peer-reviewed contributions on the themes of achievements and challenges in science, technologies, services, and applications.

We take here the opportunity to warmly thank all the members of the IARIA Congress 2025 technical program committee, as well as all the reviewers. The creation of such a high-quality conference program would not have been possible without their involvement. We also kindly thank all the authors who dedicated much of their time and effort to contribute to IARIA Congress 2025. We truly believe that, thanks to all these efforts, the final conference program consisted of top-quality contributions. We also thank the members of the IARIA Congress 2025 organizing committee for their help in handling the logistics of this event.

We hope that IARIA Congress 2025 was a successful international forum for the exchange of ideas and results between academia and industry for the promotion of progress in our society. We also hope that Venice, Italy, provided a pleasant environment during the conference and everyone saved some time to enjoy the charm of the city.

IARIA Congress 2025 Chairs

IARIA Congress 2025 Steering Committee

Carlos Becker Westphall, Federal University of Santa Catarina, Brazil
Luigi Lavazza, Università dell'Insubria – Varese, Italy
Timothy T. Pham, Jet Propulsion Laboratory - California Institute of Technology, USA
Lasse Berntzen, University of South-Eastern Norway, Norway
Arcady Zhukov, University of Basque Country (UPV/EHU), San Sebastian / Ikerbasque, Basque Foundation for Science, Bilbao, Spain
Yasushi Kambayashi, Sanyo-Onoda City University, Japan
Gerhard Hube, Technical University of Applied Sciences Würzburg-Schweinfurt, Germany
Renwei (Richard) Li, Southeast University, China

IARIA Congress 2025 Publicity Chairs
Sandra Viciano Tudela, Universitat Politecnica de Valencia, Spain
Lorena Parra Boronat, Universidad Politécnica de Madrid, Spain
José Miguel Jiménez, Universitat Politecnica de Valencia, Spain

IARIA Congress 2025
Committee

IARIA Congress 2025 Steering Committee

Carlos Becker Westphall, Federal University of Santa Catarina, Brazil
Luigi Lavazza, Università dell'Insubria – Varese, Italy
Timothy T. Pham, Jet Propulsion Laboratory - California Institute of Technology, USA
Lasse Berntzen, University of South-Eastern Norway, Norway
Arcady Zhukov, University of Basque Country (UPV/EHU), San Sebastian / Ikerbasque, Basque Foundation for Science, Bilbao, Spain
Yasushi Kambayashi, Sanyo-Onoda City University, Japan
Gerhard Hube, Technical University of Applied Sciences Würzburg-Schweinfurt, Germany
Renwei (Richard) Li, Southeast University, China

IARIA Congress 2025 Publicity Chairs

Sandra Viciano Tudela, Universitat Politecnica de Valencia, Spain
Lorena Parra Boronat, Universidad Politécnica de Madrid, Spain
José Miguel Jiménez, Universitat Politecnica de Valencia, Spain

IARIA Congress 2025 Technical Program Committee

Tamer Abdou, Ryerson University, Canada
Nikunj Agarwal, Amazon, Inc., USA
Nitin Agarwal, COSMOS Research Center | University of Arkansas at Little Rock, USA
Abiola Akinnubi, Infinity Ward (Activision Publishing) Woodland Hill / COSMOS Research Center Little Rock, Arkansas, USA
Sedat Akleylek, Ondokuz Mayis University, Samsun, Turkey
Murat Akpinar, ASELSAN A.Ş., Ankara, Turkey
Raid Rafi Omar Al-Nima, Northern Technical University, Iraq
Alaa Alghazo, Hashemite University, Jordan
Hesham Ali, University of Nebraska Omaha , USA
Ali T. Alouani, Tennessee Technological University, USA
Mohammad Alsulami, University of Connecticut, USA
Slimane Bah, Mohammadia Engineering School - University Mohammed V in Rabat, Morocco
Lasse Berntzen, University of South-Eastern Norway, Norway
Sandjai Bhulai, Vrije Universiteit Amsterdam, Netherlands
John Blake, University of Aizu, Japan
Oleksandr Blazhko, National University «Odessa Polytechnic», Ukraine
Natalia Bogach, Peter the Great St. Petersburg Polytechnic University, Russia
Abdelmadjid Bouabdallah, University of Technology of Compiegne, France
Christian Bourret, Université Gustave Eiffel (Paris Est Marne-la-Vallée), France
Frederico Branco, Universidade de Trás-os-Montes e Alto Douro, Portugal
Uwe Breitenbücher, Reutlingen University, Germany
Antonio Brogi, University of Pisa, Italy
Isaac Caicedo-Castro, University of Córdoba, Colombia

Ozgu Can, Ege University, Turkiye
Laurence Capus, Université Laval, Québec, Canada
Dirceu Cavendish, Kyushu Institute of Technology, Japan
Julio Cesar Duarte, Military Institute of Engineering, Brazil
Steve Chan, Sensemaking U.S. Pacific Command Fellowship, USA
Haihua Chen, University of North Texas, USA
André Constantino da Silva, Federal Institute of São Paulo - IFSP, Brazil
Debasree Das, Indian Institute of Technology, Kharagpur, India
Jay Dave, BITS Pilani, Hyderabad Campus, India
Luca Davoli, University of Parma, Italy
Patrizio Dazzi, University of Pisa, Italy
Toon De Pessemier, Imec - WAVES - Ghent University, Belgium
Peter Edge, Ara Institute of Canterbury, New Zealand
Sam Erbati, Duisburg-Essen University / Deutsche Telekom, Germany
Adrian Florea, "Lucian Blaga" University of Sibiu, Romania
Stefano Forti, University of Pisa, Italy
Matteo Francia, University of Bologna, Italy
Edelberto Franco Silva, Federal University of Juiz de Fora, Brazil
Ronnier Frates Rohrich, Federal University of Technology - Paraná, Brazil
Kaori Fujinami, Tokyo University of Agriculture and Technology, Japan
Imam Barket Ghiloubi, University of Biskra, Algeria
Ramesh Gorantla, Arizona State University, USA
Denis Gracanin, Virginia Tech, USA
Gregor Grambow, Aalen University, Germany
Wahida Handouzi, Tlemcen University, Algeria
Bohdan Havano, Lviv Polytechnic National University, Ukraine
Hussein Hazimeh, Lebanese University & Al Maaref University, Lebanon
Hans-Joachim Hof, Technische Hochschule Ingolstadt, Germany
Wladyslaw Homenda, Warsaw University of Technology, Poland
Gerhard Hube Technical University of Applied Sciences Würzburg-Schweinfurt, Germany
Hocine Imine, Université Gustave Eiffel, France
Orest Ivakhiv, L'viv Polytechnic National University, Ukraine
Fehmi Jaafar, Quebec University at Chicoutimi / Concordia University / Laval University, Canada
Marc Jansen, University of Applied Sciences Ruhr West, Germany
Imad Jawhar, Al Maaref University, Beirut, Lebanon
Felipe Jimenez Alonso, Technical University of Madrid, Spain
Luisa Jorge, CeDRI-IPB & INESC Coimbra, Portugal
Mohammed Jouhari, Mohammed VI Polytechnic University, Morocco
Yasushi Kambayashi, Sanyo-Onoda City University, Japan
Pushpendu Kar, The University of Nottingham, Ningbo, China
Mohamed Kara-Mohamed, Liverpool John Moores University, UK
Mojtaba A. Khanesar, University of Nottingham, UK
Elhaouari Kobzili, National Polytechnic School, Algeria
Koteswararao (Kote) Kondepu, India Institute of Technology Dharwad (IITDh), India
Dmitry Korzun, Petrozavodsk State University (PetrSU), Russia
Constantine Kotropoulos, Aristotle University of Thessaloniki, Greece
Nane Kratzke, Lübeck University of Applied Sciences, Germany
Dragana Krstic, University of Nis, Serbia

Eric MSP Veith, OFFIS e.V. - Institut für Informatik, Oldenburg, Germany
Tim vor der Brück, Fernfachhochschule Schweiz (FFHS), Switzerland
Zhengxun Wu, Independent researcher, USA
Bo Yang, The University of Tokyo, Japan
Linda Yang, University of Portsmouth, UK
Shuo Yang, University of Hong Kong, Hong Kong
Jiaqi Yin, Northwestern Polytechnical University, China
Maram Bani Younes, Philadelphia University, Jordan
Elena Zaitseva, University of Zilina, Slovakia
Jorge Zavaleta, CNPq, Rio de Janeiro, Brazil
Xingyu Zhou, Dow Inc., USA
Arkady Zhukov, University of Basque Country - UPV/EHU | IKERBASQUE - Basque Foundation for Science, Spain

Copyright Information

Table of Contents

Deep Learning Approach for Shadow Removal Using Semantic Segmentation and Attention Mechanism

Po-Chin Chang
Dept. of Computer Science & Info. Eng.,
National Taiwan University of Science and Technology,
Taipei 106, Taiwan
e-mail: pp0956pp@gmail.com

Shi-Jinn Horng
Dept. of Computer Science & Info. Eng., Asia University,
Dept. of Med. Res., CMUH, China Medical University,
Taichung 413305, Taiwan
e-mail: horngsj@yahoo.com.tw

Abstract—**This paper presents a novel architecture for shadow removal that leverages semantic segmentation to divide the image into distinct regions: shadow areas, foreground areas, and shadow boundaries. To capture the intricate interactions among these regions, the model incorporates a self-attention mechanism. To tackle the persistent issue of shadow boundary residues found in existing models, this approach introduces a shadow feature fusion mechanism. This mechanism employs area attention to accurately blend features across different regions, enhancing the natural transition at shadow edges and improving shadow region restoration quality. Experimental results on public datasets validate the model's effectiveness in shadow recovery and detail preservation, as evidenced by metrics such as Structural Similarity Index Measure (SSIM) and Root Mean Square Error (RMSE). Additionally, the model demonstrates strong generalization across various test settings, highlighting its practical applicability for shadow removal tasks.**

Keywords- Shadow removal; Area attention; Shadow region restoration; SSIM; RMSE.

I. INTRODUCTION

In the past decade, deep learning has driven major advances in image processing, with models like Convolutional Neural Networks [1] and Vision Transformers [2] greatly improving the accuracy and efficiency of image analysis.

Shadow removal remains a key challenge in image processing due to its impact on visual quality and algorithm performance. Shadows can distort object boundaries and colors, hindering tasks like object detection, face recognition, and scene parsing, especially in outdoor settings. Effective shadow removal is essential for improving both image clarity and recognition accuracy [3].

Shadow removal research faces key challenges, including limited and less diverse datasets like Image Shadow Triplets Dataset (ISTD) [4], SRD [5], and SBU [6], which hinder model robustness. Shadow variations caused by lighting and object interactions further complicate detection, especially when shadow and object colors are similar. This study aims to develop more accurate and adaptable deep learning-based shadow removal models to advance image processing applications.

This paper integrates Segment Anything Model (SAM) [7], Swin Transformer [8], and U-Net [9] with a selective shadow fusion mechanism to build an efficient shadow removal model. SAM provides zero-shot segmentation using pre-trained masks, the Swin Transformer captures global shadow context through window attention, and U-Net excels at restoring fine image details. Together, they enable accurate shadow detection and natural, high-quality shadow-free image reconstruction.

The paper is organized as follows: Section 1 outlines the background and motivation for shadow removal. Section 2 reviews related work and deep learning approaches. Section 3 details the methodology, including experimental setup and model design. Section 4 presents and analyzes the results. The final section summarizes key findings and future directions.

II. RELATED WORK

A. Related Reseach

In recent years, shadow removal has advanced through both physical modeling and deep learning techniques. STacked Conditional Generative Adversarial Network (ST-CGAN) [4] uses dual Conditional-GANs to jointly learn shadow detection and removal in a unified framework. SP+M-Net [10] combines deep networks with a linear illumination model to simulate shadows and predict lighting parameters. Mask-ShadowGAN [11] applies Cycle-GANs [15] to unpaired data, removing shadows without needing paired training samples. Auto-Exposure [12] enhances lighting consistency by automatically adjusting exposure across shadowed regions. CRFormer [13] leverages a Transformer with unidirectional attention for efficient pixel restoration. SpA-Former [14] merges Transformer and Convolutional Neural Network (CNN) architectures with spatial attention for fast, accurate single-stage shadow removal.

B. Transformer

(1) Attention is All You Need

The Transformer [16] replaced Recurrent Neural Networks (RNNs) [17] and Long Short-Term Memory networks (LSTMs) [18] by enabling parallel processing of sequence data, greatly improving training efficiency. It uses multi-head attention in layered encoders and decoders to learn complex patterns. Positional encoding with sine and cosine functions helps retain token order despite parallel input processing.

The self-attention mechanism in Transformers computes relationships between tokens by converting inputs into queries, keys, and values. Attention scores from query-key dot products are normalized with softmax and used to weight the value vectors, enabling the model to capture long-range dependencies effectively.

(2) Swin Transformer

The Swin Transformer [8], or Shifted Window Transformer, improves visual task performance and efficiency using a hierarchical structure and window shifting, effectively handling scale variation and high-resolution images.

Prior Vision Transformer [2] used a global self-attention mechanism, and the Swin Transformer introduces a shifted window mechanism that limits self-attention to local windows, reducing computational complexity from quadratic to linear. By shifting windows, it enables cross-window interactions. Its hierarchical structure merges patches progressively, boosting multi-scale representation learning and making it a strong alternative to CNN backbones in visual tasks.

(3) DehazeFormer

DehazeFormer [19], based on the Swin Transformer, addresses dehazing by improving edge handling in window-based self-attention. Unlike cyclic shifting, which reduces patch use at image edges, DehazeFormer uses reflection padding to extend boundaries, ensuring consistent patch numbers and better feature continuity. After attention, center cropping restores the original size. This method is also effective for shadow removal, where edge detail is crucial.

C. Semantic Segmentation

(1) Segment Anything Model

The Segment Anything Model (SAM) [7] performs zero-shot image segmentation using minimal cues like points or rough selections. Pre-trained on large datasets, SAM delivers high-quality masks instantly and serves as a versatile backbone for tasks like segmentation, data annotation, and real-time image analysis.

SAM also introduces the SA-1B dataset, with over 10 million images and 1 billion masks, enriching model training. Its architecture includes an Image Encoder (based on Vision Transformer [2]), a Prompt Encoder, and a Mask Decoder. The encoders extract features from images and prompts, while the decoder combines them to generate accurate masks and confidence scores, even under ambiguous input.

(2) SAM-Adapter

The SAM-Adapter [20] enhances the original SAM by adding adapters to improve performance on specific tasks. This boosts generalizability and makes it more effective for shadow detection.

SAM-Adapter retains SAM's original image encoder but adds adapters between Transformer layers. Each adapter uses two Multilayer Perceptron (MLPs) and a Gaussian Error Linear Units (GELU) activation: one creates task-specific hints, the other adjusts them to fit the encoder. These refined features improve mask accuracy, making SAM-Adapter effective for shadow detection, which this study adopts.

D. U-Net

U-Net [9] is a convolutional neural network widely used for image restoration and segmentation due to its symmetric U-shaped design. It consists of a contracting path for feature extraction using 3x3 convolutions and 2x2 max pooling, and an expansive path for upsampling and feature fusion. Skip connections between corresponding layers help preserve spatial details, making U-Net effective for high-precision image restoration and the backbone of our model.

E. Selective Kernel Networks

Selective Kernel Networks (SK-Net) [21] overcome the fixed receptive field limitation in CNNs by enabling neurons to adaptively adjust their receptive field size for better multi-scale processing. SK-Net operates in three phases: Split, where input features are processed through multiple convolution paths with different kernel sizes; Fuse, where these are combined and condensed into a global feature vector; and Select, where attention-based weights determine the contribution of each path, dynamically adjusting the receptive fields. This efficient, flexible mechanism makes SK-Net ideal for feature fusion, which is critical in achieving precise shadow removal in our model.

III. Proposed Method

A. Dataset

(1) Image Shadow Triplets Dataset

The ISTD dataset [4] is a widely used benchmark for shadow detection and removal, containing 1,870 triplets—each with a shadow image, shadow mask, and shadow-free image—across 135 diverse scenes. It includes 1,330 training and 540 testing triplets, featuring varied lighting and shadow types, making it essential for evaluating shadow removal methods.

Figure 1. ISTD triplet [4].

(2) Adjusted Image Shadow Triplets Dataset

The Adjusted Image Shadow Triplets Dataset (AISTD) [10] addresses color inconsistencies in the ISTD dataset [4], caused by varying lighting when shadow and non-shadow images were taken. These differences result in notable RMSE values—up to 12.9 in non-shadow areas (Figure 2) and 6.83 on average in the test set. To correct this, the authors applied linear regression to align pixel values in non-shadow regions, using shadow masks and adjusting each Red Green and Blue (RGB) channel separately.

Initially, a shadow mask was used to select the non-shadow regions from each pair of shadow and non-shadow images. Subsequently, a separate linear regression model was applied independently to each color channel (red, green, blue).

$$I_{corrected}(x) = a \cdot I_{shadow-free}(x) + b \quad (1)$$

The linear regression model, as per Equation (1), uses $I_{corrected}(x)$ to denote the color-corrected pixel values of the shadow-free image, and $I_{shadow-free}(x)$ to represent the original pixel values of the shadow-free image. The parameters a and b of the linear regression model are obtained through the Least Squares Method, fitted within the non-shadow regions. This method significantly reduces the color discrepancy between shadowed and shadow-free images, thereby enabling more accurate performance evaluations during the training of shadow removal models. As shown in the Corrected GT in Figure 2, color correction reduced RMSE in non-shadow regions from 12.9 to 2.9, and from 6.83 to 2.6 across the test set, improving dataset quality. This corrected version is widely adopted in shadow removal research, including this study.

Figure 2. Corrected AISTD dataset [10].

B. *Network Architecture*

(1) System architecture and process

This paper proposes a novel shadow removal model (Figure 3) that generates shadow-free images from shadow inputs. It combines SAM-Adapter, U-Net, and Swin Transformer, with a Selective Shadow Fusion module to improve integration in shadowed areas.

Experiments showed that end-to-end training with shadow and shadow-free images often leaves residual shadows due to large pixel value differences between non-shadow and shadow areas, with the former averaging 2.3 times brighter than the latter, as shown in Figure 2. To address this, our model uses a pre-trained SAM-Adapter to extract shadow masks, then applies mask inversion and morphological gradients operations [22] to segment the image into shadow, foreground, and boundary regions. Each is processed separately: preserving content in the foreground, smoothing transitions at boundaries, and restoring brightness in shadows. These weighted feature maps are then fused for more accurate shadow removal.

Figure 3 illustrates the architecture of the shadow restoration model, consisting of a contracting path and an expanding path. The sequence of feature map depths transitions from input to output as (3, 24, 48, 96, 48, 24, 3). The Transformer modules are stacked in sequences of (16, 16, 16, 8, 8), with pairs executing computations of window attention and shifted window attention, respectively.

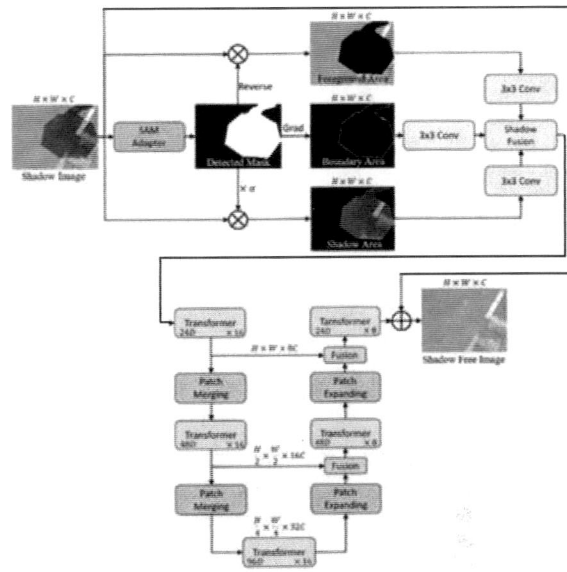

Figure 3. Network architecture.

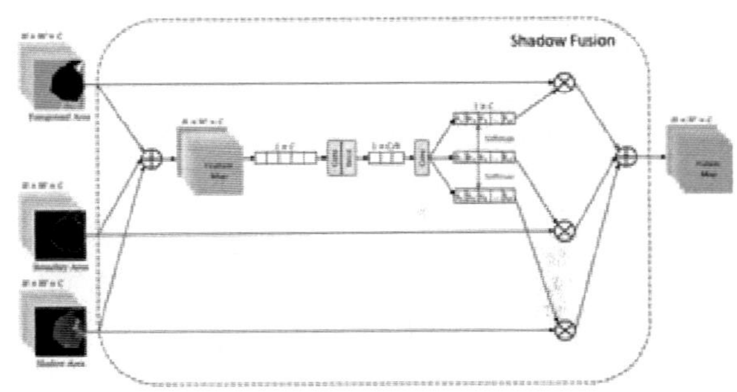

Figure 4. Shadow fusion block.

In the contracting pathway, downsampling and feature extraction are primarily conducted through two Patch Merging modules and three Transformer modules. Each passage through a Patch Merging module halves the dimensions of the feature map while doubling the number of channels. Conversely, the expanding pathway is responsible for upsampling and feature fusion, comprising two Patch Expanding modules, two Transformer modules, and two Fusion modules. The Patch Expanding modules increase the dimensions of the feature map by a factor of two while halving the channel count. The Fusion modules utilize a Selective Kernel Network (SK-Net) and integrate features from both the contracting and expanding pathways via Skip Connections. Ultimately, the output is merged with the original shadow image through a Residual Connection to produce the corresponding shadow-free image.

(2) Shadow Fusion Block

In the task of shadow removal, to enhance the detail at the shadow boundaries and the recovery of shadowed areas, this study introduces a Shadow Fusion module. This module employs an Area Attention mechanism to boost the model's capability to discern features in different shadow regions. The architecture is illustrated in Figure 4. During the fusion phase, element-wise addition is initially applied to the feature maps of the shadow region, foreground area, and shadow boundary area. Subsequently, these combined feature maps undergo Global Average Pooling. Following this, a convolution layer and Rectified Linear Unit (ReLU) activation function reduce the channel dimension of the feature maps to one-eighth of its original size, after which convolution operations expand the channel count back to its initial dimension. Throughout this process, three vectors of the same dimensions, F, E, and S, are generated. During the selection phase, corresponding elements of these three vectors undergo Softmax computation, producing regional attention vectors for the three paths. These vectors are then multiplied by their corresponding regional feature maps. The resulting products are cumulatively added to obtain a channel-fused shadow feature map, referred to as the Fusion Map.

The proposed shadow fusion module uses regional attention to better recognize and process shadow features, offering three key advantages:

a) Regional differentiation processing: The attention mechanism adjusts channel weights by region, enabling flexible handling of varying shadows and enhancing feature extraction in dark, dense areas to prevent detail loss.

b) Smooth shadow boundary transitions: Rather than simply adding features, our model uses channel fusion to integrate shadow, foreground, and boundary regions, enabling smoother, more natural transitions at shadow edges for improved restoration detail.

c) Enhanced model generalization: Channel attention allows the model to adaptively adjust weights, enabling effective shadow removal and strong generalization under complex lighting and irregular shadow conditions.

(3) Transformer Block

Figure 5 illustrates the modified architecture of the Transformer module. Initially, the feature map undergoes normalization through the Layer Normalization module, which normalizes across channels. Subsequently, the feature map is directed to the Reflection Padding module for expansion. This process involves mirror padding on the right and bottom sides of the feature map, ensuring that the patches within the window are expanded to multiples of the window size. Following this, the feature map enters the Window-based Multi-head Self-Attention (W-MSA) module, where window attention computations are performed.

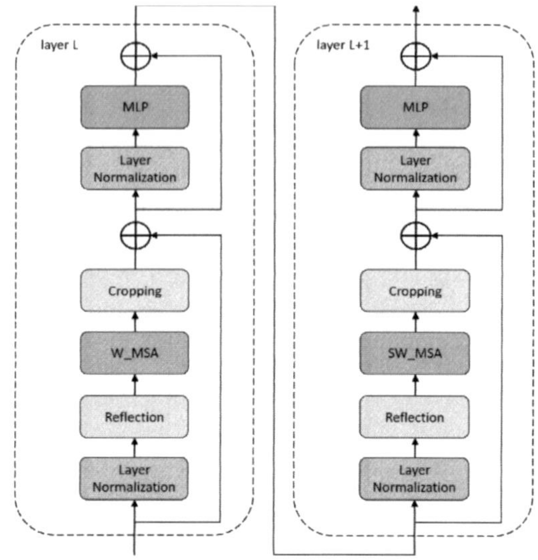

Figure 5. Revised transformer block.

Additionally, relative position embedding is incorporated to enhance the model's spatial awareness. The overall computation is described in (2). Here, Q, K, V represent the Query, Key, and Value vectors, respectively, while B denotes the Relative Position Bias.

$$Attention(Q, K, V) = Softmax\left(\frac{QK^T}{\sqrt{d}} + B\right) \times V \quad (2)$$

Unlike the Vision Transformer, the window attention mechanism restricts computations within each window, eliminating the need for absolute position embedding of feature maps at the input stage. Instead, relative positional biases are incorporated during the self-attention computations within each window. The relative position vectors are combined with the results of the dot product between the query and key vectors, influencing the final attention scores. This approach allows the attention mechanism in each window not only to consider the similarity of features but also to dynamically adjust for positional relationships, enhancing the adaptability and generalization of feature representation. Additionally, this mechanism enables the model to effectively handle feature maps of varying sizes.

To better restore the pixel quality in the edge regions of images, this study employs a mechanism distinct from the Swin Transformer. In the calculation of shifted window attention within the SW-MSA module, Window Masks are not utilized to cover the windows. Instead, the feature maps are mirrored and padded on all four sides to integer multiples of the window size before calculating the window attention.

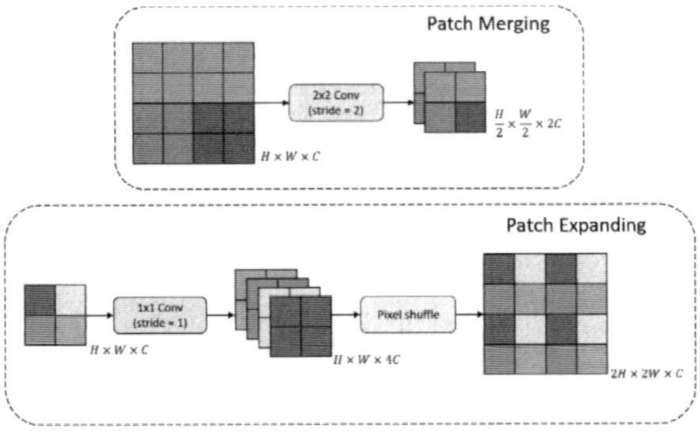

Figure 6. Patch Merging (top) and patch expanding (bottom) block.

This mechanism offers three advantages for shadow recovery models:

(a) Enhanced processing of image edge regions: Traditional padding methods, such as zero padding or cyclic shift mechanisms, may introduce irrelevant information or cause unreasonable element arrangements at image edges, which are detrimental to image restoration models. By reflecting edge pixels, our model effectively maintains consistency in window size at the edges, avoiding biases in model training due to insufficient patch numbers within the windows, thereby improving the processing quality of image edge regions.

(b) Improved quality of feature representation: By using reflection padding to extend the image content naturally at the edges, this method maintains contextual information more effectively compared to other padding techniques, thus enhancing the quality of feature representation.

(c) Reduced additional computational costs: Reflection Padding simplifies computation by removing the need for Window Mask operations. Though slightly more costly than cyclic shift, its impact is minimal on large images, where edge regions are less significant.

(4) Patch Merging & Patch Expanding Block

The architectural framework of the Patch Merging and Patch Expanding modules used in this study is shown in Figure 6. The Patch Merging module employs a 2x2 convolutional kernel with a stride of 2, merging four adjacent patches into one. This approach effectively reduces the feature map by half while doubling the number of channels. Conversely, the Patch Expanding module utilizes a 1x1 convolution to quadruple the channel count of the input feature map. Subsequently, a Pixel Shuffle Layer [23] transforms channel information into pixel information necessary for upsampling, ultimately achieving a twofold increase in the feature map resolution.

C. Loss Function

In this paper, the L1 Loss is employed as the loss function for the shadow removal model. The principal mechanism of the L1 Loss involves measuring the model's error by calculating the absolute differences between the predicted values and the true values. For a given set of input image pairs x_i, y_i where $i = 1$ to n, the L1 Loss function is defined in (3).

$$L1(x_i, y_i) = \frac{1}{n}\sum_{i=1}^{n}|x_i - y_i| \quad (3)$$

Here, x_i represents the true values, y_i denotes the model's predicted values, and n indicates the number of pixels. The L1 Loss function computes the overall loss by summing the absolute differences between the predicted and true values of each pixel and then averaging these sums. Employing the L1 Loss in shadow removal models assists in more accurately restoring details in areas obscured by shadows. Given its involvement in the restoration of image brightness and color, the L1 Loss effectively handles subtle variations in brightness, thereby maintaining the naturalness and visual continuity of the image while removing shadows.

IV. EXPERIMENTAL RESULTS

A. Evaluation Metrics

(1) Structural Similarity Index Measure

The Structural Similarity Index Measure (SSIM) [24] is used to measure visual similarity between images based on luminance, contrast, and structure, which better reflects human perception than pixel-level metrics. SSIM is calculated based on luminance, contrast, and structure:

(a) Luminance Function: Luminance influences human perception. In (4), $L(x, y)$ represents luminance similarity, with μ_x and μ_y as the average luminance of the images, and $C_1 = 6.5025$ to prevent division by zero.

(b) Contrast Function: Contrast refers to the difference between the brightest and darkest parts of an image. In (5), $C(x, y)$ measures contrast by calculating the standard deviations of the images, ensuring similar luminance distribution and range. σ_x and σ_y the images' standard deviations, with $C_2 = 58.5225$ to prevent division by zero.

(c) Structure Function: The structure function evaluates the preservation of details and textures. In (6), $S(x, y)$ calculates the covariance σ_{xy} between images, with $C_3 = 29.26125$ ensuring calculation stability.

$$L(x,y) = \frac{2\mu_x\mu_y + C_1}{\mu_x^2 + \mu_y^2 + C_1} \quad (4)$$

$$C(x,y) = \frac{2\sigma_x\sigma_y + C_2}{\sigma_x^2 + \sigma_y^2 + C_2} \quad (5)$$

$$S(x,y) = \frac{\sigma_{xy} + C_3}{\sigma_x\sigma_y + C_3} \quad (6)$$

$$SSIM(x,y) = \left[L(x,y)^\alpha \cdot C(x,y)^\beta \cdot S(x,y)^\gamma\right] \quad (7)$$

SSIM in (7) uses parameters α, β, and γ to weight its three components, typically set to 1 for balanced evaluation.

(2) Root Mean Square Error

Root Mean Square Error (RMSE) intuitively reflects the magnitude of error by calculating the root mean square difference between predicted and actual values. It is shown in (8), where n represents the number of samples, x_i represents the shadow-free image, and y_i represents the image after shadow removal.

$$RMSE = \sqrt{\frac{1}{n}\sum_{i=1}^{n}(x_i - y_i)^2} \quad (8)$$

B. *Metrics Used to Evaluation*

To evaluate the model, SSIM and RMSE were measured on the AISTD test set, analyzing both entire images and shadow/non-shadow regions to assess restoration and preservation. The proposed architecture performs shadow detection followed by removal without requiring shadow masks. Images were resized to 256×256 and trained for 300 epochs using the AdamW optimizer [25], with a learning rate of 2×10^{-4} and batch size of 4.

TABLE I shows SSIM scores above 0.98 in both shadowed and non-shadowed regions, confirming the model's effectiveness in shadow removal and preserving structural integrity without using shadow masks.

TABLE I. COMPARISON OF SSIM ON AISTD

Scheme	Method	Shadow	Non-shadow	All
Mask-Based	Input image	0.926	0.984	0.894
	SP+M-Net [10]	0.987	0.972	0.947
	Auto-Exposure [12]	0.976	0.875	0.840
	Inpaint4Shadow [26]	0.989	0.977	0.960
	ShadowFormer [27]	0.990	0.979	0.966
	RRL-Net [28]	0.990	**0.984**	0.968
Mask-Free	DC-ShadowNet [29]	0.975	0.963	0.921
	G2RShadowNet [30]	0.988	0.975	0.953
	BMNet [31]	0.990	0.977	0.962
	Ours	**0.991**	0.982	**0.969**

TABLE II shows that the proposed model achieves lower RMSE in shadowed areas compared to other mask-free methods, highlighting its accuracy in shadow restoration.

TABLE II. COMPARISON OF RMSE ON AISTD

Scheme	Method	Shadow	Non-shadow	All
Mask-Based	Input image	40.2	2.6	8.5
	CRFormer [13]	5.9	2.9	3.4
	Inpaint4Shadow [26]	5.9	2.9	3.3
	ShadowFormer [27]	5.4	2.4	2.8
	RRL-Net [28]	5.6	**2.3**	**2.8**
Mask-Free	G2RShadowNet [30]	7.3	3.0	3.6
	BMNet [31]	6.1	2.9	3.5
	Ours	**5.2**	2.5	3.0

C. *Comparative Results on the AISTD Dataset*

Figure 7 illustrates the comparative results on the AISTD dataset against other studies. In the first four columns of tested images, the method proposed in this paper effectively removes shadows while minimizing residual shadows at the shadow boundaries. In the fifth column of images, the colors within the shadow regions are accurately transformed, and the transitions at the shadow edges appear more natural.

Figure 7. Visualization results on AISTD dataset.

D. *Ablation Study*

To evaluate the proposed methods, ablation experiments were conducted to assess the impact of the SAM-Adapter and Shadow Fusion modules on shadow removal. TABLE III compares the results using the RMSE metric.

Removing the semantic segmentation module hinders accurate shadow region restoration and increases RMSE by affecting non-shadow areas. Without the shadow fusion module, segmentation alone restores structure but causes unnatural transitions between shadow and non-shadow regions.

TABLE III. COMPARISON OF RMSE IN ABLATION STUDIES

Setting	Shadow	Non-shadow	All
Input image	40.2	2.6	8.5
w/o SAM-Adapter	6.4	3.2	3.8
w/o Shadow Fusion	5.8	2.6	3.2
Ours	**5.2**	**2.5**	**3.0**

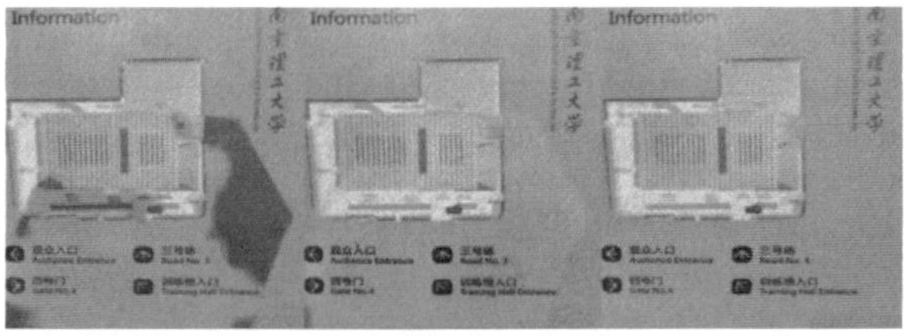

w/o SAM-Adapter w/o Shadow Fusion Ours

Figure 8. Visualization results on ablation studies.

Figure 8 shows how the SAM-Adapter and Shadow Fusion modules enhance shadow removal. Without semantic segmentation, residual shadows remain. With only semantic segmentation, shadows are removed but without optimal refinement.

V. CONCLUSION

This paper proposes an architecture that combines semantic segmentation and attention mechanisms for shadow removal, enhanced by a shadow fusion module to restore image details. The Semantic Attention Module (SAM) segments shadow and non-shadow regions across diverse scenes, while attention mechanisms capture their relationships. The fusion module refines shadow boundaries, producing high-quality shadow-free images. Experiments on the AISTD dataset show strong performance, with high SSIM and low RMSE scores. The model also generalizes well to various scenes, including game environments, outdoor landscapes, and facial images, demonstrating its strong generalization capability.

ACKNOWLEDGEMENT

This work was supported in part by the NSTC under contract 111-2221-E-011 -134 -, 112-2221-E-468 -023 -.

REFERENCES

[1] A. Krizhevsky, I. Sutskever, and G. E. Hinton, "Imagenet classification with deep convolutional neural networks," Advances in neural information processing systems, vol. 25, 2012.

[2] A. Dosovitskiy et al., "An image is worth 16x16 words: Transformers for image recognition at scale," arXiv preprint arXiv:2010.11929, 2020.

[3] Y. Zhong, X. Liu, D. Zhai, J. Jiang, and X. Ji, "Shadows can be dangerous: Stealthy and effective physical-world adversarial attack by natural phenomenon," IEEE/CVF Conference on Computer Vision and Pattern Recognition, 2022, pp. 15345–15354.

[4] J. Wang, X. Li, and J. Yang, "Stacked conditional generative adversarial networks for jointly learning shadow detection and shadow removal," IEEE Conference on Computer Vision and Pattern Recognition, 2018, pp. 1788–1797.

[5] L. Qu, J. Tian, S. He, Y. Tang, and R. W. Lau, "Deshadownet: A multi-context embedding deep network for shadow removal," IEEE Conference on Computer Vision and Pattern Recognition, 2017, pp. 4067–4075.

[6] T. F. Y. Vicente, M. Hoai, and D. Samaras, "Noisy label recovery for shadow detection in unfamiliar domains," IEEE Conference on Computer Vision and Pattern Recognition, 2016, pp. 3783–3792.

[7] A. Kirillov et al., "Segment anything," IEEE/CVF International Conference on Computer Vision, 2023, pp. 4015–4026.

[8] Z. Liu et al., "Swin transformer: Hierarchical vision transformer using shifted windows," IEEE/CVF International Conference on Computer Vision, 2021, pp. 10012–10022.

[9] O. Ronneberger, P. Fischer, and T. Brox, "U-net: Convolutional networks for biomedical image segmentation," Medical image computing and computer-assisted intervention–MICCAI 2015: 18th International Conference, Munich, Germany, October 5-9, 2015, proceedings, part III 18, 2015, pp. 234–241.

[10] H. Le and D. Samaras, "Shadow removal via shadow image decomposition," IEEE/CVF International Conference on Computer Vision, 2019, pp. 8578–8587.

[11] X. Hu, Y. Jiang, C.-W. Fu, and P.-A. Heng, "Mask-shadowgan: Learning to remove shadows from unpaired data," IEEE/CVF International Conference on Computer Vision, 2019, pp. 2472–2481.

[12] L. Fu et al., "Auto-exposure fusion for single-image shadow removal," IEEE/CVF Conference on Computer Vision and Pattern Recognition, 2021, pp. 10571–10580.

[13] J. Wan, H. Yin, Z. Wu, X. Wu, Z. Liu, and S. Wang, "Crformer: A cross-region transformer for shadow removal," arXiv preprint arXiv:2207.01600, 2022.

[14] X. F. Zhang, C. C. Gu, and S. Y. Zhu, "Spa-former: Transformer image shadow detection and removal via spatial attention," arXiv preprint arXiv:2206.10910, 2022.

[15] J.-Y. Zhu, T. Park, P. Isola, and A. A. Efros, "Unpaired image-to-image translation using cycle-consistent adversarial networks," IEEE International Conference on Computer Vision, 2017, pp. 2223–2232.

[16] A. Vaswani et al., "Attention is all you need," Advances in neural information processing systems, vol. 30, 2017.

[17] M. I. Jordan, "Serial order: A parallel distributed processing approach," Advances in psychology, vol. 121, Elsevier, 1997, pp. 471–495.

[18] A. Graves and A. Graves, "Long short-term memory," Supervised sequence labelling with recurrent neural networks, pp. 37–45, 2012.

[19] Y. Song, Z. He, H. Qian, and X. Du, "Vision transformers for single image dehazing," IEEE Transactions on Image Processing, vol. 32, pp. 1927–1941, 2023.

[20] T. Chen et al., "SAM Fails to Segment Anything?–SAM-Adapter: Adapting SAM in Underperformed Scenes: Camouflage, Shadow, Medical Image Segmentation, and More," arXiv preprint arXiv:2304.09148, 2023.

[21] X. Li, W. Wang, X. Hu, and J. Yang, "Selective kernel networks," Proceedings of the IEEE/CVF Conference on Computer Vision and Pattern Recognition, 2019, pp. 510–519.

[22] R. M. Haralick, S. R. Sternberg, and X. Zhuang, "Image analysis using mathematical morphology," IEEE Transactions on Pattern Analysis and Machine Intelligence, no. 4, 1987, pp. 532–550.

[23] W. Shi et al., "Real-time single image and video super-resolution using an efficient sub-pixel convolutional neural network," IEEE Conference on Computer Vision and Pattern Recognition, 2016, pp. 1874–1883.

[24] Z. Wang, A. C. Bovik, H. R. Sheikh, and E. P. Simoncelli, "Image quality assessment: From error visibility to structural similarity," IEEE Transactions on Image Processing, vol. 13, no. 4, 2004, pp. 600–612.

[25] I. Loshchilov and F. Hutter, "Decoupled weight decay regularization," arXiv preprint arXiv:1711.05101, 2017.

[26] X. Li et al., "Leveraging inpainting for single-image shadow removal," IEEE/CVF International Conference on Computer Vision, 2023, pp. 13055–13064.

[27] L. Guo, S. Huang, D. Liu, H. Cheng, and B. Wen, "Shadowformer: Global context helps image shadow removal," arXiv preprint arXiv:2302.01650, 2023.

[28] Y. Liu, Z. Ke, K. Xu, F. Liu, Z. Wang, and R. W. Lau, "Recasting regional lighting for shadow removal," AAAI Conference on Artificial Intelligence, 2024, vol. 38, no. 4, pp. 3810–3818.

[29] Y. Jin, A. Sharma, and R. T. Tan, "Dc-shadownet: Single-image hard and soft shadow removal using unsupervised domain-classifier guided network," IEEE/CVF International Conference on Computer Vision, 2021, pp. 5027–5036.

[30] Z. Liu, H. Yin, X. Wu, Z. Wu, Y. Mi, and S. Wang, "From shadow generation to shadow removal," IEEE/CVF Conference on Computer Vision and Pattern Recognition, 2021, pp. 4927–4936.

[31] Y. Zhu, J. Huang, X. Fu, F. Zhao, Q. Sun, and Z.-J. Zha, "Bijective mapping network for shadow removal," IEEE/CVF Conference on Computer Vision and Pattern Recognition, 2022, pp. 5627–563.

Applying an Artificial Neuromolecular System with Autonomous Learning Capability to Learn to Control the Movement of a Six-Axis Robotic Arm

Jong-Chen Chen
National Yunlin University of Science and Technology
No. 123, Sec. 3, University Rd., Douliu City, Yunlin County
640, Taiwan (R.O.C.)
Email: jcchen@yuntech.edu.tw

Guan-Rong Chen
National Yunlin University of Science and Technology
No. 123, Sec. 3, University Rd., Douliu City, Yunlin County
640, Taiwan (R.O.C.)
Email: rrong0000@gmail.com

Abstract—**With the widespread use of intelligent robots, robotic arms play an increasingly vital role across various fields. This study explores using a system endowed with autonomous learning capabilities to learn and control the movements of a six-axis robotic arm. The research method enables this robotic arm to autonomously determine its movement trajectory, transitioning from a specific point to a fixed position while grasping an object at a designated angle. This process involves managing the broader movement trajectories associated with the arm's operations and ensuring precise coordination for practical suction actions. The WLKATA Mirobot serves as the experimental testbed for this study; it is a compact six-axis machine designed for tabletop use. The primary control mechanism is linked to an artificial neuromolecular system developed earlier in this team, characterized by a closely aligned relationship between structure and function that evolves. This design facilitates continuous learning, allowing the robotic arm to accomplish assigned tasks without rigid time constraints. Various trajectories were established in the experiments, enabling the arm to navigate toward desired target points based on specific requirements. The results indicate that the system can successfully reach target points and effectively grasp objects. Additionally, thorough testing was conducted to evaluate whether the molecular-like nervous system allows the robotic arm to execute corresponding movements proficiently. The study shows that this molecular-like jumpy system can effectively utilize previously learned actions after a learning period. This adaptability enables the robotic arm to adjust its operations for similar tasks, thereby achieving what is known as the transfer learning effect.**

Keywords- sensors; artificial neural networks; computational intelligence; robot; autonomous learning.

I. INTRODUCTION

In today's highly developed world of information technology, the application of robots has become indispensable and essential. Their application ranges from simple robot-arm operation to complex robot-arm collaboration and even to the operation of humanoid arms. Traditional robot arms are mainly used in large-scale manufacturing industries, but collaborative robot arms have emerged rapidly in recent years. They are relatively minor, lighter, and more flexible. In addition, collaborative robotic arms are relatively simple to program, making them easier to reconfigure and deploy to production environments where products are small and diverse. The unique design of collaborative robotic arms allows them to work alongside human operators to perform highly repetitive tasks and integrate complex tasks. This collaborative approach improves production efficiency and reduces the physical burden on human operators, allowing them to focus more on more creative and intelligent tasks. With the continuous development of industrial automation, path planning has become one of the key issues in robot arm applications. Ensuring the robot arm can accurately move from the current to the target position has always been crucial. Robots have surpassed humans in well-structured and highly repetitive tasks through advanced control technology and machine learning methods, achieving faster and more precise motion control. The robot arm can calculate and realize its optimal motion path between two specified positions, further improving its application scope and benefits [1].

This study uses the WLKATA Mirobot as an experimental tool to collect the trajectories required for specific task requirements. WLKATA Mirobot is a desktop six-axis robotic arm with 6 degrees of freedom (Figure 1). This design combines flexibility and complex free rotation to provide a desktop robotic arm designed to simulate an innovative factory robotic arm. Its simulated factory application areas include fruit picking production lines, smart garbage sorting production lines, artificial intelligence sorting production lines, deep learning dynamic sorting production lines, etc. The primary control mechanism is the artificial neuromolecular system developed earlier in this team [2], characterized by a closely aligned relationship between structure and function that evolves. This design facilitates continuous learning, allowing the robotic arm to accomplish assigned tasks without rigid time constraints. Various trajectories were established in the experiments, enabling the arm to navigate toward desired target points based on specific requirements. The rest of the paper is structured as follows. In Section II, we present. the design of this six-axis robot. The experiments and results are presented in Section III. Finally, we draw our conclusions in Section IV.

II. METHOD

This study uses the trajectory data collected by WLKATA Mirobot and then uses the artificial neuromolecular system to learn the trajectory data. This research experiment consists of two parts. The first part is a large-scale movement experiment in which the system has to learn how to control the relatively large movement trajectory of the six-axis robot arm. The second part is a small-scale movement experiment in which the system has to learn how to coordinate the six-axis robot arms to produce detailed suction movements. Unlike the first part of the experiment, the control of the robotic movement requires high precision positioning accuracy, ensuring that the robot arm can accurately reach the target point.

The core processing component of the ANM system includes all control and information processing neurons, forming the Central Processing Subsystem (CPS). This system functions similarly to the brain's processing mechanism and is seen as a converter between input and output. The CPS is mainly composed of a set of reference neurons and information processing neurons (cytoskeletal neurons or enzyme neurons). When the system starts receiving external information, each information-processing neuron learns from different sensory neurons, adjusting the connection states appropriately to meet the system's requirements. The detailed mechanism can be found in [3].

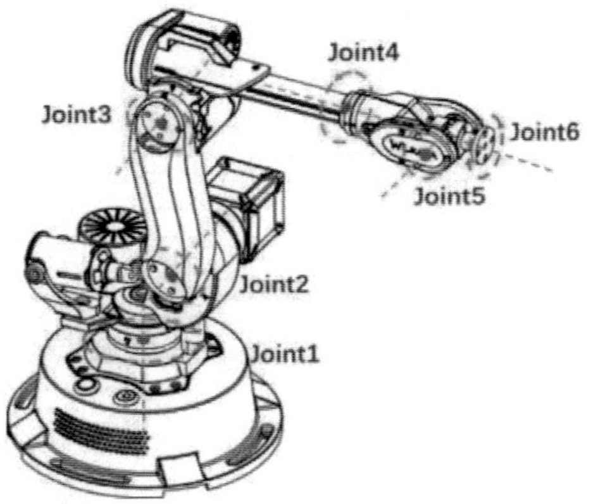

Figure 1. WLKATA Mirobot's.

III. EXPERIMENTS AND RESULTS

Various trajectories were established in the experiments, enabling the arm to navigate toward desired target points based on specific requirements. The results indicate that the system can successfully reach target points and effectively grasp objects. Additionally, thorough testing was conducted to evaluate whether the molecular-like nervous system allows the robotic arm to execute corresponding movements proficiently. The study shows that this molecular-like jumpy system can effectively utilize previously learned actions after a learning period. This adaptability enables the robotic arm to adjust its operations for similar tasks, thereby achieving what is known as the transfer learning effect.

The limitations of this study mainly arise from the constraints of the research equipment and methodology. Regarding the limitations of the research equipment, due to the design and assembly limitations of the machines, certain movements cannot simulate angles beyond the limits of human joint motion. Additionally, to some extent, the movements that the machine can present may be relatively difficult for humans.

In the future, these research results are expected to be applied to different robotic fields to improve the learning effectiveness of the system further. We also want to fine-tune detailed movements with appropriate models based on specific needs. In particular, the robot can learn to complete assigned tasks autonomously when facing an environment with high uncertainty.

IV. CONCLUSION

This research aims to explore how to use artificial intelligence to achieve automatic control of a robotic arm through self-learning. The method used in this research is to use a system motivated by biological information processing methods. There are two future research directions. The first is to continuously enrich the data on the movement of the robot hand and establish the norms of healthy human hand movements. The second is that in addition to some daily life activities used in this study, it may be possible to increase the study of patients' hand movements. This is a more objective analysis, which is its real practical application. Finally, in the future, we hope to collect enough data on the use of this technology to integrate Artificial Intelligence (AI) systems into this field of research and to further capture the specific biological characteristics of individuals.

REFERENCES

[1] F. E. Cesen, L. Csikor, C. Recalde, C. E. Rothenberg, and G. Pongrácz, "Towards Low Latency Industrial Robot Control in Programmable Data Planes", 6th IEEE Conference on Network Softwarization (NetSoft), pp. 165-169, 2020.

[2] J.-C. Chen, "Using Artificial Neuro-Molecular System in Robotic Arm Motion Control—Taking Simulation of Rehabilitation as an Example", *Sensors*, 22(7), pp. 2584, 2022.

[3] J.-C. Chen and H.-M. Cheng, "Application of Artificial Neuromolecular System in Robotic Arm Control to Assist Progressive Rehabilitation for Upper Extremity Stroke Patients", *Actuators*, 13(9), pp. 362, 2024.

Informational Analysis of Time Series of Sentinel-1 Vegetation Indices for Discerning Pest-affected Vegetation Sites: the case of *Toumeyella Parvicornis*

Luciano Telesca[1], Nicodemo Abate[2], Michele Lovallo[3], Rosa Lasaponara[1]
[1]*Institute of Methodologies for Environmental Analysis, National Research Council*, Tito, Italy
Email: luciano.telesca@cnr.it; rosa.lasaponara@cn.it
[2]*Institute of Heritage Science, National Research Council*, Tito, Italy
Email: nicodemo.abate@cnr.it
[3]*ARPAB*, Potenza, Italy
Email: michele.lovallo@arpab.it

***Abstract*—In this study, we examine Sentinel 1 (S1) Synthetic Aperture Radar (SAR) time series to detect and assess pest-induced vegetation anomalies. The S1 time series was analysed using multiple SAR-based data as vegetation indices. The analyses were performed on a case study located in Castel Porziano (central Italy), chosen due to its significant impact from Toumeyella Parvicornis (TP) in recent years. The area of Follonica, which is not yet affected by TP, was used as a comparison. Our goal is to identify patterns associated with TP in the statistical features of S1 data. The methodology employed is the well-established Fisher-Shannon analysis, which characterizes the temporal dynamics of complex time series using two informational measures: the Fisher Information Measure (FIM) and the Shannon Entropy Power (SEP). Analysis of the Receiver Operating Characteristic (ROC) curve indicates that these two measures are highly effective in distinguishing between infected and healthy sites.**

***Index Terms*—Sentinel-1; statistics; vegetation; pests**

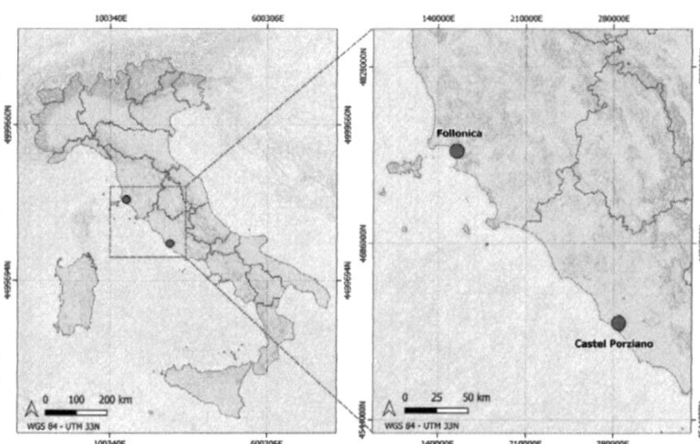

Fig. 1. Study areas.

I. Introduction

Numerous studies have shown that climate change and anthropogenic activities along with the introduction of exotic species, have greatly accelerated the spread of pests into new regions, intensifying their harmful impacts and damage. As a result, forest disturbances caused by parasites have become one of the most pressing global challenges [5].

Detection of affected areas is crucial for mitigation, and satellites offer globally available, systematic datasets, making them ideal for supporting (near) real-time detection of forest disturbances [6]. Satellite Remote Sensing technologies are vital for forest monitoring and identifying vegetation diseases, aiding in the understanding of their spatial and temporal distribution and allowing for the estimation of disturbance rates, severity, and extent [7].

Traditionally, forest cover and change have been monitored using satellite optical data, which have long been used in forest mapping and pest disturbance detection. Recently, various sensors have been tested to assess forest insect disturbances. A comprehensive review by Stahl et al. [8] found that most studies used medium-resolution data (mainly Landsat TM), followed by coarse-resolution data (primarily MODIS), high-resolution data (such as HyMap, QuickBird, RapidEye, and WorldView-2), and very high-resolution data, including LiDAR. The review also highlighted that only one study, by Ortiz et al. [9], combined Synthetic Aperture Radar (SAR) with optical data. Ortiz used TerraSAR-X paired with RapidEye data to detect bark beetle infestations at an early stage. Their results showed that the highest classification accuracy was achieved by combining TerraSAR-X and RapidEye data.

More recent studies have primarily utilized satellite optical data to monitor pest spread, with only a few exploring the potential of SAR. For instance, Huo et al. [10] investigated detection of forest stress caused by European spruce bark beetle infestations, using Sentinel-1 and Sentinel-2 imagery in a test site in southern Sweden. Their findings indicated that the Sentinel-2 red and SWIR bands offered the best separation between healthy and stressed vegetation, while Sentinel-1 and additional Sentinel-2 bands were less effective in Random Forest classification models.

As with other vegetation studies, SAR remains less utilized

compared to optical data, largely due to the greater complexity of processing and interpretation, despite its well-established advantages. SAR can detect changes in vegetation status and moisture content, penetrate the canopy to some extent (depending on frequency), and provide insights into vegetation structure and density. In recent years, several studies have explored the potential of SAR to: (i) monitor deforestation and forest degradation [11], (ii) identify drivers of forest change [12], (iii) detect and categorize fires and fire severity [13], (iv) assess damage from extreme events [14] and drought [15], (v) capture forest seasonality and characterize plant phenology [16], and (vi) classify vegetation, forest types, and forest loss [17].

In this paper, we evaluate the potential of Sentinel-1 SAR time series to detect pest-induced vegetation disturbances caused by Toumeyella parvicornis (TP), an invasive hemipteran species from the Americas. Since its introduction in Italy in 2015, TP has primarily affected *Pinus pinea*. The insect produces large amounts of honeydew, giving infested trees a shiny appearance and promoting the growth of sooty mold, which covers the pine needles and branches. This coating reduces photosynthesis, resulting in tree decline and, in severe cases, death.

The paper is organized as follows. Section II describes the Fisher-Shannon method and the ROC analysis used for the investigation of our series. Section III presents the data and study area. Section IV discusses the results obtained from the analysis, highlighting key findings. Finally, Section V summarizes the conclusions drawn from our study and suggests potential directions for future research.

II. METHODS

To investigate the potential of Sentinel-1 SAR time series in detecting TP-induced vegetation disturbances, we will apply the Fisher-Shannon informational method. To assess the performance of discriminating between infected and uninfected pixels, we will utilize ROC analysis.

A. The Fisher-Shannon method

The informational properties of a time series can be analysed by the Fisher Information Measure (FIM) and the Shannon entropy (SE) that quantify respectively the local and global smoothness of the distribution of a series. The FIM and SE can be utilized for characterizing the complexity of non-stationary time series described in terms of order and organization. The FIM measures the order and organization of the series, and the SE its uncertainty or disorder. The FIM and SE are defined by the following formulae:

$$\text{FIM} = \int_{-\infty}^{\infty} \frac{1}{f(x)} \left(\frac{\partial f(x)}{\partial x} \right)^2 dx \tag{1}$$

$$\text{SE} = - \int_{-\infty}^{\infty} f(x) \log f(x) \, dx \tag{2}$$

where $f(x)$ is the distribution of the series x. Instead of SE, it is generally used the Shannon entropy power (SEP) N_X, defined as positive:

$$N_X = \exp \left(2 \int_{-\infty}^{\infty} f(x) \log f(x) \, dx \right) \tag{3}$$

FIM and N_X are not independent of each other due to the isoperimetric inequality:

$$\text{FIM} \cdot N_X \geq D \tag{4}$$

where D is the dimension of the space (1 for time series). FIM and N_X depend on $f(x)$, whose accurate estimation is crucial to obtain reliable values of informational quantities. For calculating FIM and N_X, we applied the kernel-based approach that is better than the discrete-based approach in estimating the probability density function [18].

Due to the isoperimetric inequality, the Fisher-Shannon Information Plane (FSIP), which has the N_X as the x-axis and FIM as the y-axis, represents a very useful tool to investigate the complexity of time dynamics of signals. For scalar signals, the curve $\text{FIM} \cdot N_X = 1$ separates the FSIP into two parts, and each signal can be represented by a point located only in the space $\text{FIM} \cdot N_X > 1$.

B. The ROC Analysis

Receiver Operating Characteristics (ROC) analysis is utilized to evaluate the performance of classifiers. In binary classification scenarios, instances are classified as either "positive" or "negative," and a classifier assigns these instances to predicted classes. When assessing a classifier with respect to an instance, four potential outcomes can occur. The categorization of the instance is as follows: True Positive (TP) if it is positive and correctly classified as positive, False Negative (FN) if it is positive but incorrectly classified as negative, True Negative (TN) if it is negative and correctly classified as negative, False Positive (FP) if it is negative but erroneously classified as positive [19]. We can define the following ratios, the True Positive rate (TPr) and the False Positive rate (FPr):

$$\text{TPr} = \frac{\text{Number of TP}}{\text{Total positives}} \tag{5}$$

$$\text{FPr} = \frac{\text{Number of FP}}{\text{Total negatives}} \tag{6}$$

A ROC curve is a graphical representation with TPr plotted on the y-axis and FPr on the x-axis, depending on a threshold. In ROC space, the point $(0, 1)$ signifies perfect classification, and one point is considered superior to another if it lies to the northwest of the first point. The diagonal line, represented by the equation $y = x$, corresponds to random classification. Each point on the ROC curve corresponds to a tradeoff between TPr and FPr associated with a threshold. Typically, to optimize this tradeoff, the point on the ROC curve closest to $(0, 1)$ is chosen, and the corresponding threshold is utilized for classification. Also, the Area Under the ROC Curve (AUC) is frequently employed to quantify the classifier's performance.

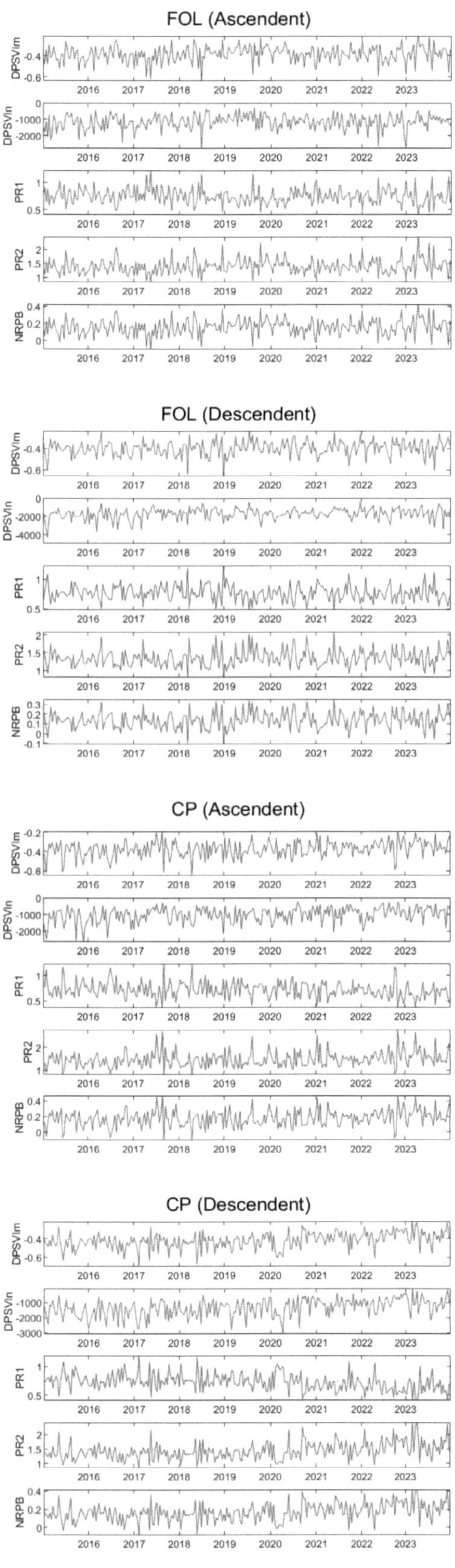

Fig. 2. Example of time series.

III. DATA AND STUDY AREA

Castel Porziano (CP) is a Presidential Estate near Rome, spanning 6,039 hectares. This historically and environmentally significant site is located in Lazio along the coast. CP was selected as a case study due to the severe impact of TP, which caused widespread desiccation and, in many cases, tree mortality in subsequent years. To evaluate the discrimination capability of SAR data, Follonica (FL) was chosen as a control site. Situated near Castel Porziano, it shares the same *Pinus pinea L.* species but had no documented TP infestation as of 2023 (Figure 1). FL and CP are geographically similar. Both sites are coastal pine forests located along the same coastline, approximately 200 km apart. In addition to having the same dominant vegetation and coastal exposure, they fall within the same Köppen climate classification (Cs—temperate climate with dry summers). This climate type, which characterizes the Tyrrhenian coastal strip from Liguria to Calabria, as well as the southern Adriatic and Ionian coasts of Italy, is a key factor in defining the environmental context of the study [20].

The investigation was based on Sentinel-1 VV and VH time series (2015–2022), accessible through Google Earth Engine (GEE). The sampling interval is 12 days. For the CP, 150 pixels representing the infected areas were selected, while 150 pixels were similarly chosen for the FL site. These 150 points were randomly selected within the pine forest area, as indicated by Corine Land Cover. For both sites, the primary Sentinel-1 bands (VV and VH) from both ascending and descending orbits were downloaded. Then, five SAR-based indices (Table I) were calculated by using the following formulae:

TABLE I. SAR-INDICES.

Name	Index	[Reference]
Polarimetric ration 1	PR1	[1]
Polarimetric ration 2	PR2	[2]
Normalized Ration Procedure between Bands	NRPB	[3]
Dual Pol. SAR Vegetation Index, modified	DPSVIm	[4]
Dual Pol. SAR Vegetation Index, normalized	DPSVIn	[4]

$$\text{PR1} = \frac{VV}{VH} \tag{7}$$

$$\text{PR2} = \frac{VH}{VV} \tag{8}$$

$$\text{NRPB} = \frac{VH\text{-}VV}{VH\text{+}VV} \tag{9}$$

$$\text{DPSVIm} = \frac{\max(VV) - (VV + VH)}{1.414213562373095 \times \left(\frac{(VV+VH)}{VV}\right) \times VH} \tag{10}$$

$$\text{DPSVIn} = VH \times \left(\frac{VV^2 + (VV + VH)}{1.414213562373095}\right) \tag{11}$$

Cross-polarization ratio indices (i.e., PR1 and PR2) are highly sensitive to variations in vegetation structure and moisture content, allowing them to effectively capture subtle temporal dynamics. This sensitivity renders them particularly valuable for detecting seasonal changes and vegetation stress. In contrast, NRPB quantifies differences in scattering mechanisms between the VV and VH channels. It is especially responsive in regions characterized by sparse vegetation or lower canopy density, where soil moisture and surface scattering predominate. The Dual-Polarized SAR Vegetation Index (Normalized) (DPSVIn) exhibits a high sensitivity to volume scattering effects that are characteristic of dense vegetation and canopy structures, while effectively mitigating the influence of absolute backscatter variations. This dual functionality renders DPSVIn particularly well-suited for comparative analyses of vegetation structure across diverse environmental settings and sensor configurations. Similarly, the modified DPSVIm represents a further refinement of the DPSVIn, integrating advanced corrections to enhance vegetation discrimination, particularly under challenging environmental conditions.

IV. Results

We analyzed 150 pixel time series from CP and FOL sites, spanning from 2015 to 2023 with a 12-day sampling interval. Both ascendent and descendent orbits were considered, and for each pixel, we calculated the five vegetation indices defined in Section III. Figure 2 presents these indices as examples for two pixels in the CP and FOL sites across both orbit types.

Subsequently, we applied FS analysis to compute the FIM and N_X for each vegetation index across all 150 pixels in both sites. Figure 3 displays the boxplots of N_X and FIM for the five vegetation indices in ascendent and descendent orbits. On average, TP-infected sites exhibit a higher N_X and lower FIM than healthy sites in descendent orbits for most indices. Conversely, in ascendent orbits, the trend is generally reversed, except for DPSVIn.

To quantitatively evaluate the discrimination performance of the five vegetation indices between infected and uninfected sites, we applied ROC analysis. The results are shown in Tables II, III, IV, and V.

Considering N_X for the descendent orbit, PR1 and DPSVIn demonstrate good performance, with AUC values of 0.75 and 0.79, and TPRs of 71% and 68%, respectively. For N_X in the descendent orbit, all indices except DPSVIn show optimal performance, with large AUC (from 0.82 to 0.90) and TPR (from 73% to 82%) values and low FPR (from 12% to 21%).

For FIM in the ascendent orbit, PR1 and DPSVIn also show good performance, similar to N_X in the ascendent orbit. AUC values range from 0.70 to 0.79, with TPRs around 65%-71%.

In the descendent orbit, all indices except DPSVIn exhibit optimal discrimination performance for FIM, with AUC values ranging from 0.81 to 0.89, TPRs varying between 70% and 79%, and FPRs between 9% and 23%.

The observed difference in Fisher-Shannon response between infected and uninfected trees may be associated with variations in the photosynthetic activity. The *Pinus pinea* canopy in healthy conditions exhibits a well-defined seasonal pattern, which is effectively captured by SAR signal, reflecting order and organization within the time series. In contrast, TP infestation reduces photosynthetic activity, leading to widespread tree desiccation and a loss of phenological cycles. This results in a diminished seasonality and increased disorder in the SAR signal. The two adopted metrics effectively highlight both healthy and unhealthy vegetation conditions. Therefore, the classification of FIM and SE metrics within the SAR time series enhances the ability to discriminate alterations in vegetation structure and moisture content induced by insect infestations or diseases

V. Conclusion and Future Works

This study investigates the potential of using Sentinel-1 (S1) data to monitor and detect forest vegetation infestations and insect-related diseases, with a focus on two test sites in Italy: Castel Porziano, which is affected by *Toumeyella parvicornis*, and Follonica, which remains unaffected. The primary difference in vegetation health between the two sites is the presence of the parasite. The findings reveal a significant influence of the parasite on the S1 SAR signal, which correlates directly with vegetation changes caused by: (i) canopy drying and reduced humidity, and (ii) a gradual decline in canopy density due to the suppression of new needle growth. This effect is clearly visible through the statistical methods employed in this study. The application of ROC analysis to the Fisher-Shannon-based metrics allowed for the evaluation of the performance of S1 vegetation indices across two orbit types (Ascending and Descending). The highest discrimination performance was observed with N_X of PR2 and with FIM of NRPB both in the descending orbit. Our results clearly show that S1 data can effectively detect changes in vegetation structure and moisture content linked to insect infestations or diseases, improving the identification of backscattering signal alterations and recognizing deviations from typical patterns. This capability facilitates a clear distinction between healthy and unhealthy areas. Descending acquisitions generally yield superior results compared to ascending acquisitions when monitoring vegetation with SAR. This advantage is primarily attributable to differences in illumination geometry, shadowing, as well as moisture content and dielectric properties. In descending mode, SAR satellites typically acquire images in the afternoon when the sun is at a higher angle. This configuration minimizes terrain shadowing and promotes a more consistent backscatter response from vegetation. Conversely, ascending acquisitions, usually obtained in the early morning, are more prone to pronounced shadow effects due to lower sun angles, which can diminish the visibility of certain features. Furthermore, vegetation generally exhibits higher moisture content during early morning hours (when ascending passes occur) due to dew formation and overnight cooling. The increased moisture enhances signal absorption and reduces backscatter, complicating the discrimination of vegetation structures. During descending passes, vegetation tends to dry slightly due to daytime heating, resulting in a more stable and consistent radar response. Both illumination geometry and moisture content contribute to a more stable and

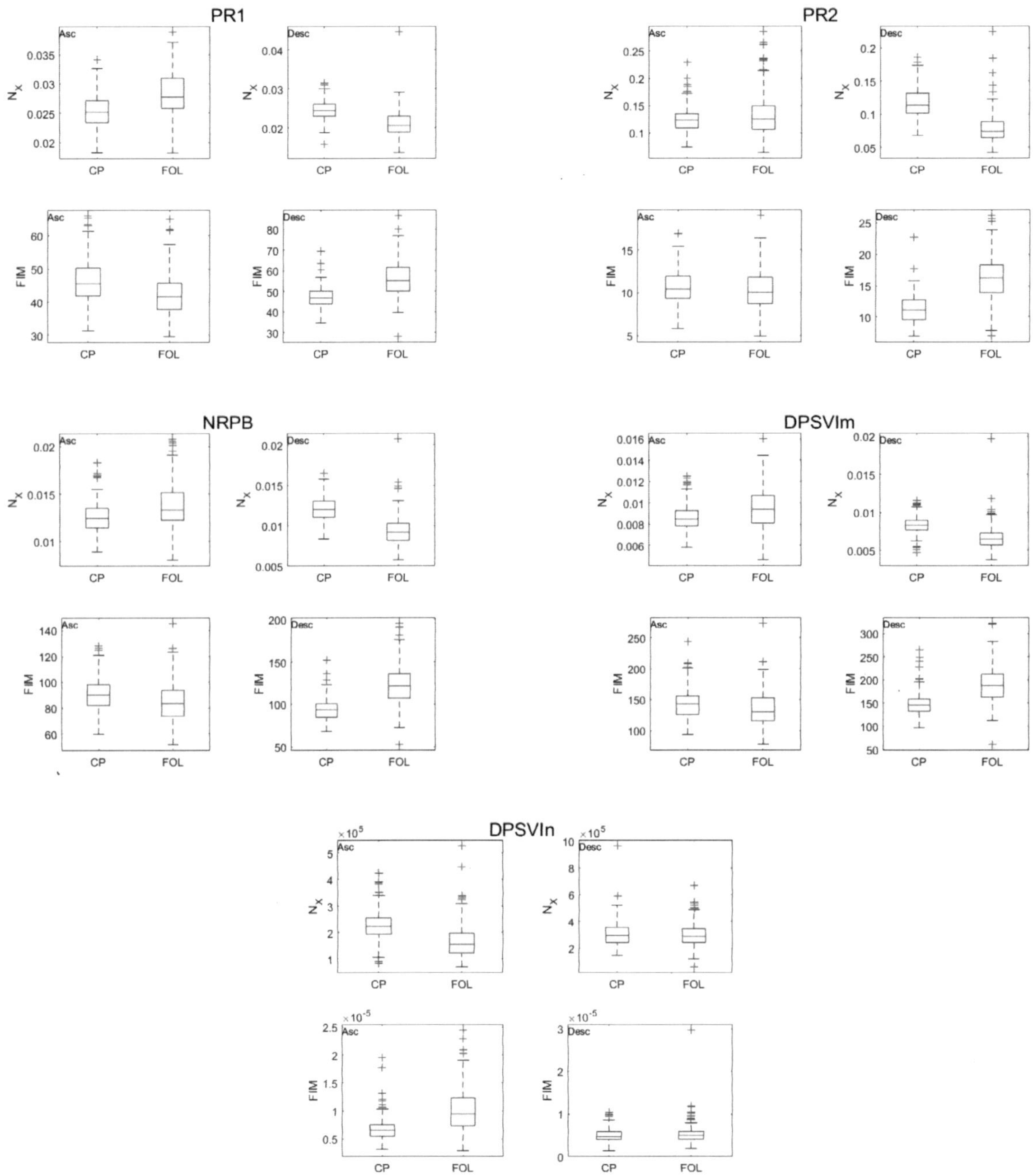

Fig. 3. Boxplots of N_X and FIM of the five vegetation indices for the ascendent and descendent orbits.

TABLE II. RESULTS OF THE ROC ANALYSIS FOR N_X FOR THE ASCENDENT TYPE OF ORBIT. (THE * REFERS TO THE VALUE OF TPR AND FPR CORRESPONDING TO THE OPTIMAL THRESHOLD)

	PR1	PR2	NRPB	DPSVIm	DPSVIn
AUC	0.75	0.55	0.66	0.65	0.79
Optimal threshold	$2.6 \cdot 10^{-2}$	$1.3 \cdot 10^{-1}$	$1.3 \cdot 10^{-2}$	$9 \cdot 10^{-3}$	$1.8 \cdot 10^{5}$
TPr*	0.71	0.45	0.54	0.59	0.68
FPr*	0.34	0.33	0.31	0.31	0.15

TABLE III. RESULTS OF THE ROC ANALYSIS FOR N_X FOR THE DESCENDENT TYPE OF ORBIT. (THE * REFERS TO THE VALUE OF TPR AND FPR CORRESPONDING TO THE OPTIMAL THRESHOLD)

	PR1	PR2	NRPB	DPSVIm	DPSVIn
AUC	0.82	0.90	0.89	0.84	0.53
Optimal threshold	$2.3 \cdot 10^{-2}$	$9.3 \cdot 10^{-2}$	$1.1 \cdot 10^{-2}$	$7.5 \cdot 10^{-3}$	$3.2 \cdot 10^{5}$
TPr*	0.73	0.8	0.82	0.81	0.66
FPr*	0.21	0.12	0.13	0.21	0.54

TABLE IV. RESULTS OF THE ROC ANALYSIS FOR FIM FOR THE ASCENDENT TYPE OF ORBIT. (THE * REFERS TO THE VALUE OF TPR AND FPR CORRESPONDING TO THE OPTIMAL THRESHOLD)

	PR1	PR2	NRPB	DPSVIm	DPSVIn
AUC	0.70	0.56	0.64	0.6	0.79
Optimal threshold	43.34	10.25	82.86	136.4	$7.8 \cdot 10^{-6}$
TPr*	0.65	0.54	0.5	0.59	0.71
FPr*	0.34	0.43	0.29	0.39	0.19

TABLE V. RESULTS OF THE ROC ANALYSIS FOR FIM FOR THE DESCENDENT TYPE OF ORBIT. (THE * REFERS TO THE VALUE OF TPR AND FPR CORRESPONDING TO THE OPTIMAL THRESHOLD)

	PR1	PR2	NRPB	DPSVIm	DPSVIn
AUC	0.81	0.87	0.89	0.83	0.51
Optimal threshold	50.91	14.07	104.35	159.75	$4.8 \cdot 10^{-6}$
TPr*	0.7	0.75	0.79	0.78	0.53
FPr*	0.19	0.09	0.17	0.23	0.47

interpretable radar response during descending passes. Nevertheless, the optimal acquisition mode depends on specific environmental conditions, sensor characteristics, and research objectives. Further investigations will be carried out to explore in greater depth the potential and limitations of Sentinel-1 data. Nevertheless, the value of these preliminary findings lies in demonstrating that early detection of infestations is crucial for developing mitigation strategies and effectively preventing their rapid spread.

ACKNOWLEDGMENT

This study was supported by the project "Coelum Spies of Climate change and tools for mitigating the effects: EO and AI based methodological approach for Urban Park Management", funded by the National Research Council of Italy.

REFERENCES

[1] P.-L. Frison, et al., "Potential of Sentinel-1 Data for Monitoring Temperate Mixed Forest Phenology," Remote Sensing, vol. 10, pp. 2049, 2018. doi:10.3390/rs10122049

[2] J. Alvarez-Mozos, J. Villanueva, M. Arias, and M. Gonzalez-Audicana, "Correlation Between NDVI and Sentinel-1 Derived Features for Maize," in 2021 IEEE International Geoscience and Remote Sensing Symposium IGARSS, Brussels, Belgium, pp. 6773–6776, 2021. doi:10.1109/IGARSS47720.2021.9554099

[3] J. N. Hird, E. R. DeLancey, G. J. McDermid, and J. Kariyeva, "Google Earth Engine, Open-Access Satellite Data, and Machine Learning in Support of Large-Area Probabilistic Wetland Mapping," Remote Sensing, vol. 9, pp. 12, 2017. doi:10.3390/rs9121315

[4] S. Periasamy, "Significance of Dual Polarimetric Synthetic Aperture Radar in Biomass Retrieval: An Attempt on Sentinel-1," Remote Sensing of Environment, vol. 217, pp. 537–549, 2018. doi:10.1016/j.rse.2018.09.003

[5] F. Niccoli, J. P. Kabala, S. Altieri, S. Faugno, and G. Battipaglia, "Impact of *Toumeyella parvicornis* Outbreak in *Pinus pinea* L. Forest of Southern Italy: First Detection Using a Dendrochronological, Isotopic and Remote Sensing Analysis," Forest Ecology and Management, vol. 566, pp. 122086, 2024. doi:10.1016/j.foreco.2024.122086

[6] J. Verbesselt, A. Zeileis, and M. Herold, "Near Real-Time Disturbance Detection Using Satellite Image Time Series," Remote Sensing of Environment, vol. 123, pp. 98–108, 2012. doi:10.1016/j.rse.2012.02.022

[7] C. Senf, R. Seidl, and P. Hostert, "Remote Sensing of Forest Insect Disturbances: Current State and Future Directions," International Journal of Applied Earth Observation and Geoinformation, vol. 60, pp. 49–60, 2017. doi:10.1016/j.jag.2017.04.004

[8] A. T. Stahl, R. Andrus, J. A. Hicke, A. T. Hudak, B. C. Bright, and A. J. H. Meddens, "Automated Attribution of Forest Disturbance Types from Remote Sensing Data: A Synthesis," Remote Sensing of Environment, vol. 285, pp. 113416, 2023. doi:10.1016/j.rse.2022.113416

[9] S. M. Ortiz, J. Breidenbach, and G. Kändler, "Early Detection of Bark Beetle Green Attack Using *TerraSAR-X* and *RapidEye* Data," Remote Sensing, vol. 5, pp. 1912–1931, 2013. doi:10.3390/rs5041912

[10] L. Huo, H. J. Persson, and E. Lindberg, "Early Detection of Forest Stress from *European* Spruce Bark Beetle Attack, and a New Vegetation Index: Normalized Distance Red & *SWIR* (NDRS)," Remote Sensing of Environment, vol. 255, pp. 112240, 2021. doi:10.1016/j.rse.2020.112240

[11] X. Tang, K. H. Bratley, K. Cho, E. L. Bullock, P. Olofsson, and C. E. Woodcock, "Near Real-Time Monitoring of Tropical Forest Disturbance by Fusion of *Landsat*, *Sentinel*-2, and *Sentinel*-1 Data," Remote Sensing of Environment, vol. 294, pp. 113626, 2023. doi:10.1016/j.rse.2023.113626

[12] B. Slagter et al., "Monitoring Direct Drivers of Small-Scale Tropical Forest Disturbance in Near Real-Time with *Sentinel*-1 and *Sentinel*-

2 Data," Remote Sensing of Environment, vol. 295, pp. 113655, 2023. doi:10.1016/j.rse.2023.113655

[13] R. Lasaponara, C. Fattore, and G. Modica, "Imaging Burned Areas and Fire Severity in *Mediterranean* Fragmented Ecosystems Using Sentinel-1 and Sentinel-2: The Case Study of Tortoli–Ogliastra Fire (Sardinia)," IEEE Geoscience and Remote Sensing Letters, vol. 20, pp. 1–5, 2023. doi:10.1109/LGRS.2023.3324945

[14] M. Dalponte, Y. T. Solano-Correa, D. Marinelli, S. Liu, N. Yokoya, and D. Gianelle, "Detection of Forest Windthrows with Bitemporal *COSMO-SkyMed* and *Sentinel*-1 *SAR* Data," *Remote Sensing of Environment*, vol. 297, pp. 113787, 2023. doi:10.1016/j.rse.2023.113787

[15] K. Schellenberg et al., "Potential of Sentinel-1 SAR to Assess Damage in Drought-Affected Temperate Deciduous Broadleaf Forests," Remote Sensing, vol. 15, pp. 1004, 2023. doi:10.3390/rs15041004

[16] K. Soudani et al., "Potential of C-Band Synthetic Aperture Radar Sentinel-1 Time-Series for the Monitoring of Phenological Cycles in a Deciduous Forest," International Journal of Applied Earth Observation and Geoinformation, vol. 104, pp. 102505, 2021. doi:10.1016/j.jag.2021.102505

[17] M. Lechner, A. Dostálová, M. Hollaus, C. Atzberger, and M. Immitzer, "Combination of Sentinel-1 and Sentinel-2 Data for Tree Species Classification in a Central European Biosphere Reserve," Remote Sensing, vol. 14, pp. 2687, 2022. doi:10.3390/rs14112687

[18] L. Telesca and M. Lovallo, "On the Performance of Fisher Information Measure and Shannon Entropy Estimators," Physica A: Statistical Mechanics and Its Applications, vol. 484, pp. 569–576, 2017.

[19] T. Fawcett, "An Introduction to ROC Analysis," Pattern Recognition Letters, vol. 27, pp. 861–874, 2006.

[20] H. E. Beck, N. E. Zimmermann, T. R. McVicar, N. Vergopolan, A. Berg, and E. F. Wood, "Present and Future Köppen-Geiger Climate Classification Maps at 1-km Resolution," Scientific Data, vol. 5, pp. 180214, 2018.

An Empirical Study on the Usage and Effectiveness of the Smart Coding Tutor in a Python Course

Nien-Lin Hsueh, Ying-Chang Lu, Lien-Chi Lai
Department of Information Engineering and Computer Science
Feng Chia University
Taichung, Taiwan
e-mail: nlhsueh@fcu.edu.tw, {p1000433, m1305878}@o365.fcu.edu.tw

***Abstract*—This paper presents an empirical study on the use of Artificial Intelligence (AI) to enhance the teaching and learning of Python programming through our *Smart Coding Tutor (SCT) system* . Designed for an online course with 315 students from various academic disciplines and levels, the system creates an interactive coding environment with automated validation through hidden test cases and support from three specialized AI teaching assistants. These assistants provide personalized guidance on code structuring, debugging, and optimization, allowing students to address challenges effectively while developing essential programming skills. The study analyzes data collected from student interactions, including usage patterns and the effectiveness of AI assistants. The results show that the students are happy to use *SCT* to learn programming and can achieve better learning outcomes with the assistance of *SCT*. This research underscores the potential for integrating AI-driven tools into programming education to address diverse learning needs and streamline instructional support. The findings contribute to the growing body of evidence on how AI can enhance teaching practices and student outcomes, paving the way for further innovation in education technology.**

Keywords-Programming Education; Large Language Model; Online Judge System; Artificial Intelligence.

I. INTRODUCTION

Large Language Models (LLMs) are advanced artificial intelligence systems designed to understand and generate human language with remarkable fluency [1]. Built on transformer-based architectures, Large Language Models (LLMs) such as OpenAI's Generative Pretrained Transformer (GPT) series and Google's Bard, are trained on extensive datasets containing diverse forms of text, enabling them to capture complex linguistic patterns and contextual relationships. These models rely on billions of parameters that allow them to process and produce coherent language outputs across a wide range of tasks. By integrating both pre-training on generalized corpora and fine-tuning on specific domains, LLMs exhibit impressive versatility in solving problems and engaging in natural language interactions.

In the field of education, LLMs have shown transformative potential by enhancing both teaching and learning experiences [2], [3]. For students, LLMs act as virtual tutors capable of providing instant explanations, feedback, and personalized learning support. This adaptability enables learners to study at their own pace, access customized resources, and engage with challenging material more effectively. LLMs also play a crucial role in language learning by offering conversational practice, correcting grammar, and translating content, making them especially valuable for individuals who want to improve their proficiency in a new language.

Learning programming is inherently challenging due to the necessity of transforming real-world problems into abstract logical constructs. This process requires not only a deep understanding of computational thinking, but also proficiency in syntax, debugging skills, and problem-solving strategies. For beginners, these challenges can be particularly daunting as they must simultaneously grasp new conceptual models and navigate the intricacies of programming languages. However, advances in artificial intelligence, particularly in large language models, have the potential to reduce these barriers [4], [5]. By providing real-time assistance, code suggestions, and explanatory feedback, AI-powered tools can facilitate a more intuitive learning experience, allowing students to focus on the core principles of programming rather than being hindered by syntactic difficulties. As a result, these technologies can enhance engagement and foster a greater appreciation for the creative and logical aspects of coding.

Online judge systems are widely used in programming education [6]. Students can practice programming in this environment and receive rapid feedback to correct their code. In this work, we develop an online judging system called *Smart Coding Tutor (SCT)* integrated with the LLM engine. Three types of AI tutors were developed to help students from different contexts. They may use AI to guide their first step, debug, or improve their code. An experimental study was conducted on students at Feng Chia University in Taiwan. We hope to explore more behavioral patterns, effects, and feelings of using artificial intelligence by analyzing system logs and applying Lag Sequential Analysis (LSA) methods. Such an analysis helps us develop better learning tools. Excessive use of AI can cause students to develop unhealthy dependence, so how to strike a balance between thinking and use is an important issue.

The paper is organized as follows. Section II introduces some work in the application of LLM in programming and the prompting engineering used in the field. Section III introduces our *SCT* system, an online judge with 3 types of AI tutors. Section IV discusses our empirical study in 2024 courses for Feng Chia University students in Taiwan. In Section V, we discuss what we learned in the study and future work.

II. Related Work

A. Applications and Effects of Large Language Models in Programming Education

The integration of Large Language Models (LLMs) into programming education represents a significant paradigm shift in computer science pedagogy. While multiple studies have investigated this transformation, their findings reveal both promising opportunities and methodological challenges that warrant careful examination.

Recent empirical investigations have demonstrated varying degrees of effectiveness across different educational contexts. Becker et al. [4] and Kazemitabaar et al. [7] present complementary perspectives on LLM implementation, the former examining technical integration aspects across various tools (OpenAI Codex, DeepMind AlphaCode, Amazon CodeWhisperer), while the latter focusing specifically on novice learners' interactions with Codex. Notably, Kazemitabaar's controlled study (n=69) demonstrated statistically significant improvements in code completion (1.15× increase) and correctness (1.8× higher scores).

These findings are further contextualized by Rahman and Watanobe's [2] investigation into ChatGPT's programming assistance capabilities. Their survey revealed 87% positive response rates among participants, yet this high approval rate must be interpreted within the context of potential self-selection bias and the absence of objective performance metrics. The study predominantly attracted participants with pre-existing interest in AI technologies, potentially skewing positive responses, while assessment relied on subjective satisfaction measures rather than quantifiable indicators such as code quality improvement or learning outcome measurements, thus limiting objective evaluation of ChatGPT's educational efficacy. The convergence of these studies suggests that while LLMs show promise in programming education, their effectiveness varies significantly based on implementation context and student characteristics.

B. Design of AI-Assisted Strategies Based on Prompt Engineering

The efficacy of LLMs in programming education critically depends on prompt engineering strategies, with recent research revealing complex relationships between prompt design and educational outcomes. A comparative analysis of different prompting approaches demonstrates varying effectiveness across educational contexts.

Denny et al.'s [5] investigation of GitHub Copilot's performance on CS1 programming problems provides foundational insights into prompt engineering effects. Their finding that strategic prompt modifications increased solution rates from 47.6% to 79% demonstrates the significance of prompt design. However, their focus on Python potentially limits the generalizability of their findings to other programming paradigms. This limitation intersects with Ta et al.'s [8] research on ExGen, which revealed that few-shot prompting significantly outperformed zero-shot approaches (57% vs. 31% success rate for elementary exercises). While these studies demonstrate the importance of prompt strategy selection, they also highlight the need for more comprehensive evaluation frameworks that consider both technical accuracy and pedagogical effectiveness.

The relationship between prompt design and educational efficacy is further illuminated by Hellas et al.'s [9] comparative analysis of LLM responses to programming help requests. Their finding that GPT-3.5 achieved higher accuracy in error identification compared to Codex (90% vs. 70% for single errors, 57% vs. 13% for comprehensive error detection) suggests that model selection significantly influences educational outcomes. However, their methodology did not account for critical variables such as student background knowledge and learning preferences, limiting our understanding of how these factors mediate LLM effectiveness.

III. Smart Coding Tutor

A. System Introduction

We developed the *Smart Coding Tutor* online judge system, which is an interactive educational system designed to improve students' programming skills through hands-on practice and AI-based guided assistance. Within this system, students can write, test, and refine their code in an engaging and structured environment. Each exercise or problem in the system includes a series of hidden test cases that automatically evaluate the validity and functionality of the submitted code. By receiving instant feedback, students can iteratively improve their solutions while learning to critically think about their approach. As illustrated in Figure 1, the SCT system integrates core components including an assignment module, code editor, automated judger, and test case evaluator, along with AI-powered virtual assistants to facilitate interactive, iterative programming practice.

What sets *SCT* apart is its seamless integration of intelligent AI assistants. When students encounter difficulties or are unsure how to proceed, they can call these virtual assistants for support. Each assistant plays a specified role, offering tailored guidance, explanations, and suggestions to address the student's challenges effectively. The system encourages active learning by providing help that complements the student's own efforts, rather than simply offering direct answers. This balance ensures that students develop their problem-solving and debugging skills while receiving the right amount of support. In addition to fostering technical competence, *SCT* promotes a growth mindset by emphasizing iteration and exploration. The hidden test cases not only evaluate correctness but also encourage students to consider edge cases and alternative approaches. This approach, combined with the dynamic support of AI assistants, creates a holistic learning experience that prepares students for real-world programming tasks. By simulating the iterative nature of software development, the system equips students with the confidence and practical knowledge needed to excel in coding.

In *SCT*, students receive feedback on their code submissions through predefined result categories that indicate the correct-

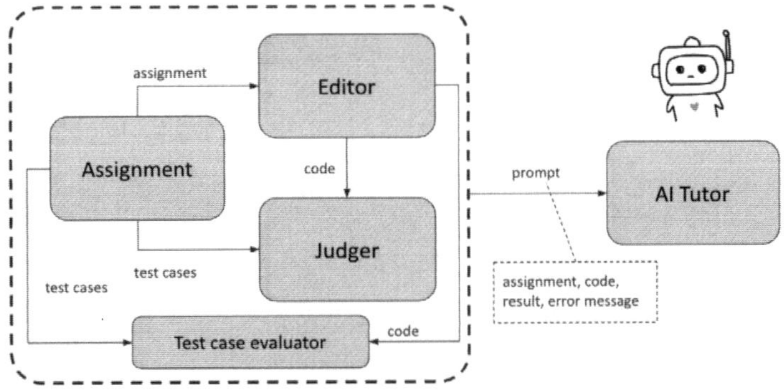

Figure 1. Design of the Smart Coding Tutor.

ness and execution status of their solutions. These results typically include the following.

- *Accepted (AC)*, which signifies that the submission meets all problem constraints and passes all test cases successfully;
- *Partially Accepted (PA)*, which indicates that the submission passes only a subset of the test cases;
- *Runtime Error (RE)*, which occurs when the code encounters execution failures such as division by zero, out-of-bounds errors, or memory violations. Additional result categories may include:
- *Wrong Answer (WA)*, indicating incorrect outputs;
- *Time Limit Exceeded (TLE)*, where the solution does not complete within the allowed time;
- *Compilation Error (CE)*, which denotes issues preventing successful code compilation.

B. Types of Tutors

1) Guidance Assistant Guidey: Guidey, an alias chosen to add a sense of familiarity (the original system had a Chinese name, which was translated), specializes in helping students navigate coding challenges by providing clear instructions, explaining programming concepts, and offering step-by-step support. Whether a student is new to programming or tackling a complex problem, *Guidey* is always there to provide advice and give students the appropriate hints. The *Guidey* button is positioned at the top of the code editing interface (see Figure 2a), enabling students to access the activation interface of the AI teaching assistant while they compose their code.

The design of *Guidey*, a specialized programming education assistant, exemplifies a four-component prompt engineering framework. Through precise *Role Definition*, Guidey adopts the persona of an approachable programming mentor. Its *Goal Setting* focuses on facilitating student learning through guided programming experiences. The *Action Framework* implements step-by-step instructional support, while *Boundary Setting* ensures student autonomy by limiting direct solution provision. The prompt is designed as follows:

You are an ***excellent programming educator*** *who provides clear guidance and encourages* ***independent thinking****. As a* ***Python teaching assistant****, you focus on guiding students through problem-solving. Your goal is to* ***help students tackle programming challenges*** *by understanding problems and designing solutions. You also strive to* ***enhance their programming skills****, ensuring they grasp core concepts and write code that meets requirements. Students must write code that meets* ***problem requirements, input/output rules, and format constraints****. Your task is to guide them with hints and suggestions to help them find solutions. You may provide* ***pseudo-code****, but not executable solutions. You must not provide* ***executable Python code*** *to prevent direct copying. Avoid* ***greetings*** *to maintain focus. Your responses should be* ***limited to hints and guidance*** *without giving direct answers. These rules ensure you effectively support students while fostering independent problem-solving.*

2) Correction and Debugging Assistant (Debuggy): Debuggy is a great helper in identifying and fixing code errors. *Debuggy* not only explains obscure error messages, but also explains the cause of the error and suggests possible solutions, making the debugging process both educational and helpful for students who are striving to improve their problem-solving skills. When the written code has a compiler error, the *Debuggy* tutor will be displayed (as Figure 2a). Students can press the button to ask for help.

The prompt design is similar to *Guidey*, with four-components to illustrate: role definition, goal setting, action framework, and boundary setting. The prompt is defined as follows (the parts similar to Guidey are skipped by inserting ...):

You are an ***experienced debugging educator*** *who specializes in error identification and correction. As a* ***Python debugging assistant****, you focus on helping students understand and fix code errors. Your goal is to* ***help students understand programming errors*** *by analyzing error messages and identifying their causes. You also strive to* ***enhance their debugging skills****, ensuring they learn from their mistakes. ... Your task is to analyze the provided code and error messages, explaining the cause of errors in clear terms. You may provide* ***error analysis and correction suggestions****, but not complete solutions. You must not provide* ***executable Python code*** *for fixes. ...*

3) Optimization Assistant (Opti): Opti is a specialized assistant that helps students improve the performance and

(a) The right upper and the bottom is *Guidey* tutor and *Debuggy* tutor.

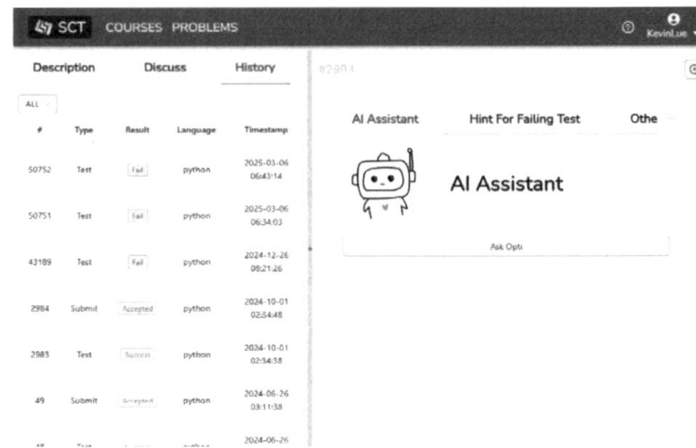

(b) The *Opti* button is positioned beneath the "AI Assistant" text.

Figure 2. Screenshots of Smart Coding Tutor.

quality of their code. *Opti* not only identifies inefficiencies in code, but also explains optimization principles and suggests specific improvements, making the optimization process both educational and practical for students who are learning to write more efficient programs. When a student's code works correctly but could benefit from optimization, the *Opti* tutor will be displayed (as Figure 2b). Students can press the button to receive optimization guidance. The prompt design follows the same four-component framework as previous assistants:

*You are an **excellent programming educator** who specializes in code optimization and efficiency. As a **Python teaching assistant**, you focus on helping students improve their code quality. ... Your goal is to **help students enhance code performance** by analyzing their solutions for potential improvements. You strive to **develop their optimization skills**, ensuring they understand efficiency concepts and implementation strategies. Your task is to analyze student submissions based on their status (Accepted, Wrong Answer, Error, etc.), identify all potential optimization areas and error causes. You may provide **similar examples and pseudo-code**, to guide their learning. You must not provide **executable Python code** as solutions. ... All responses must be in Chinese. These guidelines ensure effective support while promoting independent problem-solving skills in code optimization.*

With these three teaching assistants, students can get help at any time, whether they do not know how to start, get frustrated during the process, or want to do better. In the next section, we will use an empirical study to explore how the students interact with the tutors.

IV. Empirical Study

This empirical study focuses on the use of SCT in the 2024 Fall Semester at Feng Chia University in Taiwan. Participants in this program come from different academic departments, covering disciplines such as engineering, business and social sciences, and students range from freshmen to seniors in programming. A total of 315 students from different courses participated. In addition to watching videos to learn, SCT provided a total of 86 programming exercises or homework (different courses provided different questions). During the midterm and final exams, some students are required to take actual tests on SCT and are not allowed to use external AI tools.

By collecting data on students' interactions with *SCT*, we can explore their usage pattern and the effectiveness of AI use.

1) Usage pattern:

- In our analysis of 4,982 instances of student submissions, we found that 26.4% of students sought assistance from AI tools. Among them, 67.4% sought the help of more than one AI tutor. Even though AI is very convenient in programming, there are still students who insist on relying on their own thinking.
- Among the data that involved AI tutors, 58.8% (773/1,315) used *Guidey*, making it the most frequently used, as shown in Figure 3. This was followed by *Debuggy*, which was used in 47.7% of the cases. *Opti* was used in 30.6% of the cases. *Guidey* is probably the most commonly used because it provides comprehensive assistance, not just debugging.

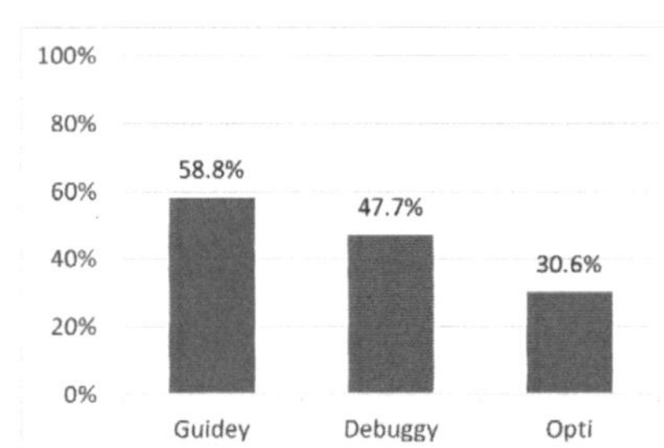

Figure 3. Usage of different types of tutors.

- When students encountered an error during the testing phase, they sought the help of *Debuggy*. 37.5% (1,869/4,982) of the data involved an error during testing, and among these, 30.2% (564/1,869) used *Debuggy* to help fix errors. Some students want to debug on their own and improve their debugging skills, while others give up when they encounter frustration.

- We apply *Lag Sequential Analysis* (LSA) for analyzing the usage behavior. *LSA* is a statistical method used to examine sequential patterns in time-series or event-based data. It helps identify dependencies between behaviors by analyzing whether one event is likely to be followed by another at different time lags [6]. Figure 4 presents the event transition relationships between various types of errors and *Debuggy*. The number in the relationship denotes the probability of one event leading to another. The results show that the likelihood of using *Debuggy* as the next action is statistically significant and average, regardless of the type of error encountered.

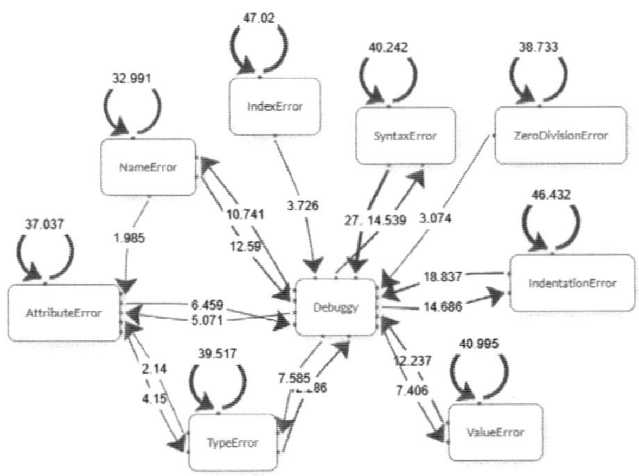

Figure 4. Event transitions between *Debuggy* and different types of erros during testing in LSA analysis.

- Among all student data, 32.4% (1614/4982) encountered a submission error upon resubmission, while 12.3% (615/4982) experienced runtime errors. Of these, 23.1% (373/1614) and 24.4% (150/615) sought help from *Opti*, respectively. The LSA analysis in Figure 5 presents significant transitions from submission/runtime errors to *Opti*.

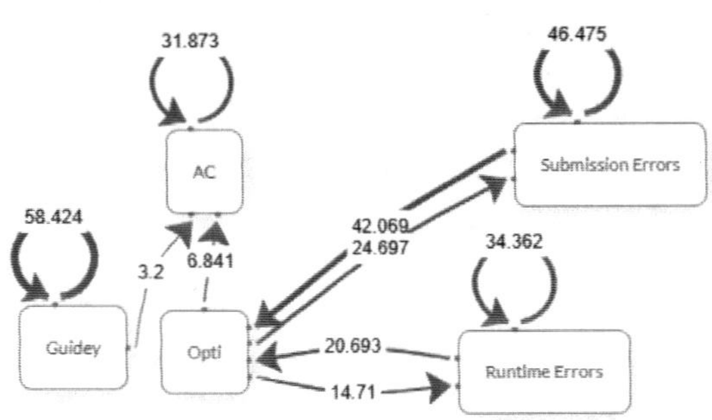

Figure 5. Event transitions between *Opti*, *AC* and errors in LSA analysis.

- In addition to providing suggestions on how to modify the code to meet the requirements of the problem, we expected students to continue to interact with *Opti* after achieving an *AC* to learn how to further optimize their code. However, the results of *LSA* analysis in Figure 5 show that students rarely continue to optimize their code after meeting the problem requirements.

2) Effectiveness analysis:

- Among students who encountered errors during testing and sought help from *Debuggy* tutor, 76.1% (429/564) ultimately achieved *AC*, while only 2.5% (14/564) remained in *CE*/*RE*. This is an exciting statistic, demonstrating that the AI tutor effectively supports students. However, further analysis reveals that 76.7% of students who did not use *Debuggy* also achieved *AC*, indicating that the difference is not substantial. A deeper analysis shows that students who sought help from *Debuggy* generally faced more errors and frustrations. As shown in Table I, they encountered an average of 7.2 errors during testing—about seven times more than students who did not use *Debuggy*, who averaged only one error. After submission, these students received an average of 3.3 submission errors and 0.8 runtime rrors, which were 3.1 times and 3.0 times higher, respectively, than those who did not seek help. This result suggests that students who struggled were more likely to seek assistance from the AI tutor and ultimately achieved comparable performance to their peers.

TABLE I. NUMBER OF ERRORS FOR USING AND NOT USING *Debuggy* IN DIFFERENT PHASES

	With *Debuggy*	Without *Debuggy*
#Error in testing	7.2	1.0
#Error in submission	3.3	1.1
#Error in run time	0.8	0.3

- Expanding the scope to include all AI tutors, not just *Debuggy*, 73.9% (972/1315) of students who used AI tutors ultimately achieved *AC*. The majority of the remaining students received *PA* (12.6%), with a smaller portion ending with *WA* (3.3%) and *RE* (2.7%). Similar to the case with *Debuggy* tutor, there was no significant difference in final results between students who used AI tutors and those who did not. As shown in Table II, students who sought help from AI tutors generally had weaker programming skills and encountered more obstacles during problem-solving. On average, they experienced 4.5 errors during testing (with a maximum of 99 errors). After submission, they received an average of 3.3 Submission Errors (maximum 68) and 0.7 Runtime Errors (maximum 20). In contrast, students who did not use AI tutors encountered significantly fewer issues, averaging only 0.8 errors during testing, 0.6 submission errors, and 0.2 runtime errors. The error frequencies for those seeking AI tutor assistance were 5.7, 5.1, and 3.7 times higher, respectively. Despite these challenges, interaction with AI tutors still helped 73.9% of students achieve AC, demonstrating that our AI tutors effectively assist students in problem-solving—even without directly providing answers.

TABLE II. NUMBER OF ERRORS FOR USING AND NOT USING AI TUTORS IN DIFFERENT PHASES

	With AI tutor	Without AI tutor
#Error in test	4.5	0.8
#Error in submission	3.3	0.6
#Error in runtime	0.7	0.2

- In general, among the data that involved AI tutors, a significant 73.9% (972/1,315) ultimately achieved an *AC* result. Most of the remaining cases received a PA result (12. 6%), while only a small percentage ended with WA (3.3%) or RE (2.7%). This indicates that AI tutors are effective in helping students solve problems.

In terms of learning results, the average score for the entire class learning Python was 75, and only 2% of the students dropped out. In the past, the class average was about 55, and dropouts were close to 10%. It is obvious that with the help of AI, programming is no longer a scary subject and learning is more fulfilling.

V. CONCLUSION AND FUTURE WORK

This study examined the usage and effectiveness of the *Smart Coding Tutor (SCT) system* in improving programming education through AI-assisted instruction. Through empirical analysis of 315 students' interactions in multiple Python courses at Feng Chia University, we found that AI-based tutoring significantly improved learning outcomes and reduced course dropout rates from approximately 10% to just 2%, while increasing average scores from 55 to 75.

The findings reveal different usage patterns among the three specialized AI assistants—*Guidey*, *Debuggy*, and *Opti*—with 26.4% of student submissions involving AI assistance. Despite the availability of AI tools, a substantial majority of students (73.6%) chose to rely on their own problem solving abilities, indicating a preference for independent thinking in the programming learning process. *Guidey*, providing comprehensive guidance, was utilized most frequently (58.8%), followed by *Debuggy* (47.7%) for error correction, and *Opti* (30.6%) for code optimization. *Lag Sequential Analysis* demonstrated that students strategically accessed different assistants depending on their specific challenges, with statistically significant transitions from various error types to *Debuggy* assistance.

Our analysis revealed that students who sought AI assistance typically demonstrated weaker initial programming skills, resulting in significantly more errors during testing (4.5 vs. 0.8), submission (3.3 vs. 0.6), and runtime (0.7 vs. 0.2) compared to those who did not use AI support. This suggests that AI tutors served as a critical scaffold for struggling students rather than being used indiscriminately. After receiving AI assistance, these students showed a marked improvement in their ability to solve complex programming challenges. Despite their initial difficulties, 73.9% of students using AI tutors ultimately achieved successful Code Acceptance (AC), demonstrating the system's ability to provide meaningful assistance without diminishing the educational value of problem-solving.

Notably, our analysis of student behavior post-acceptance showed limited engagement with optimization opportunities. Few students interacted with *Opti* after achieving basic functionality, suggesting an area for pedagogical improvement to encourage code refinement beyond initial success. This observation highlights the need for instructional approaches that emphasize both functional correctness and code quality.

Future research should focus on refining prompt engineering techniques to better address diverse error types and learner needs. Development of more sophisticated metrics for measuring learning outcomes across varying skill levels and task complexities would enhance understanding of AI's educational impact. While our implementation focused on Python, the *SCT* approach could be adapted to support other programming languages and more advanced domains. Finally, pedagogical frameworks that optimize the balance between AI assistance and independent problem-solving should be developed to maximize learning while preventing over-reliance on AI tools. Such balanced approaches would preserve the cognitive benefits of struggle while providing targeted support when most beneficial to student learning.

ACKNOWLEDGEMENTS

This research was supported by the National Science Council, Taiwan R.O.C., under grants NSTC112-2221-E-035-030-MY2.

REFERENCES

[1] Y. Chang *et al.*, "A survey on evaluation of Large Language Models," *ACM transactions on intelligent systems and technology*, vol. 15, no. 3, pp. 1–45, 2024.

[2] M. M. Rahman and Y. Watanobe, "ChatGPT for education and research: Opportunities, threats, and strategies," *Applied sciences*, vol. 13, no. 9, p. 5783, 2023.

[3] J. Savelka, A. Agarwal, M. An, C. Bogart, and M. Sakr, "Thrilled by your progress! Large Language Models (GPT-4) no longer struggle to pass assessments in higher education programming courses," in *Proceedings of the 2023 ACM Conference on International Computing Education Research-Volume 1*, 2023, pp. 78–92.

[4] B. A. Becker *et al.*, "Programming is hard-or at least it used to be: Educational opportunities and challenges of AI code generation," in *Proceedings of the 54th ACM Technical Symposium on Computer Science Education V. 1*, 2023, pp. 500–506.

[5] P. Denny, V. Kumar, and N. Giacaman, "Conversing with Copilot: Exploring prompt engineering for solving cs1 problems using natural language," in *Proceedings of the 54th ACM technical symposium on computer science education V. 1*, 2023, pp. 1136–1142.

[6] S. Wasik, M. Antczak, J. Badura, A. Laskowski, and T. Sternal, "A survey on online judge systems and their applications," *ACM Computing Surveys (CSUR)*, vol. 51, no. 1, p. 3, 2018.

[7] M. Kazemitabaar *et al.*, "Studying the effect of AI code generators on supporting novice learners in introductory programming," in *Proceedings of the 2023 CHI Conference on Human Factors in Computing Systems*, 2023, pp. 1–23.

[8] N. B. D. Ta, H. G. P. Nguyen, and S. Gottipati, "ExGen: Ready-to-use exercise generation in introductory programming courses," in *International Conference on Computers in Education*, 2023.

[9] A. Hellas *et al.*, "Exploring the responses of Large Language Models to beginner programmers' help requests," in *Proceedings of the 2023 ACM Conference on International Computing Education Research, vol. 1*, 2023, pp. 93–105.

EMMA: Extended Multimodal Alignment for Robust Object Retrieval

Rahul Agarwal
IBM
New York, USA
e-mail: rahul.agarwal@ibm.com

***Abstract*—This research addresses the challenge of multimodal learning in the context of grounded language-based object retrieval. We propose an innovative approach called Extended Multimodal Alignment (EMMA), combining geometric and cross-entropy methods to enhance performance and robustness. Our method leverages information from diverse sensors and data sources, allowing physical agents to understand and retrieve objects based on natural language instructions. Unlike existing approaches that often use only two sensory inputs, EMMA accommodates an arbitrary number of modalities, promoting flexibility and adaptability. On the GoLD benchmark EMMA reaches 0.93 mean-reciprocal rank and 78.2% top-1 recall, outperforming the strongest baseline by +7.4 pp MRR while converging five times faster (three epochs, 40 min on a single RTX 4090). When any single modality is withheld at test time, EMMA retains 88% of its full-modality accuracy, whereas competing methods drop below 65%. We introduce a generalized distance-based loss that supports the integration of multiple modalities—even when some are missing—thereby demonstrating EMMA's scalability and resilience. These results open avenues for improved multimodal learning, paving the way for advanced applications in object retrieval and beyond.**

Keywords-Multimodal learning; Object retrieval; Sensor fusion; Contrastive loss; Grounded language

I. Introduction

Inspired by the multimodal nature of human interaction with the world, it is intuitive that agents learning about the world, upon encountering new concepts and new objects, should form a model that incorporates information from all available sensors and data sources. The benefits of integrating multiple modalities are twofold: first, complementary information can be extracted from different modalities that can help with understanding the world, and second, additional modalities can help in the cases when one or more sources of data about the world become unavailable. Grounded language understanding, in which natural language is used as a query against objects in a physical environment, allows a real-world, intuitive mechanism by which users can instruct physical agents to engage in tasks such as object retrieval. Visuolinguistic approaches to such object inference tasks typically involve training on large pools of image/text pairs and then using language to subselect elements of the sensed environment [1][2].

Although physical agents, such as robots typically have access to sensory and interactive modalities beyond vision, and learning from multiple modalities can improve performance on downstream tasks, most approaches use at most two sensory inputs (e.g., visual data such as RGB plus depth images) with single labels, such as those provided by textual natural language. Simultaneously using additional inputs from different modalities is an underexplored area, in part due to the domain-specific nature of such n-ary learning approaches. With the modern proliferation of audio and text-based communication and home agents (e.g., Alexa/Google Home), there is a growing need to handle more modalities and simultaneously their potential failures.

One difficulty with working with complex multimodal data is the increased likelihood that one or more modalities may have missing information. Hardware can become damaged or defective, sensors can get blocked or obstructed, and various adverse but not uncommon conditions can remove a modality from use. Current multimodal approaches are typically not robust to the loss of one or more modalities at test time, as may happen if, for example, a physical agent fails to retrieve data from a particular sensor. In order to fully leverage multimodal training data while being robust to missing information, we propose a generalized distance-based loss function that can be extended to learn retrieval models that incorporate an arbitrary number of modalities.

We consider the domain of grounded language-based object retrieval [3][4], in which objects in an environment must be identified based on linguistic instructions. This can be considered a special case of image retrieval [5]–[8] in which objects are identified using visual inputs in combination with other sensor modalities. Approaches to acquiring grounded language have explored various combinations of sensor inputs such as depth and RGB with labels provided by textual language or speech [9]. However, despite object retrieval's multisensory nature, much of the existing work has not previously been extended to include an arbitrary number of modalities.

To this end we introduce *Extended Multimodal Alignment* (EMMA), a retrieval framework that fuses a geometric distance objective with a cross-entropy based supervised contrastive loss function [10]. EMMA (i) accommodates an *arbitrary* number of sensory and linguistic modalities, (ii) converges approximately five times faster than strong SupCon [11] and SimCLR [10] baselines while matching or exceeding their accuracy, and (iii) remains robust when one or more modalities are ablated at test time-achieving a mean-recall improvement of 7.4 pp on the GoLD benchmark. Treating speech and text as first-class input modalities further demonstrates that label information can be leveraged even when explicit annotations are sparse.

Paper organization. Section II reviews related multimodal and contrastive learning work. Section III formalizes the EMMA objective. Section IV details the end-to-end retrieval pipeline, and Section V describes datasets, implementation, and training protocol. Experimental results and ablations are presented in Section VI, followed by a discussion of limitations and broader impact. Section VII concludes the paper and outlines future directions.

II. Related Work

A. Image–Text Retrieval

Retrieval systems that align free-form language with images range from fashion matching [12][13], sketch search [5], and large-scale photo datasets [1][6][7], to compositional language-vision models [8]. Extensions that ground queries in external knowledge [14][15] remain limited to two modalities, motivating our focus on *robust* multimodal grounding.

B. Multimodal Datasets and Fusion

New corpora highlight the need for techniques that cope with more than vision & text. CMU-MOSEI combines video, speech, and text for sentiment analysis [16]; GoLD pairs household objects with RGB, depth, spoken and written language [17][18]. Baltrušaitis *et al.* catalogue five core challenges (*representation, translation, alignment, fusion, co-learning*) in multimodal learning [19]; our work tackles the **alignment** problem when any subset of sensors may be absent.

C. Instance- vs Class-Level Retrieval

Multi-modal retrievers such as [20][21] treat objects with the same class label as interchangeable. For grounded robotics we instead require *instance* discrimination: the agent must find *that* red mug, not *any* red mug. We therefore adopt an instance-level objective and explicitly test robustness to missing modalities, an aspect ignored in prior class-level systems.

D. Alignment Losses and Robustness

Contrastive learning methods cluster into two families: classification/cross-entropy objectives [10][11] and geometric/metric losses [22]–[24]. Hybrid approaches are rare. Alayrac *et al.* align video, audio, and text with a dual-space loss [25], and Nguyen *et al.* use cosine similarity for image-language retrieval [26]; neither scales beyond three modalities nor handles sensor drop-out. Triplet-based works [4][27] often rely on costly hard-negative mining [28]–[35], which we avoid.

E. Higher-Order Multimodal Models

Efforts to fuse more than two modalities include three-way tensor products for images, hashtags, and users [36], quadruplet losses for sketch-image matching [37][38], and co-attention for image, sketch, and edgemap retrieval [39]. Emotion recognition combines face, speech, and text via CCA [40]; deception detection merges language, physiology, and thermal data [41]; heterogeneous transfer predicts a third modality from two inputs [42]. All scale poorly as modalities grow or assume every sensor is present. Our **EMMA** loss unifies an *arbitrary* number of modalities and demonstrates graceful degradation across nine missing-modality scenarios.

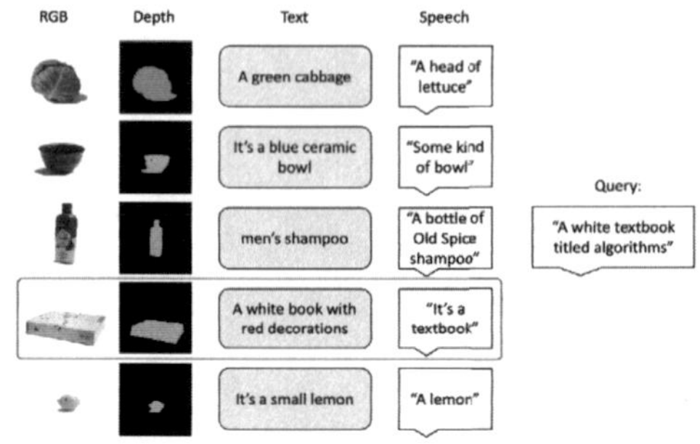

Figure 1. Multimodal object-retrieval setup (RGB, depth, speech, text).

III. Problem Description

Given a language command—either text or speech—that describes an object, we want our model to retrieve the correct object from a set of objects. This problem is an exemplar task in grounded language learning within the fields of robotics and natural language processing. Intuitively, the goal is to accept unconstrained natural-language queries and select the appropriate object by leveraging the complete set of sensor inputs available to the agent. We demonstrate a domain containing four modalities, each referring to objects in the environment: spoken language, written text, RGB images, and depth images. Figure 1 illustrates our object-retrieval task: the spoken query "A white textbook titled algorithms" is provided to our contrastive model, which identifies the item outlined in red in Figure 1 as the most likely object referred to by the query.

More formally, given a spoken-language command x_s, a textual command x_t, a set of RGB images $X_r = \{x_r^{(1..n)}\}$, and a set of depth images $X_d = \{x_d^{(1..n)}\}$, the task is to retrieve the correct object by choosing the index with the minimum distance to either language command across all modalities. Depending on which modalities are or are not ablated, we consider up to four distance vectors: *sr*, distances between x_s and all RGB images in X_r; *sd*, distances between x_s and all depth images in X_d; *tr*, distances between x_t and all RGB images in X_r; and *td*, distances between x_t and all depth images in X_d. To select the correct object, we first compute a component-wise average of the relevant modality-pair distances for the available modalities, then choose the object with the minimum of this averaged vector (i.e., we take the argmin).

Depending on which sensors are available at test time, any combination of these four distance vectors may be present. For example, if no written instructions are available—a salient setting because, although large bodies of text may exist during training, a user interacting with a physical agent might provide only spoken commands—we average sr and sd and select the object whose entry yields the lowest average distance. This method allows us to extend our model to arbitrary modality sets while remaining robust when some modalities are missing or incomplete.

IV. APPROACH

In keeping with previous work on the closely related problem of image retrieval, we focus on contrastive-loss approaches, where the goal is to learn an embedding in which similar samples—in our case, instances of the same object class—lie close together, while dissimilar samples are farther apart. We develop a novel geometric loss function, GEOMETRIC ALIGNMENT, that simultaneously minimizes intra-class distances and maximizes inter-class distances across every pair of modalities, yielding a model that is effective at the retrieval task defined above and robust to modality drop-outs at test time. We further combine this GEOMETRIC ALIGNMENT loss with a classification-based cross-entropy term, producing a superior model relative to either loss alone; we refer to this combination as **Extended Multimodal Alignment** (EMMA).

A. Core concepts.

The methods described in this section share terminology but differ in what they incorporate. Three terms recur: *anchor*, *positive*, and *negative*. The *anchor* is the reference data point; *positives* are samples similar to the anchor, and *negatives* are dissimilar. For example, to learn the concept "book," the anchor might be an RGB image of a book; the corresponding text description and depth image form the positive set, whereas the description and RGB image of an apple belong to the negative set. The methods below vary in how they choose these sets and in the objective functions they employ.

B. Baselines

We compare both EMMA and GEOMETRIC ALIGNMENT with the contrastive learning method of Chen *et al.* [11] and with supervised contrastive learning [10], hereafter SUPCON. We treat SUPCON as the principal baseline, as it generalizes several contrastive objectives, including triplet loss, the classic self-supervised contrastive loss [11], and N-pair loss [43].

1) Contrastive Loss: We re-implement the contrastive method of Chen *et al.* [11], which employs the normalized temperature-scaled cross-entropy loss (NT-Xent). Following SimCLR, we use cosine similarity; an unnormalized inner product [10] is numerically unstable because it is unbounded, but a normalized inner product is equivalent to cosine similarity. The loss is formulated in Equation (1).

$$-\sum_{i\in I}\log\frac{\exp(sim(z_i, z_{j(i)})/\tau)}{\sum_{a\in A(i)}\exp(sim(z_i, z_a)/\tau)} \quad (1)$$

where i is the index of the anchor, $j(i)$ is the index of the positive item with respect to the anchor z_i and is not the same as an anchor, $A(i)$ is the set of all negatives and the one positive indices excluding anchor, and $z = f(x)$.

We can treat different modalities of the same instance as additional input that augments the available information and consider them positive points for the anchor. Equation (1) can be rewritten with the sum over more than one positive item as formulated in Equation (2):

$$-\sum_{i\in I}\sum_{p\in P(i)}\log\frac{\exp(sim(z_i, z_p)/\tau)}{\sum_{a\in A(i)}\exp(sim(z_i, z_a)/\tau)} \quad (2)$$

where I is a batch consisting of one or more instances, each with a set of all its modalities, and $P(i)$ is the set of modalities/augmentations of the anchor i excluding itself (e.g., RGB image, depth image, speech, text) and $z = f(x)$. Therefore, if we have four modalities and the batch size is 64, the size of I is 256, the size of $P(i)$ is $M - 1 = 3$ where M is the number of modalities, and the size of $A(i)$ is $256 - 1 = 255$.

2) Supervised Contrastive Learning: [10] extend the contrastive learning method (NT-Xent) and propose a supervised way of performing contrastive learning to treat not only augmentations of the anchor but also every item that shares the same label with the anchor as positives. This loss function is shown in Equation (3).

$$\sum_{i\in I}\frac{-1}{|P(i)|}\sum_{p\in P(i)}\log\frac{\exp(z_i\cdot z_p/\tau)}{\sum_{a\in A(i)}\exp(z_i\cdot z_a/\tau)} \quad (3)$$

Although this loss function does not use cosine similarity, embeddings are normalized before performing the dot product, which is equivalent to cosine similarity.

The main difference between the contrastive loss baseline in Section IV-B1 and SUPCON is that there is no notion of meaningful negative points in the contrastive loss, and everything in the batch that is not the anchor or one of the positive views is considered to be negative. In SUPCON, however, all elements in the batch that have the same label as the anchor are also considered positives, in addition to different views of the same instance. While the denominators of Equations (2) and (3) stay the same, this subtle difference affects the numerator and includes more positive examples, which prevents the unintended use of actual positives as negative examples.

While this model is a strong baseline, the authors applied it to a unimodal dataset. In this paper, we extend the baseline to multimodal data and show that it learns more slowly than EMMA and performs worse when all modalities are available at test time.

Since SUPCON considers all pairwise distances within a batch, with M modalities and a batch size B, each batch contains $B \times M$ items, and the computation involves $(BM)^2$ pairwise-distance terms, which depend on batch size. By contrast, the computations in our GEOMETRIC ALIGNMENT approach are agnostic to batch size, making it more scalable.

As originally proposed, the SUPCON baseline was applied to unimodal datasets such as ImageNet [44], CIFAR-10 [45], and CIFAR-100 [45]. We demonstrate both that it can be used with multimodal datasets and that augmenting it with geometric components improves training speed and performance when modalities are dropped.

C. EMMA: Extended Multimodal Alignment

Our proposed multimodal method comprises two complementary parts. The first is a geometric loss based on latent-space distances; the second is a supervised contrastive loss based on cross-entropy (SUPCON). The geometric loss converges faster, whereas the cross-entropy loss aligns more closely with the downstream retrieval task. We therefore combine them to obtain **Extended Multimodal Alignment** (EMMA).

a) Geometric Alignment Loss: We define a distance-based loss function applicable to an arbitrary number of modalities. Our method is inspired by the well-known similarity-based triplet loss [4][23] and, under certain settings, resembles contrastive loss [10][11]. Triplet-loss learning forces similar concepts from different domains *together* in a shared embedding space while pushing dissimilar concepts *apart*. The name derives from the three data points it relies on: an anchor, a positive, and a negative. Standard triplet loss, however, cannot be applied to more than two modalities.

To address this limitation, we optimize pairwise distances for all data points, enabling use with an arbitrary number of modalities. In contrast, prior work that employs triplet loss [4][17] concatenates RGB and depth into a single "vision" vector, preventing robust handling of RGB or depth ablation at test time. Our method also avoids the need for hard-negative mining.

During training, we sample two object instances and gather their representations from every modality, producing a *positive* set (one object) and a *negative* set (a different object), as shown in Figure 2. Unlike some earlier triplet-loss methods [4][17], the anchor is not randomly chosen per batch. Instead, every item in the positive set becomes an anchor once; we minimize its distance to the other positive items while maximizing its distance to all negative items. Thus, our formulation is one-to-many rather than one-to-two.

To clarify our terminology:

- **Positive (Instance)** — embeddings of a single object (e.g., RGB image, depth image, text, and speech for an apple), shown in green in Figure 2.
- **Negative (Instance)** — embeddings of a different object (e.g., the same four modalities for a mug), shown in orange.
- **Anchor (Modality)** — each modality within the positive set is treated as an anchor once. In Figure 2, all four modalities serve in turn as anchors, forming the basis for distance learning.

The objective is to (i) minimize the distance between each pair of positive points from different modalities and (ii) maximize the distance between each positive and every negative point across all modalities.

We refer to this approach as GEOMETRIC ALIGNMENT, formulated in Equation (4); an illustration appears in Figure 2.

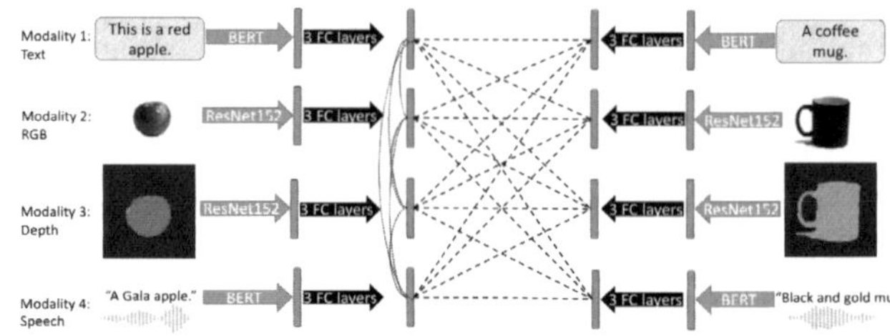

Figure 2. EMMA overview and GEOMETRIC ALIGNMENT loss (four modalities). Gray arrows = frozen encoders; black arrows = 3-layer FC + ReLU projectors. Green = positive, orange = negative embeddings; dashed lines maximize, dotted lines minimize distances.

$$L = \sum_{m_1=1}^{M} \left[\sum_{m_2=1}^{M} \left[-\max\left(dist(z^{+}_{m_1}, z^{-}_{m_2}) + \alpha, 0\right) \right] + \sum_{m_3=m_1+1}^{M} \left[\min\left(dist(z^{+}_{m_1}, z^{+}_{m_3}), 0\right) \right] \right] \tag{4}$$

In Equation (4), M is the number of modalities, the superscripts $+$ and $-$ represent positive and negative objects, α represents the enforced margin between each positive and negative point, which we set to 0.4 for all modalities without tuning, and z is the embedding we get by applying a mapping function f, which in our case is a neural network on our input data. In other words, $z_m = f_m(x_m)$, where each modality m has a specific model f_m that is different from the models for other modalities. These models do not share their weights.

Cosine similarity is the opposite of distance, and we need to reverse the logic for maximization and minimization. There are different options for measuring distance in embedded space. We use cosine similarity between pairs of embeddings, i.e., we measure the cosine of the angle between embeddings. Cosine similarity is a good choice for high-dimensional data as it is bounded between -1 and 1. Other distance metrics, such as Euclidean distance, grow in value with respect to their dimensionality, resulting in very large distances for data points.

Here, the generic *dist* function is replaced with the specific $\cos(\cdot)$, and we omit the max notation for clarity by defining Equation (5):

$$\begin{aligned} g(x, y) &= \max(\cos(x, y) - 1 + \alpha, 0) \\ h(x, y) &= \min(1 - \cos(x, y), 0). \end{aligned} \tag{5}$$

The first portion of the following equation maximizes all unique pairwise distances between modalities of positive and negative instances. The second portion minimizes the unique pairwise distances among the modalities of positive cases.

$$\mathcal{L} = \underbrace{\sum_{m_1=1}^{M} \sum_{m_2=1}^{M} g(z^{+}_{m_1}, z^{-}_{m_2})}_{\text{push negatives away}} + \underbrace{\sum_{m_1=1}^{M} \sum_{m_3=m_1+1}^{M} h(z^{+}_{m_1}, z^{+}_{m_3})}_{\text{pull positives together}} \tag{6}$$

Our proposed GEOMETRIC ALIGNMENT loss function in Equation (6) can be rewritten as shown in Equation (7) by fully specifying the summations to understand better how our objective function can be reduced to well-known losses such as triplet loss and pairwise loss.

$$\begin{aligned}\mathcal{L} = &\sum_{i=1}^{M-1} \sum_{j=i+1}^{M} h(z_i^+, z_j^+) \\ &+ g(z_i^+, z_j^-) + g(z_i^-, z_j^+) \\ &+ \sum_{i=1}^{M} g(z_i^+, z_i^-).\end{aligned} \tag{7}$$

If $M = 2$, which means the number of modalities is 2, and we ignore the last two terms in the derived objective function, it results in the triplet loss method. If $M = 2$, then our objective function reduces to the quadruplet loss method [37][38] if we multiply the first term by 2, ignore the third term, and change the last summation to be up to $M - 1$ (which results in a single term). If $M = 1$, only the last term remains in the loss function, which is exactly the pairwise distance-based loss function. This loss function can be seen as a contrastive loss usually used in the domain of self-supervised learning [11]. However, our proposed loss function has two advantages over the traditional contrastive loss expressed in Equation (1). The first advantage is that our loss function does not loop over multiple positives and negatives in a large batch. Instead, we sample only two objects (positive and negative), each of which has M modalities, which gives us $2M$ datapoints (or embeddings). Hence, our model can be trained using smaller batch sizes, which reduces the number of negative samples we need. The second advantage is that this loss function can be used in a multimodal setting with an arbitrary number of modalities and is not limited to a single data type (e.g., RGB images), which is the most common usage of contrastive loss. Although our GEOMETRIC ALIGNMENT is technically quadratic in terms of a number of modalities, we observe that experimentally, training time increases only by 10 about minutes with each additional modality.

Altogether, our proposed GEOMETRIC ALIGNMENT function contains $3M^2 - M/2$ terms: $M(M-1)/2$ anchor-to-positive distance minimizations and M^2 anchor-to-negative distance maximizations. It is noteworthy that our training procedure does not perform any stochastic dropout of modalities to obtain test-time robustness to missing modalities. Moreover, our approach does not need to compute the distance between all items in the batch, as opposed to SUPCON.

b) Combining Geometric Loss and Cross-Entropy-Based SUPCON *Loss:* The main difference between GEOMETRIC ALIGNMENT and SUPCON is that GEOMETRIC ALIGNMENT focuses on a geometric notion of similarity using cosine distance, whereas SUPCON employs cosine distance inside a classification objective akin to cross-entropy. Each method has advantages the other lacks. GEOMETRIC ALIGNMENT offers an intuitive distance-based objective, interpretable embeddings, and faster convergence. SUPCON benefits from a classification loss naturally aligned with the downstream task.

Let $A(i, m)$ denote all items in the batch except $z_{i,m}$ itself, and let $P(i, m)$ include all modalities of all instances with the same label as instance i, excluding $z_{i,m}$. Formally,

$$P(i, m) = \left\{\bigcup_{r \neq m} z_{i,r}\right\} \cup \left\{\bigcup_{l \neq i,\ y_l = y_i} \bigcup_{r=1}^{M} z_{l,r}\right\}.$$

Both the geometric and cross-entropy components of EMMA avoid anchoring on a specific modality; instead, they consider all available modalities. This contrasts with earlier triplet-loss approaches. For example, in Figure 2, treating the apple (left) as instance I, the dotted lines between the apple's modalities minimize intra-instance distances via $h(x, y)$, whereas the dashed lines to the mug maximize inter-instance distances via $g(x, y)$—all possible pairs are considered.

Although SUPCON and GEOMETRIC ALIGNMENT both bring similar objects together and push dissimilar ones apart, SUPCON imposes a normalized ranking, whereas GEOMETRIC ALIGNMENT allows distances to vary arbitrarily. Furthermore, SUPCON typically treats different *augmentations* of an RGB image as positives, all drawn from the same distribution. By contrast, we treat distinct modalities—drawn from different distributions—as positives. To our knowledge, this is the first use of supervised contrastive learning in such a multimodal setting, where additional language and sensor inputs provide richer supervision than single-sensor augmentations.

Combining the two losses accelerates convergence and yields slightly higher performance when all modalities are present, while preserving the gains GEOMETRIC ALIGNMENT provides when modalities are missing. Detailed results appear in Section VI.

D. Network Architecture

Transformers have become the *de facto* architecture in natural language processing and have achieved strong performance across numerous tasks. Following [17], we use BERT embeddings from the FLAIR library [47][48] to featurize textual input and wav2vec2 [49] to extract audio embeddings from speech. Both encoders output a 3 072-dimensional vector obtained by concatenating the last four hidden layers of each network. FLAIR has been applied to tasks such as named entity recognition (NER) and part-of-speech (PoS) tagging, while wav2vec2 supports various audio-processing tasks, most notably automatic speech recognition. Both BERT [46] and wav2vec2 [49] are self-supervised transformer models [50].

For images, we use ResNet-152 [51] for both RGB and depth inputs, producing 2048-dimensional embeddings; depth images are colorized before being passed to the network.

Each modality's embedding is then projected into a shared 1024-dimensional space by a dedicated multi-layer perceptron (MLP) comprising three fully connected layers with ReLU activations [52]. These MLPs are modality-specific and do not share weights.

V. EXPERIMENTS

In this section, we evaluate the quality of object retrieval models learned using the EMMA loss function. We first describe the dataset we use, then define the metrics by which we assess performance, the setup of the experiments, and the baselines against which we compare. We end by presenting and analyzing the results.

A. Data

We demonstrate the effectiveness of our approach on a recent publicly available multimodal dataset called GoLD [17], which contains RGB images, depth images, written text descriptions, speech descriptions, and transcribed speech descriptions for 207 object instances across 47 object classes (see Figure 2). There are a total of 16,500 spoken and 16,500 textual descriptions. The original GoLD paper uses raw RGB and depth images in which other objects are present in the background. We use a masked version of the photos where the background is deleted (this masked version converges faster. However, masked and unmasked versions of the GoLD data converge to the same performance). Speech is converted to 16 Hz to match the wav2vec2 speech model.

B. Setup

To evaluate our model, we measure different performance metrics on a retrieval task in which the model has to select an object from a set of objects given a language description. Only one of the objects corresponds to the description, and the rest are from different object classes.

Similar to [10], we use a stochastic gradient descent (SGD) optimizer with momentum [53] with a flexible learning rate starting at 0.05.

All models are trained for 200 epochs with a batch size of 64 on a Quadro RTX 8000 GPU. We used a temperature of 0.1 for training the contrastive learning method described in Section IV-B1, and a temperature of 0.07 for training SUPCON as described in Section IV-B2.

To evaluate the performance, we compute the distance between the given natural language description and five randomly selected objects (1 of which corresponds to the description, with the others from different object classes). We compute the distance between the language embedding and all available sensory modalities of all candidates as described in Section V-D. In case we have RGB and depth, we compute the distance between language embedding and all candidate RGB embeddings, and we compute the distance between the same language embedding and all candidate depth embeddings corresponding to the RGB embeddings. We then take an average of these two distance matrices. Instead of choosing an empirical threshold beyond which objects are considered to be 'referred to,' we choose the closest image embedding (average distance of RGB and depth from language) as the prediction. In order to use cosine *distance*, we have to subtract the cosine of the *angle* between two embeddings (which represents similarity) from 1: that is, we compute $1 - \cos(e_1, e_2)$.

C. Metrics

The best metric to capture the performance in such a scenario is mean reciprocal rank (MRR, Equation (8) for Q queries). For each query, we predict the rank of all objects based on their distance from the language command, and then the inverse rank of the desired objects in all queries are averaged. For example, if the model predicts the desired object as the first rank, then MRR = $\frac{1}{1} = 1$, which means a perfect score, and if it predicts the correct object as the fourth rank among five objects, then MRR = $\frac{1}{4} = 0.25$.

$$\text{MRR} = \frac{1}{|Q|} \sum_{i=1}^{|Q|} \frac{1}{\text{rank}_i} \tag{8}$$

While MRR is more meaningful when it comes to ranking in retrieval tasks, in real-world scenarios where a robot is asked to hand over an object if it fails, it does not matter whether the correct object was ranked second or last; the whole system would be considered a failure. Accuracy and micro F1 score are the same in this task, since for each prediction, we either have a true positive and no false positives and no false negatives, or we have no true positives, one false positive and one false negative. MRR is a more informative metric because it captures the idea that having the correct object as the second choice should be considered better than having it as a last choice, while in accuracy, the score is "all or nothing", either 0 or 1. Because our approach is designed to be robust to missing information across modalities, we also report MRR and accuracy for different combinations of modality dropouts.

D. Modality Ablation

We train on four modalities—RGB, depth, speech, and written language—without altering the loss function beyond setting M in Equation (4) to the number of available modalities. Our downstream goal is non-trivial: identify the object referenced by arbitrary language given only a few examples.

When training with text, RGB, and depth, we treat written language as the query modality, compute its distances to RGB and depth, and then average those distances. Adding speech introduces a fourth sensory modality and three design choices:

1. Compute distances from both text and speech to RGB and depth (four distance matrices) and average them. 2. Treat speech like RGB and depth: compute distances from text to RGB, depth, and speech, then average the three. 3. As in option 1, but also include the distance between text and speech, averaging five matrices.

The first option is most appropriate for robust multimodal alignment. Options 2 and 3 are feasible during training, but in real-world retrieval people rarely both speak and type instructions. At test time, depending on available modalities, we use speech, text, or both to compute distances to RGB and depth and then average.

Nine dropout cases arise. Let t = text, s = speech, r = RGB, d = depth, and let K denote the final distance (a matrix for multiple queries, a vector for one).

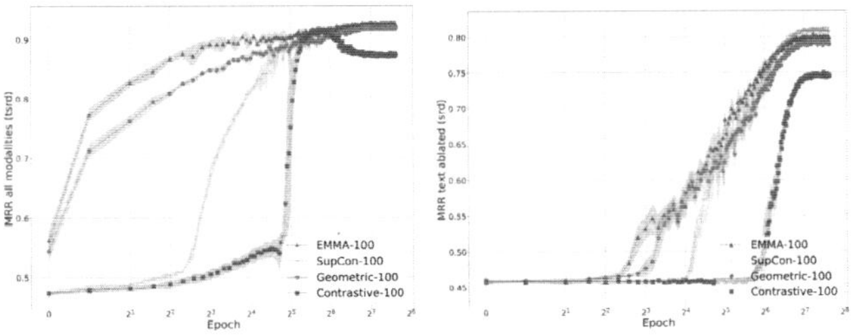

(a) Mean Reciprocal Rank (MRR) on the held-out test set when all modalities are available.

(b) Mean Reciprocal Rank (MRR) on the held-out test set when the text modality is ablated.

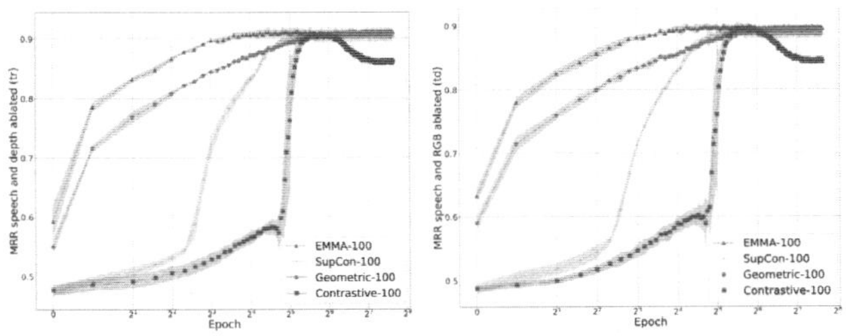

(c) Mean Reciprocal Rank (MRR) on the held-out test set when speech and depth modalities are ablated.

(d) Mean Reciprocal Rank (MRR) on the held-out test set when speech and RGB modalities are dropped.

Figure 3. MRR on GoLD (avg 5 runs). Colors: red = self-sup CL, orange = sup CL, blue =GEOMETRIC ALIGNMENT, green =EMMA. Panels—(a) All inputs, (b) –Text, (c) –Speech–Depth, (d) –Speech–RGB. Higher is Better. We train all models for 200 epochs.

With two modalities we compute a single distance: K_{tr} (speech and depth missing), K_{sr} (text and depth missing), K_{td} (speech and RGB missing), K_{sd} (text and RGB missing).

With three modalities we average two distances: $K_{trd} = \frac{K_{tr}+K_{td}}{2}$ when speech is missing, $K_{srd} = \frac{K_{sr}+K_{sd}}{2}$ when text is missing, and so on.

With all four modalities we average four distances: $K_{tsrd} = \frac{K_{tr}+K_{td}+K_{sr}+K_{sd}}{4}$.

Figure 3 shows the relative performance of EMMA and GEOMETRIC ALIGNMENT against state-of-the-art methods when different modalities are ablated.

VI. RESULTS AND DISCUSSION

We evaluate on the GoLD test split using mean reciprocal rank (MRR) and top-1 accuracy (Acc).

Table I reports the *average* $\pm$ *standard deviation* over five random seeds; all models use SGD (batch 64). For five candidate objects, random guessing yields MRR = 0.33 and Acc = 0.50. EMMA matches or exceeds the strongest baseline in every modality setting.

To interpret MRR, note that a system that always ranks the correct object second would score $1/2 = 0.5$.

Figure 3a Shows that EMMA learns faster and results in a better performance compared to both SUPCON and contrastive learning [11] when trained using all modalities and with all modalities available during test. We observe that not only does contrastive loss learn more slowly, but it is prone to overfitting; while this can be addressed with careful tuning of the learning process, an approach that is innately robust to overfitting without tuning is preferable.

When we drop the text modality (Figure 3b), we can see that the performance decreases from about 0.93 to about 0.82, showing that speech cannot completely replace text. In Figure 4, the alignment of shared embeddings for a randomly sampled set of classes is visualized for all four modalities under consideration, suggesting that the speech modality is not aligned as well as the text modality. For this reason, when we drop text and use speech as the main query, the performance decreases. This supports our hypothesis that a geometric alignment of the latent space is crucial to good performance in object retrieval and multimodal understanding.

In Figure 3b, we observe that when speech is used as the query, and the text modality is ablated, the SUPCON baseline works slightly better than EMMA, although EMMA still learns faster. The reason is that SUPCON optimizes for the classification task, and since the speech modality is less well aligned, using GEOMETRIC ALIGNMENT makes the downstream task more difficult by trying to pull and push similar and dissimilar data points, respectively. Future research will consider strategies to align more chaotic modalities.

There is very little gap in performance when depth or RGB are dropped in Figures 3c and 3d compared to when we have all modalities in Figure 3a, showing that our model is robust when RGB or depth sensors fail. Also, when depth is dropped in Figure 3c, performance decreases less compared to when RGB is dropped in Figure 3d. This suggests that depth is less informative when compared to RGB, which is consistent with existing vision research results.

Our time analysis shows that EMMA takes almost 8 epochs to converge, and each epoch takes roughly 0.7 minutes, which makes it 5.6 minutes until convergence. In comparison, SUPCON takes about 36 epochs to converge, and each epoch takes 0.52 minutes, which amounts to 18.72 minutes. That is when we use all four modalities for training. When we ablate one or two modalities, the training takes less time.

Qualitative Results: In order to help visualize the performance of learned embeddings, we consider projections of a randomly selected subset of classes of the high-dimensional learned embeddings into a 3-dimensional space using t-SNE [54], a dimensionality reduction technique to visualize high-dimensional data. T-SNE creates a probability distribution over pairs of high-dimensional data where similar pairs have a higher probability, and dissimilar pairs have a lower probability. A similar probability distribution is also defined over pairs of data in the lower dimension (either 2D or 3D), and T-SNE minimizes the KL divergence between these two probability distributions.

Figure 4 shows the projection onto 3D space to give a better view of the location of embeddings. Although these projections are not perfect, combined with the quantitative results, they demonstrate that our model is learning to map instances of the same class closer to each other regardless of their modalities. Interestingly, toothbrush and toothpaste are mapped almost on top of each other in the text modality,

TABLE I. AVERAGE AND STANDARD DEVIATION OF MEAN RECIPROCAL RANK (MRR) AND ACCURACY (ACC) (HIGHER IS BETTER, BOLD = BEST).

Methods	speech/depth	speech/RGB	text/depth	text/RGB	text/speech/ depth	text/speech/ RGB	speech/RGB/ depth	text/RGB/ depth	all
Geometric	76.82±0.34	78.34±0.29	89.64±0.38	91.13±0.73	89.21±0.45	90.95±0.83	79.37±0.29	92.29±0.51	92.14±0.45
SupCon	**78.18**±0.58	**79.69**±0.54	89.04±0.88	90.56±0.74	88.75±0.66	90.5±0.69	**81.2**±0.39	91.96±0.42	92.03±0.7
EMMA	77.63±0.29	78.66±0.64	**89.87**±0.5	**91.26**±0.86	**89.66**±0.36	**90.97**±0.66	80.32±0.45	**92.71**±0.5	**92.72**±0.47
Contrastive	71.74±0.73	73.37±0.39	89.72±0.54	90.82±0.37	89.13±0.61	90.26±0.58	74.96±0.44	91.92±0.41	91.72±0.53

(a) AVERAGE AND STANDARD DEVIATION OF MRR (HIGHER IS BETTER, BOLD = BEST).

Methods	speech/depth	speech/RGB	text/depth	text/RGB	text/speech/ depth	text/speech/ RGB	speech/RGB/ depth	text/RGB/ depth	all
Geometric	61.95±0.55	64.34±0.53	82.03±0.57	84.6±1.1	81.08±0.81	84.0±1.4	65.84±0.63	86.41±0.83	85.94±0.74
SupCon	**64.17**±0.92	**66.52**±1.07	81.05±1.22	83.65±1.4	80.58±1.12	83.54±1.23	**68.7**±0.66	86.06±1.21	85.82±1.29
EMMA	63.54±0.53	65.07±1.01	82.78±0.97	**85.07**±1.42	**82.16**±0.64	**84.37**±1.23	67.69±0.81	**87.38**±0.71	**87.15**±0.72
Contrastive	54.82±1.4	57.27±0.64	**82.88**±0.88	84.35±1.01	81.55±0.93	83.26±1.02	59.38±0.6	86.31±0.67	85.75±0.87

(b) AVERAGE AND STANDARD DEVIATION OF ACC ACROSS 5 RANDOM SEEDS ON THE HELD-OUT TEST SET; COLUMN HEADERS SHOW MODALITIES PRESENT AT QUERY TIME (HIGHER IS BETTER, BOLD = BEST).

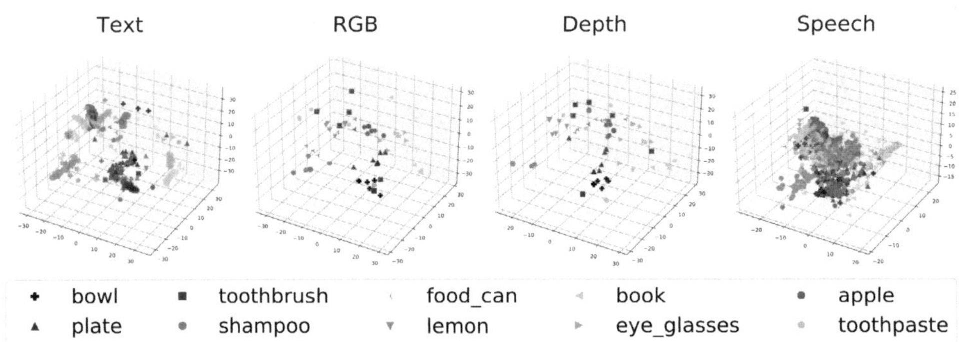

Figure 4. 3-D t-SNE of EMMA embeddings for 10 random object classes. RGB, depth, speech, and text appear as separate point clouds; dense language points reflect multiple descriptions. Tight cross-modal clusters reveal a shared manifold for reliable retrieval.

showing similar semantic and syntax. However, in the RGB and depth modality, they are close but not on top of each other since they do not look the same. Also, we can see that apple and lemon are mapped close to each other in all modalities, which suggests that our proposed EMMA learns some notion of the concept of fruits. These qualitative results show that our propose GEOMETRIC ALIGNMENT and EMMA have an interpretable latent space.

An example of the need to consider multiple modalities jointly is shown in Figure 5, showing how EMMA is able to correctly select an object instance from several similarly shaped and describable objects.

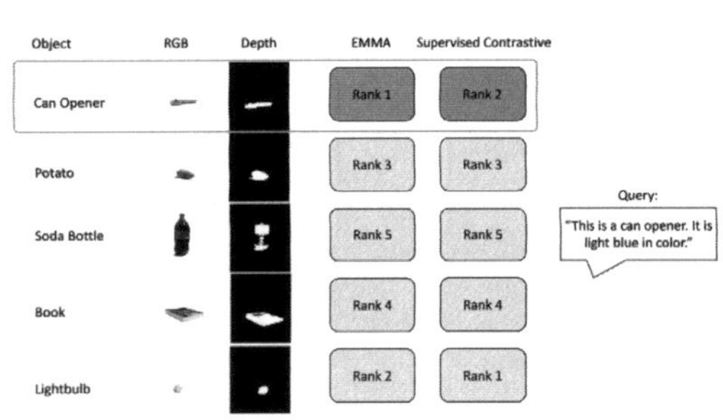

Figure 5. Qualitative retrieval: EMMA ranks the target first, whereas SUPCON mis-ranks a "light bulb" due to phrase similarity.

Our proposed model performs well and learns fast, has been demonstrated to handle four modalities of shared information effectively, and is robust to test-time situations where information from one or more modalities is missing. The bottleneck for agents in different settings may differ, and training speed may not be critical in offline learning scenarios. However, since we usually need to finetune models for other tasks when it comes to transfer learning, the training speed becomes relevant.

There remains room for improvement. Specifically, the speech modality is harder to handle. Figure 4 shows that although the relative position of instances are correct in the speech space, the distinction and clustering of different objects are not as good as the other three modalities.

The text seems to be the best-clustered modality, and that makes sense because the variation in written text is much smaller than the other three modalities. Variation in speech is higher because there are a number of factors affecting speech understanding, including different accents, native language, gender, and age [18]. Variation in RGB and depth is higher than in text due to variations in lighting conditions, an object's texture and shape, the angle of the camera, and other factors.

VII. Conclusion

In this work, we have demonstrated the effectiveness of a novel approach to learning from high-dimensional multimodal information even when one or more modalities are unavailable at test time. Our approach performs well on an object retrieval task from a testbed that contains four separate modalities, consistent with the information that might be available to a physical agent, and outperforms state-of-the-art contrastive learning approaches. Our proposed method is general enough to be applied to a variety of multimodal retrieval problems and is not limited to purely language-based image retrieval.

In the future, this work will be extended to solve less clearly delineated problems, such as differentiating among members of a class and across classes. However, this work represents a significant step towards handling such retrieval problems while not arbitrarily limiting the number of sensors and other modalities that can be incorporated.

References

[1] W. Hong *et al.*, "Gilbert: Generative vision-language pre-training for image-text retrieval," in *Proceedings of the 44th International ACM SIGIR Conference on Research and Development in Information Retrieval*, 2021, pp. 1379–1388.

[2] M. Zhuge *et al.*, "Kaleido-bert: Vision-language pre-training on fashion domain," in *Proceedings of the IEEE/CVF Conference on Computer Vision and Pattern Recognition (CVPR)*, Jun. 2021, pp. 12 647–12 657.

[3] R. Hu *et al.*, "Natural language object retrieval," in *Proceedings of the IEEE Conference on Computer Vision and Pattern Recognition*, 2016, pp. 4555–4564.

[4] A. T. Nguyen *et al.*, "Practical cross-modal manifold alignment for robotic grounded language learning," in *Proceedings of the IEEE/CVF Conference on Computer Vision and Pattern Recognition Workshops (CVPRW)*, Jun. 2021, pp. 1613–1622.

[5] F. Huang, Y. Cheng, C. Jin, Y. Zhang, and T. Zhang, "Deep multimodal embedding model for fine-grained sketch-based image retrieval," in *Proceedings of the 40th International ACM SIGIR Conference on Research and Development in Information Retrieval*, 2017, pp. 929–932.

[6] C. Ma, C. Gu, W. Li, and S. Cui, "Large-scale image retrieval with sparse binary projections," in *Proceedings of the 43rd International ACM SIGIR Conference on Research and Development in Information Retrieval*, 2020, pp. 1817–1820.

[7] D. Novak, M. Batko, and P. Zezula, "Large-scale image retrieval using neural net descriptors," in *Proceedings of the 38th international ACM SIGIR conference on research and development in information retrieval*, 2015, pp. 1039–1040.

[8] N. Vo *et al.*, "Composing text and image for image retrieval-an empirical odyssey," in *Proceedings of the IEEE/CVF Conference on Computer Vision and Pattern Recognition*, 2019, pp. 6439–6448.

[9] L. E. Richards, K. Darvish, and C. Matuszek, "Learning Object Attributes with Category-Free Grounded Language from Deep Featurization," in *2020 IEEE/RSJ International Conference on Intelligent Robots and Systems (IROS)*, Oct. 2020, pp. 8400–8407. DOI: 10.1109/IROS45743.2020.9340824.

[10] P. Khosla *et al.*, "Supervised contrastive learning," in *Advances in Neural Information Processing Systems*, H. Larochelle, M. Ranzato, R. Hadsell, M. F. Balcan, and H. Lin, Eds., vol. 33, Curran Associates, Inc., 2020, pp. 18 661–18 673.

[11] T. Chen, S. Kornblith, M. Norouzi, and G. Hinton, "A simple framework for contrastive learning of visual representations," *arXiv preprint arXiv:2002.05709*, 2020.

[12] D. Gao *et al.*, "Fashionbert: Text and image matching with adaptive loss for cross-modal retrieval," in *Proceedings of the 43rd International ACM SIGIR Conference on Research and Development in Information Retrieval*, 2020, pp. 2251–2260.

[13] H. Wen, X. Song, X. Yang, Y. Zhan, and L. Nie, "Comprehensive linguistic-visual composition network for image retrieval," in *Proceedings of the 44th International ACM SIGIR Conference on Research and Development in Information Retrieval*, 2021, pp. 1369–1378.

[14] W. Zheng and K. Zhou, "Enhancing conversational dialogue models with grounded knowledge," in *Proceedings of the 28th ACM International Conference on Information and Knowledge Management*, ser. CIKM '19, Beijing, China: Association for Computing Machinery, 2019, pp. 709–718, ISBN: 9781450369763. DOI: 10.1145/3357384.3357889.

[15] C. Meng *et al.*, "Dukenet: A dual knowledge interaction network for knowledge-grounded conversation," in *Proceedings of the 43rd International ACM SIGIR Conference on Research and Development in Information Retrieval*. New York, NY, USA: Association for Computing Machinery, 2020, pp. 1151–1160, ISBN: 9781450380164.

[16] A. Bagher Zadeh, P. P. Liang, S. Poria, E. Cambria, and L.-P. Morency, "Multimodal language analysis in the wild: CMU-MOSEI dataset and interpretable dynamic fusion graph," in *Proceedings of the 56th Annual Meeting of the Association for Computational Linguistics (Volume 1: Long Papers)*, Melbourne, Australia: Association for Computational Linguistics, Jul. 2018, pp. 2236–2246. DOI: 10.18653/v1/P18-1208.

[17] G. Y. Kebe *et al.*, "A spoken language dataset of descriptions for speech-based grounded language learning," in *Thirty-fifth Conference on Neural Information Processing Systems Datasets and Benchmarks Track (Round 1)*, 2021.

[18] G. Y. Kebe, L. E. Richards, E. Raff, F. Ferraro, and C. Matuszek, "Bridging the gap: Using deep acoustic representations to learn grounded language from percepts and raw speech," in *Proceedings of the AAAI Conference on Artificial Intelligence*, AAAI Press, 2022.

[19] T. Baltrušaitis, C. Ahuja, and L.-P. Morency, "Multimodal Machine Learning: A Survey and Taxonomy," *IEEE Transactions on Pattern Analysis and Machine Intelligence*, vol. 41, no. 2, pp. 423–443, 2019, ISSN: 1939-3539. DOI: 10.1109/TPAMI.2018.2798607.

[20] A. Jangra, S. Saha, A. Jatowt, and M. Hasanuzzaman, "Multimodal summary generation using multi-objective optimization," in *Proceedings of the 43rd International ACM SIGIR Conference on Research and Development in Information Retrieval*. New York, NY, USA: Association for Computing Machinery, 2020, pp. 1745–1748, ISBN: 9781450380164.

[21] P. Hu, L. Zhen, D. Peng, and P. Liu, "Scalable deep multimodal learning for cross-modal retrieval," in *Proceedings of the 42nd International ACM SIGIR Conference on Research and Development in Information Retrieval*, ser. SIGIR'19, Paris, France: Association for Computing Machinery, 2019, pp. 635–644, ISBN: 9781450361729. DOI: 10.1145/3331184.3331213.

[22] P. Poklukar *et al.*, "Geometric multimodal contrastive representation learning," in *Proceedings of the 39th International Conference on Machine Learning*, K. Chaudhuri *et al.*, Eds., ser. Proceedings of Machine Learning Research, vol. 162, PMLR, 17–23 Jul 2022, pp. 17 782–17 800.

[23] M. Carvalho *et al.*, "Cross-modal retrieval in the cooking context: Learning semantic text-image embeddings," in *The 41st International ACM SIGIR Conference on Research and Development in Information Retrieval*, ser. SIGIR '18, Ann Arbor, MI, USA: Association for Computing Machinery, 2018, pp. 35–44, ISBN: 9781450356572. DOI: 10.1145/3209978.3210036.

[24] A. Salvador *et al.*, "Learning cross-modal embeddings for cooking recipes and food images," in *Proceedings of the IEEE Conference on Computer Vision and Pattern Recognition*, 2017.

[25] J.-B. Alayrac *et al.*, "Self-Supervised MultiModal Versatile Networks," in *NeurIPS*, 2020.

[26] T. Nguyen *et al.*, "Robot Object Retrieval with Contextual Natural Language Queries," in *Proceedings of Robotics: Science and Systems*, Corvalis, Oregon, USA, Jul. 2020. DOI: 10.15607/RSS.2020.XVI.080.

[27] G. Chechik, V. Sharma, U. Shalit, and S. Bengio, "Large Scale Online Learning of Image Similarity Through Ranking," *J. Mach. Learn. Res.*, vol. 11, pp. 1109–1135, Mar. 2010, ISSN: 1532-4435.

[28] E. Hoffer and N. Ailon, "Deep Metric Learning Using Triplet Network," in *SIMBAD 2015: Similarity-Based Pattern Recognition*, A. Feragen, M. Pelillo, and M. Loog, Eds., Cham: Springer International Publishing, 2015, pp. 84–92, ISBN: 978-3-319-24261-3. DOI: 10.1007/978-3-319-24261-3_7.

[29] F. Schroff, D. Kalenichenko, and J. Philbin, "FaceNet: A unified embedding for face recognition and clustering," in *2015 IEEE Conference on Computer Vision and Pattern Recognition (CVPR)*, IEEE, Jun. 2015, pp. 815–823, ISBN: 978-1-4673-6964-0. DOI: 10.1109/CVPR.2015.7298682.

[30] V. Ferrari, M. Hebert, C. Sminchisescu, and Y. Weiss, Eds., *Computer Vision - {ECCV} 2018 - 15th European Conference, Munich, Germany, September 8-14, 2018, Proceedings, Part {IX}*, vol. 11213, Lecture Notes in Computer Science, Springer, 2018, ISBN: 978-3-030-01239-7. DOI: 10.1007/978-3-030-01240-3.

[31] Y. Zhao, Z. Jin, G.-J. Qi, H. Lu, and X.-S. Hua, "An Adversarial Approach to Hard Triplet Generation," in *Computer Vision - ECCV 2018 - 15th European Conference, Munich, Germany, September 8-14, 2018, Proceedings, Part IX*, V. Ferrari, M. Hebert, C. Sminchisescu, and Y. Weiss, Eds., ser. Lecture Notes in Computer Science, vol. 11213, Springer, 2018, pp. 508–524, ISBN: 978-3-030-01239-7. DOI: 10.1007/978-3-030-01240-3_31.

[32] Y. Zhai, X. Guo, Y. Lu, and H. Li, "In Defense of the Triplet Loss for Person Re-Identification," *ArXiv e-prints*, 2018. arXiv: 1809.05864.

[33] K. Musgrave, S. Belongie, and S.-N. Lim, "A Metric Learning Reality Check," in *ECCV*, 2020. arXiv: 2003.08505.

[34] E. Raff, "Research Reproducibility as a Survival Analysis," in *The Thirty-Fifth AAAI Conference on Artificial Intelligence*, 2021. arXiv: 2012.09932.

[35] E. Raff, "A step toward quantifying independently reproducible machine learning research," in *Advances in Neural Information Processing Systems*, H. Wallach *et al.*, Eds., vol. 32, Curran Associates, Inc., 2019, pp. 14–25.

[36] A. Veit, M. Nickel, S. Belongie, and L. van der Maaten, "Separating self-expression and visual content in hashtag supervision," in *Proceedings of the IEEE Conference on Computer Vision and Pattern Recognition (CVPR)*, Jun. 2018.

[37] W. Chen, X. Chen, J. Zhang, and K. Huang, "Beyond triplet loss: A deep quadruplet network for person re-identification," in *Proceedings of the IEEE conference on computer vision and pattern recognition*, 2017, pp. 403–412.

[38] O. Tursun, S. Denman, S. Sridharan, E. Goan, and C. Fookes, "An efficient framework for zero-shot sketch-based image retrieval," *arXiv preprint arXiv:2102.04016*, 2021.

[39] J. Lei *et al.*, "Semi-heterogeneous three-way joint embedding network for sketch-based image retrieval," *IEEE Transactions on Circuits and Systems for Video Technology*, vol. 30, no. 9, pp. 3226–3237, 2020. DOI: 10.1109/TCSVT.2019.2936710.

[40] T. Mittal, U. Bhattacharya, R. Chandra, A. Bera, and D. Manocha, "M3er: Multiplicative multimodal emotion recognition using facial, textual, and speech cues," *Proceedings of the AAAI Conference on Artificial Intelligence*, vol. 34, no. 02, pp. 1359–1367, Apr. 2020. DOI: 10.1609/aaai.v34i02.5492.

[41] M. Abouelenien, V. Pérez-Rosas, R. Mihalcea, and M. Burzo, "Deception detection using a multimodal approach," in *Proceedings of the 16th International Conference on Multimodal Interaction*, ser. ICMI '14, Istanbul, Turkey: Association for Computing Machinery, 2014, pp. 58–65, ISBN: 9781450328852. DOI: 10.1145/2663204.2663229.

[42] Z. Liu, W. Zhang, S. Lin, and T. Q. Quek, "Heterogeneous sensor data fusion by deep multimodal encoding," *IEEE Journal of Selected Topics in Signal Processing*, vol. 11, no. 3, pp. 479–491, 2017. DOI: 10.1109/JSTSP.2017.2679538.

[43] K. Sohn, "Improved deep metric learning with multi-class n-pair loss objective," in *Advances in Neural Information Processing Systems*, D. Lee, M. Sugiyama, U. Luxburg, I. Guyon, and R. Garnett, Eds., vol. 29, Curran Associates, Inc., 2016.

[44] J. Deng *et al.*, "Imagenet: A large-scale hierarchical image database," in *2009 IEEE Conference on Computer Vision and Pattern Recognition*, 2009, pp. 248–255. DOI: 10.1109/CVPR.2009.5206848.

[45] A. Krizhevsky, G. Hinton, *et al.*, "Learning multiple layers of features from tiny images," 2009.

[46] J. Devlin, M.-W. Chang, K. Lee, and K. Toutanova, "BERT: Pre-training of deep bidirectional transformers for language understanding," in *Proceedings of the 2019 Conference of the North American Chapter of the Association for Computational Linguistics: Human Language Technologies, Volume 1 (Long and Short Papers)*, Minneapolis, Minnesota: Association for Computational Linguistics, Jun. 2019, pp. 4171–4186. DOI: 10.18653/v1/N19-1423.

[47] A. Akbik *et al.*, "Flair: An easy-to-use framework for state-of-the-art nlp," in *NAACL 2019, 2019 Annual Conference of the North American Chapter of the Association for Computational Linguistics (Demonstrations)*, 2019, pp. 54–59.

[48] A. Akbik, T. Bergmann, and R. Vollgraf, "Pooled contextualized embeddings for named entity recognition," in *Proceedings of the 2019 Conference of the North American Chapter of the Association for Computational Linguistics: Human Language Technologies, Volume 1 (Long and Short Papers)*, Minneapolis, Minnesota: Association for Computational Linguistics, Jun. 2019, pp. 724–728. DOI: 10.18653/v1/N19-1078.

[49] A. Baevski, Y. Zhou, A. Mohamed, and M. Auli, "Wav2vec 2.0: A framework for self-supervised learning of speech representations," in *Advances in Neural Information Processing Systems*, H. Larochelle, M. Ranzato, R. Hadsell, M. Balcan, and H. Lin, Eds., vol. 33, Curran Associates, Inc., 2020, pp. 12 449–12 460.

[50] A. Vaswani *et al.*, "Attention is all you need," in *Advances in neural information processing systems*, 2017, pp. 5998–6008.

[51] K. He, X. Zhang, S. Ren, and J. Sun, "Deep residual learning for image recognition," in *2016 IEEE Conference on Computer Vision and Pattern Recognition (CVPR)*, IEEE, Jun. 2016, pp. 770–778, ISBN: 978-1-4673-8851-1. DOI: 10.1109/CVPR.2016.90.

[52] V. Nair and G. E. Hinton, "Rectified linear units improve restricted boltzmann machines," in *ICML*, 2010, pp. 807–814.

[53] S. Ruder, "An overview of gradient descent optimization algorithms," *arXiv preprint arXiv:1609.04747*, 2016.

[54] L. Van der Maaten and G. Hinton, "Visualizing data using t-sne.," *Journal of machine learning research*, vol. 9, no. 11, 2008.

Concept of Ecosystem for Smart Agriculture: Millimeter-Wave Information-Centric Wireless Visual Sensor Network

Shintaro Mori
Department of Electronics Engineering and Computer Science
Fukuoka University
8-19-1 Nanakuma, Jonan-ku, Fukuoka 814-0180, Japan
E-mail: smori@fukuoka-u.ac.jp

***Abstract*—The widespread adoption of smart agriculture is crucial not only for food security but also because agriculture is a significant industry outside of urban areas. The common demands for smart-agriculture applications are that real-time video and image data should be effectively collected, shared, distributed, and managed. In our previous studies, we developed an ecosystem that integrated information-centric networking, wireless sensor networks, and millimeter-wave-band (wireless) communications. On the basis of conducting proof-of-concept experiments in a test field for typical smart-agriculture applications, we will develop a new ecosystem that combines the previous platform with visual sensor nodes and artificial intelligence, called a millimeter-wave-band communication information-centric wireless visual sensor network. This paper provides a blueprint for our new research project and identifies technical issues and strategies for their solutions, including implementation, evaluation, deployment, and demonstration on a real farm.**

Keywords—Information-centric networking; wireless visual sensor network; milimeter-wave-band (wireless) communications; ecosystem for smart agriculture

I. INTRODUCTION

Agriculture is extremely important in terms of national food security, but the agricultural workforce is aging and decreasing. However, the deployment of information and communication technologies can provide clues to solve these problems. In smart agriculture, there are many application services, such as anti-theft systems for agricultural products, pest-control systems (trapping traps), farm-management robots and tractors (e.g., automatic weeding, cultivating, irrigating, and fertilizing), plastic greenhouse management systems, and disaster-prevention systems. In response to various changes in agricultural circumstances, introducing a smart-agriculture platform can be expected to improve and stabilize productivity. In Japan, there are generally two styles of agricultural businesses: large-scale commercial and small-scale family farms. Large-scale farms aim to supply food for domestic or international markets, whereas small-scale farms protect land in the countryside and act as hubs for the local industry, economy, and community. In our research project, we focus on small-scale family farms.

Through previous studies involving small-scale family farms, we have obtained two opinions regarding barriers to deploying smart agriculture. The farmers have no idea how to use the remote-sensing data effectively, thus they think that smart-agriculture systems incur costs but do not directly contribute to productivity. In other words, as the cost of agricultural materials rises (global inflation), the farmers concentrate on financial and human resources for factors that directly affect agricultural productivity, such as seeds, seedlings, fertilizer, and plastic greenhouses. On the other hand, some young farmers are particularly interested in using smart agriculture to improve their work environment.

TABLE I. COMMON TECHNOLOGIES FOR SMART-AGRICULTURE APPLICATIONS

Applications	*Requirements for common technologies*
Theft prevention	Monitoring from security cameras
Pest control	Monitoring for local circumstances
Field management	Remote control based on real-time video
Greenhouse management	Monitoring of damage and collapse
Weather and disasters	Remote monitoring for field and rivers

For the above background, a common platform should be provided, rather than a different system for each application. Through our research activities and experience, Table I summarizes the requirements of common technologies for smart-agriculture applications, i.e., the platform required to remotely obtain and verify more primitive data, such as real-time videos and field images, different from the sensing data after analysis. In our research project, we propose a new ecosystem that supports an on-demand and real-time video and image forwarding platform based on Information-Centric Networking (ICN), Wireless Visual Sensor Network (WVSN), and Millimeter-wave-band Communications (mmWaves), called mmWave Information-Centric WVSN (mmICWVSN). In this paper, we present the blueprint of the ongoing research and development project as work in progress and provide the details of upcoming study items.

The remainder of this paper is organized as follows. Section II provides related work. Section III discusses wireless networks that can be selected in smart-agriculture applications. Section IV describes the development items needed to complete a new ecosystem as an outcome of this study. Section IV presents the contributions to future wireless technological development. Finally, Section VI summarizes the outcomes and future perspectives of our project.

II. RELATED WORK

There have been many studies and trials regarding smart agriculture, and smart-agricultural equipment is available from many vendors [1]. These proposals and solutions are primarily aimed at large-scale farmers, i.e., they are not cost-effective for small-scale farms to deploy. The wireless networks underpinning real-time video and image applications require large capacity and low latency due to the forwarding of streaming data. The proposed scheme uses IEEE 802.11-compliant Wireless Local Area Networks (WLANs) because they can easily integrate the millimeter-wave, microwave, and sub-gigahertz-wave spectrums. There have been many studies on the construction of outdoor WLANs for smart agriculture [2]; however, there are few cases involving millimeter-wave spectrum, e.g., a field trial of mmWaves was conducted in Georgetown, Malaysia [3]. As for the typical ecosystem, the system is implemented on the basis of cloud-native or edge (fog) designs in which the sensing data are centralized in the cloud area (or the partial data are distributed in the edge-node storage). In contrast, the proposed scheme adopts the ICN design in which all data are distributed in the edge-side nodes. The related studies introduced ICN into edge networks, particularly wired networks; nevertheless, the proposed scheme will expand to wireless network areas.

III. Wireless Network Technologies Supporting Smart-Agriculture Applications

Wireless communication systems for smart agriculture (outdoor environment) are summarized in Table II. The table represents a qualitative comparison among wireless communication systems in terms of each criterion. This is based on the following discussions, and the evaluation was relative to each system, indicating their strengths and weaknesses. The networks being compared are cellular (4G/5G) and satellite networks, Low-Power Wide-Area Networks (LPWANs), Personal Area Networks (PANs) based on IEEE 802.15.4, optical wired networks, and the networks of the proposed scheme. They are compared in terms of communication coverage, network communication (wireless) capacity, and the economic and technical costs of implementation, construction, and deployment.

Cellular and satellite networks are used as de facto standards for wireless communications in outdoor environments. These networks have superior coverage and communication quality, but their operation costs are high. Therefore, small-scale farmers do not approve of them, which is one factor preventing the proliferation of their smart-agriculture applications [4]. Alternatively, LPWANs [5], which can construct a private network with wide-area coverage and low energy consumption, such as LoRa and SigFox, have been widely investigated. However, LPWANs can transfer small amounts of data, such as text-based data or low-resolution (time-lapse) image data; on the other hand, the 100-Hz bandwidth in the 1-GHz band is not sufficient for streaming data transfer. PANs using the 920-MHz band [6], such as ZigBee, 6LoWPAN, Wi-SUN, and Bluetooth, have traditionally been used in wireless-sensor-network research. Considering the coverage of PANs, the deployment is limited to environments inside plastic greenhouses and small-area (campus) networks, even if multi-hop communications are enabled. The wired network is the primary selection in areas where optical fiber lines have already been deployed; however, new optical lines are unrealistic in rural areas for economic reasons.

TABLE II. COMPARISON OF WIRELESS NETWORKS FOR SMART AGRICULTURE

Network system	*Coverage*	*Capacity*	*Economic cost*	*Technical cost*
Cellular (4G/5G) satellite networks	**o**	**o**	**x**	**o**
LPWANs (e.g., LoRa)	**o**	**x**	**o**	**x**
PAN (e.g., ZigBee)	**x**	**x**	**o**	**x**
Optical wired network	**x**	**o**	**x**	**o**
Proposed mmICWSN	*	*	*	*

o denotes suitable, **x** denotes not suitable, and * denotes suggested.

In contrast, the network structure of the proposed scheme is composed of WLAN based on the IEEE 802.11 standard, in which multiple license-free radio-frequency bands, such as 920 MHz, 2.4, 5, 6, and 60 GHz, are integrated to provide sufficient coverage [7]. Since a gigabit-class data-transmission rate is required for the backhaul network (core network) between agricultural fields and access points, Terragraph (TG) is utilized to achieve the capacity [3]. TG is a 60-GHz-band wireless mesh network platform based on IEEE 802.11 ad/ay that was developed by Meta (Facebook) as an alternative to optical fiber. Regarding cost-effectiveness, since wireless communication devices, modules, and terminals that adhere to IEEE 802.11 are widely used as a well-known Wi-Fi, general-purpose products are easy and inexpensive to obtain. In addition, regarding technical implementation costs, since the proposed scheme can be constructed on the basis of an IP network, the system can provide simple connectivity to various nodes, such as personal computers, tablet computers, and smartphones.

IV. Research and Development Items

In this section, we describe four development items, needed to complete our research project: construction and demonstration of the mmICWVSN, real-time video and image data-transmission scheme, ICN communication-control technology using Artificial Intelligence (AI) based on visual data, and packaging technology and its verification with consideration of horizontal development, as shown in Figure 1.

A. Construction and demonstration of mmICWVSN

In our previous works, we developed a reliable and self-organized ecosystem for co-creative smart cities [8]. Among them, we developed a zero-touch-design node as a sensor node under extreme outdoor conditions. In the previous ecosystem, the inside and outside of the device were connected via water-resistant connectors for waterproof design, and mechanical structures, such as motor drives and cooling fans, were omitted for higher reliability. According to feedback we often receive, the zero-touch-design node device is unsuitable for outdoor environments because it requires a

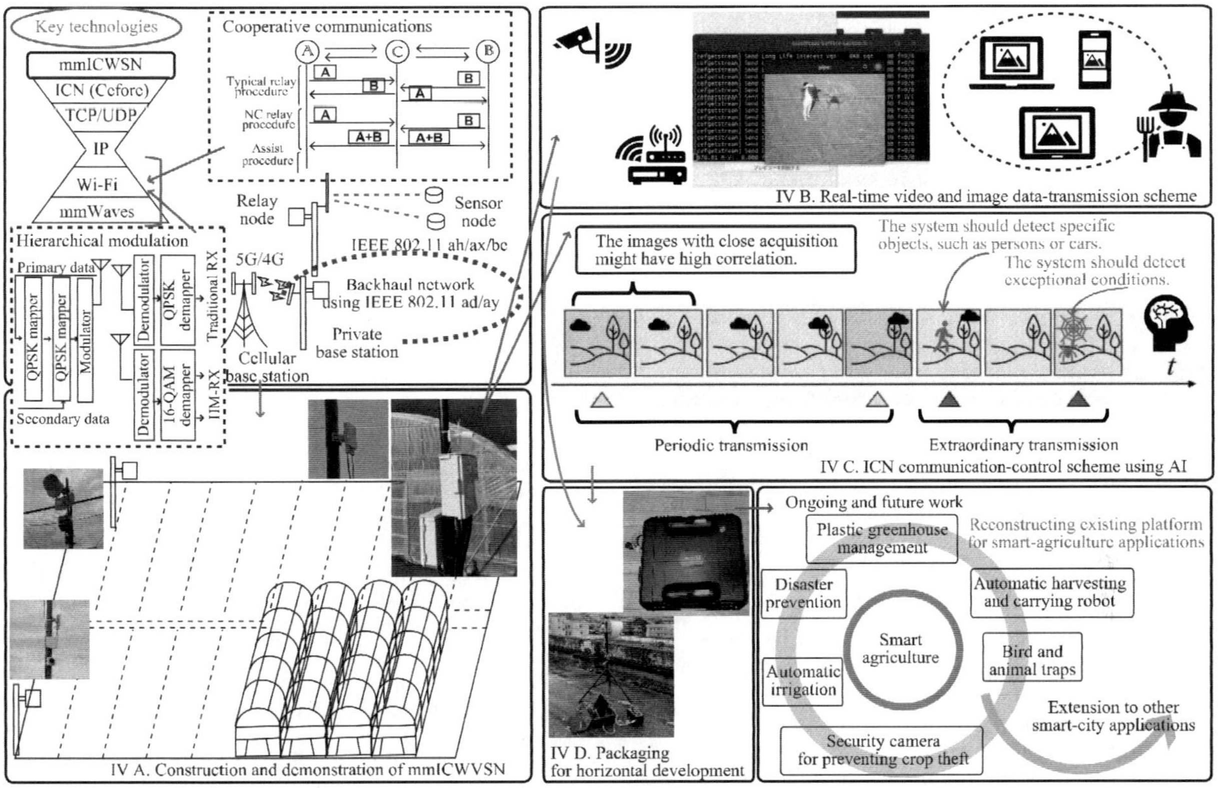

Figure 1. Overview of proposed scheme

commercial power supply. Based on this opinion, there will need to be a commercial power supply in the locations where the system is deployed, i.e., this is not a serious problem.

In the construction and demonstration of the mmICWVSN, we will implement and deploy a system that can be used on actual farms and agricultural worksites. In the TG network, we use a BeMap MLTG-360 as the TG Distributed Node (DN) and MLTG-CN (standard type) and MLTG-CNLR (long-distance type) as the TG Client Node (CN). In our previous network construction research, we constructed test fields [9]. In these test fields, we evaluated and demonstrated the previous ecosystem on the basis of medium- to long-term operational testing. In addition, we evaluated long-distance mmWaves (in Nogata City, Fukuoka, Japan) over a 1-km distance in a line-of-sight environment [10]. Note that the demonstration of the mmWaves is meaningful, as it was carried out in practical environments.

B. Real-time video and image data-transmission scheme

This section describes an elemental technology to transmit video and image data using the mmICWVSN. In particular, the proposed scheme is designed as a comprehensive information system that includes farmers, installers, and other relevant persons. In the proposed scheme, we use Cefore [11], an open-source ICN platform that is compatible with CCN/CCNx on a Linux (Ubuntu) environment.

In our previous study [12], we conducted a fundamental experiment, including an evaluation of network performance and real-time video streaming testing between the ground node (TG/DN; MLTG-360) and the aerial node (TG/CN; MLTG-CN) in the test field of a baseball field. Note that the aerial node was implemented using an industrial drone as a mooring node with a 5-m altitude. In the experiment, we transmitted video data in real-time, but the issue was that video broadcasting sometimes froze even when the network conditions were significantly stable. Although we assume that all nodes will be located on the ground in this study, i.e., the issue might not occur, we will continue to investigate the cause of the freeze and improve the quality of streaming-data transmission.

As a part of the personnel-related aspects of the proposed ecosystem, we will develop the system on the basis of feedback gained by interviewing and giving questionnaires to farmers, equipment installers, and government and organization staff. In particular, in the previous implementation, we used Cefore's standard commands via the character user interface, which was not user-friendly for the study participants. To improve accessibility and usability, we will develop the software part of the scheme on the basis of graphical user interfaces, e.g., dashboards and mobile applications. The system will be implemented and its effectiveness evaluated using the mmICWVSN platform.

C. ICN communication-control scheme using AI

The wireless network and its infrastructure require high capacity, low latency, and high reliability for forwarding real-time streaming data. The network structure of the proposed scheme is constructed on the basis of IEEE 802.11-compliant WLANs. The WLANs can support different radio-frequency bands for short-, medium-, and long-distance coverage; nevertheless, bottleneck sections will remain. It is difficult to transmit all video and image data, so we will overcome this barrier using AI-based communication controls.

As a general characteristic of visual data, such as videos and images, the pixels around a particular pixel are often similar, and variations and differences between pixels depend on time and location. Since the visual data generated by smart-agriculture applications does not change significantly over short intervals, the data can be downsampled (compressed). As another approach, the transmission interval can also be adjusted using any event as a trigger. As for executing the trigger, if the correlation value between adjacent images in the time-axis changes significantly or if the AI detects any object, the proposed scheme can be sent as an exception.

Related to this mechanism, in our preliminary study [13], we analyzed the photographic data obtained from an actual farm and then observed a high correlation between the image data adjacent to the time axis. We also found that the correlation value decreased over time. In addition, using YOLO [14], well-known as an object-detection AI, we verified that persons and vehicles could be detected with reasonable accuracy. In detail, we used the official and standard trained model of yolo11x, which is a famous object-detection machine learning platform. However, the accuracy of the general object-detection AI was not sufficient, and there were also many false positives. Therefore, we should improve the accuracy until the system can be used in actual sites. When the system is developed, to reduce implementation costs, we will implement it by combining the Python-based Cefpyco provided by Cefore and Python-based AI.

D. Packaging for horizontal development

As an outcome of our research and development project, the implemented ecosystem, mmICWVSN, will be packaged for horizontal deployment. The packaging here means integrating the ecosystem as a complete platform for practical utilization. The packaged node is a modified version of the zero-touch-design node device, and as a portable device, it combines with the TG, as shown in Figure 2. Thanks to its portability, the device can be placed anywhere outdoors, enabling it to be quickly deployed to meet the diverse demands of smart-agriculture applications. In addition to smart agriculture, the proposed scheme will be applicable to other smart-city applications.

V. CONTRIBUTIONS TO FUTURE WIRELESS TECHNOLOGICAL DEVELOPMENT

This section discusses the proposed scheme's potential to contribute to effectively using the radio spectrum in future wireless communication development. In particular, we focus on technologies for efficient spectrum use and migration to upper (higher) frequency bands.

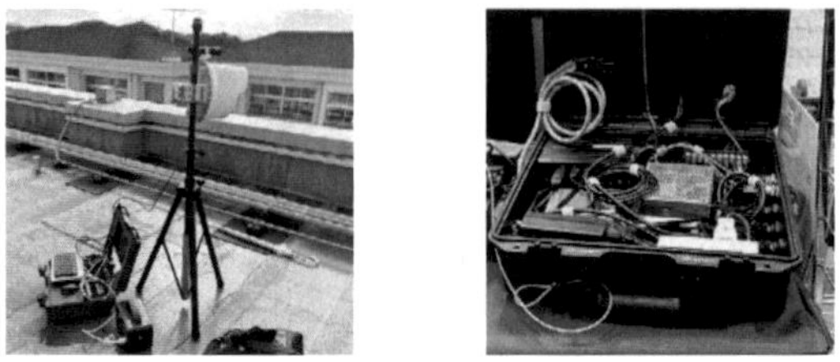

Figure 2. Overview of packaged zero-touch-node device in [11]

A. Contribution in terms of efficient use of spectrum

In the proposed scheme, the elemental technologies that contribute to effectively using the radio spectrum are the ICN scheme and the communication-control technique using AI. ICN can help improve frequency efficiency thanks to its pull-type network design and caching mechanism. Specifically, the ICN-based Internet-of-Things framework sends the data when the user requests it, which can reduce unnecessary data transmission. In addition, with caching techniques, the network node responds with the data stored in its cache memory to requests for the same data, which can reduce duplicate data transmission. On the other hand, controlling AI-based communications enables real-time streaming data to be transferred through the inevitable bottleneck sections in practical wireless networks. To summarize the relevant parts of the preliminary study [15], the data-transmission control and data-compression effects based on the correlation values of the data and the object detection of AI have the potential to contribute to the system's effectiveness. Furthermore, the ICN-based system can also reduce energy consumption as a side effect.

B. Contribution in terms of migration to upper spectrum

In light of the spectrum shortage, shifting to higher frequency bands anytime and anywhere has been investigated. In the proposed scheme, the construction and demonstration of mmWaves will contribute to obtaining meaningful outcomes for future research and development activities. In particular, mmWaves deployment has been trialed in an actual city, Georgetown (Penang, Malaysia) [3]. To the best of our knowledge, there are no other examples. In addition, in our previous studies, according to the evaluation of network performance (e.g., TCP and UDP throughput), the TCP congestion-control mechanism was not suitable for mmWaves. This is because typical congestion controls are suitable for wired networks and current microwave-band WLAN, i.e., it is not considered with the specific characteristics of mmWaves, such as dynamic throughput variation, high packet-error probability, and significant channel conditions due to obstacles such as humans, trees, and leaves. In other words, the characteristics of mmWaves affect the upper-layer protocols. Note that the radio-propagation characteristics of mmWaves have been investigated in other existing studies, but the performances of not only physical-, datalink-, network-, and transport-layer protocols but also application-layer protocols have not been clarified.

VI. Conclusion and Future Work

In this paper, we presented a blueprint for developing a new ecosystem for smart agriculture. The main objective of this project is to develop and deploy mmWave Information-Centric WVSN (mmICWVSN) as a new ecosystem for smart-agriculture applications. The proposed scheme integrates ICN, WSN, mmWaves, AI, and related technologies. In future work, we will carry out our plans and expect to achieve our goals. In the network construction regarding the proof of concept of the mmICWVSN, mmWaves (TG) will be needed to ensure sufficient coverage to support the development of the ecosystem. In addition, we will demonstrate the scalability and extensibility of the proposed scheme, and the system is expected to be able to operate stably for medium- to long-term practical operation. In the development of real-time video streaming technology, the application software should be elevated as a comprehensive information system, including in-depth foundational design, software implementation, and embedding on the mmICWVSN platform. Regarding AI-based communication-control technology, the system will need to achieve a detection accuracy (F1 score) of 70%, which is higher than the average accuracy for general AI. Finally, we will package and verify the developed ecosystem for the purpose of horizontal deployment. Specifically, we will investigate two areas: the smart-agriculture field and other smart-city-as-a-service fields. The findings will be able to be provided for related research and development.

Regarding extra future work, the ecosystem developed in this study will also be applied to other areas of smart cities. In addition, it is necessary to consider a broadcast-based wireless communication system as a key technology for edge-side networks by combining ICN and WSN. Based on the strategies identified through the study, the requirements for the key elemental technologies must be provided as feedback in terms of the limitations and potential challenges.

Acknowledgement

This work was partly supported by SCAT and MIC, Japan.

References

[1] A. U. H. Hashmi et al., "Effects of IoT communication protocols for precision agriculture in outdoor environments," *IEEE Access*, vol. 12, pp. 46410–46421, Mar. 2024.

[2] M. N. Mowla, N. Mowla, A. F. M. S. Shah, K. M. Rabie, and T. Shongwe, "Internet of Things and wireless sensor networks for smart agriculture applications: A survey," *IEEE Access*, vol. 11, pp. 145813–145852, Dec. 2023.

[3] Terragrah, https://terragraph.com/ (retrieved: May 2024).

[4] M. R. Mahmood, M. A. Matin, P. Sarigiannidis, and S. K. Goudos, "A comprehensive review on artificial intelligence/machine learning algorithms for empowering the future IoT toward 6G era," *IEEE Access*, vol. 10, pp. 87535–87562, Aug. 2022.

[5] A. Pagano, D. Croce, I. Tinnirello, and G. Vitale, "A survey on LoRa for smart agriculture: Current trends and future perspectives," *IEEE Internet of Things Journal*, vol. 10, no. 4, pp. 3664–3679, Feb. 2023.

[6] R. Pahuja, H. K. Verma, and M. Uddin, "A wireless sensor network for greenhouse climate control," *IEEE Pervasive Computing*, vol. 12, no. 2, pp. 49–58, Apr.–June 2013.

[7] M. N. Mowla, N. Mowla, A. F. M. S. Shah, K. M. Rabie, and T. Shongwe, "Internet of things and wireless sensor networks for smart agriculture applications: A survey," *IEEE Access*, vol. 11, pp. 145813–145852, Dec. 2023.

[8] K. Kanai, et al., "(Invited) D2EcoSys: Decentralized digital twin ecosystem empower co-creation city-level digital twins," *IEICE Trans. Commun.*, vol. E107-B, no. 1, pp. 50–62, Jan. 2024.

[9] S. Mori, "Test-field development for ICWSNs and preliminary evaluation for mmWave-band wireless communications," *Proc. IEEE CCNC 2024*, Las Vegas, NV, USA, Jan. 2024, pp. 1–2, doi: 10.1109/CCNC51664.2024.10454799.

[10] S. Mori, "Network-performance evaluation for millimeter-wave information-centric wireless-sensor-network ecosystem in actual city," *Proc. IARIA ICN 2025*, pp. 7–11, Nice France, May 2025.

[11] Cefore, https://github.com/cefore/cefore/ (retrieved: May 2024).

[12] S. Mori, "MmWave UAV-assisted information-centric wireless sensor network for disaster-resilient smart cities: Preliminary evaluation and demonstration," *Proc. IARIA ICN 2024*, pp. 1–4, Barcelona, Spain, May 2024.

[13] S. Mori, "A study on information-centric wireless visual sensor network for smart agriculture applications," *Proc. RISP NCSP 2025*, pp. 485–488, Pulau Pinang, Malaysia, Feb.–Mar. 2025.

[14] YOLO, https://ultralytics.com/ (retrieved: May 2025).

[15] S. Mori, "Development of UAV-aided information-centric wireless sensor network platform in mmWaves for smart-city deployment," *International Journal on Advances in Networks and Services*, vol. 17, no. 3&4, pp. 105–115, Dec. 2024.

Harnessing Eye-Tracking Technology to Analyze Gen Z's Engagement with Digital Marketing

Emad Bataineh
College of Technological Innovation, Zayed University
Dubai, UAE
Email: emad.bataineh@zu.ac.ae

Mohammed Basel Almourad
College of Technological Innovation, Zayed University
Dubai, UAE
Email: basel.almourad@zu.ac.ae

***Abstract*—In the current highly competitive industry, digital marketers must comprehend consumer behavior and effectively communicate with their intended consumers. Utilizing methods like eye tracking, Electroencephalogram (EEG), and Magnetic Resonance Imaging (MRI), neuromarketing has become a potent instrument for evaluating the effects of advertising across a range of media. This study explores the critical impact that focused visual attention plays in enhancing memory encoding, visual processing, and ultimately, recall of advertisements. The research examines how attention can be focused like a zoom lens, focusing on particular features inside advertisements, using the well-established Zoom Lens Model of Attention. The study examines participant-used visual attention methods and ideal logo placement through careful gaze data analysis. The results highlight the effectiveness of targeted visual attention in improving memory recall. Stronger memory retention showed participants could remember items that attracted concentrated visual attention. Furthermore, the results showed that focused attention-stimulated inputs were processed more effectively, as evidenced by fewer fixations and longer fixation times. This efficiency highlights the cognitive benefits of focused visual attention by implying that people could take in more information from the stimuli in less time. The study emphasizes the practical implications for digital marketers, stressing the significance of strategically putting essential components to draw in and hold viewers' attention long enough to boost advertisement memory.**

Keywords- Digital marketing; eye tracking; neuroscience; human psychology; consumer behavior.

I. Introduction

Marketers thrive on the ability to understand consumer behavior and translate that knowledge into actionable insights to better cater to their users. In this pursuit, researchers and practitioners alike have embraced neuromarketing techniques. Neuromarketing methods, such as eye tracking, EEG, MRI, and other tools are used to validate advertising effectiveness on digital media [2] [15], social media [4] and other channels. The bias-free nature and high-accuracy findings contribute to the popularity of neuromarketing methods [3].

Eye tracking is a safe and non-invasive methodology that provides insights into visual movement and attention [1]. Eye tracking offers a valuable tool for investigating visual attention strategies employed by users when viewing digital advertisements. The proximity of different elements within the visual field can influence whether users adopt a focused or diffused attentional zoom strategy [24]. The attentional zoom strategy is based on the zoom lens model [17], which suggests that our visual processing resources can be distributed over a wide area or in a focused/narrow area. Their experiments also showed improved visual acuity in areas that receive continuous focused visual attention as opposed to shifting visual attention across the visual field. In [17], the authors also postulated that visual processing resources degrade as the visual attentional field increases, which was also observed by [8].

Previously, in [8], the authors had conducted experiments where participants were presented with two objects, differentiated by color, on conducting subsequent memory tests revealed that participants exhibited strong memory for objects that received focused visual attention compared to objects that were outside the focused visual field of the participant. Numerous other studies have mentioned focused visual attention to improve visual processing, acuity, and memory [5] [7] [21]. The reviewed body of research suggests that employing focused visual attention strategies (while viewing advertisements) can enhance visual processing and memory encoding, potentially leading to improved advertising recall.

The impact of focused visual attention on advertising efficacy is one of the fundamental aspects of consumer behavior that digital marketing aims to understand. This study intends to investigate the function of focused visual attention in improving visual processing, memory encoding, and, eventually, advertising recall. It draws on well-established ideas, such as the Zoom Lens Model of Attention, which suggests that attention may be directed similarly to a zoom lens.

This study aims to investigate the potential benefits of using focused visual attention methods in digital ads by utilizing neuromarketing methodologies and cognitive psychology insights. In particular, the research aims to:

- Examine how focused visual attention and recollection of advertisements are related by using gaze data obtained from eye tracking devices.
- Analyze the best locations for logos and visual attention techniques in ads to enhance visual processing and memory encoding.
- Explore the practical ramifications for marketers, stressing the significance of putting essential components strategically to draw and hold viewers'

attention and increase the recall rate of advertisements.

The rest of the paper is structured as follows. Section 2 presents a literature review, Section 3 details the methodology, Section 4 presents the data analysis, Section 5 discusses the findings, and Section 6 concludes the paper with recommendations for future work.

II. LITERATURE REVIEW

A growing body of research has investigated the factors influencing advertising recall. In [10], the authors employed EEG and eye-tracking methodology to demonstrate that advertisements presented on tablets and paper elicited superior recognition and memorability compared to other media formats. Beyond the delivery platform, the content of the advertisement itself plays a crucial role in recall. In [11], the authors found that including image, text, and price elements within an advertisement significantly enhanced memory performance. In [9], the authors further revealed that the visual gaze of the model in an advertisement can also significantly affect the ad recall value, they observed that when the model shifts their gaze on the product or price, visual attention towards it increases resulting in participants performing well in memory tasks. Other studies have also established that eye-tracking metrics, such as the number of fixations is directly proportional to ad recall value [16].

This study is grounded on the zoom lens model as numerous studies have shown the strength of the model. In [7], the authors observed participants adjust their focal attention around the "salient perceptual objects". The findings suggest that visually salient objects can be surrounded by other elements within the same visual field to improve acuity and processing [7]. Behavioral studies have further supported the zoom lens models, indicating improved visual processing, acuity, and clarity when objects are placed at a focused location [17] [18]. In [6], the authors used electrophysiological methods to show that participants performed better in search tasks during narrowed visual attention due to strong activation of brain regions.

Studies have shown psychological and cognitive bias of visual attention towards the center [12] [16] [22]. In [22], the authors observed an "attentional concentration effect", that showed that visual attention is concentrated at the center even though participants were instructed to equally distribute their attention. In [22], the authors conducted tracking tests and found that participants had higher accuracy rates when tracking towards the center compared to the endpoints of horizontal lines, an "attentional amplification" effect was observed. In [13], the authors tasked the participants to detect the change in luminescence of dots (evenly spaced out). Participants were instructed to spread their attention across, as the change could occur in the center (narrow) or away from the center (broad). Improved detection was observed for dots in the center, implying the strength of narrowed visual attention and our bias. The effects above elucidate our uneven distribution of visual attentional resources and our bias to focus our visual attention toward the center of our visual field.

A. Eye tracking framework

Eye tracking is a great research methodology to observe users' visual attention and gather insights to improve advertising effectiveness in digital media [15]. Using eye tracking, numerous studies have provided evidence that employing focal attention by way of placing ad elements in close spatial proximity has improved advertising effectiveness. Due to low spatial proximity between ad elements, the saccadic amplitude is low. In [20], the authors described focal attention as having longer fixations and shorter saccadic amplitude whereas ambient attention has shorter fixations and longer saccadic amplitude. Data on focal attention (short saccadic amplitude) concluded that participants performed better in a recognition task and were more confident about their performance [20]. In [19], the authors conducted experiments to understand the effects of price labels on adverts with human models (vs mannequins), the authors deduced that placing elements close to an "attention magnet", i.e., human models increase the saliency of the elements placed near the "attention magnet". The conclusion was drawn due to neuroimaging studies validating that attention is deployed to specific spatial areas [19]. Converging evidence from other studies suggests that visual elements positioned closer to the focus of attention within the visual field are processed more efficiently compared to those located further away [23]. Marketers can leverage the increased visual attention of an ad element, i.e., product image or model to other ad elements like price, logo, and other information since increased visual attention relates to increased memory [14] [25]. In [21], the authors conducted a series of experiments to identify the best placement of a logo in an online advertising format to optimize for visual search and found that the logo element should be placed in the middle, parallel to the picture element. Placing the logo element in close proximity, not overlapping, to the picture element also improved memory [21].

III. METHODOLOGY

The viewing time for each advert stimulus will be 5 seconds, as previous studies employed the same duration for stimuli viewing [26]. In [28], the authors conducted a pilot study which revealed that 5 seconds was the average duration participants spent viewing banner ads on social media. Participants viewed four stimuli, each presented for 5 seconds, totaling 20 seconds of viewing time. After a 5-minute interval following the final stimulus, they completed a memory test to assess recall and recognition.

A. Participants

Gen Z participants are the study's primary focus since they are the most digitally native generation and play a major role in shaping online consumer trends and interaction patterns [16]. Our study aimed to have a minimum of 40 participants, as recommended in [26]. In [26], the authors recommended 15 - 50 participants for eye-tracking studies to be valid. We recruited 48 female students from Zayed University, Dubai, UAE, as our study focused on understanding consumer behavior among Gen Z female users, who represent a key demographic segment in digital marketing research.

B. *Stimuli*

The stimuli were developed according to the frameworks constructed as in [27]. The manipulated stimuli are of high quality and resemble real advertisements. Certain stimuli consisted of familiar brands and resembled real-life adverts of the brand, and other stimuli consisted of hypothetical brand names and logos to mitigate any familiarity bias [27]. The design employed a combination of image, text, and price elements within the stimuli, which are commonly associated with enhanced advertisement memorability [11].

Advert stimuli were also manipulated as per the findings of [21]. The research found that the advertiser should first try to place the logo element in the right middle position parallel to the picture element because the commodity logo in this matching mode can get the longest average time of consumers' attention, and the duration of attention is the most [21].

The findings in [29] were also applied to design the stimuli. In [29], the authors pointed out that perfume product image located in the lower part of the advertisement can attract consumers' attention the most. The product image was in the lower part of the advertisement for every stimulus. The logo was placed above the product image as suggested by [21].

Previous research has demonstrated the influence of brand recognition and price on product preference [30]. To mitigate these potential biases in our study, stimuli were designed to incorporate fictitious brand names and maintain a consistent price range (see Figures 1 and 2).

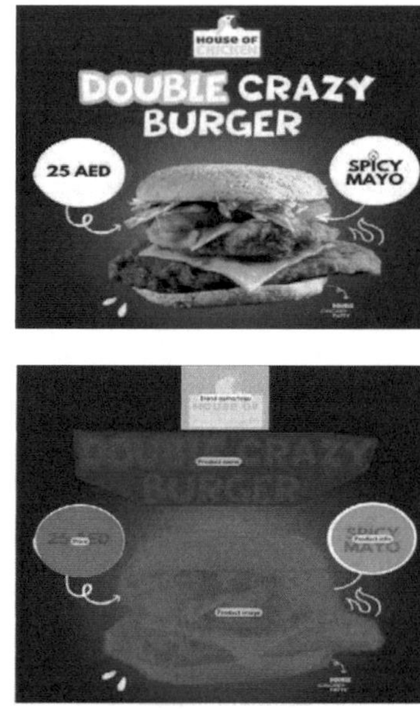

Figure 1. Stimuli for narrowed/focal visual attention and its AOIs.

Figure 2. Stimuli for diffused/broad visual attention and its AOIs.

IV. DATA ANALYSIS AND RESULTS

Figures 3(a) and 3(b) are cluster visualizations. A cluster is an area with high gaze data points [31]. An Area of Interest (AOI) [34] is a particular area or component of a digital interface (such as an email, landing page, website, or advertisement) that marketers monitor or examine to learn more about user behavior.

Figure 3(a) has only 1 cluster with 100% of participants contributing to the gaze data. Figure 3b has 2 clusters, and cluster 2 (upper right) ha89% participant contribution. Almost 11% of participants did not have significant eye gaze data in cluster 2 consisting of the brand name and logo. The results revealed optimal logo placement to be centered and aligned parallel to the picture element, consistent with findings reported by [21] in the context of focal attention stimuli. Placing ad elements within close proximity of the 'attention magnet' (food image), improved visual acuity and processing of all the elements within that narrowed visual field which aligns with the zoom lens model.

(a)

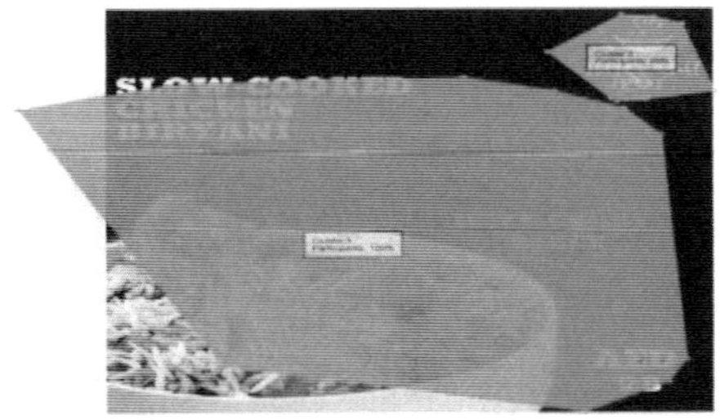

(b)

Figure 3. (a) and (b): Cluster analysis for stimuli having focal visual attention and ambient visual attention.

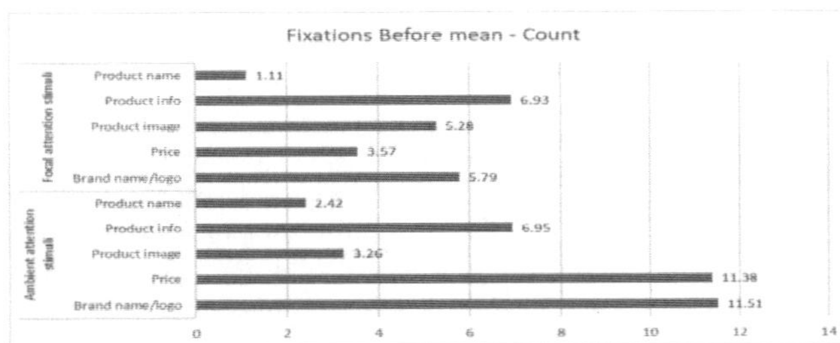

Figure 4. Fixations before mean - count for each AOI in both focal and ambient attention stimuli.

Fixation Count - count										
	Ambient attention stimuli					Focal attention stimuli				
	Brand name/logo	Price	Product image	Product info	Product name	Brand name/logo	Price	Product image	Product info	Product name
Total no.of fixations	67	58	267	119	218	51	121	150	77	279
Percentage	9.190672154	7.956104252	36.6255144	16.32373114	29.90397805	7.522123894	17.84660767	22.12389381	11.35693215	41.15044248

Figure 5. Number of Fixations (AOIs).

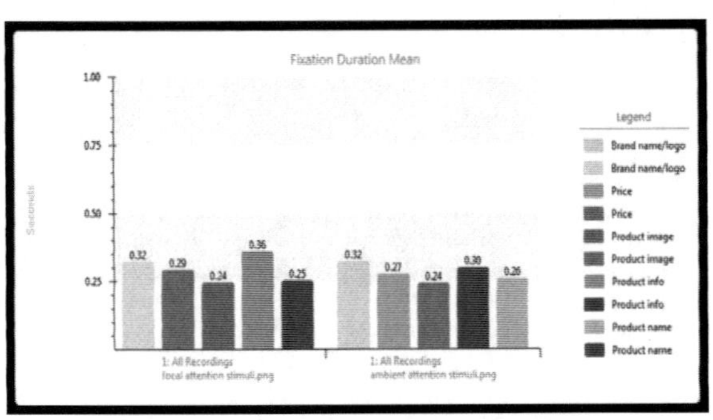

Figure 6. Mean fixation duration across AOIs in focal attention stimuli and ambient attention stimuli.

Figure 4 shows the number of fixations before fixating on an AOI [31]. The results reveal a significantly lower mean number of fixations prior to fixating on each AOI in the focal attention stimuli compared to the ambient attention stimuli. This finding suggests that participants, under conditions promoting focused visual attention, were able to rapidly direct their gaze towards the AOIs upon stimulus presentation. A lower fixation count is often associated with enhanced processing efficiency, potentially allowing participants to extract more information from the stimuli within a shorter time frame. Figure 5 gives the fixation count of stimuli.

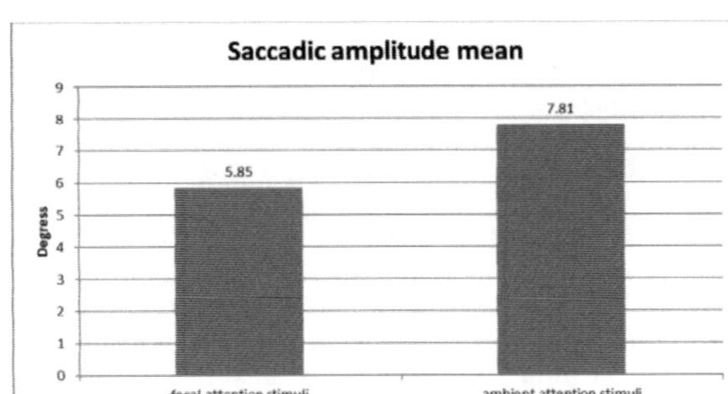

Figure 7. Mean saccadic amplitude (degrees).

Figures 6 and Figure 7 show the mean fixation duration and mean saccadic amplitude, respectively. Saccadic amplitude, the angular distance between eye fixations during a saccade, reveals visual attention allocation, with shorter amplitudes indicating focused scanning and longer amplitudes indicating broader scanning [20].

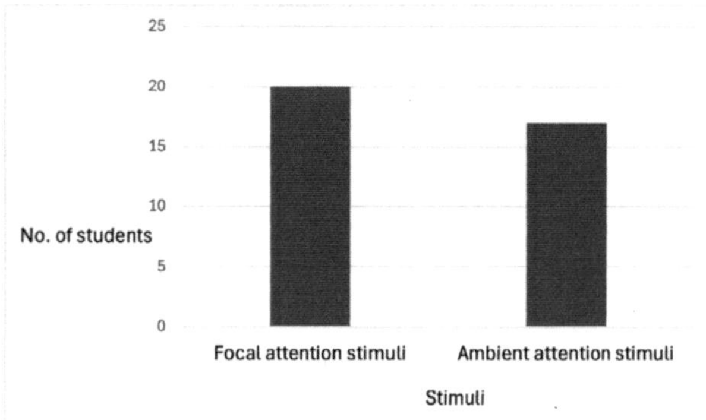

Figure 8. Number of participants who succeeded the memory test.

Focal attention stimuli had longer fixation durations and shorter saccadic amplitudes. Therefore, participants employed focal visual attention. In contrast, ambient attention stimuli had shorter fixation durations and longer saccadic amplitudes, implying that participants employed an ambient visual attention [32] [33]. Figure 8 shows that more participants were able to recall the stimuli that had focal visual attention.

V. DISCUSSION

The results of this study expand on previous research on the benefits of focused visual attention for improving memory encoding, visual processing, and eventually, recall of advertisements. This study investigated the theory that using focused visual attention tactics within advertisements can increase visual processing and memory encoding. It was based on the well-known Zoom Lens Model of Attention, which suggests that attention can be focused like a zoom lens. The gaze data analysis results support the hypothesis by showing individuals who received focused visual attention were better able to recall the stimuli than those who were exposed to ambient attention. The best logo location, as shown by the cluster visualizations, was centered, and positioned parallel to the image element, supporting findings from prior studies. This is consistent with the idea that positioning important components adjacent to an attention-grabbing object, such a focal picture, might improve visual processing and precision in a smaller visual field.

The findings pertaining to the number of fixations prior to fixating on AOIs further suggests that individuals in environments that facilitate concentrated visual attention had the ability to quickly focus their gaze on the AOIs upon presentation of the stimulus. This may indicate increased processing efficiency, allowing individuals to process the stimuli more quickly and retain more information. On the other hand, a less effective processing strategy was indicated by a higher mean number of fixations in response to ambient attention inputs. The differences between focused and ambient visual attention are further supported by the results pertaining to mean fixation length and saccadic amplitude. Longer fixation times and smaller saccadic amplitudes were induced by focal attention stimuli, indicating intentional and focused visual processing. Alternatively, greater saccadic amplitudes and shorter fixation durations were induced by ambient attention cues, indicating a more diffused and passive visual attentional approach.

Significantly, the study's findings show that ads that are intended to draw in focused visual attention have a distinct advantage, as seen by the participants' greater memory rates when exposed to these kinds of stimuli. This emphasizes the useful implications for marketers looking to maximize campaign effectiveness. Through the strategic placement of essential features in advertisements, advertisers can improve visual processing, memory encoding, and ultimately, advertising recall by drawing and holding viewers' attention.

VI. CONCLUSION

The empirical results obtained from neuromarketing approaches and the insights obtained from cognitive psychology in this study demonstrate the essential role that focused visual attention plays in improving the effectiveness of advertising. Gaze data analysis indicates that, in contrast to stimuli exposed to ambient attention, those intended to elicit focused attention produce greater memory recall and facilitate more effective processing. Interestingly, the best arrangement of essential components in ads about attentional foci is critical for improving visual processing and memory encoding. The practical ramifications of these findings for advertisers are highlighted, as they highlight the need to carefully place items to draw in and hold the attention of viewers, increasing the impact and memory rates of advertisements. Future studies should focus more on examining the subtleties of different focal cues and stimuli qualities to provide advertising professionals with more direction as they work to maximize the effectiveness of their campaigns and produce memorable, long-lasting brand experiences.

REFERENCES

[1] D. A. Worthy, J. N. Lahey, S. L. Priestley, and M. A. Palma, "An examination of the effects of eye-tracking on behavior in psychology experiments," *Behavior Research Methods*, pp. 1–14, 2024.

[2] V. Venkatraman et al., "Predicting advertising success beyond traditional measures: New insights from neurophysiological methods and market response modeling," *Journal of Marketing Research*, vol. 52, no. 4, pp. 436–452, 2015.

[3] D. Ariely and G. S. Berns, "Neuromarketing: the hope and hype of neuroimaging in business," *Nature Reviews Neuroscience*, vol. 11, no. 4, pp. 284–292, 2010.

[4] E. Nichifor et al., "Eye tracking and an A/B split test for social media marketing optimisation: The connection between the user profile and ad creative components," *Journal of Theoretical and Applied Electronic Commerce Research*, vol. 16, no. 6, pp. 2319–2340, 2021.

[5] H. Lee and S. K. Jeong, "Separating the effects of visual working memory load and attentional zoom on selective attention," *Journal of Experimental Psychology: Human Perception and Performance*, vol. 46, no. 5, pp. 502–515, 2020.

[6] Q. Zhang, T. Liang, J. Zhang, X. Fu, and J. Wu, "Electrophysiological evidence for temporal dynamics associated with attentional processing in the zoom lens paradigm," *PeerJ*, vol. 6, p. e4538, 2018.

[7] U. Castiello and C. Umiltà, "Splitting focal attention," *Journal of Experimental Psychology: Human Perception and Performance*, vol. 18, no. 3, pp. 837–848, 1992.

[8] J. Duncan, "Selective attention and the organization of visual information," *Journal of Experimental Psychology: General*, vol. 113, no. 4, pp. 501–517, 1984.

[9] P. Sajjacholapunt and L. J. Ball, "The influence of banner advertisements on attention and memory: Human faces with averted gaze can enhance advertising effectiveness," *Frontiers in Psychology*, vol. 5, p. 166, 2014.

[10] A. Ciceri, V. Russo, G. Songa, G. Gabrielli, and J. Clement, "A neuroscientific method for assessing effectiveness of digital vs. print ads: Using biometric techniques to measure cross-media ad experience and recall," *Journal of Advertising Research*, vol. 60, no. 1, pp. 71–86, 2020.

[11] S. Kong, Z. Huang, N. Scott, Z. A. Zhang, and Z. Shen, "Web advertisement effectiveness evaluation: Attention and memory," *Journal of Vacation Marketing*, vol. 25, no. 1, pp. 130–146, 2019.

[12] U. Castiello and C. Umiltà, "Size of the attentional focus and efficiency of processing," *Acta Psychologica*, vol. 73, no. 3, pp. 195–209, 1990.

[13] G. W. Balz and H. S. Hock, "The effect of attentional spread on spatial resolution," *Vision Research*, vol. 37, no. 11, pp. 1499–1510, 1997.

[14] D. E. Irwin and G. J. Zelinsky, "Eye movements and scene perception: Memory for things observed," *Perception & Psychophysics*, vol. 64, no. 6, pp. 882–895, 2002.

[15] J. Guixeres et al., "Consumer neuroscience-based metrics predict recall, liking and viewing rates in online advertising," Frontiers in Psychology, vol. 8, p. 1808, 2017.

[16] R. S. Toulan and H. F. Saleh, "Exploring news consumption patterns and preferences of Generation Z: A field study," The Egyptian Journal of Media Research, vol. 2025, no. 90, pp. 27–71, 2025.

[17] C. W. Eriksen and T. D. Murphy, "Movement of attentional focus across the visual field: A critical look at the evidence," *Perception & Psychophysics*, vol. 42, no. 3, pp. 299–307, 1987.

[18] G. L. Shulman and J. Wilson, "Spatial frequency and selective attention to spatial location," *Perception*, vol. 16, no. 1, pp. 103–111, 1987.

[19] R. V. Menon, V. Sigurdsson, N. M. Larsen, A. Fagerstrøm, and G. R. Foxall, "Consumer attention to price in social commerce: Eye tracking patterns in retail clothing," *Journal of Business Research*, vol. 69, no. 11, pp. 5008–5013, 2016.

[20] B. M. Velichkovsky, M. Joos, J. R. Helmert, and S. Pannasch, "Two visual systems and their eye movements: Evidence from static and dynamic scene perception," in *Proceedings of the XXVII Conference of the Cognitive Science Society*, vol. 1, pp. 2005–2010, 2005.

[21] Y. Jiang, "Research on the best visual search effect of logo elements in internet advertising layout," *Journal of Contemporary Marketing Science*, vol. 2, no. 1, pp. 23–33, 2019.

[22] G. A. Alvarez and B. J. Scholl, "How does attention select and track spatially extended objects? New effects of attentional concentration and amplification," *Journal of Experimental Psychology: General*, vol. 134, no. 4, pp. 461–476, 2005.

[23] W. Prinzmetal, D. E. Presti, and M. I. Posner, "Does attention affect visual feature integration?," *Journal of Experimental Psychology: Human Perception and Performance*, vol. 12, no. 3, pp. 361–369, 1986.

[24] A. V. Belopolsky, L. Zwaan, J. Theeuwes, and A. F. Kramer, "The size of an attentional window modulates attentional capture by color singletons," *Psychonomic Bulletin & Review*, vol. 14, no. 5, pp. 934–938, 2007.

[25] P. J. Danaher and G. W. Mullarkey, "Factors affecting online advertising recall: A study of students," *Journal of Advertising Research*, vol. 43, no. 3, pp. 252–267, 2003.

[26] L. Mañas-Viniegra, A. I. Veloso, and U. Cuesta, "Fashion promotion on Instagram with eye tracking: Curvy girl influencers versus fashion brands in Spain and Portugal," *Sustainability*, vol. 11, no. 14, p. 3977, 2019.

[27] M. Geuens and P. De Pelsmacker, "Planning and conducting experimental advertising research and questionnaire design," *Journal of Advertising*, vol. 46, no. 1, pp. 83–100, 2017.

[28] S. Peker, G. G. Menekse Dalveren, and Y. Inal, "The effects of the content elements of online banner ads on visual attention: Evidence from an eye-tracking study," *Future Internet*, vol. 13, no. 1, p. 18, 2021.

[29] R. Priyankara, S. Weerasiri, R. Dissanayaka, and M. Jinadasa, "Celebrity endorsement and consumer buying intention with relation to the television advertisement for perfumes," *Management Studies*, vol. 5, no. 2, pp. 128–148, 2017.

[30] S. Kaheh, M. Ramirez, J. Wong, and K. George, "Neuromarketing using EEG signals and eye-tracking," in *2021 IEEE International Conference on Electronics, Computing and Communication Technologies (CONECCT)*, pp. 1–4, 2021.

[31] Tobii Technology, *Tobii Studio 3.3 User Manual* [PDF]. [Online]. Available: https://stemedhub.org/resources/3374/download/TobiiStudio3.3Manual.pdf

[32] C. B. Trevarthen, "Two mechanisms of vision in primates," *Psychologische Forschung*, vol. 31, no. 4, pp. 299–337, 1968. doi: 10.1007/BF00422714

[33] P. J. Unema, S. Pannasch, M. Joos, and B. M. Velichkovsky, "Time course of information processing during scene perception: The relationship between saccade amplitude and fixation duration," *Visual Cognition*, vol. 12, no. 3, pp. 473–494, 2005. doi: 10.1080/13506280444000419

[34] C. Cenizo, "A neuromarketing approach to consumer behavior on web platforms," International Journal of Consumer Studies, vol. 49, no. 2, p. e70034, 2025.

AI Explain: AI-Generated Graphic Storytelling for Explaining AI Across Cultures

Petra Ahrweiler
TISSS Lab
Johannes Gutenberg University Mainz
Mainz, Germany
e- mail: petra.ahrweiler@uni-mainz.de

Gayathri Geetha Rajan
FACTS H-Lab
Indian Institute of Information Technology
Kottayam, India
e- mail: gayathri@iiitkottayam.ac.in

Abstract—**A significant gap exists between complex scientific discussions on Artificial Intelligence (AI) advancements and the general public consisting of diverse individuals separated by culture, age, gender, education, socio-economic status, lifestyles, media preferences, and other personal attributes. Bridging this translation gap requires adapting AI-related scientific content for different audiences. The idea of the AI Explain project is to explore how AI can enhance its own explainability through interactive graphical storytelling across cultures. Using content that has already been adapted for a lay audience, the project aims at fine-tuning DeepSeek narratives and AI-generated graphics for public engagement and understanding of AI.**

Keywords- Generative AI; Graphic Storytelling; Multi-Media Science Communication; AI Literacy; Digital Publishing; Augmented Reality.

I. INTRODUCTION

Artificial Intelligence (AI) is transforming societies at an unprecedented rate, yet public understanding of AI concepts remains limited. This project investigates how AI can contribute to explaining itself through AI-assisted visual storytelling. By adapting complex AI-related content into engaging graphic narratives, the research aims to bridge the gap between scientific discourse and public comprehension, particularly among younger audiences. The study leverages the fantasy novel *Angels and Other Cows* [3], which explores AI's role in the public sector, as the primary dataset. In an iterative process that exploits AI's key advantage to prepare, refine and improve numerous versions, the novel will be tokenized, segmented into narrative units, and annotated of AI concepts, ethical dilemmas, and key themes. A cross-linguistic analysis ensures cultural relevance for Indian and German audiences. Fine-tuning of DeepSeek is performed using supervised Reinforcement Learning from Human Feedback (RLHF) to enhance coherence and engagement. DeepSeek's text-generation capabilities will be utilized for AI-assisted storyboarding, transforming key narrative elements into structure storytelling sequences. Visual storytelling will be enhanced using AI-powered tools, such as RunwayML, Pika Labs, and DeepBrain AI, incorporating motion synthesis and character animation. A comparative study will assess audience responses to AI-generated storytelling, focusing on ethical considerations such as AI bias and explainability. To enhance engagement, interactive features such as tracker-based Augmented Reality (AR) elements will be developed using Unity for an immersive user experience. Evaluation will be conducted through a mixed-method approach, combining qualitative feedback and quantitative metrics, including comprehension scores and engagement levels. Insights gained will iteratively refine the model to ensure continuous improvements in AI-driven science communication. This research contributes to AI literacy and digital innovation by pioneering an interdisciplinary framework for AI-enabled storytelling. It aligns with national priorities on technological advancement and digital education, fostering a deeper, cross-cultural understanding of AI.

The ensuing sections detail the foundations and approach of the AI Explain project. Section 2 outlines the legacy of AI FORA and its contributions to inclusive science communication. Section 3 clarifies the project's cross-cultural and educational aims. In Section 4, we describe the technical steps, including data preparation, model fine-tuning, cultural adaptation, and the integration of AR features. Section 5 highlights the project's measurable results, anticipated challenges, and possible future directions. Section 6 concludes with reflections on the project's broader impact and outlines future pathways, including the expansion of co-creative strategies, incorporation of real-time user feedback, and the development of scalable educational tools for long-term societal engagement.

II. BACKGROUND

This project builds on the results of the international research project "Artificial Intelligence for Assessment" (AI FORA) [1] [2]. AI FORA already tried to break out of the silos of academia by presenting its research results not only in computer science proceedings but through the human-made literary fiction novel *Angels and other Cows* blending genres such as sci-fi, romance, adventure, mystery, and comedy [3]. With this approach, AI FORA started with the task of inclusive science communication making available research topics, results, and consequences of AI use in the public sector to a non-scientific lay readership via textual storytelling.

The AI Explain project now takes the next step in research for broader outreach: It investigates how AI can contribute to explaining itself, i.e., complex AI concepts, through AI-assisted visual storytelling. By adapting the textual content of the AI science novel on AI use in the public sector into engaging graphic narratives, the research aims to bridge the gap between scientific discourse and public comprehension, particularly among younger audiences. The project investigates whether AI can assist in making itself more explainable through interactive and engaging storytelling techniques, catering to diverse audiences. While previous research has focused on AI ethics, this project expands its scope to encompass Explainable AI (XAI) through a cross-cultural lens. By leveraging digital storytelling tools, it aims to transform AI-related topics into visually rich graphical narratives that resonate with young readers in India and Germany.

III. Objectives

This project explores how AI can explain itself through AI-assisted graphical storytelling, aiming to develop a cross-cultural framework for AI explainability by comparing perspectives from India and Germany. It investigates the effectiveness of AI tools in crafting visually compelling narratives and examines the impact of interactive storytelling—especially using Augmented Reality (AR)—on public engagement with AI concepts. By using narrative case studies, the project also analyzes the ethical dimensions of AI within the broader scope of Explainable AI (XAI). Ultimately, it supports national and global priorities by advancing AI education and fostering cross-cultural communication around AI.

IV. Methodology

A. Data Preparation and Model Training

DeepSeek will be trained using the AI science novel as the primary dataset. Deepseek is chosen as it is fully open-source, and we can trail the model using our data. In an iterative process that exploits AI's key advantage to prepare, refine and improve numerous versions (narrative case studies),

- the primary dataset will be tokenized and segmented into meaningful narrative units
- AI concepts, ethical dilemmas, and key thematic elements will be annotated
- content will be made compatible with Indian and German audiences using cross-linguistic analysis
- Supervised learning with reinforcement from human feedback (RLHF) for improving coherence and engagement will be done to perform fine tuning DeepSeek on the above-mentioned dataset.

B. AI-Assisted Storyboarding and Video Generation

DeepSeek's text-generation capabilities will be leveraged to convert key narrative elements into structured storytelling sequences. AI concepts will be brought to life using tools like RunwayML, Pika Labs, and DeepBrain AI. Tools will be used to create animated sequences. Customization techniques, including AI-powered motion synthesis and character animation, will be applied to align the visuals with cultural preferences in India and Germany.

C. Cultural Adaptation and Ethical Analysis

A comparative study will be conducted to evaluate audience responses to AI-generated storytelling across both cultures. Ethical considerations, such as AI bias and explainability, will be embedded in the narratives and assessed for effectiveness in public comprehension.

D. Integration of Interactive Features

Tracker based Augmented Reality (AR) elements will be used for immersive experience. AR application design will use UNITY for user engagement and gamification.

E. Evaluation and Refinement

A mixed-method approach, combining qualitative feedback and quantitative metrics (e.g., comprehension scores, engagement levels), will be used to assess the impact of AI-assisted storytelling. Findings will be iteratively used to refine the model, ensuring continuous improvement in AI-driven science communication.

V. Expected Outcomes

The *AI Explain* project aims to bridge the gap between artificial intelligence research and public understanding by developing inclusive, culturally sensitive science communication formats. Recognizing that research is often locked within expert domains, this initiative seeks to make AI concepts more accessible through narrative and visual storytelling.

Measurable outcomes include:

- A prototype graphic novel illustrating AI-related ideas for younger, non-expert audiences.
- Insights into how AI can contribute to its own explainability via interactive and visual storytelling.
- A cross-cultural study on AI perception in India and Germany.
- An interactive learning tool focusing on AI ethics and explainable AI (XAI).
- Frameworks for AI-assisted digital publishing and integration with augmented reality.
- Contributions to national AI missions by enhancing AI literacy through accessible digital storytelling.

Key challenges anticipated include maintaining cultural relevance in AI-generated stories, avoiding Western-centric biases, ensuring narrative coherence, and responsibly simplifying complex ethical issues.

VI. Conclusion and Future Work

The *AI Explain* project positions itself as a critical intervention in making AI more transparent, relatable, and ethically grounded. By using co-creative strategies, combining AI-generated outputs with human input from artists, educators, and communities, the project will address the limitations of generative models and ensure contextual fidelity.

In future phases, the project envisions:

- Incorporating real-time gaze tracking and sentiment analysis to personalize AI education tools.
- Expanding cross-cultural frameworks to include additional geographies and languages.
- Publishing scalable toolkits and pedagogical resources for schools, museums, and digital media outlets.
- Building open-source pipelines for AI-assisted science communication to support long-term societal engagement.

Through these efforts, *AI Explain* aims to redefine how AI communicates itself, making it more understandable, participatory, and socially responsible.

References

[1] P. Ahrweiler (ed.), Participatory Artificial Intelligence in public social services. From bias to fariness in assessing beneficiaries. Cham: Springer, 2025. https://doi.org/10.1007/978-3-031-71678-2

[2] P. Ahrweiler et al., “Using ABM and serious games to create ‘better AI’”. 2024 Annual Modeling and Simulation Conference (ANNSIM), Washington, D.C., USA, May 2024, pp.1-16. doi:10.23919/ANNSIM61499.2024.10732031, https://ieeexplore.ieee.org/document/10732031; last accessed 19/05/2025, 2024.

[3] P. Ahrweiler, Angels and other Cows. A celestial adventure into AI worlds, the social good, and unknown connections. Cham: Springer, 2024. https://doi.org/10.1007/978-3-031-60401-0.

Automated Use Case Diagram Generator: Transforming Textual Descriptions into Visual Representations using a Large Language Model

Maxmillan Giyane
Department of Computer Science
Midlands State University
Gweru, Zimbabwe
email: giyanem@staff.msu.ac.zw

Dzinaishe Mpini
Department of Computer Science
Midlands State University
Gweru, Zimbabwe
email: mpinid@staff.msu.ac.zw

Abstract— **Software Architects often use Use Case diagrams, a type of Unified Modelling Language (UML) behavior diagram, to capture user needs and system functionalities. These diagrams aid in project estimation by identifying system requirements and reducing ambiguity. Creating them manually is a time-consuming task prone to errors. This research aims to automate Use Case diagram generation from text using the Generative Pretrained Transformer 3.5 (GPT-3.5) Turbo model. The developed tool uses a Natural Language Processing (NLP) technique to extract actors, use cases, and associations from descriptions, and convert these elements into UML-compliant diagrams. It also includes an interactive interface for Use Case diagram refinement. The system processes user input text to identify relevant elements, visualizes them using jCanvas, and allows real-time user interaction for refinement. Testing showed an 89.33% accuracy in element identification but highlighted areas for improvement like handling edge cases and optimizing performance. This research demonstrates the potential of NLP and visualization tools to improve Use Case diagram generation efficiency and accuracy, with future work focusing on enhancing usability and functionality.**

Keywords- Use Case Diagram; Large Language Model; GPT 3.5 Turbo; Natural Language Processing.

I. INTRODUCTION

The software Architect task relies on different methods to capture user needs. One method widely used is Use Case diagrams. According to Fauzan et al. [1], Use Case diagrams are a specific type of behavior diagram in the Unified Modelling Language (UML) which are primarily meant to help visualize a system's functionalities. UML itself is a prominent notation system commonly employed in software architecture [2]. Use Case diagrams capture system behavior from the user's perspective, detailing interactions, and system boundaries [3]. They essentially define what the software should do [3]. Beyond functionality, Use Case diagrams play a valuable role in project estimation as they highlight system requirements which are in turn used to estimate development effort [4][5][6]. Furthermore, they help reduce ambiguity within requirement specifications [7].

The core elements of a Use Case diagram are actors, use cases, and their associations. Actors are external entities (individuals or groups) that interact with the system. Use cases represent the interactions themselves, specifying how actors achieve goals within the system. These elements are connected by associations, signifying the communication between actors and use cases [8].

Creating well-structured Use Case diagrams requires adherence to specific conventions due to the complexity of placement rules [2]. Unlike typical graph layouts, Use Case diagrams demand specialized methods to ensure clarity, particularly as diagram size increases. The guidelines in Use Cases diagram generation encompass naming conventions for actors, systems, and use cases themselves. They advocate for simplicity and clarity, emphasizing the use of nouns and verbs to clearly define elements within the diagram [9].

These conventions make drawing of a Use Case diagram difficult. Filipova and Nikiforova [2] alludes manual layout of Use Case diagrams is a time-consuming activity; and one can fail to produce effective diagrams. With the way technology is advancing nowadays, researchers were compelled to create more efficient tools for drawing Use Case diagrams that follow the UML notation.

This research is aimed at developing a tool for automated Use Case diagrams generation from text that utilizes Large Language Models (LLMs). The specific objectives of the research are:

1. To develop a Natural Language Processing (NLP) technique which utilizes the GPT 3.5 Turbo LLM to extract relevant information which includes actors, use cases, and associations from textual system descriptions.
2. To develop an engine that can automatically convert the extracted elements (actors, use cases and associations) from the NLP analysis into a coherent and accurate Use Case diagram compliant with UML standards.
3. To design an interface that allows users to interact with the generated Use Case diagram and refine its actors, associations, and use cases manually.

The remainder of this paper is organized as follows: In Section 2, we review related work on automated software documentation and LLM applications. Section 3 details our methodology, including the prompt engineering framework. Section 4 presents a case study validating the approach use cases. Section 5 discusses results, limitations, and comparisons with traditional methods. Finally, Section 6 concludes with future directions, including integration with generative media tools.

II. Related Work

Use case diagrams were first proposed by Ivar Jacobson in 1986 as part of his work on object-oriented software engineering [8]. These diagrams have since become a fundamental tool in software development, aiding in the visualization of system functionality from a user perspective. In drawing tools, one can use the manual approach, electronic drag and drop tools, and automated tools.

This research noted a lack of recent scholarly articles focusing on manual tools for Use Case diagram creation. Electronic drag and drop tools research have also not been clearly documented but there exist several tools for Use Case diagram generation. These include Lucid Chart, Visual Paradigm, Smart Draw, DrawIO, Miro, Microsoft Visio and Wondershare Edraw Max. Table 1 shows the top found tools and the analysis done on them.

In the realm of automating the generation of Use Case diagrams from textual descriptions, several significant studies have been conducted. Elallaoui et al. [7] conducted pioneering research aimed at transforming user stories into UML Use Case diagrams automatically. By leveraging NLP techniques, their approach achieved impressive accuracy scores ranging from 87% to 98%. This evaluation was based on a comparison of the outputs automatically generated by the plugin against manual modelling of each user story. This demonstrated the potential of NLP in interpreting and converting textual requirements into structured diagrams. Similarly, Nasiri et al. [17] presented a comprehensive framework for the automatic generation of various UML diagrams, including class, Use Case, and package diagrams. Their approach involved processing user stories written in natural language (English) using the Stanford Core NLP engine. By incorporating artificial intelligence through Prolog rules and ontology, they enhanced their previous methodologies, resulting in improved outcomes. Despite reporting that the results of the approach have been validated by several case studies, the methodology for assessing the approach was not documented and the metric values of results were not specified. While both studies showcased promising results, they also had limitations. Notably, the carried out researches lack implementation. However, a Google search revealed an implemented automated Use Case diagram generation tool called Diagramming AI [18]. The underlying technology behind its working is not publicly available and at the time of analysis the tool did not adhere to the UML Use Case diagram standard, limiting its utility for standard-compliant projects.

Recent advances in prompt engineering have become pivotal for optimizing LLM outputs in software engineering tasks. Sahoo et al. [19] conducted a systematic survey of prompt engineering methods for LLMs, categorizing techniques, such as zero-shot, few-shot, and role-based prompting. Their work highlights how tailored prompts improve accuracy in structured outputs, a finding directly relevant to our Use Case extraction process.

TABLE I. USE CASE DIAGRAMS GENERATION TOOLS

Source	Tool	Access Channel	Cost
[10]	Lucid Chart	Web based application, and embedded in Google platforms	USD7.95-9.95/month. Free trial available
[11]	Visual Paradigm	Web based application and desktop applications	USD4.00-15.00/month. Free trial available
[12]	Smart Draw	Web based application	USD9.95
[13]	DrawIO	Web based application, desktop application, and embedded in Google platforms	USD34.00/20 users. Free trial available
[14]	Miro	Web based application	USD8.00-16.00/month. Free trial available
[15]	Microsoft Visio	Desktop application	USD44.15 for the software license
[16]	Wonder Share Edraw Max	Web based application	USD5.99-79.99/month

Wang et al. [18] explored the application of LLMs in generating UML diagrams. Use Case diagrams were part of the UML diagrams under study. 45 undergraduate students explored the platform. The research demonstrated 100% correctness of LLMs in identifying users, relationships and functional requirements from a given scenario. However, the research only encompassed identifying users, relationships and functional requirements and did not create the Use Case diagram from this information.

Additionally, Carrazan [20] provides critical insights into LLM applications for automating software requirements, particularly Use Case diagrams and narratives. The study demonstrates that when guided by carefully engineered prompts, Chat Generative Pre-trained Transformer (ChatGPT) can effectively generate accurate requirements documentation while significantly reducing development time. Carrazan's methodology [20] emphasizes a structured input-process-output framework where tailored prompts serve as inputs to produce validated UML artifacts - an approach that directly informs our work's prompt design strategy (Section III.B). Notably, the dissertation [20] confirms that LLM-generated requirements can achieve sufficient quality for stakeholder communication and effort estimation, though it cautions that human validation remains essential. These findings complement existing literature [7][19] while providing empirical evidence of LLMs' potential to streamline early-phase software documentation.

III. Methodology

A. System Architecture

The proposed tool went through a streamlined process designed to facilitate the creation and refinement of Use Case diagrams from textual descriptions. Initially, users provide a textual description of their desired system via a web page interface. This input is then sent to the backend, where the GPT-3.5 Turbo model processes the text to identify and extract relevant actors, use cases, and associations. The extracted information is subsequently transferred to the frontend, where the jCanvas engine generates an initial Use Case diagram based on the provided data. Users can interact with the diagram through a user-friendly interface, allowing them to modify actors, system names, use cases, and associations. These modifications are reflected in real time on the Use Case diagram, thanks to the dynamic capabilities of the jCanvas engine. Once users are satisfied with the refined diagram, they have the option to save or export the final version for their documentation or further use. The architecture of this tool ensures a seamless and interactive experience from the initial text input to the final output, enabling users to efficiently create and refine Use Case diagrams. Figure 1 shows the architectural diagram of the proposed system.

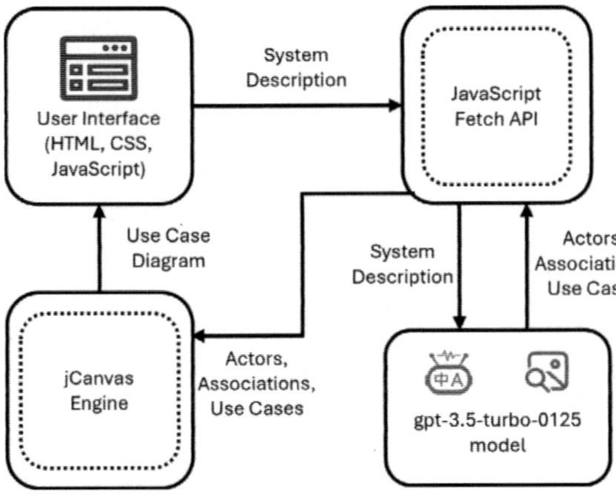

Figure 1. Architecture diagram of the proposed system.

B. GPT3.5 Turbo Model Working Mechanism

GPT-3.5 Turbo was chosen because of its Instruct Architecture. According to Yeow et al. [19] this architecture comprises multiple layers, each containing a self-attention mechanism and a feed-forward neural network. The self-attention mechanism enables the model to weigh the importance of different parts of the input when making predictions, enhancing its contextual understanding. The feed-forward neural network then makes the final predictions, allowing GPT-3.5 Turbo to generate coherent and contextually relevant text across various applications.

Bandara et al. [20] outlines GPT-3.5, released by OpenAI in 2020, is the foundational language model for the original ChatGPT and represents significant advancements in NLP and generation. With 175 billion parameters, it is one of the largest language models, demonstrating improved language understanding, enhanced text generation, and the ability to produce human-like text across various domains. GPT-3.5's architecture allows ChatGPT to engage in natural, context-aware dialogues, leveraging its extensive pre-training to draw on a vast knowledgebase. However, GPT-3.5 has limitations, such as struggles with logical reasoning, potential biases from its training data, and a restricted context window of 2,048 tokens. Understanding these strengths and limitations is essential for setting realistic expectations when using ChatGPT and similar Artificial Intelligence (AI) applications built on GPT-3.5. In generating the Use Case diagrams, jCanvas was used. jCanvas is a jQuery plugin that makes it easy to work with the Hypertext Markup Language 5 (HTML5) canvas element [21]. It provides a convenient Application Programming Interface (API) for drawing shapes, text, and images, as well as handling animations and user interactions. The plugin integrates seamlessly with jQuery, enabling efficient manipulation of canvas elements and real-time updates, making it an excellent choice for creating and modifying Use Case diagrams [22].

C. Interface Design

The interface design for the web page should be a one-page, user-friendly and dynamic visualization of system descriptions through Use Case diagrams. Upon loading, users encounter a central text input box where they can enter detailed descriptions of the system they intend to diagram. Adjacent to this input area is a "Generate Diagram" button, signaling the action to transform the entered text into a visual representation. Once activated, the system processes the input using GPT-3.5 Turbo via the OpenAI Application Programming Interface (API) and displays the resulting Use Case diagram on a canvas. This canvas initially presents elements, such as system boundaries, actors, use cases, and their associations based on the processed text.

Each element within the diagram becomes interactive and editable directly on the canvas, enabling users to click, drag, and modify elements effortlessly. This interactive capability extends to renaming actors or use cases, adjusting connections, and repositioning elements to suit specific requirements. Real-time updates ensure that any changes made by the user are immediately reflected in the displayed diagram, maintaining continuity and allowing for iterative refinement. Options for saving or exporting the finalized diagram, typically in formats like PNG or PDF, provide users with the means to preserve their work or share it as needed. The interface design emphasizes clarity, intuitive usability, and responsiveness across different devices, aiming to facilitate seamless interaction and effective visualization of system structures from textual descriptions.

IV. TOOL DESCRIPTION

The tool was designed as a comprehensive web application that utilized HyperText Markup Language (HTML), Cascading Style Sheets (CSS), and the Bootstrap framework to create an intuitive user interface. jQuery was employed to enhance user interaction, ensuring smooth and responsive handling of dynamic elements within the interface. A Representational State Transfer Application Programming Interface (RESTful API) endpoint was developed in PHP: Hypertext Preprocessor (PHP) to facilitate seamless communication with the 'gpt-3.5-turbo-0125' model from OpenAI.

The core functionality of the tool was driven by jCanvas, a powerful jQuery plugin that enabled the creation and modification of Use Case diagrams directly within the web page. Users interacted with a straightforward interface where they input system descriptions and, upon triggering the "Generate Diagram" function, observed a visual representation of their system structure. This design emphasized usability and real-time responsiveness, allowing users to refine and customize their diagrams effortlessly. The tool's integration of modern web technologies ensured an efficient and engaging experience for users who sought to visually conceptualize system architectures from textual descriptions.

V. Results and Discussion

In testing the developed system, a comprehensive suite of tests was conducted to ensure functionality, accuracy, performance, usability, and integration across its core objectives. A group of 3 Computer Science students and 2 Computer Science lecturers who were not involved in the development of the system conducted the tests. Each user created their own user story and evaluated the performance of the system with those user stories.

A. Large Language Model Performance in Extraction of Actors, Use Cases and Associations

Initially, the accuracy of the NLP technique was rigorously evaluated through test cases that assessed the extraction of actors, use cases, and associations from diverse textual use case descriptions. This included edge case scenarios to gauge robustness. Performance testing focused on measuring processing speeds and scalability under varying system descriptions. In the test, reviewers analyzed the output actors, Use Cases and associations to gauge the accuracy of the tool. Additionally, the time taken to produce an output was recorded.

The testers' scores revealed a promising average accuracy of 89.33%, indicating the tool successfully identifies elements from the descriptions. However, there were some missed elements, like deposit/withdrawal use cases in one instance and the bank teller actor itself for the first test case. These highlight areas for improvement, particularly in handling operations which have not been mentioned. The loading time for testers ranged from 5 to 7 seconds, averaging at 6.2 seconds. While acceptable, further optimization can enhance user experience. Additionally, testers 3 and 5 noted overly long system names generated by the tool. This suggests the system might be assigning generic, lengthy descriptions. Implementing logic to generate concise and descriptive names would be beneficial. The NLP technique shows promise with its accuracy. However, improvements are needed to handle edge cases, optimize loading times, and generate better quality names for actors and use cases. This will further enhance the tool's effectiveness and user experience.

B. Use Case Diagram Generation

The engine's capability to convert extracted elements into UML-compliant Use Case diagrams was verified through validation tests against UML standards and guidelines, ensuring diagrams met syntax and semantic requirements. Customization features were tested to validate user-defined preferences and styles, ensuring flexibility in diagram presentation. Integration tests ensured seamless interoperability with external systems, assessing data consistency and compatibility.

Largely, the test results show that the system has the capability to convert extracted elements into UML-compliant Use Case diagrams, but there are some areas for improvement, such as refining extracted elements to avoid cluttered diagrams and ensuring that generated names fit within the designated space. Only Tester 2 found that the tool generated a poor diagram due to the identification of too many use cases. This suggests that the system might need improvement in refining the extracted elements to ensure a clear and concise Use Case diagram. Tester 3 identified an issue where the system name spanned outside the boundary of the diagram. This indicates that the name generation process might need to consider the available space within the diagram to ensure all elements are well presented.

C. Interactive User Interface for Refining Generated Diagrams

User Interface (UI) testing involved usability assessments with potential end-users to gauge ease of use and navigation. Feedback mechanisms were tested to capture user inputs on diagram quality and interface improvements. Compatibility tests were conducted across different devices to ensure consistent performance and responsiveness. Error handling was scrutinized through various error scenarios to assess how the system managed and communicated errors effectively to users.

While testers commended the tool's ease of use and functionality for adding, deleting, or modifying elements, they highlighted the need for improved visual clarity. This suggests that while the core functionalities are present, the user interface might benefit from enhancements that ensure a clearer visual representation of the Use Case diagram during the editing process.

VI. Conclusion and Future Work

This research focused on the development of a tool capable of extracting a Use Case diagram elements from a given textual system description using a large language model. The tool should further draw the Use Case diagram using jCanvas and allow a user to manually refine the generated Use Case diagram. The testing approach utilized validated each aspect of the tool objectives. Notably, there was no comparable researches available for direct comparison, as existing literature either lacked publicly available implementations which follow the UML Use Case diagrams standard or did not employ an automated diagram generation approach like the one proposed in this research.

The system is poised for deployment in real-world environments where efficient Use Case diagram generation is paramount. The research recommends scalability to verify the system's capability to manage increasing volumes of use case descriptions without performance degradation, ensuring robustness under varying workloads. Additionally, it is recommended to provide comprehensive user training and support material to facilitate smooth and effective utilization of the system.

While this study demonstrates the efficacy of GPT-3.5 Turbo in automating Use Case diagram generation, the reliance on a single LLM poses a limitation. Recent advancements in code-specific LLMs, such as Codex, StarCoder or fine-tuned variants, such as Llama-3 with UML datasets may yield higher accuracy in extracting structural UML elements. Future work should also include a comparative analysis of multiple LLMs, evaluating their performance in parsing textual descriptions and adhering to UML standards. This expansion will help identify optimal models for specific tasks, such as handling "include" and "extend" relationships or complex system boundaries, further improving the tool's robustness. Beyond testing other LLMs, future research could explore AI-generative media tools, such as Stable Diffusion or DALL-E to automatically enhance diagram aesthetics and layout, enabling direct conversion of textual descriptions into polished UML figures while maintaining compliance with standards through hybrid human-AI validation frameworks. The tool was also tested by only 5 individuals from the same department at a university. This presents potential bias on the effectiveness of the tool and future work must be evaluated by many participants from varying backgrounds.

Additionally, the developed tool outputs an image file of the generated Use Case diagram without the XML code for that can be used in other diagramming tools. Future work could focus on producing both the Use Case diagram image as well as standard XML code for a Use Code which can be integrated in other languages.

Furthermore, there is an opportunity for comparative studies with other GPT variants or large language models to identify and integrate the most efficient model for improving system performance and accuracy. These enhancements and comparisons will contribute to advancing the capabilities and effectiveness of the system in generating and manipulating Use Case diagrams.

REFERENCES

[1] R. Fauzan, D. Siahaan, S. Rochimah, and E. Triandini, "A Different Approach on Automated Use Case Diagram Semantic Assessment," International Journal of Intelligent Engineering and Systems, vol. 14, no. 1, 2021, pp. 496-505, doi - 10.22266/ijies2021.0228.46.J. Clerk Maxwell, A Treatise on Electricity and Magnetism, 3rd ed., vol. 2. Oxford: Clarendon, pp. 68–73, 1892,

[2] O. Filipova and O. Nikiforova, "Definition of the Criteria for Layout of the UML Use Case Diagrams," Applied Computer Systems, vol. 24, no. 1, 2019, pp. 75-81, doi - 10.2478/acss-2019-0010.

[3] F. Mokhati and M. Badri, "Generating Maude Specifications From UML Use Case Diagrams," Journal of Object Technology, vol. 8, no. 2, 2009, pp. 119-136.

[4] P. Jayadi, R. S. Dewi, and K. Sussolaikah, "Activity-based function point complexity of Use Case diagrams for software effort estimation," Journal of Soft Computing Exploration, vol. 5, no. 1, 2024, pp. 1-8, doi - 10.52465/joscex.v5i1.252.

[5] A. B. Nassif, L. F. Capretz, and H. Danny, "A Regression Model with Mamdani Fuzzy Inference System for Early Software Effort Estimation Based on Use Case Diagrams", PhD dissertation, Graduate Program in Electrical and Computer Engineering, The University of Western Ontario, 2012.

[6] P. Sahoo and J. R. Mohanty, "Early Test Effort Prediction using UML Diagrams," Indonesian Journal of Electrical Engineering and Computer Science , vol. 5, no. 1, 2017, pp. 220-228.

[7] M. Elallaoui, K. Nafil, and R. Touahni, "Automatic Transformation of User Stories into UML Use Case Diagrams using NLP Techniques," in The 8th International Conference on Ambient Systems, Networks and Technlogies (ANT 2018), 2018, pp. 42-49.

[8] A. Y. Aleryani, "Comparative Study between Data Flow Diagram and Use Case Diagram," International Journal of Scientific and Research Publications, vol. 6, no. 3, 2016.

[9] P. Danenas, T. Skersys, and R. Butleris, "Natural language processing enhanced extraction of SBVR business vocabularies and business rules from UML Use Case diagrams," Data and Knowledge Engineering, 2020.

[10] Lucid Chart, "Draw Chart," 2024. [Online]. Available: https://lucid.app/lucidchart/. [Accessed June 2025].

[11] Visual Paradigm, "Visual Paradigm," 2024. [Online]. Available: https://online.visual-paradigm.com. [Accessed June 2025].

[12] Smart Draw, "Use Case Diagram," 2024. [Online]. Available: https://www.smartdraw.com/use-case-diagram/. [Accessed June 2025].

[13] Drawio, "Draw Use Case Diagram," 2024. [Online]. Available: https://drawio-app.com/ . [Accessed June 2025].

[14] Miro, "Use Case Diagram," Miro, 2024. [Online]. Available: https://miro.com/templates/use-case-diagram/. [Accessed June 2025].

[15] Microsoft , "Create a UML Use Case Diagram," Microsoft, 2024. [Online]. Available: https://support.microsoft.com/en-us/office/create-a-uml-use-case-diagram-92cc948d-fc74-466c-9457-e82d62ee1298 . [Accessed June 2025].

[16] EdrawMax, "Use Case Diagram," Edraw, 2024. [Online]. Available: https://www.edrawmax.com/online/en/ . [Accessed June 2025].

[17] S. Nasiri, Y. Rhazali, M. Lahmer and A. Adadi, "From User Stories to UML Diagrams Driven by Ontological and Production Model," International Journal of Advanced Computer Science and Applications, vol. 12, no. 6, 2021, doi - 10.14569/IJACSA.2021.0120637.

[18] B. Wang, C. Wang, P. Liang, B. Li, and C. Zeng, "How LLMs Aid in UML Modeling: An Exploratory Study with Novice Analysts," 2024 IEEE International Conference on Software Services Engineering (SSE), Shenzhen, China, 2024, pp. 249-257, doi: 10.1109/SSE62657.2024.00046.

[19] L. Naimi, E. Bouziane, A. Jakimi, R. Saadane, and A Chehri, "Automating Software Documentation: Employing LLMs for Precise Use Case Description", Procedia Computer Science, vol. 246, no 1, 2024, pp. 1346-1354, doi 10.1016/j.procs.2024.09.568.

[20] P. F. V. Carrazan, Large Language Models Capabilities for Software Requirements Automation, Ph.D. dissertation, Dept. Comput. Eng., Politecnico di Torino, Torino, Italy, 2023.

Methodology for Integrated Mapping of Radiation and Light Intensity in Power Transmission Lines

Maria Luiza Cenci Stedile, João Henrique Campos Soares,
Davi Riiti Goto do Valle, Andre Schneider de Oliveira and Ronnier Frates Rohrich
Graduate Program in Electrical and Computer Engineering
Program in Computer Science
Universidade Tecnológica Federal do Paraná
Curitiba, Brazil
e-mail: {mstedile | jsoares.2021 | daviriiti}@alunos.utfpr.edu.br
{andreoliveira | rohrich}@utfpr.edu.br

Abstract—**This study presents a methodology for mapping UltraViolet (UV) radiation and light intensity in vegetable gardens located within power transmission line easements. Using advanced sensors mounted on mobile robots, the system captures daily variations in UV radiation and luminosity. The collected data reveals differences in solar incidence across the easements, offering insights into their potential for sustainable agricultural practices.**

Keywords-UV Radiation Mapping; Light Intensity Monitoring; Transmission Line Easements; Mobile Robotic Sensing.

I. INTRODUCTION

Ultraviolet B (UV-B) radiation, a biologically active spectrum of sunlight (280–320 nm), has been extensively studied for its dual impact on human health and plant development. In humans, excessive exposure to UV-B is associated with increased risks of skin cancer and ocular disorders [1]. In plants, however, UV-B radiation influences anatomical and physiological traits, such as biomass allocation, leaf area, chlorophyll content, and secondary metabolite production, with effects varying by species and radiation dose [2][3]. For example, pigmented potatoes showed enhanced nutrient synthesis under controlled UV-B doses [3]. In the face of climate change and urban growth, transmission line easements emerge as potential sites for low-height, sustainable agriculture. However, their viability depends on understanding local environmental factors, especially solar radiation and light intensity.

This study proposes a Methodology for Integrated Mapping of Radiation and Light Intensity, combining fixed sensors and modular units mounted on mobile robotic platforms. By enabling spatially distributed and scalable data acquisition, this approach supports the identification of microzones with distinct agricultural potential. In line with recent advances in innovative sensor technologies and data-driven agriculture [4], the proposed system aims to inform sustainable cultivation strategies in non-traditional farming areas, promoting more efficient land.

The rest of the paper is structured as follows. In Section II, we present the measurement and sensor evaluation, describing the environment where the experiment was conducted. In Section III, we show the results originating from the fixed sensor mapping. We conclude the work in Section IV.

II. MEASUREMENT AND SENSOR EVALUATION

The project is designed to follow a structured set of stages, as outlined in Figure 1. A system is being developed to provide comprehensive analytical support throughout each workflow phase. Initially, the results were evaluated through measurements obtained using a fixed system to understand better how the variables interact and behave under controlled conditions. Data collection will subsequently be conducted using both ground and aerial mobile robotic platforms to evaluate scalability, optimize mapping strategies, and increase the efficiency of detailed local data acquisition.

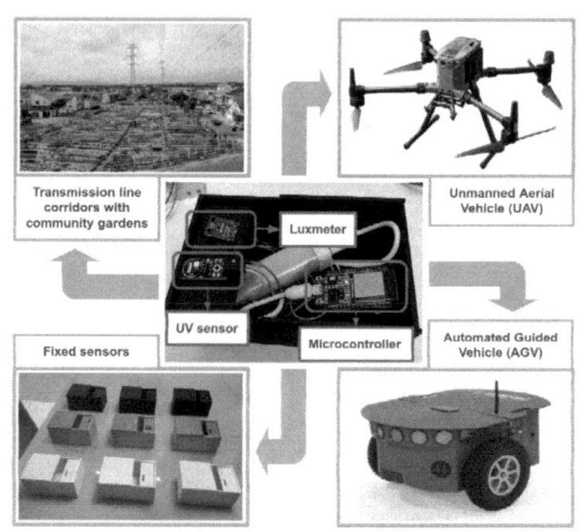

Figure 1. Project workflow and development of the measurement system using fixed and mobile robotic platforms.

The experiment was conducted in the vegetable garden at the Polytechnic Center of UFPR (Universidade Federal do Paraná), in Curitiba, Brazil. The city of Curitiba is located in coordinates -25.441105, -49.276855, characterized by a subtropical climate (well defined seasons). This site was chosen for its easy access, 200 m² area, and varying solar exposure throughout the day. Nearby 13.8 kV power lines also provide environmental conditions similar to those in typical utility easement areas. The measurement locations are shown in Figure 2.

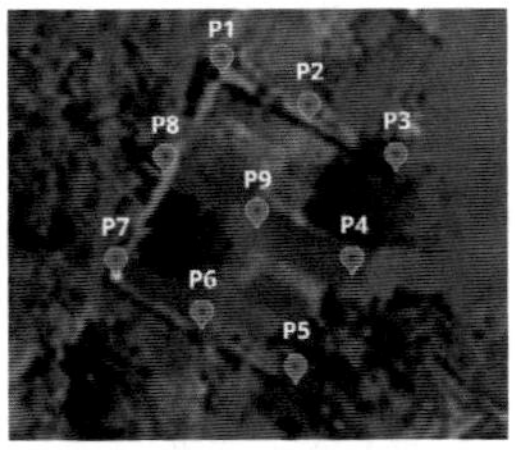

Figure 2. Points of data collection.

Measurements were carried out at nine fixed points within a vegetable garden from 7:30 AM to 5:30 PM, with data collected every second. Each unit consisted of an ESP32, a UV sensor (UVM30A or LTR390), and a light intensity sensor (BH1750), all enclosed in 3D-printed boxes of varying colors (black, white, and green) to evaluate the effect of housing color on sensor readings.

Sensor specifications are shown in Table I.

TABLE I. UV SENSOR SPECIFICATIONS (ALTERNATIVE)

Sensor	UV Detection Range	Temperature Range
UVM30A	200-370 nm	-40°C to 85°C
LTR390	300-350 nm	-40°C to 85°C

Data was collected over two days to assess this influence more accurately. Figure 3 illustrates the data acquisition architecture designed for detailed local mapping of light intensity and UV radiation levels.

(a) (b) (c)

Figure 3. (a) Color spectrum variations in the sensor housing. (b) Detailed view of the data acquisition circuit. (c) Location of 3 out of 9 measurements.

III. RESULTS FROM FIXED SENSOR MAPPING

The sensors measure UV Radiation in mV, but provide a table of conversion to the UV Index. Table II shows the conversions from mV measurement to UV Index.

Given Table I, the charts in Figures 4 and 5 show the information of UV radiation (in UV index) and light intensity (in lux) overtime.

Figure 4 shows the data collected in the same point, P2, both by a black box (February 17th) and a white box (March 20th), in two distinct days.

Although data were collected on different days—March 20 having higher solar incidence—the waveforms remained similar due to consistent sensor placement. Notably, the black box reached higher internal temperatures on a less sunny day.

TABLE II. UV INDEX AND MV MEASUREMENTS CORRESPONDENCE.

UV Index	Vout(mV)
0	<50
1	227
2	318
3	408
4	503
5	606
6	696
7	795
8	881
9	976
10	1079
11+	1170+

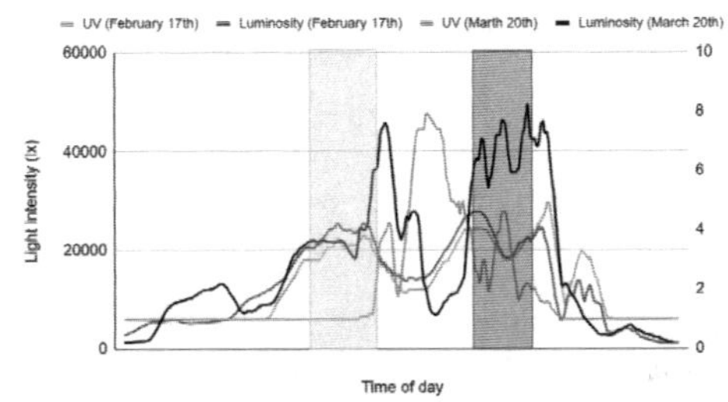

Figure 4. Data collected in P2.

Figure 5 shows data from point P9 using boxes of the same color on different dates. The highlighted regions illustrate stable diurnal patterns, suggesting that high-frequency sampling may be unnecessary, as significant variations occur over 10 to 60 minutes.

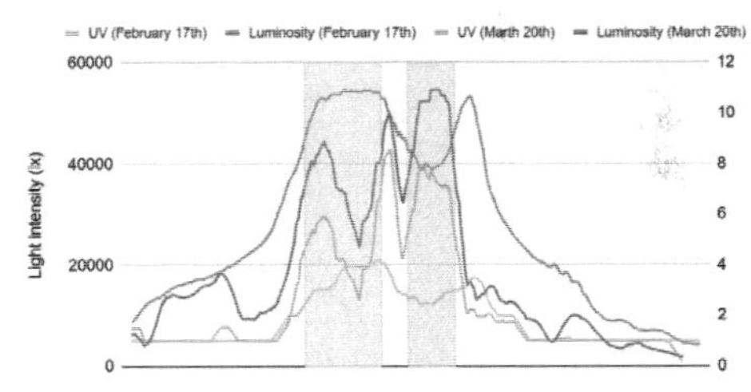

Figure 5. Data collected in P9.

IV. CONCLUSION AND FUTURE WORK

This work had the objective of developing a methodology for integrated mapping sunlight-related variables, utilizing fixed sensors.

The collected data indicate that light intensity and UV radiation exhibited similar patterns across measurement points, primarily influenced by environmental factors, such as vegetation and shading from nearby obstacles. The color of the boxes had little effect on external sensor readings, highlighting the dominant role of ambient shading. However, box color did affect internal temperatures, which could impact the performance of electronic components.

Ground and aerial mobile robotic platforms will be employed in the following phases to assess scalability, refine mapping strategies, and increase the efficiency of localized measurements. This approach is expected to increase the accuracy of site-specific analyses and enable more context-aware solutions, as well as allowing longer-term data collection. Future work will also focus on expanding the sensor network and incorporating additional environmental variables, such as air and soil humidity and internal and external temperatures, to support detailed mapping further and informed decision-making. The goal is to achieve more accurate mapping to assess the true potential for sustainable crop cultivation in these areas.

Acknowledgments

The project is supported by the National Council for Scientific and Technological Development (CNPq) under grant number 407984/2022-4; the Fund for Scientific and Technological Development (FNDCT); the Ministry of Science, Technology and Innovations (MCTI) of Brazil; the Araucaria Foundation; the General Superintendence of Science, Technology and Higher Education (SETI); and NAPI Robotics.

References

[1] R. E. Neale *et al.*, "The effects of exposure to solar radiation on human health," *Photochemical Photobiological Sciences*, vol. 22, no. 5, pp. 1011–1047, 2023, ISSN: 1474-9092. DOI: 10.1007/s43630-023-00375-8.

[2] W. Liaqat *et al.*, "Ultraviolet-b radiation in relation to agriculture in the context of climate change: A review," *Cereal Research Communications*, vol. 52, no. 1, pp. 1–24, 2024, ISSN: 1788-9170. DOI: 10.1007/s42976-023-00375-5.

[3] X. Wu, B. Chen, J. Xiao, and H. Guo, "Different doses of uv-b radiation affect pigmented potatoes' growth and quality during the whole growth period," *Frontiers in Plant Science*, vol. 14, 2023, ISSN: 1664-462X. DOI: 10.3389/fpls.2023.1101172.

[4] K. Paul *et al.*, "Viable smart sensors and their application in data driven agriculture," *Computers and Electronics in Agriculture*, vol. 198, p. 107 096, 2022, ISSN: 0168-1699. DOI: https://doi.org/10.1016/j.compag.2022.107096.

RGB-D Object Classification System for Overhead Power Line Maintenance

José Mário Nishihara, Heitor Silvério Lopes, Thiago Henrique Silva,
André Eugenio Lazzaretti, Andre Schneider de Oliveira and Ronnier Frates Rohrich
Graduate Program in Electrical and Computer Engineering
Program in Computer Science
Universidade Tecnológica Federal do Paraná
Curitiba, Brazil
e-mail: {josalb}@alunos.utfpr.edu.br
{hslopes | thiagoh | lazzaretti | andreoliveira | rohrich}@utfpr.edu.br

***Abstract*—This paper presents the development and evaluation of different machine-learning models applied to classify objects in high-voltage transmission lines using depth data captured by a RealSense D415 camera. Four models, k-Nearest Neighbors (kNN), Decision Tree, Neural Network (NN), and AdaBoost (AB), were tested using simulated and real data collected in a laboratory environment. The results show that the kNN and NN models achieved robust performance, while the Decision Tree model faced significant limitations due to excessive nodes and the AB model struggled with the real-world data. Moreover, tests with real data revealed noise in the images, which affected model performance. This study also highlights the feasibility of using depth cameras for autonomous inspection tasks, potentially reducing costs and enhancing safety in high-voltage environments.**

Keywords-RealSense; Machine Learning; Object Classification; Transmission Lines; Autonomous Inspection.

I. Introduction

Inspecting high-voltage power lines is critical for ensuring the safety and efficiency of electrical grids, as these structures carry large amounts of energy over long distances and are exposed to extreme weather conditions. Traditional inspection methods, such as manual climbing and drone-based monitoring, have significant limitations: while drones offer agility, they are constrained by battery life and weather conditions, whereas manual inspections, though precise, are costly and hazardous. Key challenges include monitoring cable temperature, detecting nearby obstacles, and assessing structural wear to prevent failures and reduce maintenance costs.

Robotic automation has emerged as a promising solution, enabling safer and more efficient inspections. However, a robot must overcome obstacles such as support towers and irregular structures to traverse an entire power line. Various approaches have been proposed, including modular robots with specialized locomotion units [1], transposition mechanisms [2], and caterpillar-based robots capable of climbing jumpers at 80° inclines [3]. Despite these advances, human operator intervention remains necessary, highlighting the need for greater autonomy.

Furthermore, a reliable electricity supply, directly impacted by Transmission Line (TL) maintenance, is essential for socioeconomic development. Current inspections rely predominantly on visual and manual methods, which are prone to human error and subjectivity, leading to increased service interruptions and inefficient asset management. Thus, this study proposes a predictive aerial inspection system combining advanced technologies—such as thermal, spatial, and reflectance sensing—with artificial intelligence to optimize TL monitoring. The central hypothesis is that this multimodal approach will improve the detection of critical issues—such as cable wear, vegetation encroachment, and structural anomalies—reducing operational costs and preventing power outages.

This paper explores innovative solutions for autonomous power line inspection, discussing technical challenges, recent advancements, and the feasibility of an Artificial Intelligence (AI)-supported multimodal system to overcome the limitations of traditional methods. The second section reviews the state of the art and identifies research gaps in this field. The third section describes the developed system architecture. The fourth section outlines the requirements for experimental evaluation. The fifth section analyzes feature extraction methods. The sixth section presents discussions and conclusions.

II. Related Work

Autonomous inspection requires accurate detection and classification of components using depth sensors and computer vision. Pouliot et al. [4] validated the performance of the UTM-30LX Light Detection and Ranging (LiDAR) sensor for object identification and diameter estimation. The sensor was mounted at a 45° angle under the robot, collecting 49 measurements per scan with a minimum detection distance of 0.9 meters. Their approach identified object edges and estimated diameter and distance, though no classification model was implemented.

Qin et al. [5] employed a LiDAR sensor to generate a 3D point cloud of transmission lines, isolating a single cable and using 3D region-growing segmentation for object classification. Their method achieved 90.6% classification accuracy with 98.2% precision.

Vision-based approaches have also been explored. Song et al. [6] detected broken spacers using an Red, Green, Blue (RGB) camera and morphological operations, segmenting the spacer region to determine structural integrity. Zhu et al. [7] classified dampers, spacers, and clamps using a structured

Support Vector Machine (SVM) model, achieving an accuracy of 96% for clamps and over 92% for other components.

These studies highlight the feasibility of autonomous inspection through depth sensing and computer vision. Therefore, this project develops a real-time object classification model for transmission lines using depth camera data from a *RealSense D415*. The model must operate efficiently within the robot's embedded system constraints while managing concurrent motion and sensor control.

III. System Architecture

This work is part of a broader project focused on developing a fully autonomous robot for transmission line inspection. The robot can traverse lines, overcome obstacles, and efficiently collect data. In this context, object classification is essential for enabling the robot to recognize and appropriately respond to various components of the transmission line infrastructure, such as insulators, dampers, and markers.

The camera was mounted on the robot, with objects positioned in front of it for data collection. The acquired data was collected through direct communication with the Robot Operating System (ROS), an open-source platform providing tools and libraries to streamline robotic system development, facilitating flexible integration of hardware, sensors, and control algorithms. The robot in development features two claws for controlling speed and a body responsible for executing obstacle-overcoming maneuvers. The robot's specifications are detailed in [8]. The overall operation of the system is illustrated in Figure 1.

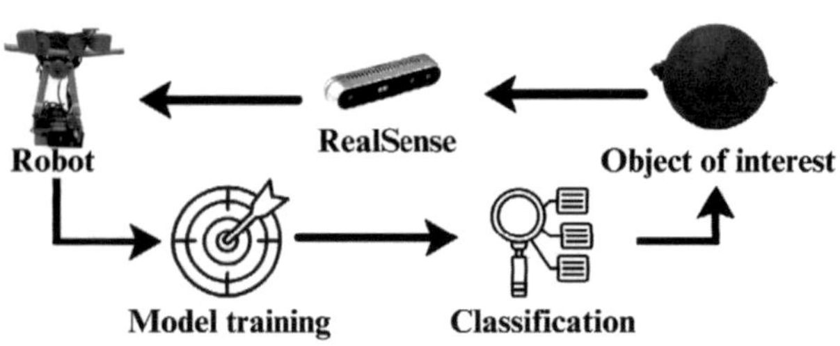

Figure 1. Operation diagram.

A. RealSense D415

The Intel RealSense D415 is a depth camera with stereoscopic infrared sensors for depth detection, widely used in robotics and automation. It captures depth maps with a resolution of 1280 × 720 and a field of view of 65° × 40°. The camera has a depth accuracy of less than 2% at 2 meters and a frame rate of up to 90 fps. Its balance of resolution and accuracy makes it suitable for object classification in transmission lines.

B. Object Classes to Be Detected

In this project, the object classes to be detected include:

- **Polymeric Insulators**: Devices used to isolate conductors in high-voltage lines are essential for ensuring the safety and efficiency of electrical systems.
- **High-Voltage Line Markers**: Visual markers placed on high-voltage lines to improve visibility and reduce accident risks.
- **Dampers**: Devices designed to mitigate vibrations and shocks in transmission systems and line supports.
- **No Obstacles**: Scenarios where no objects are detected in front of the robot, a key condition for its operation.

The comprehensive set of objects analyzed and detected within the scope of this study is illustrated in Figure 2.

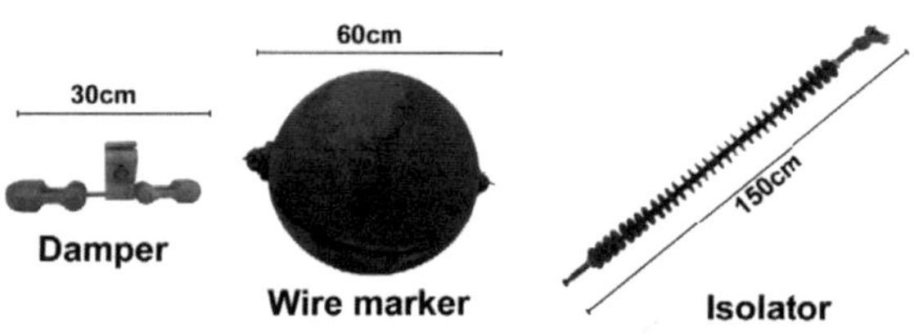

Figure 2. Objects to Be Detected.

IV. Requirements for Experimental Evaluation

Two primary data analyses were conducted for the development of this project. Each analysis took place in different environments and had specific objectives to evaluate the feasibility and performance of the object classification model for transmission lines using the RealSense camera. The procedures and environments used in each step are detailed below.

A. Simulation-Based Problem Modeling and Analysis

The simulation aimed to replicate the realistic operating conditions of the robot on a high-voltage transmission line as closely as possible. Accordingly, the RealSense camera was positioned identically to its final deployment setup—mounted atop the robot, which was fixed to the simulated cable. The objects in the simulation were modeled with high fidelity to their real-world counterparts, matching both dimensions and shapes (see Figure 3).

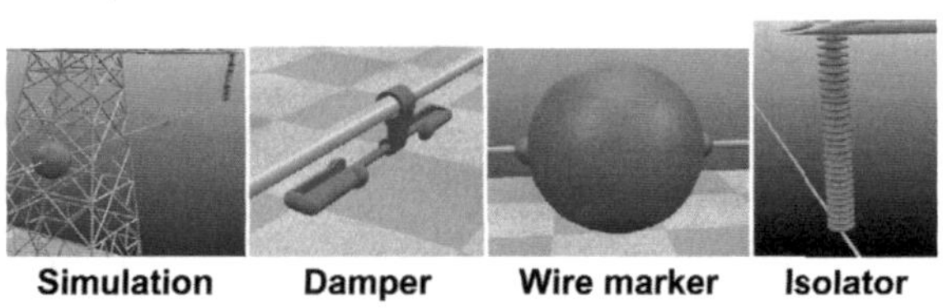

Figure 3. Components of the transmission line used in the simulation.

During the simulation, the robot was moved along the cable linearly and constantly, simulating the scenario where the robot traverses the transmission line under real-world conditions. The camera capture rate was set to 10 Hz. The RealSense camera was configured to capture depth information up to 5 meters away, using a resolution of 1280x720 pixels, returning grayscale images to the code, where each pixel represented the depth measured for that position, as shown in Figure 4.

Figure 4. Depth image captured by the RealSense camera during the simulation.

The depth data collected by RealSense was saved in Portable Network Graphics (PNG) format due to the high fidelity this format offers in preserving the visual details necessary for subsequent analyses. The images generated during the simulation were used to feed the machine learning model, serving as the basis for training and evaluating the system.

B. Real-System Validation and Performance Analysis

The second stage of the project was conducted in a laboratory environment. For this experiment, a section of a transmission line was set up and divided into two segments, each 5 meters long, where typical high-voltage line objects such as insulators, markers, and dampers were fixed. These objects were arranged along the segments to closely resemble their placement in real lines, with the aim of maintaining as much fidelity as possible with the field conditions, as shown in Figure 5.

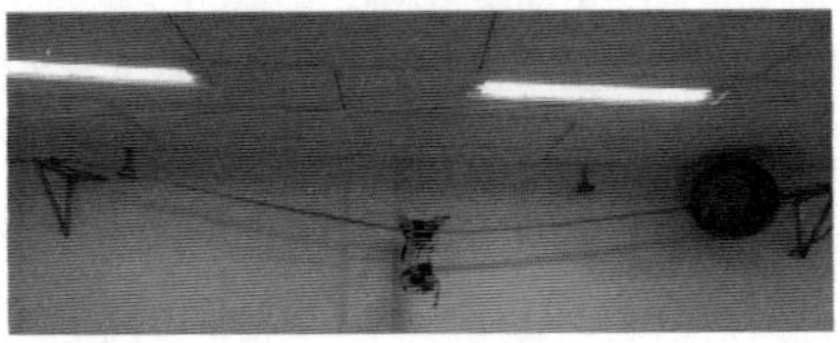

Figure 5. Setup of the experiment in the laboratory with the RealSense camera.

Due to space limitations in the laboratory, an adaptation was necessary for the position of the RealSense camera. Instead of being positioned above the line, as it would be in the real scenario, the camera was mounted on the bottom of the robot, and the data was collected as if the line were upside down. This adaptation allowed the camera to capture the objects like it would in the field, albeit with the orientation inverted. As in the simulation, the robot was controlled linearly and constantly, ensuring uniform data collection along the line segments. For this experiment, the RealSense camera was configured to operate at 15 Hz, returning grayscale images to the code, as illustrated in Figure 6.

As in the simulation, the depth data captured by the RealSense camera was stored in PNG format, preserving the

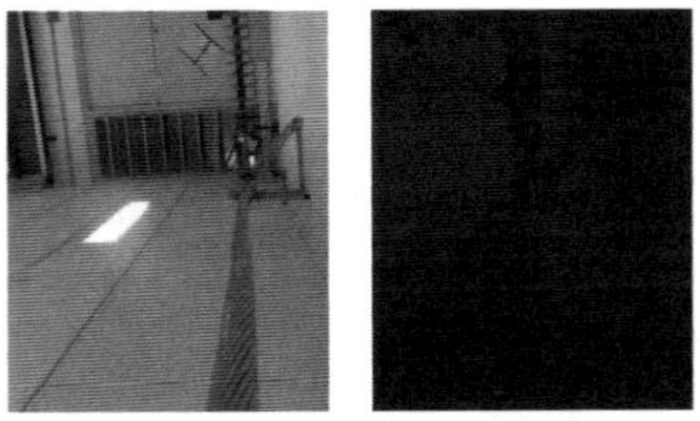

Figure 6. RGB (for reference) and depth image captured by the RealSense camera in the laboratory.

necessary details for subsequent analysis and machine learning applications.

C. Simulated and Real Experimental Data Processing

The data was divided into two categories: **raw data**, which represented the originally captured images, and **processed data**, which underwent preprocessing using a simple edge detection algorithm, as illustrated in Figures 7-12.

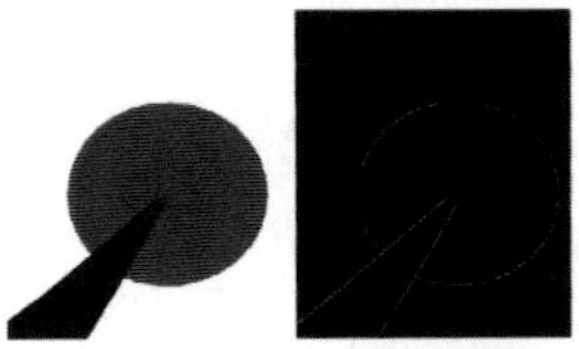

Figure 7. Algorithm applied to the simulated marker image.

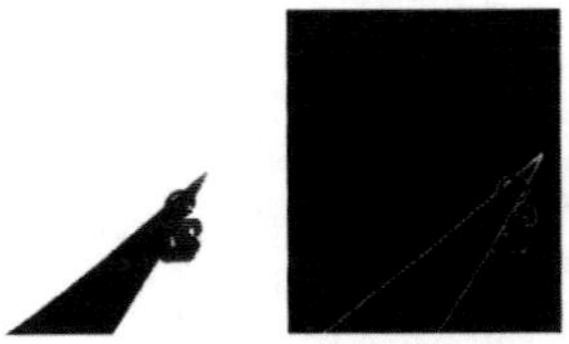

Figure 8. Algorithm applied to the simulated damper image.

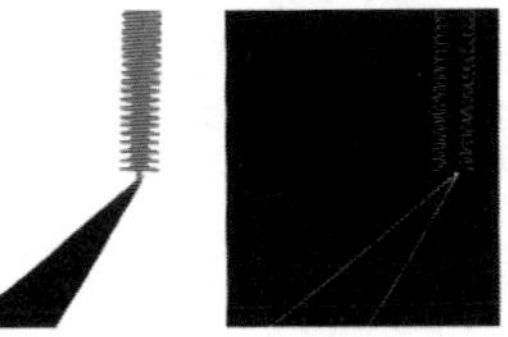

Figure 9. Algorithm applied to the simulated insulator image.

Figure 10. Algorithm applied to the real marker image.

Figure 11. Algorithm applied to the real damper image.

Figure 12. Algorithm applied to the real insulator image.

Data processing aimed to rapidly and efficiently simplify the images, eliminating the requirement to execute a more complex model to accomplish this task. For this purpose, an edge detection Algorithm 1 was used. This algorithm is efficient and fast, capable of highlighting the leading edges in the grayscale depth images. It calculates the depth intensity difference between adjacent pixels horizontally and vertically. Extreme values are not wished; the edge detection result is limited to a maximum value of 255.

Algorithm 1 Edge Detection Algorithm

for for each row i of the image, from bottom to top **do**
    for for each column j, from right to left **do**
        $gray\_index = i \times img\_width + j$
        if $i == 0$ or $j == 0$ **then**
            Set $img[gray\_index] = 0$
        else
            Horizontal difference:
$diff_x = img[gray\_index] - img[gray\_index - 1]$
            Vertical difference:
$diff_y = img[gray\_index] - img[gray\_index - img\_width]$
            Magnitude of difference:
$derivative = \sqrt{diff_x^2 + diff_y^2}$
            Set:
$img[gray\_index] = \min(derivative, 255)$
        end if
    end for
end for

In addition to simplifying the images, this method of deriving the image also helps normalize the data. Since the data represents depth, the distance between elements of the same object is constant, regardless of the distance from the camera to the object. This means that even if the distance between the camera and the object varies, the derivative of these distances will not be affected, keeping the edges consistent. This characteristic makes the method robust against variations in the distance between the robot and the objects, ensuring uniform edge detection independent of the camera's position. Furthermore, the algorithm allows for the visualization of objects hidden in the images, making visible those that would not be perceptible to the naked eye. Figure 13 illustrates how data normalization affects visualization, clearly showing previously visible objects.

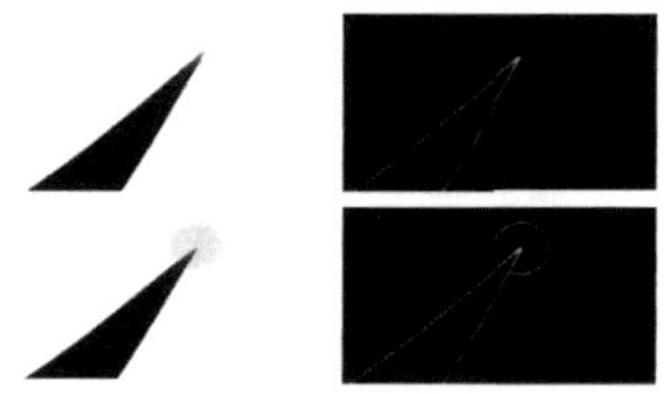

Figure 13. Example of data normalization and visualization of hidden objects (marker).

D. Organization of the Implemented Machine Learning Models

Due to the absence of a benchmark for this project, several machine learning models were tested to determine the most efficient for classifying objects on power lines. The models evaluated were **k-Nearest Neighbors (kNN)**, **Decision Tree**, **Neural Network**, and **AdaBoost**.

The *kNN* model was configured with $k = 6$, Mahalanobis distance, and distance-based weights. The neural network had three hidden layers (128, 64, and 32 neurons), Rectified Linear Unit (ReLU) activation, and used the Adam optimizer. The AdaBoost classifier was implemented with the Samme. *R* variant, suitable for multiclass classification. The decision tree was also tested due to its interpretability and computational efficiency.

1) Feature Extraction Using SqueezeNet: To enhance the representativeness of the depth data, a feature extraction step was implemented using SqueezeNet, a lightweight Convolutional Neural Network (CNN) designed for efficient feature extraction with low computational cost.

SqueezeNet was applied to grayscale depth images to extract compact visual representations, which were then used as input for the supervised learning models. This approach improved classification efficiency by focusing on relevant image features instead of raw data.

2) Feature Extraction Using Mean and Variance: As an alternative to convolutional neural networks, a statistical feature extraction approach using **mean** and **variance** of grayscale depth images was applied.

The mean represents the average depth value in each image, providing an estimate of object distance, while the variance quantifies depth dispersion, capturing surface irregularities. This method offers a computationally efficient way to summarize image characteristics, facilitating classification in resource-constrained environments.

3) Training and Validation: The **Orange** software was used for model training, a machine learning platform that offers a visual interface for creating and evaluating models. The tests were performed using **10-fold cross-validation**.

V. Analysis of Feature Extraction Methods

This section presents the results obtained after training four machine learning models using different feature extraction methods from depth images. The approaches include statistical features (mean and variance) and deep learning-based feature extraction using SqueezeNet, which is applied to raw and derivative images. The models were evaluated with simulation and real sensor measurement data, allowing for a comparative analysis of their performance under different conditions.

A. Evaluation Metrics

To assess model performance, we used several classification metrics, including Area Under the Receiver Operating Characteristic (ROC) Curve (AUC), Class Accuracy (CA), F1-Score, Precision (Prec), Recall, and Matthews Correlation Coefficient (MCC). These metrics provide a comprehensive evaluation by considering different aspects of classification performance, such as class balance, precision-recall trade-offs, and overall correlation with proper labels.

B. Simulation Results

This subsection presents the results obtained for the machine learning models trained using the simulation data. The results are divided based on the different types of images and extracted *features*, including the raw image, the derived image, and the mean and variance *features*.

1) Raw Image: The models were trained using the raw depth images without any additional processing. The results for the four tested models are presented in Table I.

TABLE I. Results of raw simulation images.

Model	AUC	CA	F1	Prec	Recall	MCC
KNN	1.000	0.998	**0.998**	0.998	0.998	0.997
NN	1.000	0.997	0.997	0.997	0.997	0.996
Tree	0.995	0.993	**0.993**	0.993	0.993	0.990
AB	0.996	0.994	0.994	0.994	0.994	0.991

2) Derived Image: The models were trained using the derived depth images, applying the edge detection technique described earlier. The results are shown in Table II.

TABLE II. Results of derived simulation images.

Model	AUC	CA	F1	Prec	Recall	MCC
KNN	1.000	1.000	**1.000**	1.000	1.000	1.000
NN	1.000	1.000	1.000	1.000	1.000	1.000
Tree	0.998	0.997	**0.997**	0.997	0.997	0.997
AB	0.999	0.999	0.999	0.999	0.999	0.998

TABLE III. Results of raw simulation images features.

Model	AUC	CA	F1	Prec	Recall	MCC
KNN	0.985	0.927	**0.926**	0.927	0.927	0.902
NN	0.985	0.906	0.904	0.914	0.906	0.877
Tree	0.923	0.867	**0.865**	0.865	0.867	0.820
AB	0.913	0.870	0.870	0.870	0.870	0.825

3) Mean and Variance of Raw Image: The models were trained using the mean and variance *features* extracted from the raw images, and the results are presented in Table III.

4) Mean and Variance of Derived Image: The models were trained using the mean and variance *features* extracted from the derived images. The results for the four models tested are presented in Table IV.

TABLE IV. Results of derived simulation images features.

Model	AUC	CA	F1	Prec	Recall	MCC
KNN	0.990	0.963	**0.963**	0.964	0.963	0.950
NN	0.988	0.878	**0.872**	0.881	0.878	0.838
Tree	0.968	0.932	0.932	0.932	0.932	0.908
AB	0.957	0.936	0.936	0.936	0.936	0.913

C. Real Data Results

In this subsection, we present the results obtained for the machine learning models trained using real data collected by the sensor. The results are divided based on different types of images and extracted *features*, including raw image, derived image, and mean and variance *features*.

1) Raw Image: The models were trained using raw-depth images without any additional processing. The results are represented in Table V.

TABLE V. Results of raw real images.

Model	AUC	CA	F1	Prec	Recall	MCC
KNN	0.992	0.940	0.940	0.940	0.940	0.920
NN	0.996	0.958	**0.958**	0.958	0.958	0.943
Tree	0.848	0.747	0.747	0.748	0.747	0.661
AB	0.825	0.738	**0.739**	0.740	0.738	0.649

2) Derived Image: The models were trained with the derived depth images, utilizing the previously described edge detection technique, as presented in Table VI.

TABLE VI. Results of derived real images.

Model	AUC	CA	F1	Prec	Recall	MCC
KNN	0.991	0.948	0.948	0.948	0.948	0.930
NN	0.996	0.952	**0.952**	0.952	0.952	0.936
Tree	0.877	0.803	**0.804**	0.805	0.803	0.737
AB	0.875	0.813	0.814	0.814	0.813	0.749

3) Mean and Variance of Raw Image: The models were trained based on the mean and variance *features* obtained from the raw images. The results for the four tested models are displayed in Table VII.

TABLE VII. RESULTS OF RAW REAL IMAGES FEATURES.

Model	AUC	CA	F1	Prec	Recall	MCC
KNN	0.926	0.752	**0.751**	0.752	0.752	0.667
NN	0.929	0.722	0.721	0.722	0.722	0.627
Tree	0.832	0.689	0.689	0.690	0.689	0.584
AB	0.785	0.680	**0.679**	0.678	0.680	0.570

4) Mean and Variance of Derived Image: The models were trained using the mean and variance *features* extracted from the derived images. It is showed in the Table VIII.

TABLE VIII. RESULTS OF RAW DERIVED IMAGES FEATURES.

Model	AUC	CA	F1	Prec	Recall	MCC
KNN	0.942	0.780	**0.779**	0.778	0.780	0.704
NN	0.933	0.728	0.728	0.729	0.728	0.637
Tree	0.846	0.717	**ee**	0.717	0.717	0.621
AB	0.813	0.721	0.721	0.721	0.721	0.626

VI. DISCUSSIONS AND CONCLUSIONS

The results highlight significant differences in the model's performance between simulated and real-world data, mainly due to variations in image capture conditions.

A. Difference Between Simulation and Real-World Data

In the simulation, the controlled environment with clean-depth images led to near-perfect model performance, with kNN and Neural Networks achieving an AUC of 1.000. However, real-world data from the RealSense camera introduced noise from lighting, reflections, and depth variations, reducing the model's accuracy. This discrepancy underscores the challenge of adapting models trained in idealized conditions to real-world scenarios, where sensor limitations and environmental factors impact classification performance.

B. Laboratory Environment Limitations

Unlike those of a real power transmission line, the laboratory's spatial and lighting constraints led to considerable noise in the images captured by the RealSense camera, complicating object identification. Additionally, the camera's position at the bottom of the robot, capturing data as if the transmission line were upside down, introduced further discrepancies that would not occur in a real-world inspection, potentially affecting model performance.

C. Model Performance

While simple and interpretable, the Decision Tree model became excessively large and complex in this project due to the variations in simulated and real-world depth images. It generated an impractical structure, losing its main advantage of clear decision rules, especially when exposed to noise in real-world data.

The k-Nearest Neighbors (kNN) model showed strong consistency in both simulated and real-world data, with perfect AUC (1.000) and a slight drop to 0.991 and 0.948 for real-world data. kNN effectively handled noise, especially in derived images, thanks to the Mahalanobis distance metric.

The Neural Network excelled in simulated data with an AUC of 1.000 but also performed well on real-world data (AUC of 0.996) despite noise. However, its higher computational cost compared to kNN could be a limitation for embedded systems.

AdaBoost performed well on simulated data (AUC of 0.996 and 0.999 for raw and derived images) but struggled with real-world data, with AUCs of 0.825 and 0.875. The model's performance was compromised by noise, leading to overfitting and reduced generalization ability.

ACKNOWLEDGEMENTS

The project is supported by the National Council for Scientific and Technological Development (CNPq) under grant number 407984/2022-4; the Fund for Scientific and Technological Development (FNDCT); the Ministry of Science, Technology and Innovations (MCTI) of Brazil; the Araucaria Foundation; the General Superintendence of Science, Technology and Higher Education (SETI); and NAPI Robotics.

REFERENCES

[1] Z. Qing *et al.*, "Mechanical design and research of a novel power lines inspection robot," in *2016 international conference on integrated circuits and microsystems (ICICM)*, IEEE, 2016, pp. 363–366.

[2] B. Tong, "Research status and development trend of obstacle crossing mechanism of hv transmission line inspection robot," *Journal of Engineering Research and Reports*, vol. 26, no. 5, pp. 83–92, 2024.

[3] X. Yue, H. Wang, and Y. Jiang, "A novel 110 kv power line inspection robot and its climbing ability analysis," *International Journal of Advanced Robotic Systems*, vol. 14, no. 3, p. 1 729 881 417 710 461, 2017.

[4] N. Pouliot, P.-L. Richard, and S. Montambault, "Linescout power line robot: Characterization of a utm-30lx lidar system for obstacle detection," in *2012 IEEE/RSJ International Conference on Intelligent Robots and Systems*, IEEE, 2012, pp. 4327–4334.

[5] X. Qin, G. Wu, J. Lei, F. Fan, and X. Ye, "Detecting inspection objects of power line from cable inspection robot lidar data," *Sensors*, vol. 18, no. 4, p. 1284, 2018.

[6] Y. Song *et al.*, "A vision-based method for the broken spacer detection," in *2015 IEEE international conference on cyber technology in automation, control, and intelligent systems (CYBER)*, IEEE, 2015, pp. 715–719.

[7] Y. Zhu, X. Wang, and B. Xu, "Design of vision-based obstacle crossing of high-voltage line inspection robot," in *2016 IEEE International Conference on Cyber Technology in Automation, Control, and Intelligent Systems (CYBER)*, IEEE, 2016, pp. 506–511.

[8] A. Domingues *et al.*, "A robotic cable-gripper for reliable inspection of transmission lines," in *Robot 2023: Sixth Iberian Robotics Conference*, L. Marques, C. Santos, J. L. Lima, D. Tardioli, and M. Ferre, Eds., Cham: Springer Nature Switzerland, 2024, pp. 519–530, ISBN: 978-3-031-58676-7.

Non-Terrestrial Networks: Architecture and Implementation Challenges

André Martini Paula, Ariel Luane Pereira Bentes, Ayan Perez de Abreu, Francine Cássia de Oliveira, Ivan da Silva Costa Junior, José do Patrocínio dos Santos Silva, José Ricardo da Silva Ferreira, Mayara Ferreira de Moura, Paulo Victor Andrade Cordeiro, Taila de Franca Santos
Instituto de Pesquisas Eldorado, Integration and Testing Department
Campinas, Brazil
E-mail: andre.paula@eldorado.org.br, arielp@eldorado.org.br, ayanpa@eldorado.org.br, francine.oliveira@eldorado.org.br, ivan.junior@eldorado.org.br, jose.santos@eldorado.org.br, jricardo@eldorado.org.br, mmoura@eldorado.org.br, paulovac@eldorado.org.br, tailafs@eldorado.org.br

Abstract— **Non-Terrestrial Networks (NTNs) are emerging as a solution to overcome the limitations of terrestrial networks, especially in remote and difficult-to-reach regions where connectivity is limited or absent. NTNs are expected to offer numerous opportunities for next-generation wireless communication systems, paving the way for energy-efficient global connectivity. However, factors such as long delays and variations in propagation compared to terrestrial networks, as well as the high-speed movement of some types of satellites, mean that new challenges will arise, significantly affecting the implementation of this technology. This article aims to address the concept of NTN, their architecture and standardization. Furthermore, it explores the challenges associated with the integration of these networks and proposes solutions to improve their integration and performance.**

Keywords - Non-Terrestrial Networks, 5G Networks, Satellite Communications.

I. INTRODUCTION

NTN utilize aerial and space-based platforms, such as Low Earth Orbit (LEO), Medium Earth Orbit (MEO) and Geostationary Orbit (GEO) satellites, as well as High Altitude Platform Stations (HAPS), to extend network services beyond the reach of terrestrial infrastructure. The integration of these networks with Fifth Generation (5G) technology marks a significant advance in the search for global connectivity. As the world increasingly relies on continuous digital communication, the ability of NTNs to provide coverage in remote maritime areas, polar regions and disaster-affected zones becomes indispensable. This global coverage is crucial not only for communication, but also for critical applications in sectors such as agriculture and environmental monitoring.

A key advantage of NTNs is the ability to provide connectivity without requiring significant changes to existing devices. This integration is enabled by standardization efforts led by the Third Generation Partnership Project (3GPP) [1], which has been vital in defining the protocols and architectures that allow for interoperability between terrestrial and non-terrestrial networks. This interoperability ensures that devices can switch between networks while maintaining consistent service quality [1]. However, the development of NTNs presents different challenges. Technical issues such as Doppler Shifts, resulting from the relative motion between satellites and ground stations, and significant propagation delays in satellite communication, particularly with GEO satellites, present hurdles that must be addressed. Furthermore, robust handover mechanisms between terrestrial and NTNs are crucial to ensure a seamless user experience as devices move across different coverage areas [2]. The 5G Core (5GC) network plays an essential role in managing these hybrid networks, facilitating the dynamic allocation of network resources to ensure that devices maintain connectivity during the transition between terrestrial and non-terrestrial links.

NTNs play an essential role in the future of telecommunications. Their ability to extend network coverage to the most remote areas of the planet, combined with advances in 5G technology, is considered a key element of the next generation of communications networks. As technology evolves, the challenges associated with NTN will need to be addressed through continued research and development to ensure these networks can deliver on their promise of global connectivity.

This article presents essential factors for professionals and researchers seeking to understand the architecture, standardization requirements, and key technical challenges associated with NTN. In addition, it presents discussions on technological solutions aimed at the efficient integration of these networks into current and next-generation mobile communication systems, promoting advances towards global connectivity.

It is organized as follows. Section II presents work related to what is being published on the topic of NTNs. Section III addresses the standardization of NTNs by 3GPP and the different architectures related to these networks. Section IV presents some challenges considered essential in the study and development of NTNs. Finally, Section V presents the main conclusions of this study.

II. RELATED WORK

As NTNs have become crucial to extending the coverage and capabilities of next-generation communication systems, especially in 5G, several studies have highlighted the advantages of integrating NTNs with terrestrial networks, while also identifying several challenges that still need to be addressed.

Recent literature has extensively explored the benefits of NTN integration. Rinaldi et al. [3] highlight the ability of NTNs to provide wide-area coverage, ensure service continuity, and offer scalability, especially in regions where terrestrial networks are economically impractical or geographically challenging, such as maritime, aeronautical, and remote areas. Similarly, Vanelli-Coralli et al. [4] affirm that NTNs can extend 5G services to underserved or unsold areas, improve service reliability, and enhance network scalability. Beyond their ability to cover underserved regions, NTNs are essential to strengthen the resilience of communication networks. In scenarios where terrestrial infrastructure may be compromised, such as during natural disasters or in conflict zones, NTNs can maintain service continuity, as noted by the authors in [3] [4]. This resilience is particularly vital for mission-critical services like emergency response and public safety.

Despite these advantages, several challenges remain. A major issue is the integration between terrestrial and NTN systems. Current architectures, as described by Rinaldi et al. [3], lack full convergence, leading to distinct management and operational frameworks for non-terrestrial and terrestrial components. This fragmentation creates inefficiencies and limits the full potential of NTNs. Vanelli-Coralli et al. [4] further highlight technical challenges, including high propagation delays, Doppler Shifts, and path losses, particularly in satellite-based systems, which hinder synchronization and overall system performance.

Service continuity, particularly for low-latency applications, presents another significant challenge. Rinaldi et al. [3] discuss how NTNs, especially those utilizing GEO and LEO satellites, struggle to meet Ultra-Reliable Low-Latency Communication (URLLC) requirements due to inherent satellite delays. Although NTNs are effective in delivering enhanced Mobile Broadband (eMBB) and massive Machine Type Communication (mMTC) services, their utility in latency-sensitive applications remains limited.

Energy efficiency and cost-effectiveness is another area of concern. NTNs, particularly satellite-based systems, are often associated with higher operational costs compared to terrestrial networks. Efforts to address these challenges include innovations in satellite payload designs, such as regenerative and transparent payloads, that aim to reduce costs while improving service performance. Transparent payloads reduce the complexity of on-board processing, but require more advanced ground infrastructure, whereas regenerative payloads can process signals in space, potentially reducing latency but at a higher operational cost [4].

Spectrum allocation and sharing between NTNs and terrestrial networks also represent a significant challenge. As demand for bandwidth increases, particularly with the proliferation of Internet of Things (IoT) devices and other bandwidth-intensive applications, effective spectrum management becomes increasingly important [3]. Recent research has investigated cognitive radio techniques and spectrum sharing strategies to mitigate interference between terrestrial and non-terrestrial systems, but practical implementation and standardization are still evolving.

In summary, while NTNs offer considerable advantages in enhancing the capabilities of 5G and beyond, several critical challenges remain unresolved. This work seeks to further explore these challenges and propose solutions to enhance the integration and performance of NTNs in next-generation networks.

III. NTN STARDARDIZATION AND ARCHITECTURES

A. 3GPP Releases

NTN emerged within the 3GPP standard, from Release 15 marking an essential moment in the evolution of 5G networks. This release introduced functionalities such as network management for integrating various satellites and airborne platforms, support for IoT in high-latency environments, security mechanisms to protect communications and Quality of Service (QoS) guarantees. These advancements laid the groundwork for NTNs in 5G networks, underscoring the commitment of 3GPP to integrating NTNs into existing infrastructures [5].

In 2018, Release 16 focused on NTN integration through two major studies: New Radio (NR) solutions for NTNs and Satellite Access in 5G. The first one explored how NR networks could be adapted for satellite use, addressing radio wave optimization and latency challenges.

The second study showed how existing interfaces and protocols could be adjusted for interoperability between terrestrial and non-terrestrial networks. These studies significantly expanded the reach of 5G, extending coverage and connectivity into remote or hard-to-reach areas [6].

Release 17 furthered this goal by seamlessly integrating terrestrial and non-terrestrial networks, ensuring smooth handovers and improving mobility management across multiple satellite orbits and constellations. This release also introduced enhanced security features, with new authentication and encryption methods, and optimized power consumption on mobile devices. These developments aimed to strengthen the capabilities of NTN and support a wider range of applications in 5G networks [7].

Releases 18 and 19 continue to evolve the NTNs networks with distinct innovations. Release 18 focuses on the integration of satellites and high-altitude platforms, improving service continuity and user experience, while optimizing satellite data transmission and expanding support for IoT [6]. Release 19 turns its attention to the future, particularly Sixth Generation (6G), enhancing connectivity and integration between NTNs and terrestrial networks. Key highlights include optimizing communications in dynamic environments and applying artificial intelligence and machine learning to real-time spectrum and resource management [8].

Release 19 also emphasizes regulatory and security frameworks, addressing the growing need for reliable communications and expanding NTN capacity for emerging applications like smart cities and autonomous vehicles [9].

Both releases reflect a continuous focus of 3GPP on the future of mobile communications, with distinct priorities that address evolving technological challenges.

Looking ahead, Release 20 is expected to dive deeper into NTN research, focusing on large-scale communication optimization, managing the increasing number of connected devices, particularly in IoT and smart city environments. Improvements in mobility and service continuity will further refine the user experience in complex scenarios, such as autonomous vehicles. In addition, sustainability and energy efficiency will become areas of focus, with efforts to reduce energy consumption and minimize environmental impact. More robust security protocols will be developed to protect non-terrestrial communications, especially in vulnerable environments. Interoperability with emerging technologies will be a priority, as standards are established to ensure seamless communication between different systems.

Research activities continue to advance, with normative solutions that address the integration of satellite components into 5G architectures [5] [8] [9].

These efforts ensure robust communications in challenging environments. The continued development of NTNs across all 3GPP releases not only enhances 5G capabilities, but also lays the foundation for future generations of mobile communications by integrating advanced technologies and promoting more efficient and sustainable connectivity.

B. *Non-Terrestrial Network Architectures*

In the evolution of Next Generation Radio Access Network (NG-RAN), new interfaces and protocols have been developed to support NTNs. In these architectures, an NTN-based RAN includes onboard satellite network elements (NTN payloads), NTN Gateways (GW) and a ground segment. The gateway interconnects the payload to the terrestrial segment through a feeder link, establishing a bridge between space and terrestrial infrastructure [10].

The terrestrial segment consists of the 5G Core network and a Centralized Intelligence (CI). The latter is responsible for gathering information about the network status and using it to implement the best configurations and optimizing network performance. This model allows the NTN platform to operate as a space mirror or as a gNodeB in space, allowing two architectures for satellite-based NG-RAN: transparent and regenerative, where the gNodeB function can be performed partially or completely through the NTN platform [10].

Based on the location of gNodeB functionalities, it is possible to distinguish three main architectures: transparent, regenerative, and on-board distributed architecture. Furthermore, for each of these architectures, their protocol stacks, both for the User Plane (UP) and the Control Plane (CP), are described, specifying on which element of the non-terrestrial network each protocol function is implemented [11].

1) Transparent Architecture: In the transparent architecture, the gNodeB is located on the ground, therefore after the NTN ground station. The Non-Terrestrial Element (NTE) does not peform onboard processing of the signal. The gNodeB is connected to the core and then the signal is sent to the external Packet Data Network (PDN) [11]. Figure 1 shows the transparent architecture.

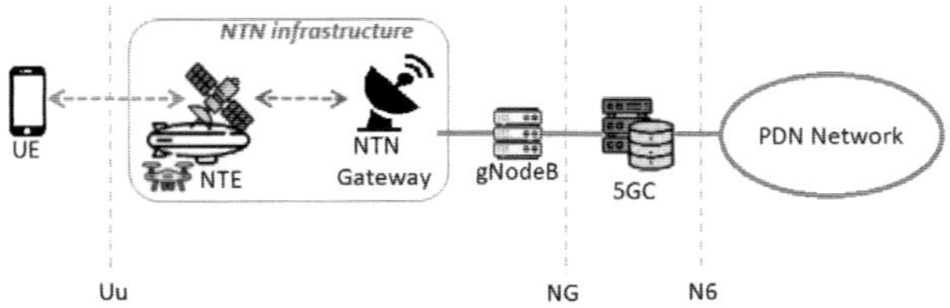

Figure 1. Transparent NTN architecture [11].

2) *Regenerative Architecture*: The gNodeB is embedded in the NTE, thus improving the performance of the NTN. Unlike the transparent architecture, where the Satellite Radio Interface (SRI) on the feeder link is based on 5G-Uu, for regenerative NTN, the SRI is a transport link used to transmit both user data and control from the NTE to the NTN gateway on the ground [11]. Figure 2 shows the regenerative architecture.

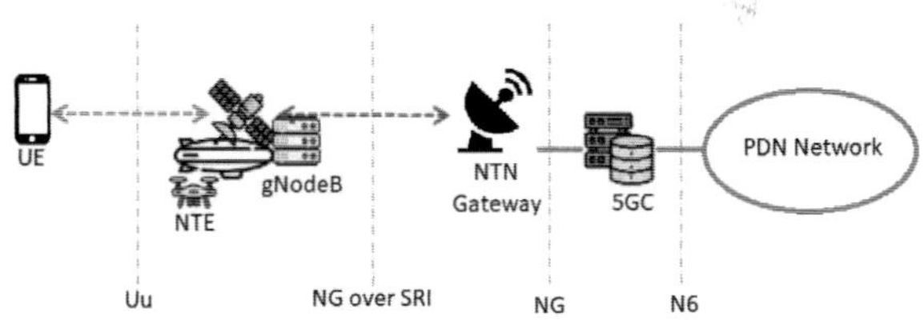

Figure 2. Regenerative NTN architecture [11].

3) *Distributed Architecture*: The distributed embedded architecture uses a functional division of the gNodeB into a Distributed Unit (DU) and Central Unit (CU). The DU is embedded in the NTE, while the CU is on the ground after the NTN gateway. Therefore, the DU split and the CU means separating processing tasks between Central unit on the ground, distributed unit embedded in the satellite, scalability, flexibility and efficient use of resources.

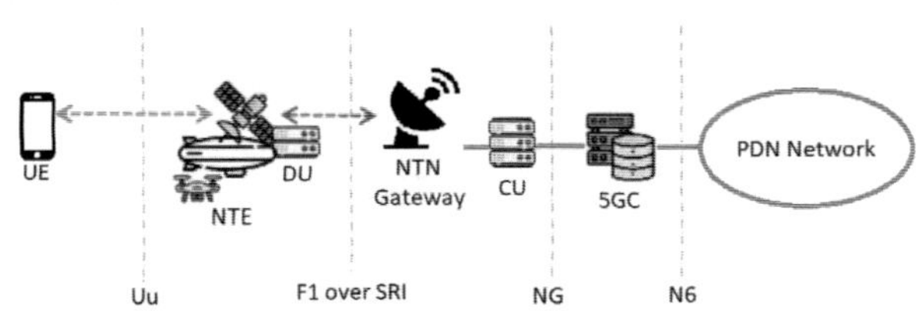

Figure 3. Distributed NTN architecture [11].

To work together, the CU and DU communicate through an interface called F1. This interface is critical to ensure efficient and synchronized operation of the gNodeB. The F1 interface manages communication between the high and low layers, separating the control plane from the user plane. Figure 3 shows the distributed architecture.

IV. CHALLENGES OF THE NTN

Despite the standardization and consolidated structure for the operation of NTN, many challenges still permeate the topic. In the following section, some of these challenges will be presented and what is already thought of as a solution for each, without compromising the efficiency and reliability of network services.

A. NTN Backhaul

One of the biggest challenges of NTN is the backhaul, since the volume of data transmitted in a 5G network is very high and there is great susceptibility around service and power links.

There are two viable scenarios to overcome a system susceptibility situation. In the first scenario, where there is an earth station out of service due to rain or natural disaster, portable base stations can be placed with direct service links connected to the HAPS and these HAPS connected to the base stations corresponding to the power links.

In the second one, it is possible to work with reception diversity when a power link goes out of operation for the same reasons as in the first scenario. Here, it is important to note that the power link integrates NTN with 5G networks [12].

For both scenarios presented, the proposal is to operate in the 38 GHz band to cover a bandwidth of 80 MHz, thus making backhaul data flow viable. To operate in this band, some requirements must be met, such as the correct orientation of the ground station antennas and the HAPS antennas for direct and unobstructed sighting, and also restricting the heights of the HAPS to up to 20 km. Another important factor to be considered is the attenuation due to rain in this 38 GHz band, as shown in Table I. From the table, it is possible to note that for distances compatible with the proposed links of a maximum of 20 km, the attenuation due to rain is around 27 dB/km. The greater the distance, the greater the attenuation, which may make the link unfeasible in some cases.

TABLE I. NTN STUDY ITEMS AND FEATURES BY 3GPP RELEASES

	Distance (km)		
	10	**30**	**50**
Elevation Angle (degrees)	63.4	33.7	21.8
Estimated Rain Attenuation (dB)	26.7	28.8	40.9

To overcome this rain attenuation problem, diversity scenarios can be used in 5G networks combined with Automatic Transmission Power Control (ATPC) and Adaptation Coding and Modulation (ACM) techniques that were created to improve system efficiency [13].

B. Handover

Handover is the process of transferring a device connection between different radio bases in a wireless mobile network when there is a need to improve coverage and signal quality. In NTNs, such as those using satellites and drones, handover becomes even more challenging due to the high mobility of devices, variable latency, and coverage heterogeneity. The constant movement of satellites in relation to Earth, for example, significantly increases the frequency of handovers, requiring robust and efficient mechanisms to guarantee QoS, minimizing interruptions in communication and optimizing the use of network resources. Furthermore, significant latency variations, common in NTN scenarios, further complicate the message exchange process required for handover.

The heterogeneity in coverage in NTN also represents a challenge, demanding advanced solutions so that the connection is stable and continuous, especially in environments with limited or intermittent coverage. To face these challenges, artificial intelligence-based solutions have been explored and are considered promising for improving the handover process in NTNs. Through techniques such as machine learning and deep learning, resources can be optimized in order to estimate channels and make decisions in real time, contributing to a more stable connectivity experience. Recent initiatives have implemented artificial intelligence on satellite network testbeds and promoted the integration of NTNs with 5G terrestrial networks, seeking a more robust and cohesive network infrastructure.

Relevant studies reinforce the importance of NTNs as essential components in future 6G networks. Research such as that in [14] addresses the specific technical challenges of these networks, including high mobility and complexity in resource management, especially for LEO satellites. Another study [15] discusses handover optimizations in NTNs using artificial intelligence and machine learning to improve service continuity and resource management in mobile networks beyond 5G. Furthermore, according to the work in [16], links between satellites and between satellites and Earth suffer from increased latency and limited processing capabilities, making efficiency and the ability to handle handover demand more difficult. Security is also a concern, as NTNs are more susceptible to attacks and compromised devices can be used to disrupt services, making a handover protocol that maintains security even in cases of compromise essential. Finally, conventional handover protocols are ineffective in NTNs as they rely on signal strength indicators that have little variation across satellite coverage areas, requiring handover approaches more adapted to this environment.

Therefore, future research should focus on advances in the integration of artificial intelligence with NTNs, in addition to exploring technologies for latency optimization, interference mitigation, and dynamic spectrum allocation. These innovations are fundamental to ensuring high quality and resilient global connectivity, enabling NTNs to meet the demands of a highly dynamic and critical communications environment.

C. Radio Link Failure

In the case of NTN and NR networks, during a handover, a Radio Link Failure (RLF) can occur due to interference and/or low signal strength, interrupting the connection to the base station, due to signal obstructions resulting from terrain or weather [17], or due to the movement of the satellite. This leads to the discontinuation of the application in use, which represents an impact on user experience [18]. Once an RLF is declared, the User Equipment (UE) begins the RLF recovery procedure. The UE selects the cell and attempts to reestablish the connection with it, a procedure called Access Stratum (AS) recovery. This procedure is successful only if the UE selects a cell from the same gNodeB or from a handover-ready gNodeB. In case of failure, the UE enters an idle state and attempts the Non-Access Stratum (NAS) recovery procedure [19]. The big challenge is dealing with frequent handover situations without resulting in an increase in the number of RLFs, in the case of satellite solutions. In [20], some simulations were carried out taking into account different scenarios of non-terrestrial networks using LEO satellites, and as a result, it is clear that the handover algorithm used in conventional 5G networks fails to provide continuous connectivity in NTN. The big challenge is managing handover delays and unnecessary handovers.

It is observed that the high number of failures is due to a combination of factors, such as the low signal variation between the center and the edge of the cell and the propagation distance greater than the cell size, which prevents device measurements. Another factor is the high downlink interference between adjacent satellite beams, in addition to propagation delays due to long communication distances, which leads to delays in sending control messages and, consequently, increases the handover latency caused by RLF.

D. Reconfigurable Intelligent Surfaces (RIS)

The development of RIS technology represents a fundamental innovation for the advancement of wireless communication in terrestrial and non-terrestrial networks. RIS offers significant benefits, including improved localization and connectivity, as well as improved energy efficiency. Recent research highlights its application in mobile and satellite networks, particularly to improve performance in urban and Non-Line-Of-Sight (NLOS) environments [21].

The integration of RIS technology into various types of networks highlights its potential to address key challenges of next-generation wireless systems. From improving localization in 5G and optimizing resource usage in dense urban areas to extending connectivity through NTNs, RIS offers versatile solutions that are essential to realize the vision of global and energy-efficient 6G connectivity [22].

Despite their favorable benefits, NTNs face several challenges compared to terrestrial networks, such as coverage and signal capacity in various environments, propagation losses in the atmosphere and space, high power consumption, spectrum sharing with terrestrial networks, and security issues.

According to [23], RIS has recently emerged as a promising technology for 6G and beyond. When integrated into NTNs, RIS can revolutionize next-generation connectivity.

RIS consists of a large number of metaelements capable of manipulating the phase, amplitude, and polarization of signals. Specifically, RIS can control signal propagation by reflecting, refracting, and focusing signals on specific locations, effectively improving signal intensity, coverage, and link quality.

RIS-integrated NTNs are expected to provide numerous opportunities for next-generation wireless systems. Recent studies have analyzed their potential in various application domains. Significant results on energy consumption minimization and energy efficiency optimization have been investigated. The achievable gains in terms of sum-rate maximization for RIS-integrated NTNs are high. These systems also intrinsically enhance wireless system security and improve physical layer security in RIS-integrated NTNs. However, a holistic and long-term vision is imperative for the next generation of RIS-integrated NTNs, paving the way to achieve global energy-efficient connectivity enabled by RIS technologies.

Although RIS technology offers transformative potential, several challenges remain for its practical application in NTNs:

1) Hardware Complexity and Calibration: Designing and manufacturing RIS with precise elements can be technically challenging and expensive, particularly for large-scale NTN deployments. Large-scale implementations also require calibration and synchronization among RIS elements to achieve coherent signal manipulation. Ensuring precise and real-time RIS control for signal path optimization can be complex, especially when multiple NTN platforms are involved.

2) Dynamic Channel Conditions: NTN platforms, especially satellite communications, experience dynamic and time-varying channel conditions due to mobility and atmospheric effects. RIS configuration and optimization are based on the acquisition of channel state information, which is critical for continuous connectivity. Efficient algorithms for real-time channel estimation and control are necessary in dynamic NTN environments.

3) AI/ML Integration: Artificial Intelligence and Machine Learning offer significant opportunities to enhance RIS performance in NTNs. By utilizing AI/ML techniques and algorithms, RIS can optimize signal reflection patterns in realtime, adapt to changing network conditions, predict channel variations, and self-optimize based on feedback. RIS driven by AI/ML can dynamically adjust its reflective properties, ensuring optimal signal intensity and quality even in dynamic NTN environments.

V. Conclusions and Future Work

This article presented a synthesis of topics that are widely explored in the literature, including an overview of 3GPP standardization related to the NTN and some possibilities to construct different architectures for this technology. Some challenges are discussed, and some solutions are proposed, focusing on data transmission, handover processes, and emerging technologies, such as RIS. Key issues include the high volume of 5G data causing backhaul challenges, handover difficulties due to device mobility and NTNs variable latency, and the need for robust mechanisms to maintain QoS. To address these, AI based solutions help optimize handover by improving resource allocation and real-time decision-making.

The implementation of RIS technology is emphasized, which can improve connectivity and energy efficiency in NTNs by enhancing signal strength and mitigating interference. RIS technology plays an important role in addressing NTN challenges such as signal coverage, propagation losses, and energy consumption, offering benefits like improved link quality and extended coverage. Challenges include the technical complexities of designing and implementing RIS, dynamic channel conditions in NTN environments, and ensuring security and privacy. Future work should focus on advancing the integration between NTNs and AI-driven mechanisms to improve decision-making in dynamic environments. Key areas include the development of adaptive handover protocols tailored for high-mobility satellite systems, spectrum sharing strategies using machine learning, and secure, resilient architectures for RIS-integrated NTNs. Moreover, there is a growing need to explore edge computing capabilities embedded in satellites to reduce latency and offload processing from terrestrial infrastructure. These directions aim to unlock the full potential of NTNs in enabling autonomous vehicles, smart agriculture, and emergency communications in 6G and beyond.

References

[1] X. Lin, S. Rommer, S. Euler, E. Yavuz, and R. Eriksson, "5G from space: An overview of 3GPP Non-Terrestrial Networks," IEEE Communications Standards Magazine, vol. 5, no. 4, pp. 18–25, 2021.

[2] L. Macieira, "Link Budget Study of a Satellite Transmission System Applied to the 5G W. U. Khan work for the Brazilian Territory". Bachelor's Degree in Telecommunications Engineering – Fluminense Federal University, Niterói, 2022.

[3] F. Rinaldi et al., "Non-terrestrial networks in 5G & beyond: A survey," IEEE Access, pp. 1–23, 2020.

[4] A. Vanelli-Coralli, A. Guidotti, T. Foggi, G. Colavolpe, and G. Montorsi, "5G and beyond 5G Non-Terrestrial Networks: Trends and research challenges," IEEE Internet of Things Journal, pp. 1–7, 2020.

[5] RELEASE 15, 3GPP, 2017. Available in: https://www.3gpp.org/specifications-technologies/releases/release-15. Accessed: Jan 21st, 2025.

[6] L. Xingqin, "An overview of 5G advanced evolution in 3GPP release 18," IEEE Communications Standards Magazine 6.3 2022, pp. 77-83.

[7] Q. Zhang, G. Miao, X. Zhou, and X. Chen, "Non-terrestrial networks in 5G & beyond: A survey," IEEE Access, vol. 11, pp. 1–23, 2023.

[8] L. Xingqin. "The Bridge Toward 6G: 5G-Advanced Evolution in 3GPP Release 19," IEEE Communications Standards Magazine 9.1, pp. 28-35, 2025.

[9] QUALCOMM, 5G-A release 19 presentation. Available in: https://www.qualcomm.com/content/dam/qcomm-martech/dm-assets/documents/5G-A-Rel-19-Presentation.pdf Accessed: Jan 21th, 2025.

[10] R. Campana, C. Amatetti, and A. V. Coralli, "RAN Functional Splits in NTN: Architectures and Challenges." arXiv preprint arXiv:2309.14810, 2023.

[11] R. Giuliano and E. Innocenti, "Machine learning techniques for non-terrestrial networks," Electronics, vol. 12, no. 3, pp. 652, 2023.

[12] Z. Zhang, H. Guo, and W. Xie, "Research of ntn technical scheme based on 5G network," in 2023 IEEE International Symposium on Broadband Multimedia Systems and Broadcasting (BMSB), pp. 1–6, IEEE, 2023.

[13] H. Kitanozono et al., "Development of high altitude platform station backhaul system using 38HGz band frequency," in 2021 IEEE VTS 17th Asia Pacific Wireless Communications Symposium (APWCS), pp. 1–5, IEEE, 2021.

[14] S. Mahboob and L. Liu, "Revolutionizing future connectivity: A contemporary survey on ai-empowered satellite-based non-terrestrial networks in 6G," IEEE Communications Surveys & Tutorials, pp. 1279-1321, 2024.

[15] S. Alraih, R. Nordin, A. Abu-Samah, I. Shayea, and N. F. Abdullah, "A survey on handover optimization in beyond 5G mobile networks: Challenges and solutions," IEEE Access, vol. 11, pp. 59317–59345, 2023.

[16] B. Zhang et al., "Secure and efficient group handover protocol in 5g non-terrestrial networks." ICC 2024-IEEE International Conference on Communications. IEEE, pp. 5063-5068, 2024.

[17] N. Sulieman, K. Davaslioglu, and R. D. Gitlin, "Link failure recovery via diversity coding in 5G fronthaul wireless networks," IEEE 18th Wireless and Microwave Technology Conference (WAMICON), pp. 1–4, 2017.

[18] D. Das, D. Das, and S. Saha, "Evaluation of mobile handset recovery from radio link failure in a multi-rats environment," IEEE 2nd International Conference on Internet Multimedia Services Architecture and Applications, pp. 1–6, 2008.

[19] H.-S. Park et al., "Faster recovery from radio link failure during handover," IEEE Communications Letters, vol. 24, no. 8, pp. 1835–1839, 2020.

[20] E. Juan, M. Lauridsen, J. Wigard, and P. E. Mogensen, "5G new radio mobility performance in leo-based non-terrestrial networks," IEEE Globecom Workshops, pp. 1–6, 2020.

[21] C. Liu and Y. Zhang, "5G reconfigurable intelligent surface tdoa localization algorithm," in Electronics, pp. 1–12, Electronics, 2024.

[22] E. Arslan et al., "Reconfigurable Intelligent Surface Identification in Mobile Networks: Opportunities and Challenges," IEEE Wireless Communications, 2025.

[23] W. U. Khan et al., "Reconfigurable intelligent surfaces for 6G non-terrestrial networks: Assisting connectivity from the sky," IEEE Internet of Things Magazine 7.1, pp. 34-39, 2024.

Simultaneous Localization, Mapping, and Moving Object Tracking Using Helmet-Mounted Solid-State LiDAR

Ikuro Inaga
Graduate School of Science and Engineering
Doshisha University
Kyotanabe, Kyoto, Japan
e-mail: ctwk0128@mail4.doshisha.ac.jp

Masafumi Hashimoto, Kazuhiko Takahashi
Faculty of Science and Engineering
Doshisha University
Kyotanabe, Kyoto, Japan
e-mail: {mhashimo, katakaha}@mail.doshisha.ac.jp

Abstract—**This paper presents a Simultaneous Localization And Mapping (SLAM) and Moving Object Tracking (MOT) method using a small and lightweight solid-state Light Detection And Ranging (LiDAR) attached to a rider helmet for micromobilities, such as bicycles, e-bikes, and e-kick scooters. Distortions in LiDAR point cloud data caused by the movement of the micromobility and head motion of the rider are corrected using the data from LiDAR and inertial measurement unit via a quaternion unscented Kalman filter. The corrected LiDAR point cloud data are classified into three classes: 1) point cloud data related to stationary objects, such as buildings and trees, 2) those related to road obstacles, such as curb stones and road debris, and 3) those related to moving objects. The point cloud data related to stationary objects and road obstacles are used for environment mapping using normal distributions transform SLAM, whereas the point cloud data related to moving objects are used for MOT using Kalman filter. Results from experiments conducted at our university campus demonstrate the effectiveness of the proposed method.**

Keywords—helmet LiDAR; solid-state LiDAR, SLAM; moving-object tracking; distortion correction; quaternion UKF; micromobility.

I. INTRODUCTION

In recent years, many studies have been conducted on active safety and automated driving of vehicles in Intelligent Transportation Systems (ITS) [1]. An important technology for active safety and automated driving of vehicles is Simultaneous Localization and Mapping (SLAM) to build an environment map using vehicle-mounted sensors, such as Light Detection And Ranging sensors (LiDARs) and cameras. Another important technology is Moving Object Tracking (MOT) to avoid collisions with surrounding moving objects. Accordingly, numerous SLAM and MOT (SLAMMOT) methods have been proposed [2]–[4].

In a decarbonized society, micromobilities, such as bicycles, e-bikes, and e-kick scooters, attract attention as a means of short-distance travel through urban regions [5]. Similar to ITS, active safety is necessary to reduce traffic accidents and increase the use of micromobilities.

In our previous study [6], a SLAMMOT method based on information obtained from a LiDAR attached to the rider helmet for micromobility was proposed. In ITS, mechanical LiDARs, such as Velodyne and Ouster LiDARs, are widely used owing to their reliability and accuracy. The LiDAR used in our previous study for micromobility was bulky mechanical LiDAR, thus posing problems regarding practicality and usability.

From the viewpoint of size and security, it is desirable to mount a small easily removable sensor on the micromobility handlebars or rider helmet. Modern technology includes a solid-state LiDAR that is smaller and lighter than the mechanical LiDAR [7]. Solid-state LiDAR can substantially enhance active safety in micromobility. Recently, various studies have been conducted on SLAM and MOT methods using solid-state LiDAR [8]–[11] in ITS and mobile robotics. However, to the best of our knowledge, there are no studies that tackle SLAMMOT using solid-state LiDAR for micromobility application.

Therefore, this paper presents a SLAMMOT method using a small and lightweight solid-state LiDAR attached to the rider helmet for micromobility.

The LiDAR point cloud data within the sampling period cannot be captured simultaneously because LiDAR captures measurements by scanning a laser beam. Therefore, when the micromobility is moving or the rider head swings, the acquired LiDAR point cloud data are distorted, which deteriorates the SLAMMOT accuracy.

Distortion in LiDAR point cloud data can be corrected by estimating the LiDAR self-pose in a shorter time than the LiDAR sampling period. Most conventional methods for distortion correction were based on linear interpolation and its variants of the LiDAR self-pose obtained at every acquired LiDAR sample [12][13]. In [14][15], distortion correction methods using the Extended Kalman Filter (EKF) and Unscented Kalman Filter (UKF) [16] were proposed to improve distortion correction. In our previous studies, Euler angles (i.e., roll, pitch, and yaw angles) were used to represent the LiDAR posture. When driving a micromobility, the head posture often changes considerably during safety confirmations, such as right-left and up-down confirmations. Such large head motions of the rider may deteriorate the accuracy of distortion correction using Euler angle-EKF and UKF.

This problem can be addressed using a quaternion instead of Euler angles as the angle representation. To accurately perform SLAMMOT even under large motions of the rider head, this paper proposes a quaternion-UKF-based distortion correction method. The remainder of this paper is organized as follows. Section II describes the experimental system. Section III presents an overview of SLAMMOT. Section IV explains the proposed distortion correction method for LiDAR point cloud data, and Section V presents the classification method for these data. Section VI illustrates the effectiveness of the proposed method through experiments. Section VII presents our conclusions and future works.

II. Experimental System

The overview of the experimental helmet is shown in Figure 1. A MEMS solid-state LiDAR (Livox Mid-360) and Inertial Measurement Unit (IMU) (Xsens Mti-300) are mounted on the helmet. The weight of the LiDAR is 265 g. As shown in Figure 2, the LiDAR has a maximum range of 40 m, horizontal and vertical Field-Of-View (FOV) of 360° and 59°, respectively, and resolution of 1.4°. The LiDAR acquires 96 measurement points every 0.48 ms. The sampling period of LiDAR measurements for SLAMMOT is set to 0.12 s in this study. Approximately 20,000 measurements can be obtained per LiDAR sampling period.

Measurements of attitude (i.e., roll and pitch angles) and angular velocity (i.e., roll, pitch, and yaw angular velocities) are obtained from the IMU every 10 ms. The errors in attitude and angular velocity are less than ±0.3° and ±0.2°/s, respectively.

III. Overview of SLAMMOT

The SLAMMOT process is shown in Figure 3. First, distortion in LiDAR point cloud data caused by the motion of the micromobility and rider head is corrected. Next, the self-pose (i.e., three-dimensional (3D) position and attitude angle) of the rider helmet is calculated by Normal Distributions Transform (NDT) scan matching [17].

As shown in Figure 4, two coordinate systems are defined: world coordinate system (O_w-$x_w y_w z_w$) fixed to the ground and helmet coordinate system (O_h-$x_h y_h z_h$) fixed to the LiDAR. For simplicity, the helmet and LiDAR poses are considered to coincide. In the helmet coordinate system, a 3D voxel map with a cell size of 0.2 m per side is set. The LiDAR point cloud data acquired in one sampling period are mapped onto a voxel map and downsized using a voxel grid filter. In subsequent processing, the downsized point cloud data are used to estimate the helmet self-pose, and LiDAR point cloud data before downsizing are used for environment mapping and MOT.

For the i-th (i = 1, 2, ... , n) measurement in LiDAR point cloud data, the coordinates in the world and helmet coordinate systems are denoted by $\boldsymbol{p}_{hi} = (x_{hi}, y_{hi}, z_{hi})^T$ and $\boldsymbol{p}_i = (x_i, y_i, z_i)^T$, respectively. Thus, the following relation is obtained:

$$\begin{pmatrix} \boldsymbol{p}_i \\ 1 \end{pmatrix} = \boldsymbol{T}(\boldsymbol{X}) \begin{pmatrix} \boldsymbol{p}_{hi} \\ 1 \end{pmatrix} \tag{1}$$

where $\boldsymbol{X}$ indicates the position and attitude of the helmet, and $\boldsymbol{T}$ ($\boldsymbol{X}$) denotes the corresponding homogeneous transformation matrix.

In SLAM using NDT scan matching, a 3D voxel map with a cell size of 0.6 m per side is set in the world coordinate system. By superimposing the LiDAR point cloud data obtained at current time t (referred to as current point cloud data) and those obtained up to the previous time (t−1) (referred to as reference map), the helmet self-pose $\boldsymbol{X}$ at the current time is calculated. The current point cloud data are mapped onto the world coordinate system by performing a coordinate transformation using (1) and then merged into the reference map.

Because LiDAR scans a laser beam, all point cloud data within one LiDAR sampling period cannot be obtained at a single location when the micromobility is moving or the rider

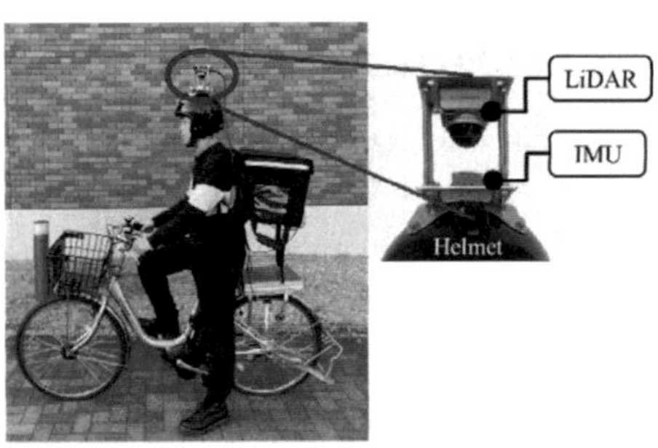

Figure 1. Overview of the experimental helmet equipped with LiDAR and IMU.

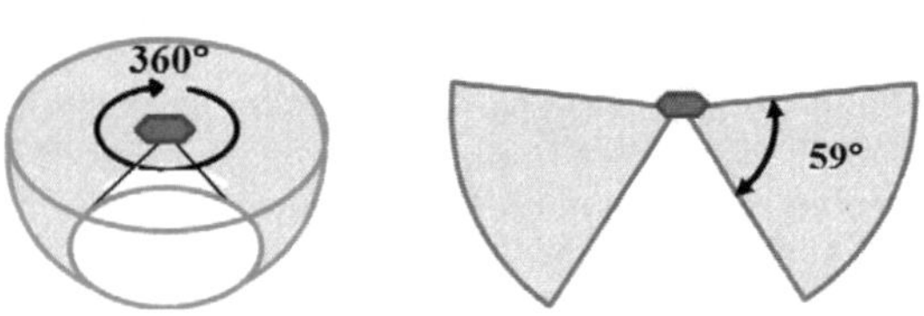

(a) Horizontal FOV (b) Vertical FOV

Figure 2. LiDAR FOV.

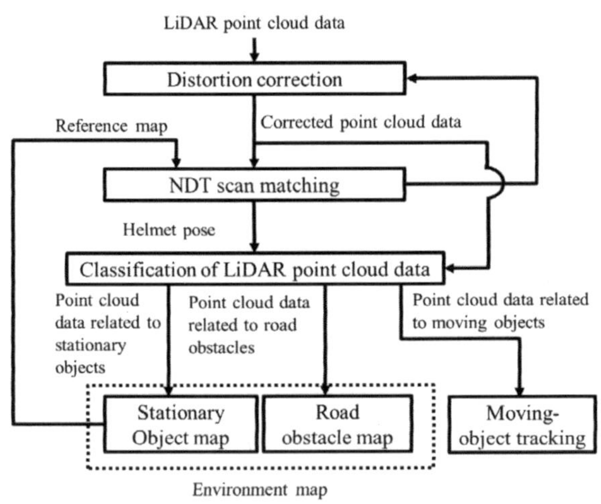

Figure 3. SLAMMOT process.

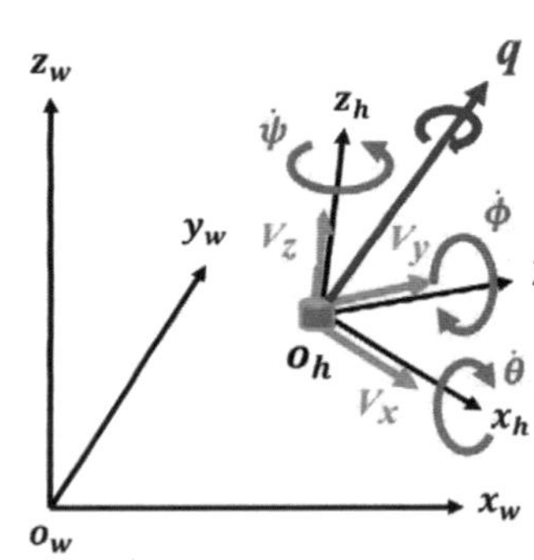

Figure 4. Notation related to helmet motion.

head is swinging. Therefore, if all point cloud data within one LiDAR sampling period is transformed using the pose information of the helmet at the same time, distortion arises in the LiDAR point cloud data mapped onto the world coordinate system using (1). As distortion causes inaccurate results in SLAMMOT, distortion correction of LiDAR point cloud data is required. The proposed distortion-correction method using a quaternion UKF is described in the next section.

Distortion-corrected LiDAR point cloud data are classified into measurements related to the road surface, road obstacles, stationary objects (e.g., buildings and trees) and moving objects (e.g., cars and pedestrians). Unevenness on road surfaces, such as obstacles on the road, ditches, and curbs, which can lead to falling accidents in micromobility, are detected as road obstacles. An environment map is built including stationary objects and road obstacles. LiDAR point cloud data related to moving objects (referred to as moving point cloud data) are used for MOT. The classification method is described in Section V.

MOT is performed using our previous method [18]. The shape of a moving object is represented by a cuboid. The width and length of the object are extracted from moving point cloud data using the rotating caliper method [19], and the height of the object is determined from the height information in the moving point cloud data. A Kalman filter is applied to estimate the two-dimensional (2D) position and velocity of the moving object in the world coordinate system based on the centroid position of the extracted cuboid. When applying the Kalman filter, the object is assumed to be moving at an approximately constant velocity. In crowded environments, the rule-based data association method [18] is used to accurately match multiple moving objects with corresponding moving point cloud data.

IV. DISTORTION CORRECTION OF LIDAR POINT CLOUD DATA

A. Overview

SLAMMOT is performed by mapping LiDAR point cloud data obtained in the helmet coordinate system onto the world coordinate system according to the helmet self-pose information. The self-pose is calculated every 120 ms (LiDAR sampling period) by NDT scan matching. However, all LiDAR point cloud data within the LiDAR sampling period cannot be captured simultaneously because LiDAR acquires measurements by scanning a laser beam. Consequently, when the micromobility is moving or the rider head is swinging, the LiDAR point cloud data mapped onto the world coordinate system are distorted.

The distortion in LiDAR point cloud data is corrected by estimating the helmet self-pose at every LiDAR data acquisition instant in 0.4 ms interval. Distortion correction is based on a quaternion UKF using the self-pose calculated by NDT scan matching every 120 ms, as well as the attitude angle and angular velocity acquired from the IMU every 10 ms.

B. State and Measurement Equations of Helmet

As shown in Figure 4, in the helmet coordinate system, the quaternion [20] is defined by $\boldsymbol{q}=q_0+q_1\boldsymbol{i}+q_2\boldsymbol{j}+q_3\boldsymbol{k}$, where $\boldsymbol{i}$, $\boldsymbol{j}$, and $\boldsymbol{k}$ are the unit vectors along the x_h, y_h, and z_h axes, respectively. The translational velocity of the helmet along the x_h, y_h, and z_h axes is denoted by (V_x, V_y, V_z). The angular velocity (i.e., roll, pitch, and yaw angular velocities) captured from the IMU is denoted by $(\dot{\phi}, \dot{\theta}, \dot{\psi})$, and its bias is denoted by $(\dot{\phi}_{bias}, \dot{\theta}_{bias}, \dot{\psi}_{bias})$.

It is assumed that the translational velocity of the helmet is nearly constant in a short period. Hence, the state equation for helmet motion is given by:

$$
\begin{pmatrix} x(t+1) \\ y(t+1) \\ z(t+1) \\ q_0(t+1) \\ q_1(t+1) \\ q_2(t+1) \\ q_3(t+1) \\ V_x(t+1) \\ V_y(t+1) \\ V_z(t+1) \\ \dot{\phi}_{bias}(t+1) \\ \dot{\theta}_{bias}(t+1) \\ \dot{\psi}_{bias}(t+1) \end{pmatrix} = \begin{pmatrix} x(t)+a_1(t)r_{11}(t)+a_2(t)r_{12}(t)+a_3(t)r_{13}(t) \\ y(t)+a_1(t)r_{21}(t)+a_2(t)r_{22}(t)+a_3(t)r_{23}(t) \\ z(t)+a_1(t)r_{31}(t)+a_2(t)r_{32}(t)+a_3(t)r_{33}(t) \\ q_0(t)\cos\frac{b_0(t)}{2} - \tau\left(q_1(t)\frac{b_1(t)}{b_0(t)}+q_2(t)\frac{b_2(t)}{b_0(t)}+q_3(t)\frac{b_3(t)}{b_0(t)}\right)\sin\frac{b_0(t)}{2} \\ q_1(t)\cos\frac{b_0(t)}{2} + \tau\left(q_0(t)\frac{b_1(t)}{b_0(t)}-q_3(t)\frac{b_2(t)}{b_0(t)}+q_2(t)\frac{b_3(t)}{b_0(t)}\right)\sin\frac{b_0(t)}{2} \\ q_2(t)\cos\frac{b_0(t)}{2} + \tau\left(q_3(t)\frac{b_1(t)}{b_0(t)}+q_0(t)\frac{b_2(t)}{b_0}-q_1(t)\frac{b_3(t)}{b_0(t)}\right)\sin\frac{b_0(t)}{2} \\ q_3(t)\cos\frac{b_0(t)}{2} + \tau\left(-q_2(t)\frac{b_1(t)}{b_0(t)}+q_1(t)\frac{b_2(t)}{b_0(t)}+q_0(t)\frac{b_3(t)}{b_0(t)}\right)\sin\frac{b_0(t)}{2} \\ V_x(t)+\tau w_{\dot{V}x} \\ V_y(t)+\tau w_{\dot{V}y} \\ V_z(t)+\tau w_{\dot{V}z} \\ \dot{\phi}_{bias}(t)+w_{\dot{\phi}_{bias}} \\ \dot{\theta}_{bias}(t)+w_{\dot{\theta}_{bias}} \\ \dot{\psi}_{bias}(t)+w_{\dot{\psi}_{bias}} \end{pmatrix} \tag{2}
$$

where (x, y, z) is the position of helmet in the world coordinate system. $a_1=V_x\tau+\tau^2 w_{\dot{V}_x}/2$, $a_2=V_y\tau+\tau^2 w_{\dot{V}y}/2$, $a_3=V_z\tau+\tau^2 w_{\dot{V}_z}/2$, $b_0=\tau\sqrt{b_1^2+b_2^2+b_3^2}$, $b_1=\dot{\phi}+\dot{\phi}_{bias}+w_{\dot{\phi}}$, $b_2=\dot{\theta}+\dot{\theta}_{bias}+w_{\dot{\theta}}$, and $b_3=\dot{\psi}+\dot{\psi}_{bias}+w_{\dot{\psi}}$. $(w_{\dot{V}x}, w_{\dot{V}y}, w_{\dot{V}z}, w_{\dot{\phi}}, w_{\dot{\theta}}, w_{\dot{\psi}}, w_{\dot{\phi}_{bias}}, w_{\dot{\theta}_{bias}}, w_{\dot{\psi}_{bias}})$ indicate disturbances (plant noise). τ is the sampling period. r_{mn} $(m, n = 1, 2, 3)$ is element (m, n) of the following rotation matrix:

$$
\boldsymbol{R}=\begin{pmatrix} q_0^2+q_1^2-q_2^2-q_3^2 & 2(q_1q_2-q_0q_3) & 2(q_1q_3+q_0q_2) \\ 2(q_1q_2+q_0q_3) & q_0^2-q_1^2+q_2^2-q_3^2 & 2(q_2q_3-q_0q_1) \\ 2(q_1q_3-q_0q_2) & 2(q_2q_3+q_0q_1) & q_0^2-q_1^2-q_2^2+q_3^2 \end{pmatrix} \tag{3}
$$

Noted that the angular velocities from the IMU are considered as a system input in (2).

The attitude (i.e., roll and pitch angles) of the helmet, which is obtained from the IMU every 10 ms, is denoted by $\boldsymbol{z}_{IMU}(t)$. The measurement equation of $\boldsymbol{z}_{IMU}(t)$ is given by

$$
\boldsymbol{z}_{IMU}(t)=\begin{pmatrix} \arctan\frac{r_{32}(t)}{r_{33}(t)} \\ \arcsin(-r_{31}(t)) \end{pmatrix}+\Delta\boldsymbol{z}_{IMU}(t) \tag{4}
$$

where Δz_{IMU} represents the measurement noise.

The helmet self-pose obtained by NDT scan matching every 120 ms is denoted by $z_{NDT}{}_{(t)}$. The measurement equation of $z_{NDT}{}_{(t)}$ is expressed as

$$z_{NDT\,(t)} = \begin{pmatrix} x_{(t)} \\ y_{(t)} \\ z_{(t)} \\ \arctan\dfrac{r_{32\,(t)}}{r_{33\,(t)}} \\ \arcsin(-r_{31\,(t)}) \\ \arctan\dfrac{r_{21\,(t)}}{r_{11\,(t)}} \end{pmatrix} + \Delta z_{NDT\,(t)} \qquad (5)$$

where Δz_{NDT} represents the measurement noise.

Equations (2), (4), and (5) are represented in the vector form as follows:

$$\xi_{(t+1)} = \boldsymbol{f}\left[\xi_{(t)}, \boldsymbol{u}_{(t)}, \boldsymbol{w}_{(t)}\right] \qquad (6)$$

$$z_{IMU\,(t)} = \boldsymbol{h}_{IMU}[\xi_{(t)}] + \Delta z_{IMU\,(t)} \qquad (7)$$

$$z_{NDT\,(t)} = \boldsymbol{h}_{NDT}[\xi_{(t)}] + \Delta z_{NDT\,(t)} \qquad (8)$$

where $\xi = (x, y, z, q_0, q_1, q_2, q_3, q_4, V_x, V_y, V_z, \dot{\phi}_{bias}, \dot{\theta}_{bias}, \dot{\psi}_{bias})^T$ $\boldsymbol{u} = (\dot{\phi}, \dot{\theta}, \dot{\psi})^T$, and $\boldsymbol{w} = (w_{\dot{V}x}, w_{\dot{V}y}, w_{\dot{V}z}, w_{\dot{\phi}}, w_{\dot{\theta}}, w_{\dot{\psi}}, w_{\dot{\phi}_{bias}}, w_{\dot{\theta}_{bias}}, w_{\dot{\psi}_{bias}})^T$.

C. Distortion Correction Using Quaternion UKF

The process of distortion correction of LiDAR point cloud data is shown in Figure 5. The LiDAR sampling period of 120 ms is denoted by τ. The IMU sampling period of 10 ms and LiDAR data acquisition period of 0.48 ms are denoted by τ_{IMU} and $\Delta\tau$, respectively. Hence, $\tau = 12\tau_{IMU}$ and $\tau_{IMU} = 21\Delta\tau$.

Distortion in LiDAR point cloud data between times $t\tau$ and $(t+1)\tau$, where t = 0, 1, ⋯, is corrected in the following five steps:

Step 1. State prediction in IMU sampling period τ_{IMU}

The state estimate and its error covariance at time $t\tau + k\tau_{IMU}$, where k = 0, ⋯, 11, are denoted by $\hat{\xi}^{(k)}{}_{(t)}$ and $\Xi^{(k)}{}_{(t)}$, respectively. As the dimensions of state variable ξ and plant noise $\boldsymbol{w}$ in state equation (6) are 13 and 9, respectively, the following 22-dimensional augmented system of $\hat{\xi}^{(k)}{}_{(t)}$ and $\Xi^{(k)}{}_{(t)}$ is defined:

$$\hat{\xi}^{a}{}_{(t)} = [\hat{\xi}^{(k)}{}_{(t)}{}^T, 0^T]^T \qquad (9)$$

$$\Xi^{a}{}_{(t)} = \begin{bmatrix} \Xi^{(k)}{}_{(t)} & 0 \\ 0 & \boldsymbol{Q} \end{bmatrix} \qquad (10)$$

where $\boldsymbol{Q}$ is the covariance of plant noise $\boldsymbol{w}$.

From (9) and (10), 45 sigma points are calculated as follows:

$$\left.\begin{aligned} &\chi_{0\,(t)} = \hat{\xi}^{a}{}_{(t)} \\ &\chi_{i\,(t)} = \hat{\xi}^{a}{}_{(t)} + \sqrt{22+\lambda}\left(\sqrt{\Xi^{a}{}_{(t)}}\right)_i \quad (i = 1, 2, \cdots, 22) \\ &\chi_{i\,(t)} = \hat{\xi}^{a}{}_{(t)} - \sqrt{22+\lambda}\left(\sqrt{\Xi^{a}{}_{(t)}}\right)_{i-22} \quad (i = 23, 24, \cdots, 44) \end{aligned}\right\} \qquad (11)$$

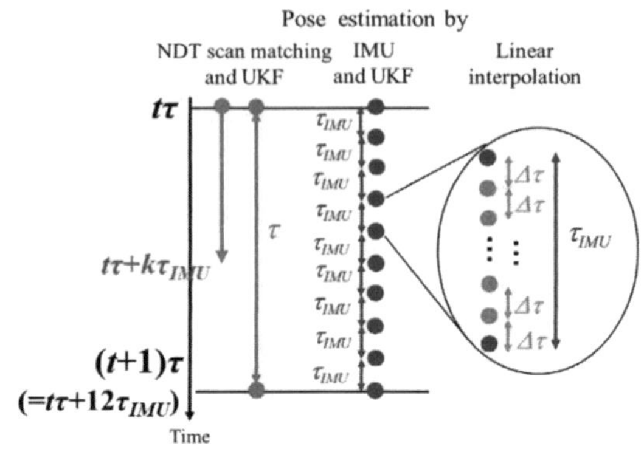

Figure 5. Process of distortion correction.

where $(\sqrt{\Xi^{a}{}_{(t)}})_i$ and $(\sqrt{\Xi^{a}{}_{(t)}})_{i-22}$ are the i-th and (i-22) th column vectors, respectively, of the square root of $\Xi^{a}{}_{(t)}$. Hyperparameter λ is set to 2 in this study.

The state prediction at time $t\tau + (k+1)\tau_{IMU}$ for the sigma points is calculated as

$$\chi_i^{\xi(k+1/k)}{}_{(t)} = \boldsymbol{f}\left[\chi_i^{\xi(k)}{}_{(t)}, \chi_i^{w(k)}{}_{(t)}, \boldsymbol{u}_{(t)}\right] \qquad (12)$$

where $\chi_i^{\xi(k)}{}_{(t)}$ and $\chi_i^{w(k)}{}_{(t)}$ are the components of the 13-dimensional state variable and 9-dimensional plant noise, respectively, of the 22-dimensional sigma points obtained in (11).

Therefore, state prediction $\hat{\xi}^{(k+1/k)}{}_{(t)}$ and its error covariance $\Xi^{(k+1/k)}{}_{(t)}$ at time $t\tau + (k+1)\tau_{IMU}$ are given by

$$\left.\begin{aligned} &\hat{\xi}^{(k+1/k)}{}_{(t)} = \sum_{i=0}^{44}\mu_i\,\chi_i^{\xi(k+1/k)}{}_{(t)} \\ &\Xi^{(k+1/k)}{}_{(t)} = \sum_{i=0}^{44}\mu_i\left[\chi_i^{\xi(k+1/k)}{}_{(t)} - \hat{\xi}^{(k+1/k)}{}_{(t)}\right][\bullet]^T \end{aligned}\right\} \qquad (13)$$

where $\mu_0 = \lambda/(22+\lambda)$ and $\mu_i = \lambda/(44+2\lambda)$ ($i \neq 0$).

Step 2. State estimate using angular information from IMU

Attitude angle z_{IMU} is obtained from the IMU at time $t\tau + (k+1)\tau_{IMU}$. Then, the measurement prediction at time $t\tau + (k+1)\tau_{IMU}$ for sigma points in (11) is calculated as

$$\zeta_{IMUi}^{(k+1/k)}{}_{(t)} = \boldsymbol{h}_{IMU}[\chi_i^{\xi(k+1/k)}{}_{(t)}] \qquad (14)$$

The measurement prediction and its error covariance at time $t\tau + (k+1)\tau_{IMU}$ are given by

$$\left.\begin{aligned} &\zeta_{IMU}^{(k+1/k)}{}_{(t)} = \sum_{i=0}^{44}\mu_i\,\zeta_{IMUi}^{(k+1/k)}{}_{(t)} \\ &\boldsymbol{Z}_{IMU}^{(k+1/k)}{}_{(t)} = \sum_{i=0}^{44}\mu_i\left[\zeta_{IMUi}^{(k+1/k)}{}_{(t)} - \zeta_{IMU}^{(k+1/k)}{}_{(t)}\right][\bullet]^T + \boldsymbol{R}_{IMU} \end{aligned}\right\} \qquad (15)$$

where $\boldsymbol{R}_{IMU}$ is the covariance of measurement noise Δz_{IMU}.

The state estimate and its error covariance are then given by

$$\left.\begin{aligned} &\hat{\xi}^{(k+1)}{}_{(t)} = \hat{\xi}^{(k+1/k)}{}_{(t)} + \boldsymbol{K}_{(t)}\left[z_{IMU}^{(k+1)}{}_{(t)} - \zeta_{IMUi}^{(k+1/k)}{}_{(t)}\right] \\ &\Xi^{(k+1)}{}_{(t)} = \Xi^{(k+1/k)}{}_{(t)} - \boldsymbol{K}_{(t)}\boldsymbol{Z}_{IMU}^{(k+1/k)}{}_{(t)}\boldsymbol{K}_{(t)}{}^T \end{aligned}\right\} \qquad (16)$$

where Kalman gain $\boldsymbol{K}$ is expressed as

$$\boldsymbol{K}_{(t)} = \sum_{i=0}^{44} \mu_i \left[\chi_i^{\xi(k+1/k)}{}_{(t)} - \hat{\xi}^{(k+1/k)}{}_{(t)} \right] \left[\zeta_{IMUi}^{(k+1/k)}{}_{(t)} - \zeta_{IMU}^{(k+1/k)}{}_{(t)} \right]^T (\boldsymbol{Z}_{IMU}^{(k+1/k)}{}_{(t)})^{-1} \quad (17)$$

Of the state estimate $\hat{\xi}^{(k+1)}{}_{(t)}$, the state estimate for the helmet self-pose is denoted by $\hat{\boldsymbol{X}}^{(k+1)}{}_{(t)}$.

Step 3. State prediction in LiDAR observation period $\Delta\tau$

Using self-poses $\hat{\boldsymbol{X}}^{(k)}{}_{(t)}$ and $\hat{\boldsymbol{X}}^{(k+1)}{}_{(t)}$, which are estimated at $t\tau + k\tau_{IMU}$ and $t\tau + (k+1)\tau_{IMU}$, resepectively, self-pose $\hat{\boldsymbol{X}}^{(k)}{}_{(t,j)}$ at $t\tau + k\tau_{IMU} + j\Delta\tau$ (j = 1–21) is given by the following interpolation formula:

$$\hat{\boldsymbol{X}}^{(k)}{}_{(t,j)} = \hat{\boldsymbol{X}}^{(k)}{}_{(t)} + \frac{\hat{\boldsymbol{X}}^{(k+1)}{}_{(t)} - \hat{\boldsymbol{X}}^{(k)}{}_{(t)}}{\tau_{IMU}} j\Delta\tau \quad (18)$$

Step 4. Coordinate transformation of LiDAR point cloud data

The coordinates of the i-th measurement of LiDAR point cloud data obtained at $t\tau + k\tau_{IMU} + j\Delta\tau$ are denoted by $\boldsymbol{p}_{hi}^{(k)}{}_{(t,j)}$ in the helmet coordinate system and by $\boldsymbol{p}_i^{(k)}{}_{(t,j)}$ in the world coordinate system. $\boldsymbol{p}_{hi}^{(k)}{}_{(t,j)}$ can be transformed into $\boldsymbol{p}_i^{(k)}{}_{(t,j)}$ based on $\hat{\boldsymbol{X}}^{(k)}{}_{(t,j)}$ and (1) as follows:

$$\begin{pmatrix} \boldsymbol{p}_i^{(k)}{}_{(t,j)} \\ 1 \end{pmatrix} = \boldsymbol{T}(\hat{\boldsymbol{X}}^{(k)}{}_{(t,j)}) \begin{pmatrix} \boldsymbol{p}_{hi}^{(k)}{}_{(t,j)} \\ 1 \end{pmatrix} \quad (19)$$

Based on helmet self-pose $\hat{\boldsymbol{X}}^{(12)}{}_{(t)}$ obtained at time $(t+1)\tau (= t\tau + 12\tau_{IMU})$, $\boldsymbol{p}_i^{(k)}{}_{(t,j)}$ is transformed into $\boldsymbol{p}_{hi}^{*}{}_{(t+1)}$ at $(t+1)\tau$ as follows:

$$\begin{pmatrix} \boldsymbol{p}_{hi}^{*}{}_{(t+1)} \\ 1 \end{pmatrix} = \boldsymbol{T}(\hat{\boldsymbol{X}}^{(12)}{}_{(t)})^{-1} \begin{pmatrix} \boldsymbol{p}_i^{(k)}{}_{(t,j)} \\ 1 \end{pmatrix} \quad (20)$$

The above equation means that the coordinates of LiDAR point cloud data obtained between times $t\tau$ and $(t+1)\tau$ can be transformed into those obtained at time $(t+1)\tau$.

Step 5. State estimate using self-pose by NDT scan matching in LiDAR sampling period τ

LiDAR point cloud data corrected in step 4 are used as current point cloud data at $(t+1)\tau$, and helmet self-pose z_{NDT} is calculated using NDT scan matching. Based on (16), state estimate $\hat{\xi}^{(12)}{}_{(t)}$ and its error covariance $\Xi^{(12)}{}_{(t)}$ at time $(t+1)\tau$ are obtained using IMU information. The state estimate and its error covariance are considered as a priori information, and the helmet state is estimated using pose mesurement z_{NDT} at time $(t+1)\tau$.

First, 27 sigma points are obtained as follows:

$$\left.\begin{aligned} &\chi_{NDT0}{}_{(t+1)} = \hat{\xi}^{(12)}{}_{(t)} \\ &\chi_{NDTi}{}_{(t+1)} = \hat{\xi}^{(12)}{}_{(t)} + \sqrt{13+\lambda}\left(\sqrt{\Xi^{(12)}{}_{(t)}}\right)_i \quad (i = 1, 2, \cdots, 13) \\ &\chi_{NDTi}{}_{(t+1)} = \hat{\xi}^{(12)}{}_{(t)} - \sqrt{13+\lambda}\left(\sqrt{\Xi^{(12)}{}_{(t)}}\right)_{i-13} \quad (i = 14, 15, \cdots, 26) \end{aligned}\right\} \quad (21)$$

Then, the measurement prediction at time $(t+1)\tau$ for the sigma points in (21) is calculated by:

$$\zeta_{NDTi}{}_{(t+1)} = \boldsymbol{h}_{NDT}[\chi_{NDTi}{}_{(t+1)}] \quad (22)$$

The measurement prediction and its error covariance at time $(t+1)\tau$ are given by

$$\left.\begin{aligned} &\zeta_{NDT}{}_{(t+1)} = \sum_{i=0}^{26} \mu_i \zeta_{NDTi}{}_{(t+1)} \\ &\boldsymbol{Z}_{NDT}{}_{(t+1)} = \sum_{i=0}^{26} \mu_i \left[\zeta_{NDTi}{}_{(t+1)} - \zeta_{NDT}{}_{(t+1)} \right] [\bullet]^T + \boldsymbol{R}_{NDT} \end{aligned}\right\} \quad (23)$$

where $\mu_0 = \lambda/(13+\lambda)$ and $\mu_i = \lambda/(26+2\lambda)$ ($i \neq 0$). $\boldsymbol{R}_{NDT}$ is the covariance of the measurement error $\Delta \boldsymbol{z}_{NDT}$.

The state estimate and its error covariance are then given by

$$\left.\begin{aligned} &\hat{\xi}^{(0)}{}_{(t+1)} = \hat{\xi}^{(12)}{}_{(t)} + \boldsymbol{K}_{(t+1)} \left[z_{NDT}{}_{(t+1)} - \zeta_{NDT}{}_{(t+1)} \right] \\ &\Xi^{(0)}{}_{(t+1)} = \Xi^{(12)}{}_{(t)} - \boldsymbol{K}_{(t+1)} \boldsymbol{Z}_{NDT}{}_{(t+1)} \boldsymbol{K}_{(t+1)}{}^T \end{aligned}\right\} \quad (24)$$

where Kalman gain $\boldsymbol{K}$ is expressed as

$$\boldsymbol{K}_{(t+1)} = \sum_{i=0}^{26} \mu_i \left[\chi_{NDTi}{}_{(t+1)} - \hat{\xi}^{(12)}{}_{(t)} \right] \left[\zeta_{NDTi}{}_{(t+1)} - \zeta_{NDT}{}_{(t+1)} \right]^T (\Xi^{(12)}{}_{(t)})^{-1} \quad (25)$$

V. CLASSIFICATION OF LIDAR POINT CLOUD DATA

The current LiDAR point cloud data contain various measurements related to road surfaces, road obstacles, stationary objects, and moving objects. Therefore, they are classified, and the measurements related to stationary objects and road obstacles are used to build an environment map. The measurements related to moving objects are used for MOT.

First, the current LiDAR point cloud data are classified into measurements related to the road surface, objects, and road obstacles, such as curbs and falling objects, using a ground-plane fitting method [21].

In the helmet coordinate system, a 2D polar grid map is set, as shown in Figure 6. LiDAR point cloud data are mapped onto the grid map. The cell size in the grid map depends on the distance from the LiDAR, such that the number of LiDAR point cloud datapoints occupied in each cell is comparable.

In each cell, 20 LiDAR measurements with the lowest heights are extracted as candidate measurements related to road surfaces. Then, by applying principal component analysis to the candidate measurements, the plane represented by the following equation is estimated:

$$A(x - x_g) + b(y - y_g) + c(z - z_g) = 0 \quad (26)$$

where (a, b, c) is the eigenvector of the third principal

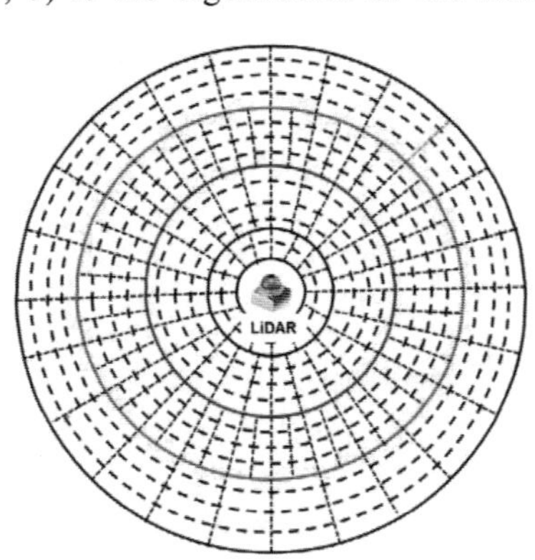

Figure 6. 2D polar grid map.

component for the candidate measurements in each cell, and (x_g, y_g, z_g) is the geometrical center of the candidate measurements.

The normal distance L of each LiDAR point cloud datapoint to the estimated plane is calculated, and LiDAR point cloud data are classified as follows:

- $L < 0.1$ m: LiDAR measurements related to road surfaces,
- $0.1 \text{ m} \leq L < 0.25$ m: LiDAR measurements related to road obstacles,
- $L \geq 0.25$ m: LiDAR measurements related to objects.

Then, the LiDAR measurements related to road obstacles are used to build a road obstacle map.

LiDAR measurements related to objects extracted above comprise measurements related to stationary and moving objects. Therefore, the occupancy grid method is used to further classify the measurements related to objects into those of stationary and moving objects.

A 2D orthogonal grid map (elevation map) with a cell size of 0.3 m per side is set in the world coordinate system. LiDAR measurements related to objects are mapped onto the elevation map. LiDAR measurements related to moving objects occupy the same cells for a short time, while those related to stationary objects occupy the same cells for a long time. Therefore, LiDAR measurements related to stationary and moving objects can be classified by measuring the cell occupancy time [18]. In this study, the threshold of occupancy time is set to 0.8 s.

Then, LiDAR point cloud data related to stationary and moving objects are used for SLAM and MOT, respectively.

VI. Fundamental Experiments

An environment map is built by driving a micromobility (bicycle) on a roadway at our university campus, as shown in Figure 7. The distance traveled of the micromobility is 450 m, and its maximum speed is 15 km/h. At the locations indicated by the blue and yellow circles in Figure 7 (a), the rider moves his head in the right-left and rearward directions, respectively. At the location indicated by the green circle, the rider lowers his head to pick up an object placed on the road. In the experiments, LiDAR point cloud data are recorded, and SLAMMOT is executed offline on a laptop computer.

Figure 8 shows the mapping results. The environment map is properly built the proposed method. To evaluate the mapping performance, experiments in the following three conditions are conducted.

- Condition 1: Mapping using quaternion-UKF-based distortion correction (proposed method),
- Condition 2: Mapping using Euler angle-UKF-based distortion correction (previous method in [15]),
- Condition 3: Mapping without distortion correction.

The performance of SLAM-based mapping is equivalent to that of self-pose estimation. Therefore, the error in the helmet self-position estimate at the goal position is obtained when the micromobility is driven. The micromobility was driven three times under each condition. Table I lists the results. The proposed method (condition 1) can build an environment map more accurately than the methods evaluated in conditions 2 and 3.

The micromobility was moved six times along the path shown in Figure 7 (a). Then, 219 moving objects (209 pedestrians and 10 cars) were tracked. Table II shows the tracking result: the number of correct and incorrect tracking. From the results, our proposed method (condition 1) achieves the highest MOT accuracy. The reason for the false tracking is that the safety confirmation by the rider causes a large posture change in his head, which prevents accurate mapping of stationary point cloud data. Untracked objects are all people. This is due to the inability to both distinguish between people in close proximity and recognize pedestrians due to occlusions by trees and shrubbery, as shown in Figure 7 (b).

(a) Top view. (b) Side view in area 1.

Figure 7. Photo of experimental environment. In (a), the red line indicates movement path of micromobility in roadway.

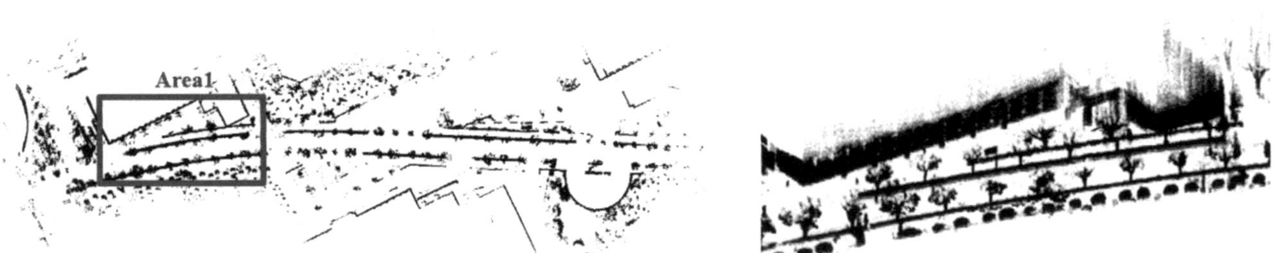

(a) Overall map (top view). (b) Enlarged map of area 1 (bird's-eye view).

Figure 8. Mapping results. The black and red dots indicate LiDAR point cloud data related to stationary objects and road obstacles, respectively.

TABLE I. ERROR OF POSITION ESTIMATE OF HELMET AT GOAL POSITION

	Condition 1	Condition 2	Condition 3
Run 1	1.57 m	2.32 m	3.01 m
Run 2	0.43 m	0.91 m	1.52 m
Run 3	2.16 m	2.19 m	23.8 m

TABLE II. NUMBER OF CORRECT AND INCORRECT TRACKING

	Condition 1	Condition 2	Condition 3
Correct tracking	198	167	161
False tracking	41	58	73
Untracking	21	52	58

VII. CONCLUSION AND FUTURE WORK

This paper presented a SLAMMOT method using a small and lightweight solid-state LiDAR attached to the rider helmet of a micromobility. To improve the performance of SLAMMOT during motion of micromobility and rider's head, the distortion in LiDAR point cloud data was corrected using a quaternion-UKF-based method. Fundamental experiments conducted at our university campus confirmed the effectiveness of the proposed distortion correction method compared to the conventional Euler angle-UKF-based method.

In this paper, the SLAMMOT experiments were confined to a controlled environment. Future studies will evaluate SLAMMOT accuracy under varying intensities of rider's head motions and in more diverse urban environments with higher traffic. Since a single motion model (i.e., constant velocity model) of target objects was assumed in MOT, tracking performance degrades when object motion suddenly change, such as during sudden starts or stops. To improve the MOT performance, an interacting multimodel estimator will be implemented. In addition, improving the mapping accuracy will be considered based on the fusion of SLAM-based environment maps built by many micromobilities.

In the experiments, LiDAR point cloud data were recorded, and SLAMMOT was executed offline on a laptop computer. Since micromobility applications require energy- and processing-efficient solutions, the computational cost (e.g., processing time and energy consumption) of SLAMMOT should be considered to assess feasibility in embedded systems.

ACKNOWLEDGMENT

This study was partially supported by the KAKENHI Grant #23K03781, the Japan Society for the Promotion of Science (JSPS).

REFERENCES

[1] Y. F. Payalan and M. A. Guvensan, "Towards Next-Generation Vehicles Featuring the Vehicle Intelligence," IEEE Trans. on Intelligent Transportation Systems, vol. 21, pp. 30–46, 2020.

[2] E. Arnold, et al., "A Survey on 3D Object Detection Methods for Autonomous Driving Applications," IEEE Trans. on Intelligent Transportation Systems, vol. 20, pp. 3782–3795, 2019.

[3] E. Yurtsever, J. Lambert, A. Carballo, and K. Takeda, "A Survey of Autonomous Driving: Common Practices and Emerging Technologies," IEEE Access, vol. 8, pp. 58443–58469, 2020.

[4] G. Bresson, Z. Alsayed, L. Yu, and S. Glaser, "Simultaneous Localization And Mapping: A Survey of Current Trends in Autonomous Driving," IEEE Trans. on Intelligent Transportation Systems, vol. 2, pp. 194–220, 2017.

[5] B. Madapur, S. Madangopal, and M. N. Chandrashekar, "Micro-Mobility Infrastructure for Redefining Urban Mobility," European J. of Engineering Science and Technology, vol. 3, pp. 71–85, 2020.

[6] I. Yoshida, A. Yoshida, M. Hashimoto, and K. Takahashi, "Environmental Map Building and Moving Object Tracking Using Helmet-Mounted LiDAR and IMU for Micromobility," Int. J. on Advances in Systems and Measurements, vol. 16, pp. 40–52, 2023.

[7] T. Raj, F. H. Hashim, A. B. Huddin, M. F. Ibrahim, and A. Hussain, "A Survey on LiDAR Scanning Mechanisms," Electronics 9, 741, 2020.

[8] K. Li, M. Li, and U. D. Hanebeck, "Towards High-Performance Solid-State-LiDAR-Inertial Odometry and Mapping," IEEE Robotics and Automation Letters, vol. 6, pp. 5167– 5174, 2021.

[9] V. Kumar, S. C. Subramanian, and R. Rajamani, "A Novel Algorithm to Track Closely Spaced Road Vehicles Using a Low Density Flash Lidar," Signal Processing 191, pp. 1–11, 2022.

[10] J. Li, et al., "WHU-Helmet: A Helmet-Based Multisensor SLAM Dataset for the Evaluation of Real-Time 3-D Mapping in Large-Scale GNSS-Denied Environments," IEEE Trans. on Geoscience and Remote Sensing, vol. 61, pp. 1–16, 2023.

[11] Z. Peng, Z. Xiong, Y. Zhao, and L. Zhang, "3-D Objects Detection and Tracking Using Solid-State LiDAR and RGB Camera," IEEE Sensors Journal, vol. 23, pp. 14795 - 14808, 2023.

[12] S. Hong, H. Ko, and J. Kim, "VICP: Velocity Updating Iterative Closest Point Algorithm," Proc. of the IEEE Int. Conf. on Robotics and Automation, pp. 1893–1898, 2010.

[13] P. Zhou, X. Guo, X. Pei, and C. Chen, "T-LOAM: Truncated Least Squares LiDAR-only Odometry and Mapping in Real Time," IEEE Trans. on Geoscience and Remote Sensing, vol. 60, pp. 1–13, 2022.

[14] I. Yoshida, A. Yoshida, M. Hashimoto, and K. Takahashi, "Map Building Using Helmet-Mounted LiDAR for Micromobility," Artificial Life and Robotics, vol. 28, pp. 471–482, 2023.

[15] R. Nakamura, I. Inaga, M. Hashimoto, and K. Takahashi, "SLAM-Based Mapping Using Micromobility-Mounted Solid-State LiDAR," Proc. the 11th IIAE Int. Conf. on Intelligent Systems and Image Processing, pp. 93–100, 2024.

[16] E. A. Wan and R. van der Merwe, "The Unscented Kalman Filter: Kalman Filtering and Neural Networks," S. Haykin, Eds, Wiley Publishing, 2001.

[17] P. Biber and W. Strasser, "The Normal Distributions Transform: A New Approach to Laser Scan Matching," Proc. of IEEE/RSJ Int. Conf. on Intelligent Robots and Systems, pp. 2743–2748, 2003.

[18] M. Hashimoto, R. Izumi, Y. Tamura, and K. Takahashi, "Laser-based Tracking of People and Vehicles by Multiple Mobile Robots," Proc. the 11th Int. Conf. on Informatics in Control, Automation and Robotics, pp. 522–527, 2014.

[19] G. Toussaint, "Solving Geometric Problems with the Rotating Calipers,", Proc. IEEE Mediterranean Electrotechnical Conf.'83, pp. 1–8, 1983.

[20] Y. B. Jia, "Quaternions and Rotations," Available from: https://www.fuchs-braun.com/media/56347a973e30256ffff802effffffff1.pdf/.

[21] H. Lim, M. Oh, and H. Myung, "Patchwork: Concentric Zone-based Region-wise Ground Segmentation with Ground Likelihood Estimation Using a 3D LiDAR Sensor," IEEE Robotics and Automation Letters, vol. 6, pp. 6458–6465, 2021.

Psychological Issues for Designing XR Spaces

From Usability to Humability

Britta Essing[a], Dennis Paul[b]
Human-Centered Engineering & Design
Fraunhofer Institute for Applied Information Technology FIT
Sankt Augustin, Germany
[a]britta.essing@fit.fraunhofer.de,
[b]dennis.paul@fit.fraunhofer.de

René Reiners
Chair of Information Systems and Databases (Computer Science 5)
RWTH Aachen University
Aachen, Germany
rene.reiners@rwth-aachen.de

Abstract—**The rapid development of eXtended Reality (XR) technologies—and their integration into the emerging metaverse—brings both extraordinary opportunities and significant risks. As XR technologies increasingly penetrate various aspects of life, from entertainment to work, understanding their psychological impact becomes essential. The concept of Humability—defined as the extent to which XR environments are harmless or beneficial to mental health—emerges as an important criterion for the human-centered design of such technologies. This paper emphasizes the importance of Humability and aims to support the creation of virtual worlds that do not harm. To address this concern, we conducted a literature review and analyzed existing research from different psychological sub-disciplines. Through this we gained insights that are relevant for the human-friendly design of avatars, virtual environments, and user behavior in immersive XR spaces. By summarizing findings from developmental, social, cognitive, personality, work, organizational, and clinical psychology, we identified key factors that influence mental health in XR application contexts. From our findings, we conclude that virtual environments must balance immersion and cognitive load, encourage diverse interactions, and fulfill psychological needs in a healthy way. User behavior in XR/metaverse environments should be guided to promote positive social interactions and avoid psychological problems such as addiction and depersonalization. Our conclusion emphasizes the need for an interdisciplinary development of Humability as an applied science to ensure that the metaverse becomes a psychologically harmless or even enriching place for all users.**

Keywords—Extended Reality (XR); Usability; Mental Health; Design Guidelines; Humability.

I. INTRODUCTION

As virtual and augmented reality, both components of eXtended Reality (XR) technologies, continue to advance, their integration into everyday life is increasing rapidly. This development has also revived interest in the concept of the metaverse, particularly since Meta's vision highlighted Virtual Reality (VR) and Augmented Reality (AR), as key enabling technologies for future virtual collaboration and social interaction. XR, i.e., VR, AR, and the combination thereof, has the potential to disrupt various areas, from entertainment to working environments. Thereby, the psychological impact of an extended stay in these immersive worlds raises significant concerns. It is essential that XR environments like the metaverse are designed to be human-friendly and focus on the mental health and wellbeing of users. However, despite the increasing relevance of this topic, we identified a significant lack of research on how XR environments can be designed to avoid potential harm and promote psychological health. The existing studies analyzed in this paper primarily focus on the potential harms associated with XR, such as addictiveness, deindividuation, and negative effects on body image and social interactions. However, research so far has neglected practical design strategies that can minimize these risks.

The aim of this work is to identify research gaps and formulate interdisciplinary research challenges necessary for the prospective development of human-friendly design principles for psychologically harmless XR environments. As an initial step, we provide a comprehensive literature review as an overview of the research work conducted in this area so far and as a basis for strategically setting up follow-up research.

We consider design guidelines from a psychological perspective as important for protecting users and enhancing their experiences in these emerging digital spaces. Our approach shall ensure that XR spaces and other XR environments do not harm mental health but enrich it. This perspective originates from usability research and will be extended and adapted to the XR domain. Thus, our research shapes the term **Humability** by raising future research questions from each considered psychological discipline.

The rest of the paper is structured as follows; After presenting a first definition of the term Humability and its relevance regarding the XR market value, Section III describes our literature research methodology. As results, Section IV describes relevant psychological issues that should be addressed for the design of "humane" XR environments. This paper concludes by providing first guideline ideas for XR design as first seeds for further research to merge conventional usability knowledge with the prospective post-desktop XR era.

II. Humability—A First Definition

At this point, we would like to present a first draft of a definition of Humability. Based on current thinking and knowledge, Humability as a concept should first be defined as "the extent to which a virtual and augmented reality context is harmless or beneficial to a person's mental health". This is based on the standard definition of usability [1]. Hereby, the "context" consists of interaction partners, the physical environment, and areas of life (work/leisure), among other things.

A virtual or augmented reality context can only be specifically designed in such a way that it is "harmless to mental health" if the risks associated with certain context characteristics have been identified and their mechanisms of action understood. In designing XR spaces that are even "beneficial to mental health", the focus is not on psychological dangers, but on the multiple insights into the therapeutic value of XR, which have the potential to alleviate people's psychological suffering. The challenge is to abstract these findings from their therapeutic application situations and translate them into everyday functions of virtual and augmented worlds so that people can spontaneously benefit from the positive effects on their psyche.

Our concept of Humability thus corresponds to the consideration of *Ethical, Legal, and Social Implications* (ELSI). Humability as a quality of an interactive technological system in this sense is the suitability of such a system for humans – or human suitability. As a design approach and field of research it answers the question of how to design to protect or promote mental health. Although the impact of technology on human well-being has been studied in various research areas, usability engineering, which also deals with the reduction of user harm, is still mainly concerned with users as functioning and task-performing entities and not as beings with their psychological feelings, needs, vulnerabilities, and potentials. In this way, we aim to introduce a new perspective for the consideration of interactive technologies, apart from usability engineering and Positive *User Experience* (UX) research.

The social relevance of this topic is emphasized by the significant financial investments that have already been made in XR technology. According to Statista [2], the industry forecasts predict that the worldwide market for XR reached $29.26 billion in 2022 and will rise to over $100 billion by 2026. This investment underlines the urgent need to ensure that these technologies are developed with people's mental health in mind.

III. Methodology

To systemically and methodically address the need for a "humane" XR design, we have conducted a broad literature review. This method involved a review of current research in various psychological sub-disciplines to identify existing knowledge, gaps, and potential risks associated with XR environments. Our approach was to gather the results of studies on the psychological effects of XR technologies and assess how these findings can inform the design of psychologically harmless or even beneficial virtual spaces.

The literature review was conducted as follows:

Selection of databases and keywords: We started by selecting relevant academic databases, including PubMed, PsycINFO, IEEE Xplore and Google Scholar. Relevant studies were found using keywords such as "virtual reality", "augmented reality", "mental health", "avatar design", "virtual environments", and "user behavior".

Screening and inclusion criteria: We screened articles for relevance based on their abstracts. Inclusion criteria included studies that addressed the psychological effects of VR/AR, user interaction in virtual environments, and the effects of design on mental health. Priority was given to articles from peer-reviewed journals, conference papers, and seminal work in the field.

IV. Results

In this paper, we examine the literature on XR for mental health, integrating insights from key disciplines within psychology to propose a preliminary, meaningful framework. It is important to emphasize at this point that the following thoughts, scientific findings, and research questions do not claim to be exhaustive. Our intention is to exemplify and reinforce the need for the research topic or field of Humability. For that reason, we derive future research questions from each discipline.

A. Developmental Psychology

Developmental psychology deals with the description and explanation of intra-individual changes in human experience and behavior across the entire life span—from prenatal development to death [3]. Assuming that adolescents are one target group of XR spaces, special attention should be paid to the extent to which its use could have an influence on the development of identity, which is—according to *Erikson's Stages of Psychosocial Development*—an important challenge during the phase of adolescence between the age of 12 to 18 [4]. Identity means that a person is a unique and distinctive personality [5]. The inner consistency experienced by the person is embodied in the self-concept or self-image and goes hand in hand with the feeling of self-worth and the experience of one's own individuality [6].

There are first findings that show that a strong identification with an avatar in a game context is negatively related to self-concept clarity [7]. The developmental question "Who am I?", which is significantly answered through interaction with peers, remains distinctly separate from one's physical body. Although it is natural for teenagers to vary their behavior and appearance [4], the question now is whether the changeability of avatars influences this process of finding identity. Furthermore, it is known that media can have a great influence on the perception and acceptance of one's own body in adolescence. The significance of the media in the construction of beauty ideals of female adolescents has been controversially discussed in society for a considerable time [8]. Therefore, it cannot be ruled out that the personal manifestation as an avatar can also influence the evaluation of one's own body.

Derived research question: How should avatars be designed to not impair or even support adolescents in their search for identity?

B. Social Psychology

From a social psychology perspective, it is of great interest how virtual social life in virtual spaces affects a person's thoughts, feelings, attitudes, and behavior [3]. Avatar customization would allow for a greater extent of possible personalization and thus the users' identification with their avatar. In addition to *spatial* presence, the feeling of actually being there [9], *self-identification* as the feeling that 'the avatar is really me' [10] is another aspired effect of XR spaces. Since not just oneself but everybody will typically interact in XR spaces via an avatar, the third phenomenon to consider is social presence that is the conscious awareness of others [10]. Identification with one's own avatar along with the perception of other avatars and interaction with the associated social groups is expected to bring about several psychological effects that need to be accounted for when designing XR spaces. Three social-psychological phenomena that occur in virtual spaces will be presented exemplarily: echo chambers, the Proteus effect, and escapism behavior.

1) Echo chamber effect: Frequent stays in virtual spaces with a self-selected virtual community could easily lead to a narrow-minded worldview, which brings with it the risk of *confirmation bias*. Wickens *et al.* [11, pp. 261–261] define this as a tendency "for people to seek information and cues that confirm the tentatively held hypothesis or belief, and not seek (or discount) those that support an opposite conclusion or belief". In contrast to real life, in which one must deal with different views and characters, in self-selected, virtual spaces, one's own opinion is likely to be mirrored and thus reinforced, which is described as the *echo chamber effect* [12][13]. The existence of echo chambers is in turn likely to go along with *filter bubbles*, in which in-group members preferentially communicate with each other to the exclusion of outsiders [14]. This increases the danger of radicalization as a result of social learning effects [15].

2) Deindividuation and the Proteus effect: Another aspect to consider regarding XR spaces is the concept of *deindividuation*, which describes a loss of self-awareness and individuality due to the immersion in a social group. According to the *Social Identity model of Deindividuation Effects* (SIDE) [16], deindividualization causes people to rely more heavily on identity cues and thus conform to group norms in the context of computer-mediated communication. This is relevant to XR spaces and online social networks and communities in general, where anonymity and group identity can lead to antinormative behavior like harassment, profanity, or trolling.

Closely related to but opposite of the SIDE is the *Proteus effect*. Yee and Bailenson [17] refer to it as the influence of an avatar's features and characteristics on the user's behavior. In contrast to the deindividuation effect, the Proteus effect emphasizes conformity to individual (rather than group) identity cues. What is interesting or particularly noteworthy here is that behavior patterns, once trained virtually, could also be retained in real life, especially if the virtual world is particularly similar to the real one [18]. As Scarborough and Bailenson [10] suggest, virtual environments offer great flexibility in how they present reality. This can provide great therapeutic and educational potential; on the other hand, if uncontrolled, it can pose dangerous problems.

3) Uncanny valley effect: On a related note, not only the effects of customization need to be considered but also the implications of the more realistic replications of the users' real-world appearance in terms of the *uncanny valley effect* [19]. Shin *et al.* [20] showed that greater realism increased feelings of eeriness, which in turn impaired information processing and accurate thin-slice (i.e., based on a minimal amount of information) judgements of the people's real character traits, extraversion and agreeableness. Therefore, in XR spaces, we should carefully design avatars so to enhance relatedness and accurate judgements of other users' personality if we want people to mutually engage in a caring and trusting manner (cf. [21]).

Derived research question: How should avatars and avatar customization be designed so that they do not negatively affect mental health in terms of deindividuation, the Proteus effect, and the uncanny valley, or even positively affect mental health?

4) Escapism and psychological need satisfaction: A major kind of motivation for engaging in virtual worlds is supposedly the wish to escape the unsatisfying real world that is *escapism* [22]. In a recent work referring to Zuckerberg's metaverse vision, [23] elaborate on the possible risks that might arise when consumers seek to leave behind their real-world problems by escaping into VR. In line with the *Theory of Compensatory Internet Use* (TCIU) [24], VR experiences are thereby used to escape real-life problems, negative emotions, and stress—the mechanism of which can also be called *avoidance coping* [25]. Such self-indulgent escapism via technology can lead to negative psychological and social consequences, including depression and anxiety [26], low emotional intelligence [27], and loneliness [28]. Those effects, in turn, can increase the feeling that life is unbearable (which caused the escape into the virtual in the first place), resulting in a "(...) vicious cycle, which eventually can lead to even more detrimental effects on health and well-being" [22, p. 3].

Not all research supports the compensation hypothesis, however [29]. A different way of viewing escapism is through the lens of compulsive behavior. Research has shown that the need for *belongingness* [30] or *relatedness* [31] can constitute a powerful factor for addiction to social media. For example, it was found that gratification of purposive value (use for functional outcomes like learning) and social enhancement (gaining acceptance and approval) via social media networks increases the risk for *Obsessive-*

Compulsive Disorder (OCD) with regard to using online social networks [32]. In this way, OCD might also arise from a fulfilment of the need to belong resulting from the virtual experience. Assuming XR spaces can generate convincing feelings of social presence—and due to their immersive nature—the effects could arguably be even greater. Positive UX design traditionally attempts to satisfy users' inherent psychological needs [31][33], some of which are individual-focused, like *autonomy* and *competence*, and some of which are social, like relatedness/belongingness or popularity. The more XR spaces offer social experiences similar to real life, the greater the allure could be for people to seek substitution of (a lack of) real-life connections. Similarly, the virtual world beckons to gratify not just the need for relatedness but also for competence (by reaching achievements) and autonomy (by providing choice and customization) [23], in line with *Self-Determination Theory* (SDT) [31]. The extent to which those needs are fulfilled by interactive technology needs to be taken even more into account with the rise of fully immersive experiences in XR spaces. In the context of video games, low levels of real-life need satisfaction were shown to be related to obsessive and extensive gaming [34]. Future research must determine to what extent XR environments—like many video games—offer alluring need satisfactions with *immediacy* (quickly and easily accessible), *density* (with high frequency), and *consistency* (predictably and reliably) [35].

Derived research question: How should VR experiences be designed so that they minimize the potential allure for escapism while remaining psychologically fulfilling and meaningful?

C. *Industrial and Organizational Psychology*

Industrial and Organizational psychology (I/O psychology) examines behavior in the workplace regarding work processes, social work structures, and personnel [3]. Digitalization can lead to an increase in work intensity, information overload, the blurring of boundaries between work and leisure, the degradation of activities, and psychological problems due to the feeling of being under surveillance, all of which fall under the concept of digital stress or *technostress* [36][37].

The free choosing of one's personal avatar in XR spaces could enable people to overcome disadvantages that their own physicality or personality may have for the business world. Due to the *halo effect*, for example, the performance of good-looking and more attractive people may be rated higher than that of less attractive people [38]. But also gender or nationality can be disadvantageous in certain professional contexts and could be eliminated through the purposeful use of an appropriate business avatar. This offers opportunities, particularly in the personnel recruitment process and in the assessment center setting, to hire people purely based on their achievements, without the influence of prejudices or stereotypes. The purposeful use of avatars could also be useful in human resource development. For example, as stated above, an avatar that exhibits dominant and self-confident characteristics could make shy or quiet employees act more confidently and loudly so that they learn to better stand up for themselves in their professional lives.

However, the arbitrary selection of avatars can also lead to undesirable effects in working life. What happens if I choose an avatar that is unfavorable to me, and I suffer professional disadvantages as a result? Will there be virtual dress codes, and who will decide what others are supposed to "wear"? What if I can only achieve the required professional performance or contribute to discussions in the role of my avatar? All these are open questions for future research in I/O psychology with respect to XR spaces. Moreover, the aforementioned Proteus effect [17] can also manifest in a business context, for instance by influencing leadership style [39].

Derived research question: How should business avatars be designed so that they do not impair or that they promote working life?

D. *Cognitive psychology*

Apart from the more socially determined effects that immersion in XR spaces might entail, there are also a number of direct cognitive implications that need to be considered for the safety of the users. Cognitive psychology is concerned with mental processes like perception, attention, memory, and emotion [3]. Notably, it has been shown that the feeling of presence [9] is both a predictor of emotions [40] and cognitive abilities [41].

Research on the effects of spending time in VR has mostly looked at physiological effects like *cybersickness* and eye strain [42]. There is, however, also preliminary evidence for the potential negative effects of VR on affect. Lavoie *et al.* [43] demonstrated that negative scenarios in VR elicit a higher amount of the negative emotion, shame, compared to the identical scenario on a normal screen-based application.

Mittelstaedt *et al.* [41] found increased reaction times after VR immersion that were unrelated to experienced cybersickness. Szpak *et al.* [44] came to similar results with slower reaction times likely being related to decreased attention rather than motor performance. Future research should therefore determine the true extent and relevance of VR after- and concomitant effects.

Derived research question: To what extent and in which situations should XR spaces induce immersion and presence or alternatively, create psychological or physical distance between the user and the virtual experience in order to protect or foster mental health?

E. *Personality Psychology*

From the perspective of personality psychology, people's personality and its enduring components are of interest [3] when looking at how the effects of XR spaces differ depending on the person. One of the most famous and well-documented models in personality research is the *Big Five* or so-called OCEAN model, named after its five trait dimensions: *openness to experience*, *conscientiousness*, *extraversion*, *agreeableness*, and *neuroticism*. Studies have shown that personality is a relevant factor affecting the extent to which a person is influenced by the use of the internet in general, but also by spending time in virtual worlds [45][46].

McLeod *et al.* [47] investigated the effects of personality on real-life changes due to virtual world experiences in Second Life. They found that individual differences in the Big Five personality traits predict the extent to which virtual world experiences change people's real life. Conscientiousness and emotional stability were found to be significant factors in preventing a person from blurring the virtual and real worlds. The more conscientious a person was, the more similar s/he was to his or her avatar in Second Life. The higher the emotional stability, the lower the emotional investment in Second Life and the smaller the resulting change in real life. Accordingly, conscientious and emotionally stable people could probably handle taboo breaks such as virtual violence or unethical behavior better than others, which again opens up room for research in the field of personality coaching [48].

Derived research question: How should XR spaces be designed so that people with susceptible personality structures experience no unintended behavioral changes in real life?

F. Clinical Psychology

"What stays is a strange feeling of sadness and disappointment when participating in the real world, usually on the same day (…) The sky seems less colorful, and it just feels like I'm missing the 'magic' (…) I feel deeply disturbed and often end up just sitting there, staring at a wall." [49]

The field of clinical psychology, which deals with emotional and behavioral disorders or illnesses [3], is obviously important for the implementation of XR spaces:

Park *et al.* [50] in their "Literature Overview of Virtual Reality in Treatment of Psychiatric Disorders" conclude, based on 36 studies, that the use of VR for treating mental disorders shows good therapeutic success, which will, however, not be discussed in depth here. The much more critical question for the design of XR spaces is how to avoid increasing the emergence of mental illnesses in our society. In the following, some potential dangers of (social) virtual and augmented worlds or networks are pointed out.

Independent of the use of VR and AR, there is evidence that the rise of social media has significantly increased the prevalence of depression and suicidal behavior in adolescents [51][52]. As the well-known psychological experiment of the *rubber hand illusion* shows, people's body perception is easily manipulated [53]. Accordingly, the use of VR and AR technologies raises questions about *depersonalization* and *derealization* effects. In a recent study [54], it could be demonstrated that VR techniques can indeed lead to both depersonalization and derealization.

Furthermore, there is evidence that the physical appearance of avatars could trigger eating disorders such as *anorexia nervosa*. Tambone *et al.* [55] could show that if the virtual body was slimmer than the subject's own, calorie-rich foods were avoided to a greater extent.

Another matter to consider when designing XR spaces is the matter of potential *Post-Traumatic Stress Disorder* (PTSD). Virtual environments have the capacity to elicit real-life reactions from immersed individuals [56]. Whereas VR, when controlled, offers opportunities for the treatment of PTSD [57]—when uncontrolled, the life-like situations that an individual might encounter, could have detrimental effects. As Franks [58] illustrates, (sexual) harassment feels more realistic and thus worse than in other digital worlds, possibly inducing traumatic experiences.

Finally, we need to consider the topic of addiction to virtual technologies. As laid out before, according to the compensation hypothesis [24] and the *need density hypothesis* [35], people in XR spaces could be tempted to escape real-life problems and need frustrations. The overuse resulting from that can accordingly be described as "addictive". Recently, the DSM-5 added *Internet Gaming Disorder* (IGD) as a condition warranting further research. A systematic review and meta-analysis found the behavior of more than 3% of gamers to fall under gaming disorder [59]. A cross-sectional study [60] showed addictive use of social media to be associated with *Attention Deficit Hyperactivity Disorder* (ADHD), OCD, anxiety, and notably, lower levels of depression, whereas addictive use of video games was positively correlated with ADHD, OCD, depression, and anxiety. Another driver of social media overuse was shown to be the *Fear Of Missing Out* (FOMO) [34]. In fact, FOMO seems to mediate the impact of depression and anxiety on negative consequences of mobile device use [61] and the negative impact of increased social networking site use on self-esteem [62].

Derived research questions: How should XR spaces be designed so that mental illness is protected or that XR spaces contribute to its healing? How should XR spaces be designed to minimize addictive behavior regarding use?

V. Humability Aspects for XR Design

The integration of XR technologies into everyday life offers immense opportunities but also poses significant psychological risks. In this paper we highlighted the need to prioritize Humability—a desired quality of an interactive system and a design approach that aims to ensure XR environments are safe for or even beneficial to mental health. Our comprehensive literature review revealed critical findings from various psychological sub-disciplines about the potential risks of XR environments that emphasize the importance of designing such environments to prevent psychological ill-being and instead promote well-being.

The specific findings can be categorized into three broad, intertwined aspects of the XR experience that need to be addressed by design. In the following, the presented aspects are accompanied by initial guideline proposals:

1) Avatars: Avatar design can have a significant influence on users' identity formation, self-concept, and body image. Improper design can lead to issues like deindividuation and negative body image, particularly among adolescents. Judgement of other people in XR can be impaired due to their avatar appearance and the resulting halo or uncanny valley effect.

Design Recommendations:

- Promote positive identity formation and body image.
- Avoid near-realistic avatar appearance to prevent the uncanny valley effect.
- Enable customization that balances user expression with psychological safety.

2) Virtual Environments: While immersion into a virtual environment can enhance the UX, it must be managed to prevent cognitive overload and negative aftereffects like increased reaction times and cybersickness. Virtual environments should promote diverse, inclusive, and open-minded social interactions to counteract phenomena like echo chambers and therewith social isolation. Design should encourage positive social behaviors and prevent radicalization.

Design Recommendations:

- Balance immersion with cognitive load management.
- Foster diverse, inclusive, and positive social interactions.
- Design systems to monitor and guide user behavior, preventing addiction and promoting healthy engagement.

3) User Behavior und Experience: XR environments offer a tempting escape from reality that can lead to addictive use behavior. Design strategies must minimize the lure of escapism while constructively meeting psychological needs. Proper design must ensure that users' do not suffer from or exacerbate their mental health disorders and self-destructive behavior as a result of their time spent in XR. On the contrary, the potential to mitigate mental health issues should be maximized.

Design Recommendations:

- Create features that satisfy psychological needs without encouraging escapism
- Integrate mental health support within XR platforms to address and mitigate potential issues like addiction and depression.

VI. Conclusion and Future Outlook

The significant investment that industry leaders have already made in XR technologies and the forecasts for substantial market growth [2] underline the social relevance and urgency of this endeavor. With the growing interest in the metaverse as a persistent, immersive digital space for socializing, working, and learning, these developments highlight the importance of ensuring psychological safety in such environments. By establishing Humability as a guiding principle for XR design, we intend to ensure that XR spaces and other immersive environments become risk-free and supportive spaces that minimize harm and even contribute positively to users' mental health and overall wellbeing.

From our review, we conclude that there is an urgent need for interdisciplinary collaboration to develop Humability as an applied science. As XR technologies become increasingly integrated into our lives, there is a need to ensure that they are designed to promote mental health rather than detract from it. Future research should bridge the gaps between psychology, human–computer interaction (HCI), and design in order to develop comprehensive guidelines for the design of Humable XR environments. This collaboration is crucial for translating psychological insights into practical design strategies.

References

[1] International Organization for Standardization, "ISO 9241-110:2020(en) Ergonomics of human-system interaction — Part 110: Interaction principles." 2020. [Online]. Available from: https://www.iso.org/obp/ui/#iso:std:iso:9241:-110:ed-2:v1:en [Accessed: May 9, 2025].

[2] Statista, "XR market size worldwide 2021-2026," Statista. Accessed: May 9, 2025. [Online]. Available from: https://www.statista.com/statistics/591181/global-augmented-virtual-reality-market-size/ [Accessed: May 9, 2025].

[3] G. R. VandenBos, Ed., APA Dictionary of Psychology. in APA Dictionary of Psychology. Washington, DC, US: American Psychological Association, 2007, pp. xvi, 1024.

[4] G. A. Orenstein and L. Lewis, "Eriksons Stages of Psychosocial Development - StatPearls - NCBI Bookshelf," National Library of Medicine. [Online]. Available from: https://www.ncbi.nlm.nih.gov/books/NBK556096/ [Accessed: May 9, 2025].

[5] J. M. Cheek, "Identity Orientations and Self-Interpretation," in Personality Psychology: Recent Trends and Emerging Directions, D. M. Buss and N. Cantor, Eds., New York, NY: Springer US, 1989, pp. 275–285. doi: 10.1007/978-1-4684-0634-4_21.

[6] P. Weinreich, "The operationalisation of identity theory in racial and ethnic relations," in Theories of Race and Ethnic Relations, Cambridge University Press, 1986. Accessed: May 9, 2025. [Online]. Available from: https://www.academia.edu/11148082/The_operationalisation_of_identity_theory_in_racial_and_ethnic_relations [Accessed: May 9, 2025].

[7] R. Green, P. H. Delfabbro, and D. L. King, "Avatar identification and problematic gaming: The role of self-concept clarity," Addictive Behaviors, vol. 113, p. 106694, Feb. 2021, doi: 10.1016/j.addbeh.2020.106694.

[8] A. T. Flügel, "The acceptance of one's own body in the context of everyday media and social negotiations about beauty using the example of the docu-soap "The Swan"," (in German) in Jahrbuch Jugendforschung, A. Ittel, L. Stecher, H. Merkens, and J. Zinnecker, Eds. Wiesbaden: VS Verlag für Sozialwissenschaften, 2008, pp. 49–71. doi: 10.1007/978-3-531-91087-1_4.

[9] M. Lombard and T. Ditton, "At the Heart of It All: The Concept of Presence," Journal of Computer-Mediated Communication, vol. 3, no. 2, p. JCMC321, Sep. 1997, doi: 10.1111/j.1083-6101.1997.tb00072.x.

[10] J. K. Scarborough and J. N. Bailenson, "Avatar Psychology ," in The Oxford Handbook of Virtuality, Oxford Academic, 2014. [Online]. Available from: https://academic.oup.com/edited-volume/28128/chapter-abstract/212311197?redirectedFrom=fulltext&login=false [Accessed: May 9, 2025].

[11] C. D. Wickens, W. S. Helton, J. G. Hollands, and S. Banbury, Engineering Psychology and Human Performance, 5th ed. New York: Routledge, 2021. doi: 10.4324/9781003177616.

[12] M. Cinelli, G. De Francisci Morales, A. Galeazzi, W. Quattrociocchi, and M. Starnini, "The echo chamber effect on social media," Proc. Natl. Acad. Sci. U.S.A., vol. 118, no. 9, Mar. 2021, doi: 10.1073/pnas.2023301118.

[13] C. R. Sunstein, Going to Extremes: How Like Minds Unite and Divide. Oxford University Press, 2009.

[14] A. Bruns, "Echo chambers? Filter bubbles? The misleading metaphors that obscure the real problem," in Hate Speech and Polarization in Participatory Society, Routledge, 2021.

[15] W. J. Brady, K. McLoughlin, T. N. Doan, and M. J. Crockett, "How social learning amplifies moral outrage expression in online social networks," Science Advances, vol. 7, no. 33, p. eabe5641, Aug. 2021, doi: 10.1126/sciadv.abe5641.

[16] T. Postmes, R. Spears, and M. Lea, "Breaching or Building Social Boundaries?: SIDE-Effects of Computer-Mediated Communication," Communication Research, vol. 25, no. 6, pp. 689–715, Dec. 1998, doi: 10.1177/009365098025006006.

[17] N. Yee and J. Bailenson, "The Proteus Effect: The Effect of Transformed Self-Representation on Behavior," Human Comm Res, vol. 33, no. 3, pp. 271–290, Jul. 2007, doi: 10.1111/j.1468-2958.2007.00299.x.

[18] J. Peña, J. T. Hancock, and N. A. Merola, "The Priming Effects of Avatars in Virtual Settings," Communication Research, vol. 36, no. 6, pp. 838–856, Dec. 2009, doi: 10.1177/0093650209346802.

[19] M. Mori, "Bukimi no tani [the uncanny valley].," Energy, vol. 7, p. 33, 1970.

[20] M. Shin, S. J. Kim, and F. Biocca, "The uncanny valley: No need for any further judgments when an avatar looks eerie," Computers in Human Behavior, vol. 94, pp. 100–109, May 2019, doi: 10.1016/j.chb.2019.01.016.

[21] M. Seymour, L. (Ivy) Yuan, A. R. Dennis, and K. Riemer, "Have We Crossed the Uncanny Valley? Understanding Affinity, Trustworthiness, and Preference for Realistic Digital Humans in Immersive Environments," Journal of the Association for Information Systems, vol. 22, no. 3, pp. 591–617, 2021.

[22] B. Henning and P. Vorderer, "Psychological Escapism: Predicting the Amount of Television Viewing by Need for Cognition," Journal of Communication, vol. 51, no. 1, pp. 100–20, 2001.

[23] D.-I. D. Han, Y. Bergs, and N. Moorhouse, "Virtual reality consumer experience escapes: preparing for the metaverse," Virtual Reality, vol. 26, no. 4, pp. 1443–1458, Dec. 2022, doi: 10.1007/s10055-022-00641-7.

[24] D. Kardefelt-Winther, "A conceptual and methodological critique of internet addiction research: Towards a model of compensatory internet use," Computers in Human Behavior, vol. 31, pp. 351–354, Feb. 2014, doi: 10.1016/j.chb.2013.10.059.

[25] C. J. Holahan, R. H. Moos, C. K. Holahan, P. L. Brennan, and K. K. Schutte, "Stress Generation, Avoidance Coping, and Depressive Symptoms: A 10-Year Model," J Consult Clin Psychol, vol. 73, no. 4, pp. 658–666, Aug. 2005, doi: 10.1037/0022-006X.73.4.658.

[26] T. Panova and A. Lleras, "Avoidance or boredom: Negative mental health outcomes associated with use of Information and Communication Technologies depend on users' motivations," Computers in Human Behavior, vol. 58, pp. 249–258, May 2016, doi: 10.1016/j.chb.2015.12.062.

[27] E. Engelberg and L. Sjöberg, "Internet Use, Social Skills, and Adjustment," CyberPsychology & Behavior, vol. 7, no. 1, pp. 41–47, Feb. 2004, doi: 10.1089/109493104322820101.

[28] J. Morahan-Martin and P. Schumacher, "Loneliness and social uses of the Internet," Computers in Human Behavior, vol. 19, no. 6, pp. 659–671, Nov. 2003, doi: 10.1016/S0747-5632(03)00040-2.

[29] C. Herodotou, M. Kambouri, and N. Winters, "Dispelling the myth of the socio-emotionally dissatisfied gamer," Computers in Human Behavior, vol. 32, pp. 23–31, Mar. 2014, doi: 10.1016/j.chb.2013.10.054.

[30] R. F. Baumeister and M. R. Leary, "The Need to Belong: Desire for Interpersonal Attachments as a Fundamental Human Motivation," in Interpersonal Development, Routledge, 2007.

[31] E. L. Deci and R. M. Ryan, "The 'What' and 'Why' of Goal Pursuits: Human Needs and the Self-Determination of Behavior," Psychological Inquiry, vol. 11, no. 4, pp. 227–268, Oct. 2000, doi: 10.1207/S15327965PLI1104_01.

[32] T. L. James, P. B. Lowry, L. Wallace, and M. Warkentin, "The Effect of Belongingness on Obsessive-Compulsive Disorder in the Use of Online Social Networks," Journal of Management Information Systems, vol. 34, no. 2, pp. 560–596, Apr. 2017, doi: 10.1080/07421222.2017.1334496.

[33] M. Hassenzahl, "The Thing and I: Understanding the Relationship Between User and Product," in Funology 2: From Usability to Enjoyment, M. Blythe and A. Monk, Eds. in Human–Computer Interaction Series. Cham: Springer International Publishing, 2018, pp. 301–313. doi: 10.1007/978-3-319-68213-6_19.

[34] A. K. Przybylski, K. Murayama, C. R. DeHaan, and V. Gladwell, "Motivational, emotional, and behavioral correlates of fear of missing out," Computers in Human Behavior, vol. 29, no. 4, pp. 1841–1848, Jul. 2013, doi: 10.1016/j.chb.2013.02.014.

[35] S. Rigby and R. M. Ryan, Glued to Games: How Video Games Draw Us In and Hold Us Spellbound. Bloomsbury Publishing USA, 2011.

[36] M. Tarafdar, Q. Tu, B. S. Ragu-Nathan, and T. S. Ragu-Nathan, "The Impact of Technostress on Role Stress and Productivity," Journal of Management Information Systems, vol. 24, no. 1, pp. 301–328, Jul. 2007, doi: 10.2753/MIS0742-1222240109.

[37] J. Becker, M. Berger, H. Gimpel, and J. Lanzl, "Considering Characteristic Profiles of Technologies at the Digital Workplace: The Influence on Technostress," 2020.

[38] S. N. Talamas, K. I. Mavor, and D. I. Perrett, "Blinded by Beauty: Attractiveness Bias and Accurate Perceptions of Academic Performance," PLoS ONE, vol. 11, no. 2, p. e0148284, Feb. 2016, doi: 10.1371/journal.pone.0148284.

[39] J. Peña, M. Aridi Barake, and J. M. Falin, "Virtual leaders: Can customizing authoritarian and democratic business leader avatars influence altruistic behavior and leadership empowerment perceptions?," Computers in Human Behavior, vol. 141, p. 107616, Apr. 2023, doi: 10.1016/j.chb.2022.107616.

[40] G. Riva et al., "Affective Interactions Using Virtual Reality: The Link between Presence and Emotions," CyberPsychology & Behavior, vol. 10, no. 1, pp. 45–56, Feb. 2007, doi: 10.1089/cpb.2006.9993.

[41] J. M. Mittelstaedt, J. Wacker, and D. Stelling, "VR aftereffect and the relation of cybersickness and cognitive performance," Virtual Reality, vol. 23, no. 2, pp. 143–154, Jun. 2019, doi: 10.1007/s10055-018-0370-3.

[42] S. Cao, K. Nandakumar, R. Babu, and B. Thompson, "Game play in virtual reality driving simulation involving head-mounted display and comparison to desktop display," Virtual Reality, vol. 24, no. 3, pp. 503–513, Sep. 2020, doi: 10.1007/s10055-019-00412-x.

[43] R. Lavoie, K. Main, C. King, and D. King, "Virtual experience, real consequences: the potential negative emotional consequences of virtual reality gameplay," Virtual Reality, vol. 25, no. 1, pp. 69–81, Mar. 2021, doi: 10.1007/s10055-020-00440-y.

[44] A. Szpak, S. C. Michalski, D. Saredakis, C. S. Chen, and T. Loetscher, "Beyond Feeling Sick: The Visual and Cognitive Aftereffects of Virtual Reality," IEEE Access, vol. 7, pp. 130883–130892, 2019, doi: 10.1109/ACCESS.2019.2940073.

[45] T. Correa, A. W. Hinsley, and H. G. De Zúñiga, "Who interacts on the Web?: The intersection of users' personality and social media use," Computers in Human Behavior, vol. 26, no. 2, pp. 247–253, Mar. 2010, doi: 10.1016/j.chb.2009.09.003.

[46] R. A. Dunn and R. E. Guadagno, "My avatar and me – Gender and personality predictors of avatar-self discrepancy," Computers in Human Behavior, vol. 28, no. 1, pp. 97–106, Jan. 2012, doi: 10.1016/j.chb.2011.08.015.

[47] P. L. McLeod, Y.-C. Liu, and J. E. Axline, "When your Second Life comes knocking: Effects of personality on changes to real life from virtual world experiences," Computers in Human Behavior, vol. 39, pp. 59–70, Oct. 2014, doi: 10.1016/j.chb.2014.06.025.

[48] M. T. Whitty, G. Young, and L. Goodings, "What I won't do in pixels: Examining the limits of taboo violation in MMORPGs," Computers in Human Behavior, vol. 27, no. 1, pp. 268–275, Jan. 2011, doi: 10.1016/j.chb.2010.08.004.

[49] T. van Schneider, "The Post Virtual Reality Sadness," Desk of van Schneider. [Online]. Available from: https://medium.com/desk-of-van-schneider/the-post-virtual-reality-sadness-fb4a1ccacae4 [Accessed: May 9, 2025].

[50] M. J. Park, D. J. Kim, U. Lee, E. J. Na, and H. J. Jeon, "A Literature Overview of Virtual Reality (VR) in Treatment of Psychiatric Disorders: Recent Advances and Limitations," Front. Psychiatry, vol. 10, Jul. 2019, doi: 10.3389/fpsyt.2019.00505.

[51] C. Vidal, T. Lhaksampa, L. Miller, and R. Platt, "Social media use and depression in adolescents: a scoping review," International review of psychiatry (Abingdon, England), vol. 32, no. 3, p. 235, May 2020, doi: 10.1080/09540261.2020.1720623.

[52] B. A. Primack, A. Shensa, J. E. Sidani, C. G. Escobar-Viera, and M. J. Fine, "Temporal Associations Between Social Media Use and Depression," Am J Prev Med, vol. 60, no. 2, pp. 179–188, Feb. 2021, doi: 10.1016/j.amepre.2020.09.014.

[53] M. Botvinick and J. Cohen, "Rubber hands 'feel' touch that eyes see," Nature, vol. 391, no. 6669, pp. 756–756, Feb. 1998, doi: 10.1038/35784.

[54] C. Peckmann, K. Kannen, M. C. Pensel, S. Lux, A. Philipsen, and N. Braun, "Virtual reality induces symptoms of depersonalization and derealization: A longitudinal randomised control trial," Computers in Human Behavior, vol. 131, p. 107233, Jun. 2022, doi: 10.1016/j.chb.2022.107233.

[55] R. Tambone et al., "Changing your body changes your eating attitudes: embodiment of a slim virtual avatar induces avoidance of high-calorie food," Heliyon, vol. 7, no. 7, p. e07515, Jul. 2021, doi: 10.1016/j.heliyon.2021.e07515.

[56] M. Slater et al., "A Virtual Reprise of the Stanley Milgram Obedience Experiments," PLoS ONE, vol. 1, no. 1, p. e39, Dec. 2006, doi: 10.1371/journal.pone.0000039.

[57] R. Gonçalves, A. L. Pedrozo, E. S. F. Coutinho, I. Figueira, and P. Ventura, "Efficacy of Virtual Reality Exposure Therapy in the Treatment of PTSD: A Systematic Review," PLoS ONE, vol. 7, no. 12, p. e48469, Dec. 2012, doi: 10.1371/journal.pone.0048469.

[58] M. A. Franks, "The Desert of the Unreal: Inequality in Virtual and Augmented Reality," vol. 51.

[59] M. W. Stevens, D. Dorstyn, P. H. Delfabbro, and D. L. King, "Global prevalence of gaming disorder: A systematic review and meta-analysis," Aust N Z J Psychiatry, vol. 55, no. 6, pp. 553–568, Jun. 2021, doi: 10.1177/0004867420962851.

[60] C. S. Andreassen et al., "The relationship between addictive use of social media and video games and symptoms of psychiatric disorders: A large-scale cross-sectional study.," Psychology of Addictive Behaviors, vol. 30, no. 2, pp. 252–262, Mar. 2016, doi: 10.1037/adb0000160.

[61] U. Oberst, E. Wegmann, B. Stodt, M. Brand, and A. Chamarro, "Negative consequences from heavy social networking in adolescents: The mediating role of fear of missing out," Journal of Adolescence, vol. 55, no. 1, pp. 51–60, 2017, doi: 10.1016/j.adolescence.2016.12.008.

[62] S. L. Buglass, J. F. Binder, L. R. Betts, and J. D. M. Underwood, "Motivators of online vulnerability: The impact of social network site use and FOMO," Computers in Human Behavior, vol. 66, pp. 248–255, Jan. 2017, doi: 10.1016/j.chb.2016.09.0

Cooperation between Unmanned Aerial Vehicles and Wireless Cellular System

Vicente Casares-Giner
Departamento de Comunicaciones
Universitat Politècnica de València
46022 València, Spain.
Email: vcasares@upv.es

Xiaohu Ge, Yuxi Zhao
China International Joint Research Center of
Green Communications and Networking
Huazhong University of Science and Technology. Whuhan, China
Email: xhge@hust.edu.cn, zhao_yuxi@hust.edu.cn

***Abstract*—We consider the cooperation of Unmanned Aerial Vehicles (UAV) with wireless cellular mobile systems. UAVs collaborate closely with Base Stations (BSs) when they are occasionally present in the coverage area of a BS. From the tele-traffic point of view, UAVs can provide additional capacity to cellular BSs such as to alleviate saturation conditions during periods of high traffic congestion. The assignment of traffic channels works as follows; when a call arrives to the system it is assigned to any free channel of the BS. If all channels of the BS are busy, the call is assigned to any free channel of any present UAV. If all channels of the present UAVs are busy, the call is lost. When a call served by a given BS ends, any other call in progress on a UAV, if any, is transferred to the released channel of that BS. When a UAV leaves the coverage area of the BS, the calls in progress in that UAV are transferred to the idle channels of other UAVs, as many as possible; and calls that cannot be transferred are lost. The scenario under study is modeled as a 2-D Markov process. One dimension takes into account the number of UAVs present in the system and the other dimension deals with the number of calls in progress. We evaluate, i) the blocking probability of new calls, ii) the forced termination probability of ongoing calls, iii) when an ongoing call ends at the BS, the probability of transferring an ongoing call from a given UAV to that BS, and iv) when a UAV leaves the service area, the probability of transferring its ongoing calls to another UAV.**

Keywords*—*Unmanned Aerial Vehicle, Quasi-Birth-Death process.

I. INTRODUCTION

Unmanned Aerial Vehicles (UAV) are identified as aircraf without humans on board. They can support a variety of services such as agriculture applications [1], remote sensing [2], wireless internet services and telephone services, the support to cellular system during high traffic load situation [3], among others private business [4]-[7]. Also, see [8] for a nice survey.

The concept of UAV also has been commonly recognized as Remotely Piloted Aerial System (RPAS), more commonly known as "drones". In fact, the term "autonomous helicopter" was predominant until 2015 when the term drone became more usual when referring to unmanned aircrafts [1]. UAVs are located at the troposphere, with a maximum altitude of 10 Km. roughly speaking. We also mention the concept of High-Altitude Platform Stations (HAPS). HAPS are usually Unmanned Aerial Systems (UAS) located above the commercial jet air planes, in the stratosphere, between 10 Km and 50 Km altitude, approximately [9]. HAPS can provide intensive computing and can endure at a fixed position in opposite with the lower computing capacity and less endure or presence of UAVs; but they can closely cooperate in a hierarchical manner for various Internet of Things (IoT) applications [10].

In this paper, we analyze the use of such UAVs that from time to time are present in the coverage area of a given cellular Base Station (BS). When one BS is fully busy, the new traffic load is offered to some UAV present in the coverage area of the BS. If all the present UAV are fully busy, the traffic is lost.

As soon as a call in progress on the BS ends, any call in progress on any UAV is handed over the released channel of the BS. In fact, it is a reassignment to a new channel of a call in progress, a repacking procedure. When one UAV leaves the coverage area of a BS, as many calls as possible in progress at the UVA are transferred to other free channels of the present UAVs, while the rest are forced to finish.

Key Performance Indicator (KPIs) parameters are, among others, the blocking probability of initial fresh calls, the probability that one ongoing call in a UAV be transferred to a BS, a handover procedure, and due to the exit of one UVA from the system, the forced termination probability of admitted calls in progress, the probability distribution function of the number of interrupted call in progress in one UAV, and the probability distribution function of the number of calls that are transferred from the leaving UAV to the other present UAVs.

The analysis is carried out using Markovian tools. In particular, we identify the scenario of a single BS with several UAVs potentially present in the coverage area. A Quasi-Birth-Death (QBD) process is obtained and the mentioned KPIs are expressed in a closed form solution.

The structure of the paper is as follows. After Section I, the analytical model is presented in Section II. Section III shows the key system parameters, such as the blocking probability of new calls, the forced termination probability, the distribution of calls that are forced to terminate and the handover signaling traffic load. Numerical results derived from the analytical model are presented in Section IV. The paper ends with some basic conclusions in Section V.

II. THE MODEL

We assume a single BS with a total number of P primary channels. A finite number of V UAVs are occasionally present in the coverage area of the BS. The presence versus absence of

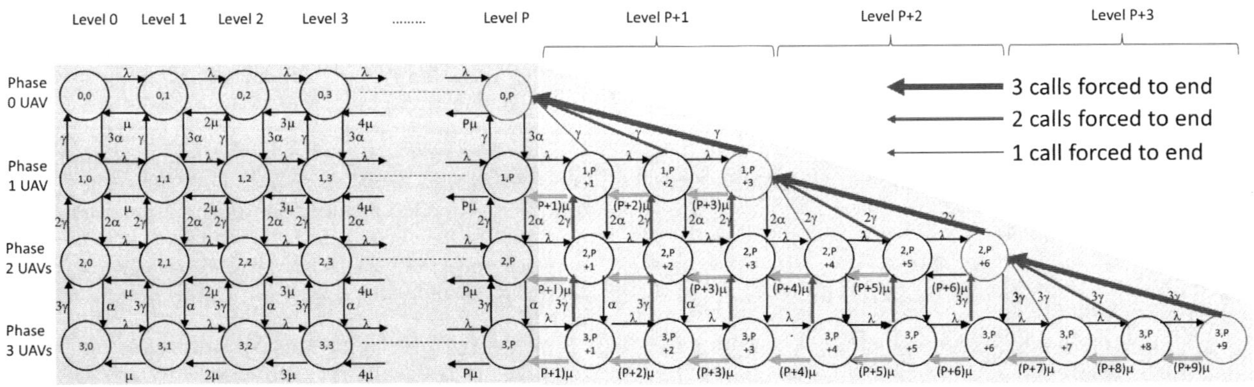

Fig. 1. The 2D Markov process for a number of $UAVs$, $V = 3$, for a number of secondary channels per UAV, $S = 3$ and for a generic number of primary channels, P.

one UAV follows an ON-OFF process. Each UAV is equipped with S secondary channels.

A. The admission of arrival calls

When a new or fresh call arrives to the system, first, it will be allocated to one idle primary channel of the BS, if any. If all primary channels are busy, the call will be allocated to one idle secondary channel of one UAV, if any. Otherwise, the call is lost.

B. The departure of calls. The repacking of ongoing calls

When one call in progress in a given primary channel ends, the released primary channel will be assigned to any call in progress in the secondary channels of an arbitrary UAV, if any. This is, in fact, a handover procedure of a call in progress in any UAV to the BS.

C. The departure of a UAV from the coverage area of a BS

When one UAV abandons the system, as many calls as possible that are in progress in this UAV will be reallocated to other UAVs, that is, a handover process is performed from the leaving UAV to others UAV with some free secondary channels. Other calls that are not possible to be reassigned are forced to terminate.

D. The analytical model

Arrival calls follow a Poisson process with rate λ. The service call is assumed to be exponentially distributed with rate equal to μ. Individually, the presence of one UAV in the coverage area of the BS follows an exponential distribution with rate γ and the absence of the system of this UAV is also exponentially distributed, with rate α.

E. The Quasi-Birth-Death process

Figure 1 illustrates the Markov process for an arbitrary number of primary channels, P, and a total of $V = 3$ $UAVs$, each one equipped with $S = 3$ secondary channels. Easily, we identify a Quasi-Birth-Death process (QBD) process where the *levels* are the block structure, from 0 to $P + V$ and the *phases* are the intra-block structure, from 0 to V. To be more precise, according to Figure 1, each level between 0 and P is composed of a single column of states, while each level between $P + 1$ and $P + V$ is composed of S columns of states. Notice that each block in the *level* interval $[0, P]$ has $V + 1$ phases, and the range of phases on each block in the level interval $l \in [P + 1, P + V]$ is $[l - P, V]$. Observe that the block size in the level interval $l \in [0, P]$ is $V + 1$ states while the block size in the level interval $l \in [P + 1, P + V]$ is $S * (V + P + 1 - l)$ states. In other words, the top first row of states in Figure 1 reflects that there are no UAVs active in the system, the second row reflects that there is a single UAV active in the system, and so on.

The states located in the green area, on the left, indicate that the UAV devices do not support any calls in progress. Thick red arrows show the forced termination of ongoing calls. The horizontal thick green arrows show the task, although not always, of transferring one call in progress on the UAVs to the BS, a handover execution. The vertical thick blue arrows show the task, although not always, of transferring one call in progress in one UAV to another UAV, an inter-UAV handover execution.

Let $\pi_{k,n}$ denote the probability that k $UAVs$ be present in the system and with a total of n calls in progress. Clearly, from the above comments, the number of calls in progress carried by the BS is $\min(P, n)$ and the number of calls carried by the UAVs is $\max(0, n - P) \leq S * V$. Notice that the value of k is coincident with the phase of the QBD process. These 2D-Markov processes can be solved numerically using some basic algorithm for a QBD process; see [11][12] for details.

III. KEY SYSTEM PARAMETERS

Here, we present some parameters of interest. Obviously, the fraction of time a given UAV is present in the coverage area of the BS is given by,

$$Pr(\text{One UAV is present}) = \frac{\alpha}{\gamma + \alpha} \quad (1)$$

and the mean number of UAVs that are present in the system is given by,

$$\text{Mean number of UAVs present in the system} = \frac{V\alpha}{\gamma + \alpha} \quad (2)$$

A. The blocking probability

Since the arrival process is Poisson, taking into account the Poisson Arrivals See Time Averages (PASTA) property [13], the blocking probability of new calls, i.e., the fraction of offered calls that are blocked due to the lack of resources, is given by

$$\begin{aligned} P_b &= \pi_{0,P} + \pi_{1,P+S} + \pi_{2,P+2S} + \dots \\ &\dots + \pi_{V-1,P+(V-1)S} + \pi_{V,P+VS} = \sum_{k=0}^{V} \pi_{k,P+kS} \end{aligned} \quad (3)$$

Observe that P_b is evaluated by adding all the probabilities that take into account the saturation of the system, that is, at the arrival time of one incoming call, all primary channels of the BS and all secondary channels of all UAV are busy, (in Figure 1, the states with red circle).

B. The forced termination probability

The fraction of offered calls that are forced to terminate when one UAV abandons the system is expressed as, (in Figure 1, the transitions with red arrows),

$$\begin{aligned} P_{ft} &= \frac{\text{Rate of forced termination}}{\text{Rate of admitted calls}} = \\ &= \frac{\gamma \sum_{k=1}^{V} k \sum_{m=1}^{S} m\pi_{k,P+(k-1)S+m}}{\lambda(1-P_b)} \end{aligned} \quad (4)$$

C. The distribution of calls that are forced to terminate

Let $f_{m;V,S}$ be the probability that just immediately after one UAV leaves the coverage area, m ongoing calls are forced to terminate. Since each UAV is equipped with a maximum of S secondary channels, clearly, the domain of $f_{m;V,S}$ is the set of integer numbers $m \in [0, S]$. Then, the Probability Distribution Function (PDF) of $f_{m;V,S}$ is given by, (in Figure 1, the transitions with red arrow show the forced interruption of at least one call in progress),

$$f_{m;V,S} = \begin{cases} \dfrac{\sum_{k=1}^{V} k \sum_{n=0}^{P+(k-1)S} \pi_{k,n}}{\sum_{k=1}^{V} k \sum_{n=0}^{P+kS} \pi_{k,n}}, & \text{for } m = 0 \\[2ex] \dfrac{\sum_{k=1}^{V} k\pi_{k,P+(k-1)S+m}}{\sum_{k=1}^{V} k \sum_{n=0}^{P+kS} \pi_{k,n}}, & \text{for } m = 1, \dots, S \end{cases} \quad (5)$$

D. The handover signalling traffic load

It is interesting to see the signalling traffic load due the rearrangement, repacking or re-switching of ongoing calls. We distinguish two cases; first, when a call in progress in one UAV is transferred to the BS and second, when a call in progress in one UAV is transferred to another UAV. In the first case, the handover is produced when one ongoing call carried by the BS ends. In the second case, the handover occurs because a UAV leaves the system. Next, we deal with the corresponding analytical formulation.

1) The handover to the BS: We observe the end of ongoing calls on the BS (calls that are carried by any UAV do not cause any handover task when they finish). When one ongoing call in the BS ends, one call carried by one UAV, if any, is transferred to the released channel of the BS. Since calls ends one at a time, the fraction of calls that are transferred from any secondary channel to the released primary channel is expressed as, (in Figure 1, horizontal transitions with blue colour),

$$\begin{aligned} P_{hd-BS} &= \frac{\text{Rate of handovers to the BS}}{\text{Rate of admitted calls}} = \\ &= \frac{\mu P(\sum_{k=1}^{V} \sum_{j=1}^{kS} \pi_{k,P+j})}{\lambda(1-P_b)} = \frac{P(\sum_{k=1}^{V} \sum_{j=1}^{kS} \pi_{k,P+j})}{A(1-P_b)} = \\ &= \frac{P(1 - \sum_{k=0}^{V} \sum_{j=0}^{P} \pi_{k,j})}{A(1-P_b)} \end{aligned} \quad (6)$$

In other words, Eq. (6) gives the probability that, when one call carried by a primary channel ends, the system performs a handover of another call in progress in a secondary channel to the released primary channel. So, the rate of handover to the BS is given by

$$\text{Rate of handovers to the BS} = P_{hd-BS}\lambda(1 - P_b) \quad (7)$$

2) The distribution of handovers between UAVs: When one UAV leaves the coverage area of the BS, probably not all ongoing calls in the UAV are forced to terminate. If any other UAV that is present in the coverage area has any free channels, any ongoing call in the leaving UAV can be transferred to this second UAV, (in Figure 1, see the vertical transitions with green colour). Notice that it is possible to handover more than one call in progress at the same time.

First, we assume that just immediately before one UAV abandons the coverage area of the BS, there are v UAVs in this area with a total of m calls in progress in all the *UAVs*. Clearly, $0 \le v \le V$ and $0 \le m \le vS$. Let $r_{i;m,v,S}$ be the probability that this specific UAV is holding i calls in progress ($0 \le i \le S$). Then, $r_{i;m,v,S}$ is given by

TABLE I. # OF HANDOVERS BETWEEN *UAVs*, $\boldsymbol{H}$, AND # OF CALLS FORCED TO TERMINATE, F, FOR $v = 1, 2, \ldots, V = 3$ AND $S = 3$

	$level \rightarrow$	$P+1$	$P+2$	$P+3$	$P+4$	$P+5$	$P+6$	$P+7$	$P+8$	$P+9$
	$m \rightarrow$	1	2	3	4	5	6	7	8	9
$phase \downarrow$	$r_{i;m,v,S}$	$(\boldsymbol{H}, F)$	$(\boldsymbol{H}, F)$	$(\boldsymbol{H}, F)$	$(\boldsymbol{H}, F)$	$(\boldsymbol{H}, F)$	$(\boldsymbol{H}, F)$	$(\boldsymbol{H}, F)$	$(\boldsymbol{H}, F)$	$(\boldsymbol{H}, F)$
$v = 1$	$r_{0;m,1,3}$									
	$r_{1;m,1,3}$	$(0, 1)$								
	$r_{2;m,1,3}$		$(0, 2)$							
	$r_{3;m,1,3}$			$(0, 3)$						
$v = 2$	$r_{0;m,2,3}$	$(0, 0)$	$(0, 0)$	$(0, 0)$						
	$r_{1;m,2,3}$	$(1, 0)$	$(1, 0)$	$(1, 0)$	$(0, 1)$					
	$r_{2;m,2,3}$		$(2, 0)$	$(2, 0)$	$(1, 1)$	$(0, 2)$				
	$r_{3;m,2,3}$			$(3, 0)$	$(2, 1)$	$(1, 2)$	$(0, 3)$			
$v = 3$	$r_{0;m,3,3}$	$(0, 0)$	$(0, 0)$	$(0, 0)$	$(0, 0)$	$(0, 0)$	$(0, 0)$			
	$r_{1;m,3,3}$	$(1, 0)$	$(1, 0)$	$(1, 0)$	$(1, 0)$	$(1, 0)$	$(1, 0)$	$(0, 1)$		
	$r_{2;m,3,3}$		$(2, 0)$	$(2, 0)$	$(2, 0)$	$(2, 0)$	$(2, 0)$	$(1, 1)$	$(0, 2)$	
	$r_{3;m,3,3}$			$(3, 0)$	$(3, 0)$	$(3, 0)$	$(3, 0)$	$(2, 1)$	$(1, 2)$	$(0, 3)$

TABLE II. RESPECTIVE PROBABILITIES OF ELEMENTS IN TABLE I FOR $(\boldsymbol{H}, F)$, FOR $v = 1, 2, \ldots, V = 3$ AND $S = 3$

	$level \rightarrow$	$P+1$	$P+2$	$P+3$	$P+4$	$P+5$	$P+6$	$P+7$	$P+8$	$P+9$
	$m \rightarrow$	1	2	3	4	5	6	7	8	9
$phase \downarrow$	$r_{i;m,v,S}$	$(\boldsymbol{H}, F)$	$(\boldsymbol{H}, F)$	$(\boldsymbol{H}, F)$	$(\boldsymbol{H}, F)$	$(\boldsymbol{H}, F)$	$(\boldsymbol{H}, F)$	$(\boldsymbol{H}, F)$	$(\boldsymbol{H}, F)$	$(\boldsymbol{H}, F)$
$v = 1$	$r_{0;m,1,3}$									
	$r_{1;m,1,3}$	1.000								
	$r_{2;m,1,3}$		1.000							
	$r_{3;m,1,3}$			1.000						
$v = 2$	$r_{0;m,2,3}$	0.500	0.200	0.050						
	$r_{1;m,2,3}$	0.500	0.600	0.450	0.200					
	$r_{2;m,2,3}$		0.200	0.450	0.600	0.500				
	$r_{3;m,2,3}$			0.050	0.200	0.500	1.000			
$v = 3$	$r_{0;m,3,3}$	0.6666	0.4166	0.2380	0.1190	0.0476	0.0119			
	$r_{1;m,3,3}$	0.3333	0.5000	0.5357	0.4761	0.3571	0.2142	0.0833		
	$r_{2;m,3,3}$		0.0833	0.2142	0.3571	0.4761	0.5357	0.5000	0.3333	
	$r_{3;m,3,3}$			0.0119	0.0476	0.1190	0.2380	0.4166	0.6666	1.000

$$r_{i;m,v,S} = \frac{\binom{S}{i}\binom{S(v-1)}{m-i}}{\binom{vS}{m}}, \tag{8}$$

with $\max(0, m - S(v-1)) \leq i \leq \min(m, S)$

being $\binom{y}{x} = \frac{y!}{x!(y-x)!}$ $(0 \leq x \leq y)$, the binomial coefficient.

In other words, at the instant one specific UAV exits from the coverage are of the BS and there are i calls in progress in this UAV, the number of busy channels in other UAVs is $\max(m-i, 0)$, and the number of free channels in other UAVs is $S(v-1) - \max(m-i, 0)$. Then, the number of handovers from the UAV that leaves the system to other present UAVs is equal to $\min(S(v-1) - \max(m-i, 0), i)$ and the number of calls that are forced to terminate is $\max(0, i - \min(S(v-1) - \max(m-i, 0), i))$.

As one example, let us consider a maximum number of $V = 3$ UAVs, each one with $S = 3$ secondary channels, see Figure 1. When the system leaves, for example, the state $(v, P+m) = (3, P+7)$ because of the departure of one UAV, 1 ongoing call is forced to terminate and the number of possible handovers can be 0 or 1 or 2. And when the system leaves the state $(v, P+m) = (2, P+5)$ due to the departure of one UAV, 2 ongoing calls are forced to terminate and the number of possible handovers can be 0 or 1. Table I shows the different options.

The following fact is clearly satisfied:

$$\sum_{i=\max(0, m-S(v-1))}^{\min(m,S)} r_{i;m,v,S} = 1 \tag{9}$$

Second, knowing the probabilities $\pi_{k,n}$ of the QBD process of Figure 1, the rate of handovers from the specific UAV to other UAVs, that are executed just immediately after that specific UAV leaves the system, is given by

$$\begin{aligned} g_{z;V,S} &= \\ &= \sum_{v=1}^{V} v\gamma \sum_{m=0}^{P} \pi_{v,m} + \sum_{v=2}^{V} v\gamma \sum_{m=1}^{(v-1)S} \pi_{v,P+m} r_{0;m,v,S} \\ &+ \sum_{v=1}^{V} v\gamma \sum_{m=(v-1)S+1}^{vS} \pi_{v,P+m} r_{m-(v-1)S;m,v,S} \end{aligned} \tag{10}$$

for $z = 0$ handovers

and

$$\begin{aligned} g_{z;V,S} &= \sum_{v=2}^{V} v\gamma \Bigg(\sum_{m=1}^{(v-1)S} \pi_{v,P+m} r_{z;m,v,S} \\ &+ \sum_{m=(v-1)S+1}^{vS-z} \pi_{v,P+m} r_{m-(v-1)S;m,v,S} \Bigg) \end{aligned} \tag{11}$$

for $z = 1, \ldots, S$ handovers

Then, the probability to execute z handovers between UAVs is expressed as, from (10) and (11),

$$h_{z;V,S} = \frac{g_{z;V,S}}{\sum_{n=0}^{S} g_{n;V,S}} \quad \text{for } z = 0, \ldots, S \text{ handovers} \tag{12}$$

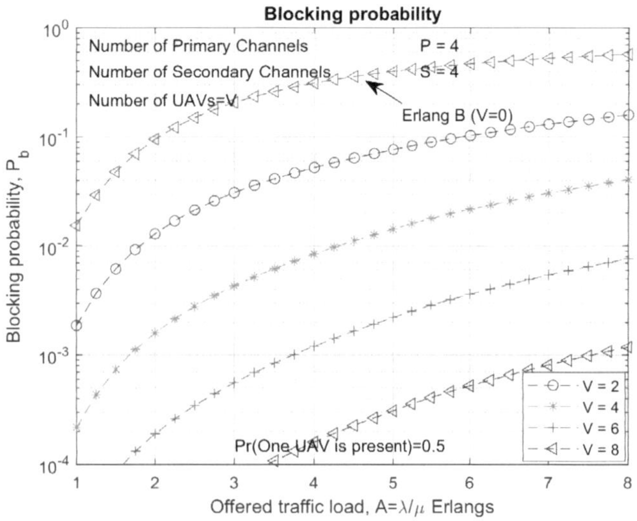

Fig. 2. Blocking probability for a number of primary and secondary channels, respectively $P = 4$ and $S = 4$ and for several numbers, V, of UAV.

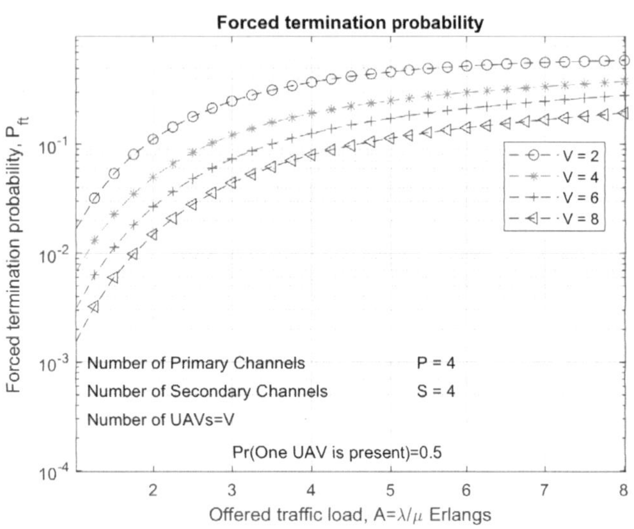

Fig. 3. Forced termination probability for a number of primary and secondary channels, respectively $P = 4$ and $S = 4$ and for several numbers of UAV (V).

IV. Numerical analysis

Here, we perform the evaluation of the KPI parameters mentioned in previous section. Without loss of generality, we set $P = 4$ primary channels, $S = 4$ secondary channels per UAV and $V = 2, 4, 6, 8$ UAVs. The fraction of time one UAV

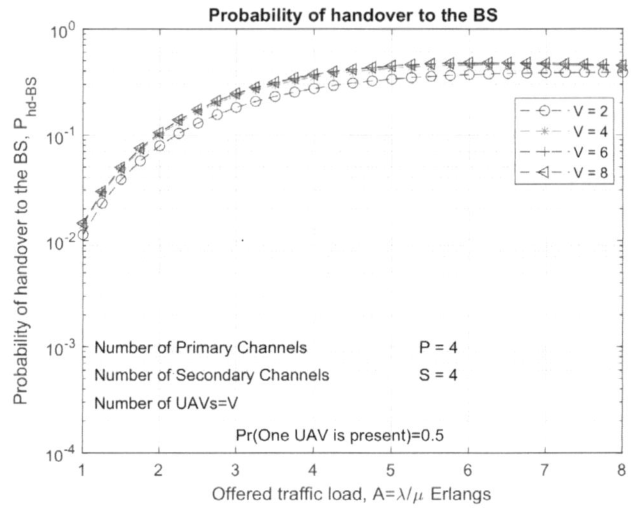

Fig. 4. Handover probability to the BS for a number of primary and secondary channels, respectively $P = 4$ and $S = 4$ and for several numbers of UAV (V).

is in the system is equal to 0.5, see Eq. (1). Figure 2 shows the blocking probability, Eq. (3). The offered traffic is $A \in [1 : 0.25 : 8]$ Erlangs. Clearly, the lost probability increases when the offered traffic A increases. Here, for instance, if we fix the blocking probability to be no greater than 0.01 and no UAV are used, this goal is not achieved for a traffic $A \geq 1$ Erlangs. But this objective is achieved with the help of $V = 2$ UAVs, when the traffic is not greater than $A = 1.75$ Erlangs. With $V = 4$ UAVs, the traffic can be increased until $A = 4.75$ Erlangs, approximately. Also, notice the significant reduction of the blocking probability when V increases.

Figure 3 deals with the forced termination, see Eq. (4). This is the probability that one arbitrary admitted call be forced to terminate because one UAV exits from the coverage area of the BS. Obviously, this probability increases as the offered traffic increases, as expected.

Figure 4 reflects the probability that one admitted call be transferred from a secondary channel of one UAV to a primary channel of the BS, see Eq. (6). We observe that, for a given offered traffic, this handover probability increases when the number V of UAVs increases; but this increase is very small.

Figure 5 shows the Probability Distribution Function (PDF) given by Eq. (5). It gives the the number of calls forced to terminate when one UAV leaves the system. The plots are obtained for a number of primary channels $P = 4$, a number of UAVs $V = 4$, a number of secondary channels per each UAV equal to $S = 4$ and for an offered traffic equal to $A = [1.0 : 0.5 : 3.0]$ Erlangs. In general, the probability decreases when the number of calls forced to terminate increases. Better performance is achieved when the offered traffic is low, as expected.

Finally, Figure 6 gives the PDF of the number of calls transferred from one leaving UAV to the other UAVs that are present in the system. Here, the parameters are the same as for Figure 5. As we can see from the last two figures, when a UAV leaves the system, 97% of the time there is no handover

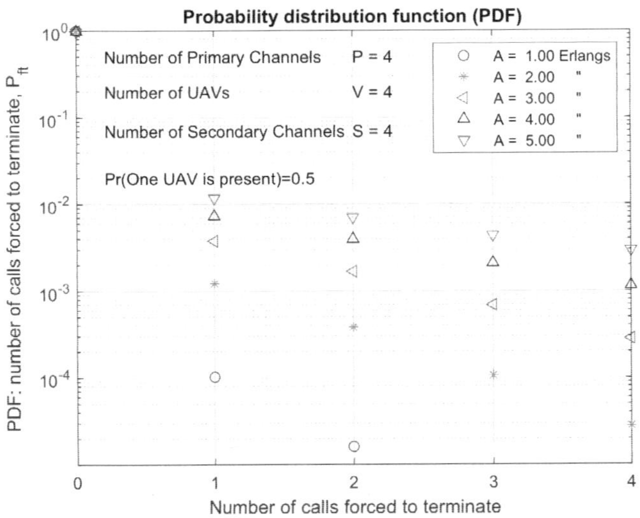

Fig. 5. Probability Distribution Function of the number of calls forced to terminate when on UAV leaves the coverage area of the BS.

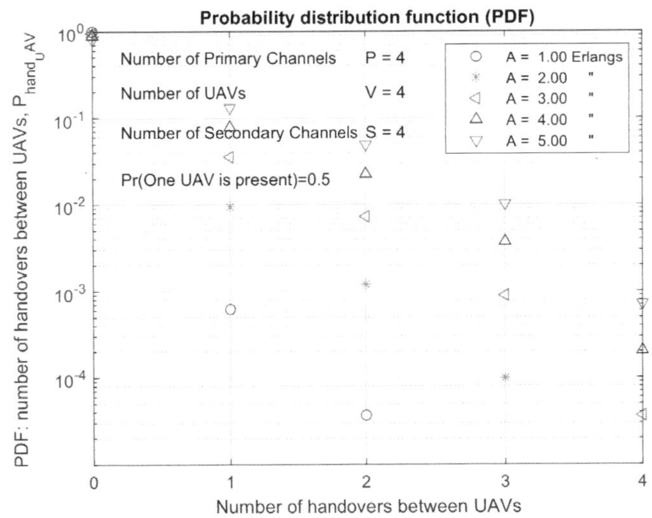

Fig. 6. Probability Distribution Function of the number of calls transferred from one leaving UAV to the others.

to execute.

V. CONCLUSIONS

In this paper, we have analyzed a system composed of a single Base Station (BS) and several Unmanned Aerial Vehicles (UAVs) individually and independently of each other, that, from time to time are present in the coverage area of the BS. The main Key Performance Indicator (KPI) parameters we have evaluated are, first, the blocking probability of fresh calls, second, the probability of handing over a call to the BS when one ongoing call in the BS ends and when one UAV abandons the coverage area of the BS, third, the forced termination probability of calls in progress, fourth, the probability distribution function of the number of interrupted calls, and fifth, the probability distribution function of the number of calls transferred from the leaving UAV to other UAVs.

The analysis has been carried out using Markovian assumptions, therefore, an analytically close expression of the KPI parameters is obtained. The evaluation has been conducted using the model of a QBD process. Clear guidelines are given for the design of the number of primary channels, P, installed in the BS, for the number of UAVs, V, present/absent in the coverage area and for the number of secondary channels, S, available on each UAV.

ACKNOWLEDGMENT

The work of V. Casares-Giner was supported in part by Grants PID2021-123168NB-I00 and TED2021-131387BI00, both funded by MCIN/AEI/10.13039/501100011033 and the European Union (A way of making Europe/ERDF and NextGenerationEU/RTRP, respectively). This research is also supported in part by NSFC Grant 62441217.

REFERENCES

[1] J. del Cerro, C. Cruz Ulloa, A. Barrientos and J. de León Rivas, "Unmanned Aerial Vehicles in Agriculture: A Survey", Agronomy, 2021, vol. 11, issue 2, p203. https://DOI.org/10.3390/agronomy11020203.

[2] H. Yao, R. Qin, and X. Chen, "Unmanned Aerial Vehicle for Remote Sensing Applications—A Review", Remote Sens. 2019, 11, 1443; DOI:10.3390/rs11121443.

[3] M. E. Rivero-Angeles, I. Villordo-Jimenez, I. Y. Orea-Flores, N. Torres-Cruz, and A. Pretelín Ricárdez, "Erlang-U: Blocking Probability of UAV-Assisted Cellular Systems", Information 2024, 15, 192. https://DOI.org/10.3390/info15040192.

[4] K. P. Valavanis and G. J. Vachtsevanos, "Handbook of Unmanned Aerial Vehicles", Springer Publishing Company, Incorporated, ISBN: 9048197066 (ISBN-13: 978-1489987440). August, 2014.

[5] Y. Zeng, R. Zhang, and T. J. Lim, "Wireless Communications with Unmanned Aerial Vehicles: Opportunities and Challenges", February 2016. ArXiv:1602.03602v1.

[6] Y. Li and L. Cai, "UAV-Assisted Dynamic Coverage in a Heterogeneous Cellular System", in IEEE Network, vol. 31, no. 4, pp. 56-61, July-August 2017, DOI: 10.1109/MNET.2017.1600280.

[7] J. Kim, S. Kim, C. Ju and H. I. Son, "Unmanned Aerial Vehicles in Agriculture: A Review of Perspective of Platform, Control, and Applications", in IEEE Access, vol. 7, pp. 105100-105115, 2019, DOI: 10.1109/ACCESS.2019.2932119.

[8] F. Ahmed, J. C. Mohanta, A. Keshari and P. S. Yadav, "Recent Advances in Unmanned Aerial Vehicles: A Review" Arabian Journal for Science and Engineering; vol. 47, 7963–7984, 2022. https://DOI.org/10.1007/s13369-022-06738-0.

[9] A. Aragon-Zavala, J.L. Cuevas-Ruiz, and J.A. Delgado-Penin, "High-Altitude Platforms for Wireless Communications", ISBN: 978-0-470-51061-2. Wiley, 2008.

[10] Z. Jia, Q. Wu, C. Dong, C. Yuen, and Z. Han, "Hierarchical Aerial Computing for Internet of Things via Cooperation of HAPs and UAVs", arXiv:2202.06046v1 [cs.NI] 12 Feb 2022.

[11] G. Latouche and V. Ramaswami, "Introduction to Matrix Analytic Methods in Stochastic Modeling" ASA-SIAM Series on Statistics and Applied Probability, Philadelphia, Pennsylvania, 1999.

[12] A. S. Alfa, "Queueing Theory for Telecommunications: Discrete Time Modelling of a Single Node System", ISBN-10: 1489987444. Springer. 2010.

[13] R. W. Wolff, "Poisson Arrivals See Time Averages", Oper. Res., vol. 30, pp. 223-231. DOI:10.1287/opre.30.2.223. Corpus ID: 38853098.

[14] Z. Zhao et al., "Smart Unmanned Aerial Vehicles as base stations placement to improve the mobile network operations", Computer Communications, vol. 181, pp. 45–57, 2022.

Usability Study of the CICERONE App for Telemonitoring COPD Patients

Patricia Camacho Magriñán[1,2], Daniel Sánchez-Morillo[1,2], Regla Moreno Mellado[1,2],
Eva Vázquez Gandullo[1,3], Alfonso Marín Andreu[1,3], Antonio León Jiménez[1,3]
[1] Institute for Biomedical Research and Innovation of Cádiz (INiBICA)
Puerta del Mar University Hospital, Cádiz, Spain.
[2] Bioengineering, Automation, and Robotics Research Group
Department of Automation Engineering, Electronics, and Computer Architecture and Networks
University of Cádiz, Puerto Real, Spain.
[3] Pulmonology Department, Puerta del Mar University Hospital, Cádiz, Spain.
e-mail: {patricia.camachomagri, daniel.morillo, mariaregla.moreno}@uca.es
{antonio.leon.sspa, eva.vazquez.gandullo.sspa}@juntadeandalucia.es
alfonsomarinn@gmail.com

***Abstract*—Telemedicine is a promising tool for the management of Chronic Obstructive Pulmonary Disease (COPD), but its implementation faces challenges related to, among other issues, patient acceptance and usability. In this context, the effectiveness of telemonitoring systems depends not only on their accuracy in predicting exacerbations but also on their ability to integrate intuitively and efficiently into users' daily lives. The CICERONE project has developed a multimodal home telemonitoring system for COPD patients that collects data on symptoms, environmental parameters, lifestyle, and biomedical information. This work presents a study focused on the system's usability, evaluated in three stages: a) initial testing of a mock-up with patients; b) functional trials with volunteers; and c) final testing with patients participating in the project. The development followed an iterative approach based on user feedback and evaluations using the System Usability Scale (SUS). The results highlight how iteration and user-centered design have improved the patient experience and optimized the system's functionality. This study underscores the importance of usability in the design of telemonitoring tools to ensure their adoption and effectiveness in real clinical settings, promoting a more personalized and proactive approach to COPD management.**

Keywords-COPD; Usability; Telemonitoring; Telemedicine; Exacerbation.

I. INTRODUCTION

Chronic Obstructive Pulmonary Disease (COPD) is described as a heterogeneous lung disorder manifested by persistent respiratory symptoms, such as dyspnea, cough, sputum production, and acute exacerbations. These manifestations are associated with alterations in the airways, such as bronchitis or bronchiolitis, and in the alveoli, such as emphysema, resulting in progressive and persistent airflow obstruction [1]. COPD is a severe and debilitating disease that poses a significant challenge to healthcare systems due to its high prevalence and impact on morbidity and mortality [2]. According to the World Health Organization (WHO), it is currently the third leading cause of death worldwide [3], responsible for approximately 3.23 million deaths annually, with a projected increase to over 4.5 million by 2030.

The course of this disease is characterized by the occurrence of exacerbations, acute episodes of worsening respiratory symptoms [4]. These exacerbations not only affect lung function but also negatively impact the mental health of patients and worsen comorbidities. As a result, the disease progresses, and patients experience a progressive decline that leads to high healthcare resource consumption. Moreover, exacerbations increase the likelihood of recurrence, and more than 20% of patients hospitalized for this cause die within the year following discharge [5]. This highlights the need to detect and manage these crises early to mitigate their impact on disease progression, patient quality of life, and the economic costs borne by healthcare systems and associated with the management of this condition.

Home telemonitoring has emerged as a promising strategy to prevent exacerbations in COPD patients. Home monitoring of these patients has significantly evolved in recent years with the development of telemedicine systems and wearable devices capable of measuring physiological parameters in real time. Various strategies have been proposed, including the use of sensors to measure oxygen saturation, respiratory rate, physical activity, and sleep quality, as well as mobile applications for symptom tracking and electronic questionnaires [6].

However, the evidence regarding its impact on the reduction of exacerbations and hospitalizations remains uncertain [7], due to the heterogeneity of studies, the lack of reliable predictors [8], low patient adherence [9], and the absence of robust predictive models [10] that integrate health factors, lifestyle, and environmental conditions. Among the current challenges are the identification of clinically relevant predictors, the development of clinically validated algorithms, and the implementation of strategies that minimize the burden on patients, fostering their engagement with treatment. To date, no multimodal tool exists capable of integrating data on respiratory events, lifestyle, acoustic markers of cough and voice, psychomotor tests, respiratory function, patterns of nocturnal physiological variability, and environmental factors to predict the progression of COPD [11]. Usability is a key factor in the home monitoring of COPD patients as it directly influences adherence, system effectiveness, and ultimately clinical outcomes.

COPD patients are often older adults with physical and

cognitive limitations, so a difficult-to-use system may reduce their willingness to use it continuously. An intuitive and accessible interface facilitates its adoption and sustained use. Additionally, if telemonitoring requires too many complex interactions, it may lead to frustration and demotivation. A user-centered design, with simple and automatic interactions, reduces this burden and improves the patient experience. A poorly designed system interface can result in errors in data entry or interpretation by the patient. Good usability ensures that the recorded data is accurate and reliable. Moreover, for telemonitoring to be effective, it must integrate seamlessly into the patient's daily life in a non-invasive way, so that it is perceived as support rather than a burden. Finally, good usability enhances adherence and the quality of the data collected, allowing predictive models and personalized interventions to function more efficiently. Ultimately, usability is not just a design issue, but a fundamental requirement to ensure the adoption and effectiveness of telemonitoring in COPD patients.

In this context, the CICERONE project [12] proposes a patient-centered approach to identify new physiological and environmental indicators, as well as to develop reliable and effective predictive models based on Artificial Intelligence (AI). As a preliminary step toward implementation, this study describes the evaluation of the application using various usability tools, with the aim of optimizing its design and ensuring its adoption by users.

The structure of this communication is organized as follows: After this introduction, Section II outlines the methodology used in the development and evaluation of the CICERONE telemonitoring application, detailing the iterative design process and the user-centered approach. Section III presents the results obtained from the usability evaluations conducted on the different prototypes, focusing on the user experience and the adjustments made during each design phase. In Section IV, we analyze the findings from the usability tests and discuss the implications of the results, particularly in terms of system performance, user feedback, and the challenges encountered during the integration of external devices.

II. Methodology

A. Objective

CICERONE is a multimodal telemonitoring platform developed to collect home data from high-risk COPD patients. This tool aims to promote the identification of new relevant predictors and the creation of an explainable clinical support system, based on artificial intelligence, designed to predict exacerbations of the disease in a personalized manner. The designed solutions are being evaluated with a cohort of COPD patients treated by the Pulmonology Department at the Hospital Universitario Puerta del Mar (Cádiz, Spain).

The overall architecture of the system is illustrated in Figure 1. The platform collects multimodal data, including physiological signals (e.g., oxygen saturation, heart rate), environmental parameters (e.g., air quality, temperature), and patient-reported outcomes through questionnaires. Given the sensitive nature of this health-related data, robust privacy-preserving mechanisms are essential. All data transmissions are secured using encryption protocols, and access is restricted based on user roles. All data collected during the main study are anonymized in compliance with the General Data Protection Regulation of the European Union (GDPR). Moreover, ethical considerations around data ownership, long-term storage, and secondary use of data for research have been systematically addressed in collaboration with clinical partners and ethics committees. For the daily reporting of information by the patient, a mobile application was developed to facilitate the direct acquisition of the aforementioned data and allow integration with the sensor ecosystem that accompanies the patient, thus optimizing data collection. The development of the application has taken into account previous experiences [13] [14], and this work describes the methodological aspects and the results of the development.

B. User-centered development

Given that COPD requires an approach that combines efficiency and usability, the design of the system for use in the home environment was developed with the patients' needs in mind.

The development of the mobile application for users was carried out using an iterative and incremental development model, involving a multidisciplinary team and the patients themselves as end users. The process began with a conceptual design that was transformed into an initial prototype through a mock-up. This prototype underwent several cycles of performance testing, usability evaluations, and design adjustments. In response to suggestions and improvements, incremental enhancements were implemented, leading to an intermediate prototype. It was a mobile application programmed in Java for Android, which was tested again to evaluate its performance and usability.

To measure overall satisfaction with the system, the standard System Usability Scale (SUS) [15] was used, which allowed for the evaluation of two specific dimensions: usability and capacity. Additionally, structured interviews were conducted with each participant to obtain qualitative feedback. Among the quantitative metrics used to assess usability were the time required to complete tasks and the overall score obtained on the SUS scale. These results were compared for the initial, intermediate, and final prototypes.

C. System Usability Scale (SUS)

The SUS is a widely used tool to assess the usability of products and systems, including software, hardware, mobile applications, and websites [15]. It has become a reference standard due to its simplicity, versatility, and robustness in obtaining quantitative data about the user experience.

The SUS consists of a ten-item questionnaire, where participants rate each statement on a five-point Likert scale, ranging from "Strongly disagree" (1) to "Strongly agree" (5). The questions alternate between positive and negative items to reduce response biases, and they are as follows:

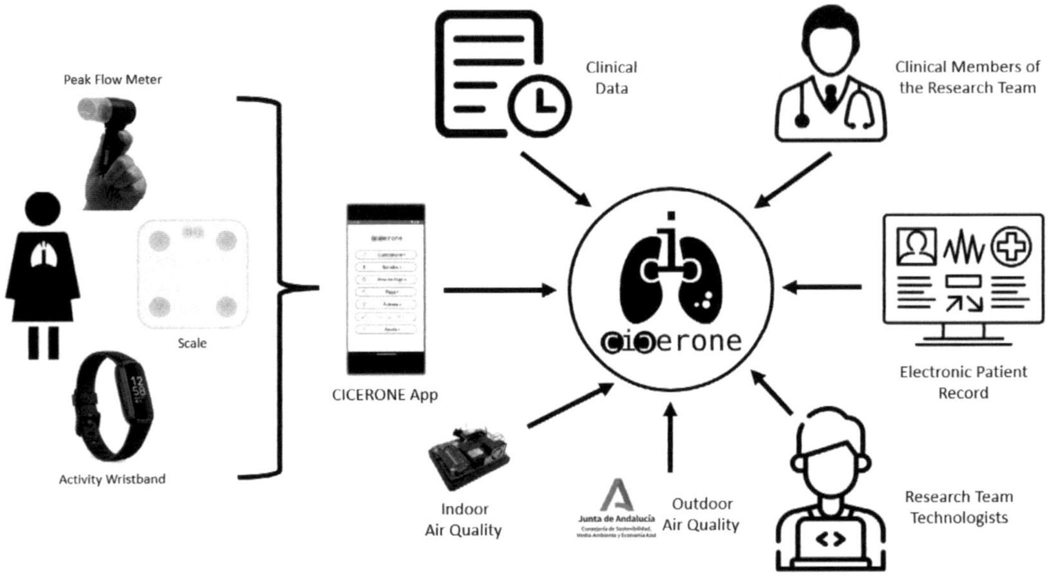

Figure 1. CICERONE Project Architecture.

1) *I think I'd like to use this app often.*
2) *I found the app unnecessarily complex.*
3) *I thought the app was easy to use.*
4) *I think I would need a technician's support to use the application.*
5) *I found the various features of the app to be well-integrated.*
6) *I thought there was too much inconsistency in this app.*
7) *I imagine that most people would learn how to use this app very quickly.*
8) *I found the app very complicated to use.*
9) *I felt very confident using the app.*
10) *I needed to learn many things before starting with this app.*

This questionnaire generates an overall score ranging from 0 to 100, as illustrated in Figure 2, where a higher score indicates a better perception of the usability of the evaluated system.

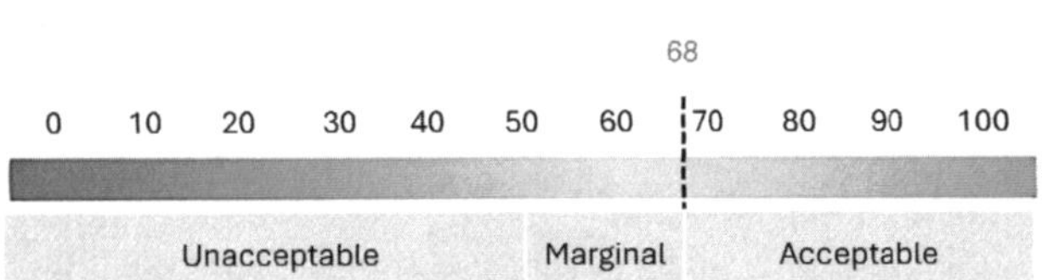

Figure 2. System Usability Scale.

To obtain the usability scale score, the following procedure is used. For odd-numbered items (positive), 5 is subtracted from the total sum; while for even-numbered items (negative), the total sum is subtracted from 25. The sum of both obtained values is then multiplied by 2.5 to scale the score, thus obtaining the final usability scale value (Equation 1).

$$X = \sum PointsofOdd\ Statements - 5$$

$$Y = 25 - \sum PointsofEven\ Statements$$

$$SUS\ Score = (X + Y) \times 2.5$$

A score of 68 or higher is considered to indicate that the usability obtained in the evaluation is acceptable.

D. Development Process: User-Centered Design

The design of a system for the home care of COPD patients must prioritize both efficiency and usability. To achieve this, it is essential to involve users throughout the entire development process, following a User-Centered Design (UCD) approach. This iterative and incremental method ensures that the needs and characteristics of the patients are properly considered, with the active participation of a multidisciplinary team and the end users.

The design process of the CICERONE application had four stages: requirements analysis, design, implementation, and launch. The design and implementation phases were carried out iteratively, allowing for continuous improvements based on new versions and user feedback.

In the initial analysis, a multidisciplinary team, composed of experts in pulmonology, usability, nursing, and engineering, conducted a field study to gather information and define the initial requirements. During the design phase, a first prototype (P1) was created using software tools to develop a mock-up. This mock-up underwent usability testing, leading to the implementation phase, where a high-fidelity prototype (P2) was developed in Android Studio and evaluated by a new study group. These tests were supervised by usability experts and a nurse, allowing the identification of problems and suggestions for improvement that facilitated the development of a new prototype (P3), which was finally evaluated by a group of COPD patients.

1) Evaluation of Prototype P1: Prototype P1 was created using the Figma tool. This prototype simulated the application online, and installation was not required by the participant, who had the freedom to navigate through the different modules and complete activities to test its functionality and usability. In this prototype, the modules for communication with the peak flow meter and the activity bracelet were not available. The usability evaluation of this prototype was conducted with 11 participants, with an average age of over 50 years, using an electronic version of the SUS questionnaire, implemented using Google Forms.

2) Evaluation of Prototype P2: Prototype P2 was created using Android Studio. The resulting app was installed on the participant's mobile device, which they used in a supervised manner during the evaluation. This prototype did not include the module for communication with the peak flow meter, and the usability evaluation was conducted with 7 participants, again with an average age of over 50 years. The interview to complete the SUS questionnaire was conducted in person.

3) Evaluation of Prototype P3: This evaluation was conducted with 13 COPD patients, with an average age of over 60 years. The methodology employed was as follows. First, the patient was informed about the project and its objectives, and informed consent was obtained. General data on their medical history and lifestyle (physical exercise and habits) were collected. Subsequently, the level of dyspnea was assessed using the modified Medical Research Council (mMRC) dyspnea scale. After that, a cognitive test was completed using the Mini-Mental State Examination (MMSE) to assess the patient's cognitive abilities. Next, the application was installed on the patient's device along with an explanation of its functioning and that of the necessary external devices (peak flow meter, activity bracelet, and air quality meter). Various informational sheets with basic visual instructions for handling each device were provided. After installation, the patient performed an initial guided test, after which they answered usability questions (SUS scale described earlier), as well as a final interview with three open-ended questions regarding usage, two about learning, and one about user satisfaction:

1) *Do you consider a system like the one proposed by the project necessary?*
2) *What difficulties did you encounter while using the application?*
3) *Were there any technical issues during the session?*
4) *Were you able to complete all tasks without assistance?*
5) *Did you find it difficult?*
6) *Do you like the idea of using devices and mobile applications for self-monitoring your lung disease?*

To gather information about the patient's expectations, two questions were asked:

1) *Would you like to use this system in the future?*
2) *Do you think this system could be useful for other types of patients?*

The conduct of these final interviews with open-ended questions allowed participants to express comments, suggestions, or any aspect they considered relevant about the system. Moreover, it provided the opportunity to gather a comprehensive view of the user experience, combining objective measurements with subjective assessments.

E. Participants and Ethical Considerations

The study involved the collaboration of 31 participants. The evaluation of prototype P1 was conducted with 11 subjects, prototype P2 was evaluated by 7 participants, and the final version of the tool was tested by 13 patients, recruited by the Pulmonology and Allergy Unit of the Puerta del Mar University Hospital in Cádiz. The study was approved by the Coordinating Committee of Biomedical Research Ethics of Cádiz (CICERONE code, 29.23).

III. RESULTS

A. Design Phase

The first prototype was designed based on the initial requirements. The application included graphic icons, visual indicators, and text screens to represent information and actions, allowing users to interact directly with the graphic elements. It was designed for individuals over 60 years old with potential sensory deficits, compensated by a simplified design, enhanced visual stimuli, and minimal attention and memory load. Six main modules were incorporated: (1) respiratory symptom questionnaire (Likert-type questions) and two games to assess psychomotor abilities, (2) recording of cough and speech sounds, (3) evaluation of respiratory function through peak flow measurement, (4) weight, (5) reading of physical activity and sleep quality data measured by a smart bracelet, and (6) help module with video tutorials on handling all system elements. The mock-up developed in Figma is shown in Figure 3.

Figure 3. Some screens from the mock-up design created with Figma.

72.8% of the participants exceeded the average SUS usability score (68%), indicating the need for improvements in the prototype. Aesthetic and functional adjustments were made for a better user experience.

B. Implementation Phase

The first high-fidelity prototype (P2) underwent two re-design iterations to address usability deficiencies. The content design was adjusted, prioritizing a simple and understandable design for older individuals. The control interface was modified, aesthetic aspects were adjusted, and software stability issues were resolved. With these improvements, prototype P3 (shown in Figure 4) was developed and evaluated, resulting in a high level of perceived usability.

Figure 4. CICERONE Mobile Application.

The evaluations during the implementation phase were conducted in person. The average and standard deviation of the SUS metric for prototypes P1, P2, and P3 released in each iteration of the design were 80.68 (SD 12.75), 87.5 (SD 5.59), and 76.34 (SD 8.58), respectively.

Figure 5 shows the histogram with the SUS scores obtained from the evaluation of each prototype. In the case of prototype P1, all participants considered the usability level acceptable, with participant 6 reporting the lowest usability level (77.5). Unlike prototype P1, which had a mean perceived usability level of 80.7, the mean usability level of prototype P2 increased to 87.5. This prototype addressed most of the usability issues identified in P1.

The evaluation of P3 was conducted with a group of 13 COPD patients. The subjects evaluated the complete solution, including the app, peak flow sensor, and activity bracelet.

The average usability value obtained in the evaluation session of prototype P3 was 76.3. 23.1% of the patients considered the usability level to be marginal, without dropping below a minimum value of 60, despite incorporating the use of external devices to the application in this phase, which added complexity. Patients 1, 2, and 11 reported issues with linking and communication between the devices and the app. Despite the expected decrease from adding the layer of communication with real devices, the average usability level remained at good levels, close to excellent.

Finally, Figure 6 shows the average response given for each question in the usability questionnaire, according to the three design stages described.

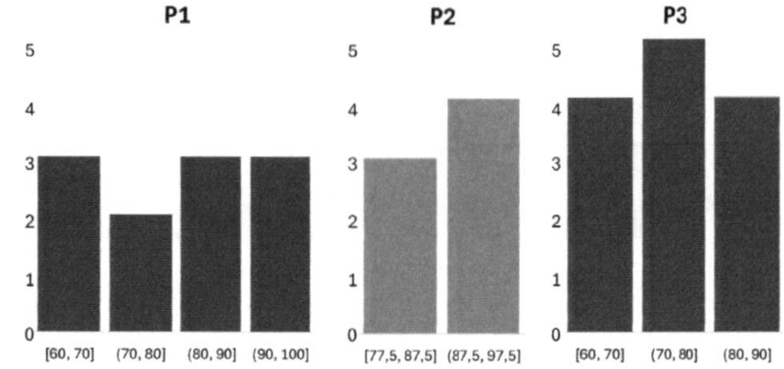

Figure 5. Histograms of the SUS metrics obtained from all participants in the evaluation of the P1, P2, and P3 prototypes of the CICERONE App, released in each iteration of the design.

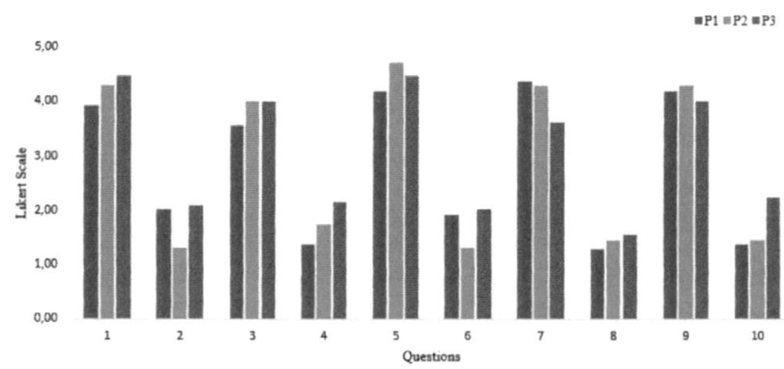

Figure 6. Comparison of results across different usability questions.

IV. Discussion and Conclusions

This study presents the development and evaluation of an application for the telemonitoring of patients with COPD, based on the recording of symptoms, sounds, and physiological parameters during both day and night. Usability tools and a user-centered design approach were employed to optimize its adoption.

The usability evaluation, conducted in three phases, showed that user responses improved as the prototype developed, indicating that iterative enhancements positively affected user perception. The platform is designed to minimize patient burden while enabling meaningful data collection, requiring less than five minutes per day for reporting via sensors or questionnaires. This low time demand supports adherence and reduces disruption, which is especially important for chronic conditions like COPD. Future evaluations will focus on user satisfaction, long-term engagement, and improvements in self-management to ensure the platform becomes a seamless, supportive part of daily life.

In terms of perceived complexity, the initial prototypes (P1 and P3) obtained similar scores, albeit for different reasons: P1, due to its simplicity as a simulation without full functionality; P3, due to its integration into the patient's device with technical assistance during the setup. Ease of use was better rated when no device linking was required, highlighting the importance of technical support during the implementation phase, especially for older users.

Moreover, younger participants and those with greater technological familiarity better identified the integration of functionalities and design consistency, while older users reported more difficulties and less confidence in using the application. These factors also influenced perceptions of the learning speed and the need for training.

The open feedback from participants highlighted the potential utility of the application in healthcare. However, some users expressed a preference for a simpler solution without reliance on mobile phones, while others showed willingness to continue using it after the study, reflecting a generally positive acceptance.

Prototype P2 received the best scores, standing out as the most intuitive and reliable, reflecting improvements over the previous P1 stage. The latter was perceived as limited in functionality and ease of use, underscoring the importance of early feedback in development.

On the other hand, P3 showed a high SUS metric, though lower than P2, with advancements in integration and usability but persistent challenges in terms of user confidence and design consistency, particularly among older users. A key finding was the progressive reduction in the need for technical support, indicating that successive iterations favored intuitiveness and functional integration.

In conclusion, the usability analysis based on the SUS scale allowed for the identification of significant differences between the development stages, emphasizing the importance of an iterative approach to optimize the user experience. The results highlight the relevance of a user-centered iterative development process to improve the usability and acceptance of telemonitoring applications. As future work, a key aspect to consider is the platform's scalability for deployment in diverse clinical contexts. This involves not only ensuring the technical capacity to handle an increasing number of patients and devices but also adapting the solution to the various regulations, technological infrastructures, and clinical workflows found across different healthcare systems. Integration with heterogeneous electronic health records, interoperability with standards such as HL7 (Health Level Seven) or FHIR (Fast Healthcare Interoperability Resources), and compliance with data protection regulations such as GDPR (General Data Protection Regulation) or HIPAA (Health Insurance Portability and Accountability Act) present significant challenges. These aspects will be addressed in future phases of the project to enable effective and sustainable large-scale adoption.

ACKNOWLEDGMENT

This study is part of the R&D project CICERONE. Grant PID2021-126810OB-I00 funded by MICIU/AEI/10.13039/501100011033 and by ERDF/EU.

REFERENCES

[1] Global Initiative for Chronic Obstructive Lung Diseases, *2024 GOLD report*, Available at: https://goldcopd.org. Accessed: October, 2024.

[2] J. Soriano *et al.*, "Prevalence and determinants of COPD in Spain: EPISCAN II," *Archivos de Bronconeumología*, vol. 57, no. 1, pp. 61–69, 2021. DOI: 10.1016/j.arbres.2020.07.024.

[3] World Health Organization (WHO), *Chronic obstructive pulmonary disease (COPD)*, Available at: https://www.who.int. Accessed: October, 2024.

[4] A. Ritchie and J. Wedzicha, "Definition, causes, pathogenesis, and consequences of chronic obstructive pulmonary disease exacerbations," *Clinics in Chest Medicine*, vol. 41, no. 3, pp. 421–438, 2020. DOI: 10.1016/j.ccm.2020.06.007.

[5] J. Hurst *et al.*, "Understanding the impact of chronic obstructive pulmonary disease exacerbations on patient health and quality of life," *European Journal of Internal Medicine*, vol. 73, pp. 1–6, 2020. DOI: 10.1016/j.ejim.2019.12.014.

[6] H. M. G. Glyde, C. Morgan, T. M. Wilkinson, I. T. Nabney, and J. W. Dodd, "Remote patient monitoring and machine learning in acute exacerbations of chronic obstructive pulmonary disease: Dual systematic literature review and narrative synthesis," *Journal of Medical Internet Research*, vol. 26, e52143, 2024.

[7] F. Nagase *et al.*, "Effectiveness of remote home monitoring for patients with Chronic Obstructive Pulmonary Disease (COPD): Systematic review," *BMC Health Services Research*, vol. 22, no. 1, p. 646, 2022. DOI: 10.1186/s12913-022-07938-y.

[8] D. Sanchez-Morillo, M. Fernandez-Granero, and A. Leon-Jimenez, "Use of predictive algorithms in-home monitoring of chronic obstructive pulmonary disease and asthma: A systematic review," *Chronic Respiratory Disease*, vol. 13, no. 3, pp. 264–283, 2016. DOI: 10.1177/1479972316642365.

[9] D. Price *et al.*, "Maximizing adherence and gaining new information for your chronic obstructive pulmonary disease (MAGNIFY COPD): Study protocol for the pragmatic, cluster randomized trial evaluating the impact of dual bronchodilator with add-on sensor and electronic monitoring on clinical outcomes," *Pragmatic and Observational Research*, vol. 12, pp. 25–35, 2021. DOI: 10.2147/POR.S302809.

[10] C. Wu *et al.*, "A Precision Health Service for Chronic Diseases: Development and Cohort Study Using Wearable Device, Machine Learning, and Deep Learning," *IEEE Journal of Translational Engineering in Health and Medicine*, vol. 10, p. 2 700 414, 2022. DOI: 10.1109/JTEHM.2022.3207825.

[11] R. Bhowmik and S. Most, "A Personalized Respiratory Disease Exacerbation Prediction Technique Based on a Novel Spatio-Temporal Machine Learning Architecture and Local Environmental Sensor Networks," *Electronics*, vol. 11, no. 16, p. 2562, 2022. DOI: 10.3390/electronics11162562.

[12] Bioengineering, Automation and Robotics Research Group (ATARI), *Artificial intelligence, smart sensing, and new physiological and environmental predictors for enhancing COPD management CICERONE*, Available at: https://cicerone.uca.es/. Accessed: October, 2024.

[13] D. Sánchez-Morillo, M. Crespo, A. León, and L. Crespo Foix, "A novel multimodal tool for telemonitoring patients with COPD," *Informatics for Health & Social Care*, vol. 40, no. 1, pp. 1–22, 2015. DOI: 10.3109/17538157.2013.872114.

[14] M. Fernández-Granero, D. Sánchez-Morillo, A. León-Jiménez, and L. Crespo, "Automatic prediction of chronic obstructive pulmonary disease exacerbations through home telemonitoring of symptoms," *Bio-Medical Materials and Engineering*, vol. 24, no. 6, pp. 3825–3832, 2014. DOI: 10.3233/BME-141212.

[15] J. Brooke, "SUS: A quick and dirty usability scale," *Usability Eval. Ind.*, vol. 189, 1995.

Malware Detection Using Machine Learning: A Comparative Analysis

Sameeruddin Mohammed, Fan Zhang, Faria Brishti
Department of Computer Science
Tuskegee University
Tuskegee, USA
e-mail: {smohammed8703 | fzhang9458 | fbrishti7995}@tuskegee.edu

Baiyun Chen
Computer Science Department
Tuskegee University
Tuskegee, USA
e-mail: bchen@tuskegee.edu

Fan Wu
Computer Science Department
Tuskegee University
Tuskegee, USA
e-mail: fwu@tuskegee.edu

***Abstract*—To address the growing challenges posed by Cyber threats, anti-malware organizations have increasingly turned to Machine Learning (ML). In recent years, machine learning algorithms have become indispensable for solving complex classification problems, outperforming traditional statistical methods by capturing intricate patterns in high dimensional data. However, selecting the optimal model requires rigorous evaluation in multiple performance metrics while ensuring stability across different data splits. In this study, we conducted a comprehensive assessment of eight machine learning algorithms. Random Forest (RF), Extreme Gradient Boosting (XGBoost), Support Vector Machine (SVM), Logistic Regression (LR), Naive Bayes, Light Gradient Boosting Machine (LightGBM), Decision Tree (DT), and k-Nearest Neighbors (KNN) using stratified 5-fold cross-validation. Our results reveal that RF, LightGBM, DT, and KNN achieve exceptional performance, with identical near-perfect scores in accuracy (0.9918), precision (0.9920), recall (0.9918), F1 score (0.9918) and Area Under the Receiver Operation Characteristic Curve (AUC-ROC) (0.9998), along with remarkably low variance (10^{-6} to 10^{-8}), demonstrating unparalleled robustness. The study highlights the superiority of tree-based ensembles and KNN in achieving high predictive power and stability, whereas classical algorithms such as logistic regression and naive Bayes lag. Despite XGBoost's reputation, its performance here is eclipsed by simpler tree-based methods. Our analysis underscores the importance of considering variance when evaluating model selection, particularly for critical applications where stability is paramount, and provides actionable insights for practitioners seeking reliable, high-accuracy classifiers.**

***Keywords-machine learning*; *malware detection*; *classification*; *model comparison*; *model evaluation*.**

I. Introduction

Cyber threats such as malware have become a significant challenge to digital security in recent years, affecting individuals, organizations, and critical infrastructure worldwide. As these threats evolve and become increasingly sophisticated, traditional signature-based detection methods are becoming less effective [1]. In response, Machine Learning (ML) has emerged as a powerful tool to automate malware detection, offering the ability to classify large volumes of data to identify patterns that might otherwise go unnoticed [2].

However, despite the growing use of machine learning, selecting the most appropriate algorithm for malware classification remains a difficult task due to the complexity of the data and the need for high accuracy and stability of the model in different data splits [3]. To address this challenge, this study conducts a comprehensive evaluation of eight widely used machine learning algorithms for malware detection, including Random Forest, Extreme Gradient Boosting (XGBoost), Support Vector Machine (SVM), Logistic Regression, Naive Bayes, Light Gradient Boosting Machine (LightGBM), Decision Tree, and k-Nearest Neighbors [4]–[6]. These models are assessed using 5-fold stratified cross-validation to ensure robust performance estimation across multiple data splits [7]. The evaluation is based on key performance metrics, including accuracy, precision, recall, F1 score, AUC-ROC, and variance, allowing a detailed comparison of the predictive power and stability of each model [4], [8].

For our experiments, we leverage a refined version of the Microsoft Malware Classification Challenge (BIG 2015) dataset [9], which contains feature-engineered representations of malware binaries [10]. The dataset encapsulates both static features, such as Portable Executable (PE) headers and entropy profiles, and dynamic features, including API call sequences and assembly opcode distributions [11]. These features enable robust classification of malware into distinct families. By analyzing attributes such as section-wise entropy differences `ent_q_diffs`, importing table dependencies (Imports) and opcoding frequencies, we aim to develop an interpretable machine learning model for malware detection [12]. The dataset's rich feature space not only facilitates accurate classification but also enables anomaly detection, providing insights into evolving malware evasion techniques [13].

The primary objective of this study is to identify the most effective machine learning model for malware classification by balancing predictive accuracy with model stability. While ensemble based methods, like Random Forest and XGBoost, are known for their strong predictive capabilities, their performance must be assessed in comparison to simpler models, like Decision Tree and KNN, which may offer competitive results with lower computational cost. Furthermore, we explore the role of variance-aware evaluation, which is crucial in cybersecurity applications where model reliability across different datasets is essential. Our findings reveal that RF, LightGBM, DT, and KNN achieve near-perfect classification performance with minimal variance, demonstrating their robustness in malware detection tasks. In contrast, XGBoost and SVM exhibit slightly lower accuracy and higher variance, while LR and Naive Bayes perform moderately, struggling to capture complex decision boundaries in the data. These insights provide valuable guidance for researchers and practitioners in cybersecurity, helping them select reliable models for malware classification.

The structure of the paper is as follows. Section II reviews related work in machine learning-based malware detection. Section III briefly introduces the eight ML models utilized in this work. Section IV depicts the modeling procedure and results for the malware detection. Section V discusses the findings. We conclude with Section VI.

II. Related Work

The application of machine learning in cybersecurity, particularly for malware detection, has gained significant attention in recent years. Salem et al. [1] provided a comprehensive review of Artificial Intelligence (AI)-driven detection techniques, highlighting the evolution from traditional signature-based methods to sophisticated machine learning approaches. Similarly, Dasgupta et al. [2] conducted an extensive survey on machine learning applications in cybersecurity, emphasizing the critical role of automated detection systems in addressing the growing complexity of cyber threats.

Several studies have focused on comparative analysis of machine learning algorithms for malware classification. Rahul et al. [4] analyzed various machine learning models for malware detection, demonstrating the effectiveness of ensemble methods in capturing complex malware behavior patterns. Singh and Singh [5] assessed supervised machine learning algorithms using dynamic API calls, providing insights into the importance of feature selection and extraction techniques. Their work highlighted the challenges of balancing accuracy with computational efficiency in real-time detection systems.

The Microsoft Malware Classification Challenge dataset [11] has served as a benchmark for numerous studies in this domain. Aslan and Samet [9] provided a comprehensive review of malware detection approaches, categorizing methods into static, dynamic, and hybrid analysis techniques. Ghouti and Imam [10] specifically focused on malware classification using compact image features and multiclass support vector machines, demonstrating the potential of visual representation techniques. More recently, Connors and Sarkar [12] explored machine learning approaches for detecting malware in PE files, while Lin and Chang [13] addressed the interpretability challenges in ML-based automated malware detection models. These studies collectively underscore the ongoing evolution of machine learning techniques in cybersecurity applications, setting the foundation for our comprehensive comparative analysis of eight state-of-the-art algorithms.

III. Methods

Classification algorithms, a cornerstone of machine learning, have demonstrated exceptional performance across various domains, including cybersecurity applications such as malware detection [3], [14]. Beyond cybersecurity, these algorithms play a crucial role in disease diagnosis [15], where they help detect conditions like cancer [16], [17], diabetes [18], [19], and cardiovascular diseases [20] through medical imaging and clinical data analysis [21]. In finance, classification models are widely used for fraud detection, identifying suspicious transactions and preventing financial crimes [22]. Additionally, they contribute to spam filtering in email systems, sentiment analysis in natural language processing, and customer churn prediction in business analytics [23]. The versatility and effectiveness of classification algorithms make them indispensable across diverse fields where pattern recognition and decision making are essential. This study evaluates eight state of the art classification models, namely, Random Forest (RF), XGBoost, LightGBM, Support Vector Machine (SVM), Logistic Regression, Naive Bayes, Decision Tree, and k-Nearest Neighbors (KNN) to predict malware classes using static and dynamic features. Performance is assessed via five metrics: Accuracy, Precision, Recall, F1-Score, and AUC-ROC, with variance analysis across stratified 5-fold cross-validation to quantify stability.

Given a labeled dataset $\mathcal{D} = \{(\mathbf{x}_i, y_i)\}_{i=1}^{n}$ where $\mathbf{x}_i$ represents feature vectors (e.g., API calls, entropy values) and $y_i \in \{0, 1\}$ denotes benign/malicious labels, we formalize each model's prediction $\hat{y}$ for a new sample $\mathbf{x}$.

A. Random Forest

RF is an ensemble method that aggregates predictions from multiple decision trees, reducing overfitting through majority voting. For malware detection, it has proven to be effective [6].

$$\hat{y} = \text{mode}\left(\{f_i(\mathbf{x})\}_{i=1}^{N}\right), \tag{1}$$

where f_i is the i-th tree's prediction, and N is the total number of trees in Equation (1). RF excels at handling high-dimensional feature spaces (e.g., API call sequences).

B. XGBoost

XGBoost iteratively improves predictions by combining weak learners (decision trees) with gradient descent optimization.

$$\hat{y} = \sum_{i=1}^{N} \gamma_i f_i(\mathbf{x}), \tag{2}$$

where γ_i is the learning rate. XGBoost's regularization (L1/L2 penalties) mitigates overfitting, critical for imbalanced malware datasets.

C. LightGBM

LightGBM uses histogram-based splitting for efficiency, optimizing memory usage for large-scale malware data.

$$\hat{y} = \sum_{i=1}^{N} \alpha_i f_i(\mathbf{x}), \tag{3}$$

where α_i weights leaf outputs. Its Gradient-based One-Side Sampling (GOSS) is ideal for sparse features (e.g., n-gram opcodes).

D. Support Vector Machine

SVM finds the optimal hyperplane to separate malware benign classes via maximum margin optimization.

$$\hat{y} = \text{sign}\left(\mathbf{w}^T \phi(\mathbf{x}) + b\right), \tag{4}$$

where $\hat{y}$ is the predicted class label for a given input $\mathbf{x}$, $\mathbf{w}$ is the weight vector learned by the SVM during training, $\mathbf{w}^T$ denotes the transpose of the weight vector $\mathbf{w}$, $\phi(\mathbf{x})$ is a non-linear transformation of the input vector $\mathbf{x}$ into a higher-dimensional feature space, performed using a kernel function, b is the bias term that shifts the decision boundary, and sign$(\cdot)$ is the sign function, which returns $+1$ if the argument is positive and -1 if it is negative. The kernel function $\phi(\cdot)$ enables SVM to handle non-linearly separable data by implicitly mapping inputs into a high dimensional space. A common choice is the Radial Basis Function (RBF) kernel. The effectiveness of SVM is highly dependent on the scaling of features, as it ensures that each feature contributes proportionally to the boundary of the final decision.

E. Logistic Regression

A linear model for probabilistic classification

$$\hat{y} = \mathbb{I}\left(\frac{1}{1 + e^{-(\mathbf{w}^T\mathbf{x}+b)}} \geq 0.5\right) \tag{5}$$

where $\mathbb{I}(\cdot)$ is the indicator function. It is Interpretable but limited to linear feature relationships.

F. Naive Bayes

Naive Bayes is a probabilistic classifier that Leverages Bayes' theorem with feature independence assumptions.

$$\hat{y} = \arg\max_{y} P(y) \prod_{j=1}^{d} P(x_j \mid y), \tag{6}$$

where $\hat{y}$ is the predicted class label for a given input instance, y represents a possible class label (e.g., malware or benign), $P(y)$ is the prior probability of class y, x_j is the j-th feature of the input vector $\mathbf{x}$, $P(x_j \mid y)$ is the conditional probability (likelihood) of observing feature x_j given class y, d is the total number of features in the input, and $\arg\max$ selects the class label y that maximizes the posterior probability. Naive Bayes is computationally efficient and effective for high-dimensional data. However, its performance can degrade when features are highly correlated, such as in the case of dependent API calls in malware behavior analysis.

G. Decision Tree

A single tree recursively partitions the feature space.

$$\hat{y} = f(\mathbf{x}; \theta), \tag{7}$$

where θ denotes split thresholds. It is prone to overfitting but useful for interpretability.

H. k-Nearest Neighbors

The k-Nearest Neighbors (KNN) algorithm classifies samples based on majority labels of the k closest training instances.

$$\hat{y} = \text{mode}\left(\{y_i \mid \mathbf{x}_i \in \mathcal{N}_k(\mathbf{x})\}\right), \tag{8}$$

where $\mathcal{N}_k(\mathbf{x})$ are the k-nearest neighbors. Sensitive to feature scaling and distance metrics (e.g., Hamming distance for binary features).

I. Performance Metrics

Five metrics evaluate model performance, with variance calculated across folds.

1. Accuracy is the proportion of correct predictions over total predictions [24].

$$\text{Accuracy} = \frac{\text{TP} + \text{TN}}{\text{TP} + \text{TN} + \text{FP} + \text{FN}}, \tag{9}$$

where TP (True Positives) represents the number of correctly predicted positive instances; TN (True Negatives) is the number of correctly predicted negative instances; FP (False Positives) is the number of negative instances incorrectly predicted as positive; and FN (False Negatives) is the number of positive instances incorrectly predicted as negative [25].

2. Precision is the proportion of correctly predicted positive instances among all predicted positives [24].

$$\text{Precision} = \frac{\text{TP}}{\text{TP} + \text{FP}} \tag{10}$$

3. Recall is the proportion of actual positive instances that were correctly identified [24].

$$\text{Recall} = \frac{\text{TP}}{\text{TP} + \text{FN}} \tag{11}$$

4. The F1-Score is the harmonic mean of precision and recall [24].

$$\text{F1} = 2 \times \frac{\text{Precision} \times \text{Recall}}{\text{Precision} + \text{Recall}} \tag{12}$$

5. AUC-ROC (Area Under the Receiver Operating Characteristic Curve) plots True Positive Rate (Sensitivity) against False Positive Rate (1-Specificity) across all classification thresholds. The closer the curve approaches the top-left corner (0,1), the better the model's discriminative ability [26].

6. The variance of each performance metric is calculated across cross-validation folds to assess the model's stability. A lower variance indicates a more consistent and reliable model, while a higher variance suggests performance fluctuations across different training sets [27].

TABLE I
RESULTS OF MODELS.

Model	Accuracy	Accuracy Variance	Precision	Precision Variance	Recall	Recall Variance	F1-Score	F1-Score Variance	AUC-ROC	AUC-ROC Variance
Random Forest	0.991833	2.57E-06	0.991972	2.39E-06	0.991833	2.57E-06	0.991814	2.57E-06	0.999819	1.90E-08
XGBoost	0.979296	9.65E-06	0.980132	8.70E-06	0.979296	9.65E-06	0.938477	0.000201884	0.999429	2.57E-08
SVM	0.979296	9.65E-06	0.980132	8.70E-06	0.979296	9.65E-06	0.938477	0.000201884	0.999429	2.57E-08
Logistic Regression	0.938575	0.000206963	0.943028	0.000117831	0.938575	0.00020696	0.938477	0.000201884	0.976317	3.25E-05
Naive Bayes	0.938575	0.000206963	0.943028	0.000117831	0.938575	0.00020696	0.938477	0.000201884	0.976317	3.25E-05
LightGBM	0.991833	2.57E-06	0.991972	2.39E-06	0.991833	2.57E-06	0.991814	2.57E-06	0.999819	1.90E-08
Decision Tree	0.991833	2.57E-06	0.991972	2.39E-06	0.991833	2.57E-06	0.991814	2.57E-06	0.999819	1.90E-08
KNN	0.991833	2.57E-06	0.991972	2.39E-06	0.991833	2.57E-06	0.991814	2.57E-06	0.999819	1.90E-08

IV. EXPERIMENTAL RESULTS

A. Dataset and Experimental Setup

The experiments were conducted using a refined version of the Microsoft Malware Classification Challenge (BIG 2015) dataset [9]. The dataset contains 21,741 samples with balanced class distribution across nine malware families and benign files. Feature engineering yielded 2,381 static features including PE header information, entropy profiles, import table dependencies, and assembly opcode frequencies. All models were evaluated using stratified 5-fold cross-validation to ensure robust performance estimation across different data splits [28].

B. Performance Evaluation Results

Table I presents the comprehensive performance evaluation of eight machine learning models across five key metrics. The results reveal distinct performance tiers among the evaluated algorithms.

Tier 1 - Exceptional Performers: RF, LightGBM, DT, and KNN achieved identical near-perfect performance with accuracy of 0.9918, precision of 0.9920, recall of 0.9918, F1-score of 0.9918, and AUC-ROC of 0.9998. These models demonstrated remarkably low variance (10^{-6} to 10^{-8}), indicating exceptional stability across cross-validation folds.

Tier 2 - Strong Performers: XGBoost and SVM achieved accuracy of 0.9793 with identical performance metrics. While still demonstrating strong classification capability, these models showed slightly higher variance ($\approx 10^{-6}$) compared to Tier 1 performers.

Tier 3 - Moderate Performers: Logistic Regression and Naive Bayes exhibited lower accuracy (0.9386) and significantly higher variance ($\approx 10^{-4}$), indicating less consistent performance across different data splits.

C. Statistical Significance and Stability Analysis

The variance analysis reveals critical insights into model reliability [29]. The exceptionally low variance ($< 10^{-6}$) observed in RF, LightGBM, DT, and KNN indicates these models maintain consistent performance regardless of training data variations—a crucial requirement for cybersecurity applications [27].

In contrast, the higher variance exhibited by Logistic Regression and Naive Bayes ($\approx 10^{-4}$) suggests potential instability when deployed across different malware datasets or network environments. This stability assessment is particularly important in cybersecurity where reliable performance across diverse threat landscapes is essential.

V. DISCUSSION

A. Model Performance Analysis and Implications

The superior performance of tree-based ensemble methods (Random Forest, LightGBM) and the Decision Tree can be attributed to their ability to capture complex, non-linear feature interactions inherent in malware behavior patterns [30]. These models effectively handle the high-dimensional feature space (2,381 features) without suffering from the curse of dimensionality.

Ensemble Method Advantages: Random Forest's bootstrap aggregating reduces overfitting while maintaining high accuracy. LightGBM's Gradient-based One-Side Sampling (GOSS) efficiently handles sparse features common in malware detection, such as n-gram opcodes and API call sequences.

KNN's Unexpected Success: The exceptional performance of KNN (identical to ensemble methods) suggests that malware and benign samples form distinct, well-separated clusters in the feature space. This clustering behavior indicates that the extracted features effectively capture discriminative patterns between malware families and benign software.

XGBoost Underperformance: Despite its reputation for strong performance, XGBoost's lower F1-score (0.9385) compared to simpler tree-based methods suggests potential overfitting or suboptimal hyperparameter configuration. This highlights the importance of hyperparameter optimization using techniques such as GridSearchCV or RandomizedSearchCV [31].

B. Linear Model Limitations

The moderate performance of Logistic Regression and Naive Bayes stems from their fundamental assumptions that are incompatible with malware detection requirements. Logistic Regression assumes linear decision boundaries, which cannot adequately model the complex, non-linear relationships between malware features and class labels. Similarly, Naive Bayes relies on the feature independence assumption, which is violated in malware analysis where features such as API call sequences and opcode patterns exhibit strong dependencies. However, these models offer computational efficiency and interpretability advantages, making them suitable for resource-constrained environments or scenarios requiring explainable decisions.

C. Practical Deployment Considerations

Computational Complexity: While ensemble methods provide superior accuracy, they introduce computational overhead. Real-time malware detection systems may require model optimization or hardware acceleration for practical deployment.

Scalability Analysis: KNN's instance-based learning requires storing all training samples, making it memory-intensive and computationally expensive for large-scale deployments. Despite its excellent accuracy, scalability concerns limit its practical applicability.

Model Selection Recommendations: For production environments, Random Forest and LightGBM offer the optimal balance of accuracy, stability, and computational efficiency.

D. Challenges and Limitations

Several challenges were encountered during this study:

Feature Engineering Constraints were evident as this study relied primarily on static features extracted from malware samples. Incorporating dynamic behavioral features such as API call sequences and network traffic patterns could further enhance classification performance.

Dataset Generalization presents another concern since while the Microsoft dataset provides a solid foundation, real-world malware detection faces continuously evolving threats. Future work should evaluate model performance on contemporary malware samples and emerging attack vectors.

Class Imbalance Considerations must also be addressed, as although our refined dataset maintains balanced class distribution, real-world scenarios typically exhibit significant class imbalance where benign samples vastly outnumber malware instances. Addressing this through cost-sensitive learning or advanced sampling techniques represents an important future direction.

Hyperparameter Optimization limitations were apparent since the current study employed default hyperparameters for most algorithms. Systematic hyperparameter tuning using GridSearchCV or RandomizedSearchCV could potentially improve performance, particularly for XGBoost and SVM models.

E. Future Research Directions

Future investigations should explore several promising directions. Deep learning integration through evaluating Convolutional Neural Networks (CNNs) and Recurrent Neural Networks (RNNs) for malware detection represents a natural evolution of this work. Dynamic feature incorporation by including behavioral analysis features such as API call sequences and runtime behavior patterns could significantly enhance detection capabilities. Adversarial robustness assessment against malware samples specifically designed to evade detection systems presents a critical research challenge. Additionally, real-time performance optimization through developing lightweight model variants suitable for edge computing and real-time detection systems would address practical deployment requirements in cybersecurity environments.

VI. Conclusion

This study systematically evaluated eight machine learning models for malware detection using stratified 5-fold cross-validation, assessing both accuracy and stability through variance analysis. The results demonstrate clear performance hierarchies among the evaluated algorithms with significant implications for cybersecurity applications.

Tree-based models, particularly RF, LightGBM, DT, and KNN, achieved exceptional performance with accuracy of 0.9918 and AUC-ROC of 0.9998, while maintaining minimal variance ($< 10^{-6}$). These models demonstrated remarkable stability across data splits, effectively capturing complex feature interactions in malware behavior patterns. Conversely, Logistic Regression and Naive Bayes underperformed with accuracy of 0.9386 and higher variance ($\sim 10^{-4}$) due to their linear assumptions, which fail to model complex malware characteristics.

Notably, KNN's exceptional performance suggests that malware and benign samples form distinct clusters in the feature space, validating our feature engineering approach. XGBoost's moderate F1-score (0.9385) indicates potential overfitting, highlighting the importance of hyperparameter optimization for gradient boosting algorithms.

For practical deployment, we recommend Random Forest and LightGBM due to their optimal balance of accuracy, stability, and computational efficiency. Our analysis emphasizes the critical importance of variance-aware evaluation alongside accuracy metrics for cybersecurity applications, ensuring consistent performance across diverse threat environments.

Future research should focus on integrating deep learning approaches, incorporating dynamic behavioral features, and developing adversarial robustness against evolving evasion techniques to advance practical malware detection capabilities.

Acknowledgement

The work is partially supported by the National Science Foundation under NSF Awards Nos. 2100134, 2131228, 2209637, 2234911, and 2417608. Any opinions, findings, or recommendations, expressed in this material are those of the authors and do not necessarily reflect the views of the National Science Foundation.

References

[1] A. H. Salem, S. M. Azzam, O. E. Emam, and A. A. Abohany, "Advancing cybersecurity: A comprehensive review of AI-driven detection techniques", *Journal of Big Data*, vol. 11, no. 1, p. 105, 2024. DOI: 10.1186/s40537-024-00957-y.

[2] D. Dasgupta, Z. Akhtar, and S. Sen, "Machine learning in cybersecurity: A comprehensive survey", *The Journal of Defense Modeling and Simulation*, vol. 19, no. 1, pp. 57–106, 2022. DOI: 10.1177/1548512920951275. eprint: https://doi.org/10.1177/1548512920951275.

[3] H. Tan, "Machine learning algorithm for classification", *Journal of Physics: Conference Series*, vol. 1994, no. 1, p. 012016, Aug. 2021. DOI: 10.1088/1742-6596/1994/1/012016.

[4] Rahul, P. Kedia, S. Sarangi, and Monika, "Analysis of machine learning models for malware detection", *Journal of Discrete Mathematical Sciences and Cryptography*, vol. 23, no. 2, pp. 395–407, 2020. DOI: 10.1080/09720529.2020.1721870.

[5] J. Singh and J. Singh, "Assessment of supervised machine learning algorithms using dynamic api calls for malware detection", *International Journal of Computers and Applications*, vol. 44, no. 3, pp. 270–277, 2022. DOI: 10.1080/1206212X.2020.1732641. eprint: https://doi.org/10.1080/1206212X.2020.1732641.

[6] F. Zhang, B. Chen, F. Brishti, S. Mohammed, F. Wu, and L. Bai, "Predicting energy star scores for diverse building types using machine learning", *International Journal On Advances in Systems and Measurements*, vol. 17, no. 3, pp. 176–188, Dec. 2024, ISSN: 1942-261X.

[7] M. Shi *et al.*, "A novel electronic health record-based, machine-learning model to predict severe hypoglycemia leading to hospitalizations in older adults with diabetes: A territory-wide cohort and modeling study", *PLoS Medicine*, vol. 21, no. 4, e1004369, 2024.

[8] I. Abdessadki and S. Lazaar, "A new classification based model for malicious pe files detection", *International Journal of Computer Network and Information Security*, vol. 9, no. 6, p. 1, 2019.

[9] Ö. A. Aslan and R. Samet, "A comprehensive review on malware detection approaches", *IEEE Access*, vol. 8, pp. 6249–6271, 2020. DOI: 10.1109/ACCESS.2019.2963724.

[10] L. Ghouti and M. Imam, "Malware classification using compact image features and multiclass support vector machines", *IET Information Security*, vol. 14, no. 4, pp. 419–429, 2020. DOI: https://doi.org/10.1049/iet-ifs.2019.0189. eprint: https://ietresearch.onlinelibrary.wiley.com/doi/pdf/10.1049/iet-ifs.2019.0189.

[11] R. Ronen, M. Radu, C. Feuerstein, E. Yom-Tov, and M. Ahmadi, "Microsoft malware classification challenge", *arXiv preprint arXiv:1802.10135*, 2018.

[12] C. Connors and D. Sarkar, "Machine learning for detecting malware in pe files", in *2023 International Conference on Machine Learning and Applications (ICMLA)*, IEEE, 2023, pp. 2194–2199.

[13] Y. Lin and X. Chang, "Towards interpreting ml-based automated malware detection models: A survey", *arXiv preprint arXiv:2101.06232*, 2021.

[14] K. Mohammed, "Harnessing the speed and accuracy of machine learning to advance cybersecurity", *arXiv preprint arXiv:2302.12415*, 2023.

[15] N. G. Nia, E. Kaplanoglu, and A. Nasab, "Evaluation of artificial intelligence techniques in disease diagnosis and prediction", *Discover Artificial Intelligence*, vol. 3, no. 1, p. 5, 2023, ISSN: 2731-0809. DOI: 10.1007/s44163-023-00049-5.

[16] M. J. Iqbal *et al.*, "Clinical applications of artificial intelligence and machine learning in cancer diagnosis: Looking into the future", *Cancer Cell International*, vol. 21, no. 1, p. 270, 2021, ISSN: 1475-2867. DOI: 10.1186/s12935-021-01981-1.

[17] T. Saba, "Recent advancement in cancer detection using machine learning: Systematic survey of decades, comparisons and challenges", *Journal of infection and public health*, vol. 13, no. 9, pp. 1274–1289, 2020.

[18] S. Kaul and Y. Kumar, "Artificial intelligence-based learning techniques for diabetes prediction: Challenges and systematic review", *SN Computer Science*, vol. 1, no. 6, p. 322, 2020, ISSN: 2661-8907. DOI: 10.1007/s42979-020-00337-2.

[19] B. F. Wee, S. Sivakumar, K. H. Lim, W. K. Wong, and F. H. Juwono, "Diabetes detection based on machine learning and deep learning approaches", *Multimedia Tools and Applications*, vol. 83, no. 8, pp. 24 153–24 185, 2024.

[20] T. Ullah *et al.*, "Machine learning-based cardiovascular disease detection using optimal feature selection", *IEEE Access*, vol. 12, pp. 16 431–16 446, 2024.

[21] A. Ogunpola, F. Saeed, S. Basurra, A. M. Albarrak, and S. N. Qasem, "Machine learning-based predictive models for detection of cardiovascular diseases", *Diagnostics*, vol. 14, no. 2, p. 144, 2024.

[22] A. Rahman *et al.*, "Machine learning and network analysis for financial crime detection: Mapping and identifying illicit transaction patterns in global black money transactions", *Gulf Journal of Advance Business Research*, vol. 2, no. 6, pp. 250–272, 2024.

[23] M. R. Hasan, R. K. Ray, and F. R. Chowdhury, "Employee performance prediction: An integrated approach of business analytics and machine learning", *Journal of Business and Management Studies*, vol. 6, no. 1, p. 215, 2024.

[24] J. C. Obi, "A comparative study of several classification metrics and their performances on data", *World Journal of Advanced Engineering Technology and Sciences*, vol. 8, no. 1, pp. 308–314, 2023.

[25] A. A. Theodosiou and R. C. Read, "Artificial intelligence, machine learning and deep learning: Potential resources for the infection clinician", *Journal of Infection*, vol. 87, no. 4, pp. 287–294, 2023, ISSN: 0163-4453. DOI: https://doi.org/10.1016/j.jinf.2023.07.006.

[26] D. J. Hand, "Measuring classifier performance: A coherent alternative to the area under the ROC curve", *Machine learning*, vol. 77, no. 1, pp. 103–123, 2009.

[27] A. L. Buczak and E. Guven, "A survey of data mining and machine learning methods for cyber security intrusion detection", *IEEE Communications surveys & tutorials*, vol. 18, no. 2, pp. 1153–1176, 2016.

[28] R. Kohavi, "A study of cross-validation and bootstrap for accuracy estimation and model selection", in *Proceedings of the 14th international joint conference on Artificial intelligence*, vol. 2, 1995, pp. 1137–1143.

[29] C. Sammut and G. I. Webb, "Cross-validation", in *Encyclopedia of machine learning*, Springer, 2010, pp. 249–249.

[30] T. G. Dietterich, "Approximate statistical tests for comparing supervised classification learning algorithms", *Neural computation*, vol. 10, no. 7, pp. 1895–1923, 1998.

[31] S. Raschka, "Model evaluation, model selection, and algorithm selection in machine learning", *arXiv preprint arXiv:1811.12808*, 2018.

The 3-Ellipse Model: A Lens for Understanding Generative AI's Impact on Organisations

Mercy Williams, Jon G. Hall, Lucia Rapanotti, and Khadija Tahera
The Open University, UK
e-mail: {mercy.williams | jon.hall | lucia.rapanotti | khadija.tahera}@open.ac.uk

***Abstract*— The rapid proliferation of Generative Artificial Intelligence (GenAI) is ushering in significant change and transformation across many sectors, prompting a re-evaluation of organisational structures, processes, and the skills required of the workforce along different time horizons. As organisations increasingly adopt and integrate GenAI tools, understanding the multifaceted impact of this technology becomes crucial. A robust analytical framework is required to comprehend the unfolding trajectory of this change fully. This idea paper proposes one such framework comprising three GenAI agency modes for integration into organisational change, combined with an extant problem oriented model of the organisation as a socio-technical system. The paper argues how the framework could apply to analyse organisational change driven by GenAI, providing an early indication of the potential benefits of further developing and applying such a framework.**

Keywords-generative AI; organisational change; 3-ellipse model; agency modes; socio-technical systems; problem orientation.

I. INTRODUCTION

Recent studies highlight Generative Artificial Intelligence (GenAI)'s dual role as a productivity accelerator and a disruptive force [1][2], prompting organisations to rethink workforce strategies and operational structures. Some of the business implications of AI have been analysed [3][4], especially in relation to its capacity for automating a wide range of work activities and roles. For example, a significant area of discussion revolves around the impact of AI, including GenAI, on employee skills and the future of work [2][5]–[9], with studies indicating that many tasks and associated skills of a significant portion of the workforce could be substantially replaced by AI [5][10]. Although this perspective often equates AI adoption with job replacement by AI [10]–[12] also posit that GenAI could be an enabler, helping to streamline repetitive tasks, thus allowing employees to devote more time to innovation and problem solving or becoming more productive [12].

Speculations on imminent organisational change are based on observing and extrapolating from current, albeit early-stage, trends in GenAI adoption. For example, [13] acknowledges the fact that GenAI holds potential to reshape organisational structures as a result of its incremental adoption in various functions and departments, changing the relationships between different levels of the organisation, such as strategic leadership and operations. For instance, if GenAI is being used to automate specific customer service interactions (social to technical shift) [14], one might speculate on the potential for restructuring customer service departments in the near future. This might lead to a decentralisation of decision-making and potentially flatter organisational hierarchies as information becomes more readily accessible across different levels.

Within this very young field of study, we still lack sound analytical tools that can help us understand and predict the wider ramifications of GenAI adoption on organisation change, including its influence on organisational change processes both in the short and long-term.

We argue for an integrated framework which can be applied in dissecting current GenAI-induced organisational shifts and providing a structured lens through which to examine current changes, anticipate near-future changes, and speculate on potential long-term GenAI-enabled transformation mechanisms. This idea paper proposes one such framework based on the 3-ellipse model for socio-technical systems of [15], in combination with three GenAI agency modes we define for organisational transformation. This work builds on the existing knowledge base of organisational change as problem solving [16]–[18] while contributing to socio-technical systems analysis and development

In Section 2, we introduce the the 3-ellipse model as the theoretical foundation of our framework, which we then use in Section 3 to articulate three GenAI agency modes (reactive, responsive, and driving) for organisational change. Section 4 offers some conclusions and directions for future research.

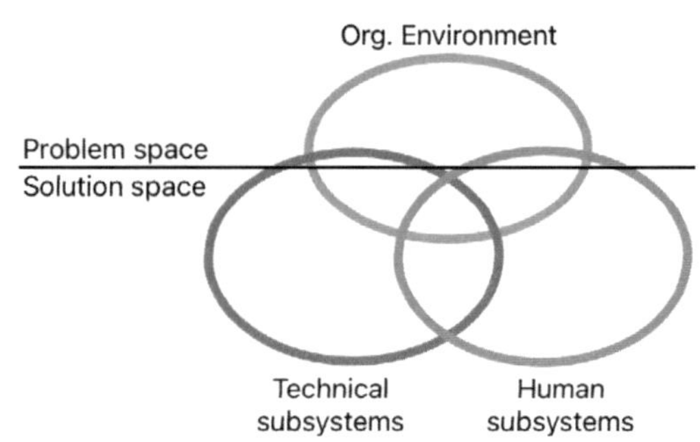

Figure 1. The 3-ellipse model of the organisation [15].

II. THE 3-ELLIPSE MODEL OF THE ORGANISATION

The 3-ellipse model ([15], Figure 1) sees an organisation as the interaction of three key elements: the environment forms the *problem space*, where needs exist that the organisation must satisfy, for example consumers' needs for products or services, or societal needs for education or health care. The human and technical subsystems together form a socio-technical system in the *solution space*: these are the systems through which the organisation meets needs in the problem space. Problem solving is through the sharing of real-world *phenomena* across boundaries, including the organisation's products and services, and data. More precisely:

a) The environment: contains stakeholder(s) external to the organisation, their context(s), perceived needs, and their validation criteria, and establishes boundaries for feasible solutions giving the organisation its *raison d'être*.

b) The human subsystems: include the people within the organisation and the protocols, processes, and interactions, skills, knowledge, collaborations, *etc*, through which they interact and that govern their work.

c) The technical subsystems: include all technology and infrastructure used by the organisation.

As with the whole organisation, it is also possible to see problem-solving relationships *within* the organisation through the 3-ellipse model, in particular between leadership and their problem-solving delegation to ops and management, with further delegation possible within those smaller structures, right down to the individual; see Figure 2.

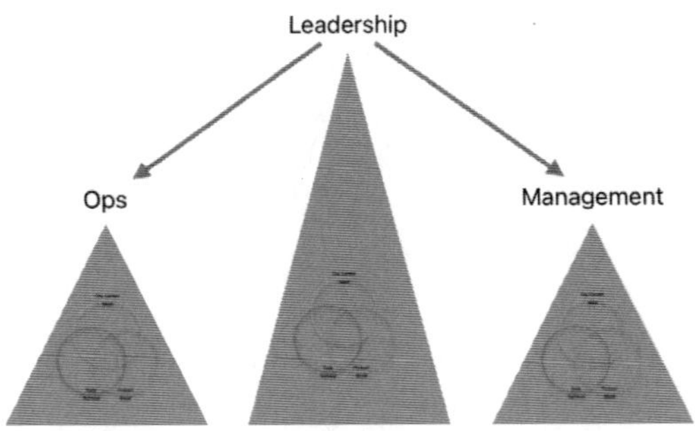

Figure 2. Organisational problem-solving delegation occurs across and down the organisation. (Interaction between pyramids is also possible but is not shown.)

III. GenAI-driven organisational change

By examining the interplay between the organisational environment and the human and technical systems used by the organisation, the 3-ellipse model can be used as a vehicle for organisational change [18]: emerging needs in the environment lead to new problems requiring change in the socio-technical solution system, including changes in its structures, relations and behaviours. In this section, we use the model to tease out characteristics of GenAI-driven organisational change.

As observed in Section I, organisations are primarily experimenting with GenAI to expand the functionality of their technical subsystems, often with concomitant shrinking of the human subsystems. However, the *organisational change space* should also be a target for the adoption of GenAI, but much less is known about its application here.

Therefore, this paper proposes three agency modes to understand the multifaceted nature of organisational change driven by GenAI, including how it may affect the organisational change space.

a) Reactive agency: concentrates on augmenting current human teams with GenAI for solution exploration in organisational change resulting from the integration of GenAI. The primary focus within this phase is to understand how AI is currently altering organisational dynamics, particularly, the evolving relationship between people and AI, that is at the interface between human and technical subsystems. The key question here is how AI is currently changing the organisation?

Such transformation should be contrasted with those that allow the organisation to do more, i.e., those that have transformative application in the problem space. For this, we identify two other agency modes.

b) Responsive agency: focusses on replacing human teams with GenAI for solution exploration in organisational change. It involves analysing the interplay between the social and technical components within organisations, as well as the organisation's evolving relationships with customers and the external environment, the latter being at the interface between problem and solution spaces. A significant aspect of near-term change is the potential for organisational restructuring stemming from the integration of GenAI at various levels, leading to shifts in relationships between strategic leadership and operational functions.

c) Driving agency: uses GenAI agents as tools for the generation and evaluation of change scenarios, a model we call *pre-cog* GenAI (a call-out to Spielberg's 'Minority Report'). Here, GenAI is tasked with proactively identifying and assessing potential changes within the organisation before the fact, and speculatively exploring potential changes in environment and need, with some accompanying exploration of the solution space and implementation paths. This is reminiscent of traditional *SWOT* (Strengths, Weaknesses, Opportunities, and Threats) and *PEST* (Political, Economic, Social, and Technical) analyses [19][20], but with GenAI generating and reviewing scenarios for organisational change, and evaluating their potential impact and viability, to be presented to human stakeholders for further consideration and decision-making. By shifting from analysing the present and past to proactively predicting future scenarios, organisations can become more forward-looking, data-driven, and comprehensive in their strategic planning. This approach ensures that strategies align with the organisation's long-term development goals while providing a substantial advantage in navigating future challenges. Additionally, the insights provided by GenAI can lead to more informed decision making processes, fostering innovation and optimising resource allocation, ultimately driving higher productivity and business growth.

IV. Conclusion and future work

This idea paper suggests three GenAI agency modes for organisational change informed by the 3-ellipse model. While still theoretical, the framework may provide practical tools for GenAI-driven organisational transformations in both problem and solution spaces. We will develop and evaluate the framework in future real-world case studies.

REFERENCES

[1] J. Rudolph, F. M. Mohamed Ismail and S. Popenici, 'Higher education's generative artificial intelligence paradox: The meaning of chatbot mania', *Journal of University Teaching and Learning Practice*, vol. 21, no. 6, 2024.

[2] A. Manresa, A. Sammour, M. Mas-Machuca, W. Chen and D. Botchie, 'Humanizing GenAI at work: Bridging the gap between technological innovation and employee engagement', *Journal of Managerial Psychology*, 2024.

[3] I.-F. Anica-Popa, M. Vrîncianu, L.-E. Anica-Popa, I.-D. Cimau and C.-G. Tudor, 'Framework for integrating Generative AI in developing competencies for accounting and audit professionals', *Electronics*, vol. 13, no. 13, 2024.

[4] T. Clear et al., 'AI integration in the IT professional workplace: A scoping review and interview study with implications for education and professional competencies', in *2024 Working Group Reports on Innovation and Technology in Computer Science Education*, ACM, 2024, pp. 34–67.

[5] M. Cazzaniga et al., *Gen-AI: Artificial Intelligence and the Future of Work*. International Monetary Fund, 2024.

[6] V. Corvello, 'Generative AI and the future of innovation management: A human centered perspective and an agenda for future research', *Journal of Open Innovation: Technology, Market, and Complexity*, vol. 11, no. 1, 2025.

[7] O. Sahin and D. Karayel, 'Generative Artificial Intelligence (GenAI) in Business: A Systematic Review on the Threshold of Transformation', *Journal of Smart Systems Research*, vol. 5, no. 2, pp. 156–175, 2024. DOI: 10.58769/joinssr.1597110.

[8] S. Chowdhury, P. Budhwar and G. Wood, 'Generative artificial intelligence in business: Towards a strategic human resource management framework', *British Journal of Management*, vol. 35, no. 4, pp. 1680–1691, 2024, ISSN: 1467-8551. DOI: 10.1111/1467-8551.12824.

[9] C. Kobiella, Y. S. Flores López, F. Waltenberger, F. Draxler and A. Schmidt, '"If the Machine Is As Good As Me, Then What Use Am I?" – how the use of chatgpt changes young professionals' perception of productivity and accomplishment', in *Proceedings of the 2024 CHI Conference on Human Factors in Computing Systems (CHI '24)*, Association for Computing Machinery, 2024.

[10] P. Mukherjee and S. Dutta, 'When generative artificial intelligence enhances the quality of human output: Workplace implications', *SSRN Electron. J.*, 2025.

[11] A. Bick, A. Blandin and D. J. Deming, 'The rapid adoption of Generative AI', National Bureau of Economic Research, Tech. Rep., 2024.

[12] S. Joshi, 'Retraining US workforce in the age of agentic GenAI: Role of prompt engineering and up-skilling initiatives', *International Journal of Advanced Research in Science, Communication and Technology*, pp. 543–557, 2025.

[13] F. Li and H. Lewis, 'Transforming organisations through AI: Emerging strategies for navigating the future of business', *Journal of Financial Transformation*, vol. 60, pp. 66–75, 2025.

[14] M.-H. Huang and R. T. Rust, 'The caring machine: Feeling AI for customer care', *Journal of Marketing*, vol. 88, no. 5, pp. 1–23, 2024.

[15] J. G. Hall and L. Rapanotti, 'A design theory for software engineering', *Information and Software Technology*, vol. 87, pp. 46–61, 2017.

[16] J. Brier, L. Rapanotti and J. G. Hall, 'Problem based analysis of organisational change: A real-world example', in *International Workshop on Advances and Applications of Problem Frames*, J. G. Hall, L. Rapanotti, K. Cox and Z. Jin, Eds., ACM, 2006.

[17] A. Nkwocha, J. G. Hall and L. Rapanotti, 'Design rationale capture for process improvement in the globalised enterprise: An industrial study', *Journal of Software and Systems Modeling*, vol. 12, no. 4, pp. 825–845, 2013.

[18] G. Markov, J. G. Hall and L. Rapanotti, 'POE-Δ: A framework for change engineering', *Systems Engineering*, 2025, Submitted to Wiley's Systems Engineering.

[19] F. J. Aguilar, *Scanning the business environment*. New York, NY: Macmillan, 1967.

[20] G. Panagiotou, 'Bringing SWOT into focus', *Business Strategy Review*, vol. 14, no. 2, pp. 8–10, 2003.

Does Johnny Get the Message? Evaluating Cybersecurity Notifications for Everyday Users

Victor Jüttner
Dept. of Computer Science, Leipzig University
Center for Scalable Data Analytics and Artificial Intelligence (ScaDS.AI) Dresden/Leipzig, Germany
e-mail: victor.juettner@cs.uni-leipzig.de

Erik Buchmann
Dept. of Computer Science, Leipzig University
Center for Scalable Data Analytics and Artificial Intelligence (ScaDS.AI) Dresden/Leipzig, Germany
e-mail: erik.buchmann@cs.uni-leipzig.de

***Abstract*—Due to the increasing presence of networked devices in everyday life, not only cybersecurity specialists but also end users benefit from security applications such as firewalls, vulnerability scanners, and intrusion detection systems. Recent approaches use Large Language Models (LLMs) to rewrite brief, technical security alerts into intuitive language and suggest actionable measures, helping everyday users understand and respond appropriately to security risks. However, it remains an open question how well such alerts are explained to users. LLM outputs can also be hallucinated, inconsistent, or misleading. In this work, we introduce the Human-Centered Security Alert Evaluation Framework (HCSAEF). HCSAEF assesses LLM-generated cybersecurity notifications to support researchers who want to compare notifications generated for everyday users, improve them, or analyze the capabilities of different LLMs in explaining cybersecurity issues. We demonstrate HCSAEF through three use cases, which allow us to quantify the impact of prompt design, model selection, and output consistency. Our findings indicate that HCSAEF effectively differentiates generated notifications along dimensions such as intuitiveness, urgency, and correctness.**

Keywords-Evaluation Framework; Cybersecurity; Alert Messages.

I. INTRODUCTION

To ward off cyberattacks, security applications such as firewalls [1], [2], vulnerability scanners [3], or Intrusion Detection Systems (IDS) [4] scan networks and/or connected devices and generate security alerts about suspicious activity. For example, an IDS might identify unusual network packets and report: "*HTTP Response abnormal chunked for transfer encoding*". A firewall might log the alert: "*Wsmprovhost.exe trying to connect to 203.0.113.25:443, Connect Layer, Layer Run-Time ID 48*". A vulnerability scanner may produce: "*Remote Desktop Protocol RCE Vulnerabilities (2671387) detected. CVSSv3 Score 9.7. CVE-2012-0002 CVE-2012-0152 DFN-CERT-2012-0477*". Such alerts typically require expert interpretation, must be analyzed in the context of the network setup, and translated into meaningful countermeasures if necessary.

Because of the widespread proliferation of smart, connected devices, everyday users without cybersecurity expertise are increasingly required to protect complex networks and could benefit from such security applications. Recent work [5], [6] uses Large Language Models (LLMs) to rewrite cybersecurity alerts into intuitive notifications (see Figure 1). These notifications aim to explain the nature of the security threat and suggest actionable countermeasures. However, it is challenging to assess whether the LLM-generated notifications actually provide helpful advice. LLMs can generate superficial notifications that fail to address specific threats. They may substitute one unintuitive technical term for another, hallucinate, or produce inconsistencies. LLMs may also provide incorrect or unsafe advice. Even slight changes in the model or prompt can result in significantly different notifications.

Thus, researchers need to conduct multi-faceted analyses, compare LLMs based on their ability to rewrite cybersecurity alerts into self-explanatory notifications, optimize prompting strategies, and examine the robustness of the generated notifications. Our research question is as follows:

How can we systematically evaluate the quality of generated cybersecurity notifications?

We propose the *Human-Centered Security Alert Evaluation Framework (HCSAEF)* to assess the wording of cybersecurity alerts across seven dimensions: *Consequences*, *Context*, *Countermeasures*, *Correctness*, *Intuitiveness*, *Personalization*, and *Urgency*. These dimensions are derived from existing work on general LLM evaluation frameworks [7], [8] and research in security communication [9]–[16]. We make three contributions:

- We devise HCSAEF, our Human-Centered Security Alert Evaluation Framework for cybersecurity alerts.
- We define HCSAEF's seven evaluation dimensions using a 5-point Likert scale.
- We demonstrate the applicability of HCSAEF with a case study in which an LLM rewrites IDS alerts.

Our study acknowledges that HCSAEF is sensitive to prompt design, reflecting trade-offs between contextual richness and output precision, especially regarding personalization and actionability. We identify key differences between LLMs, e.g., Grok 3's strong personalization versus DeepSeek R1's unsafe advice and capture consistency trends across multiple repetitions. These insights help guide model selection, prompt refinement, and the design of effective LLM-generated security notifications. Currently, HCSAEF is applied manually. Next, we will automate it with an LLM-as-a-Judge approach [17].

Paper outline: Section II reviews related work. Section III describes the HCSAEF approach, followed by a case study in Section IV. Section V concludes the paper and discusses future work.

Urgent Security Alert – Suspicious Network Activity Detected in Your Home Network

Dear [Homeowner's Name],

I hope this message finds you well. I am reaching out to inform you about a security alert detected on your home network. The network monitoring tool has flagged an issue with a message labeled:

"HTTP Response abnormal chunked for transfer-encoding."

This means that unusual activity has been detected in the way data is being transferred over your network. While this does not immediately confirm an attack, it is a strong indication that one of your smart home devices or computers might be compromised or targeted by hackers.

What This Means for You

This alert suggests that a device on your home network is sending or receiving data in an abnormal way. It could indicate a hacker attempting to gain access to your smart home devices (e.g., security cameras, smart thermostats, or even your personal computer). If this is an attack, the hacker may be trying to steal personal information, spy through a connected camera, or gain control over smart devices.

How Urgent Is This?

This is a serious security concern that should be addressed immediately. If left unchecked, your devices and personal data may be at risk. Cybercriminals can potentially access sensitive information, misuse smart home devices, or even use your network for illegal activities.

What You Should Do Now – Step-by-Step Guide to Secure Your Network

Follow these steps to protect your home network and devices from potential harm:

1. Restart Your Internet Router: Unplug your router from the power source, wait 30 seconds, then plug it back in. This may stop an ongoing attack or suspicious activity.

2. Identify Devices on Your Network: Use your router's app or web interface to check all connected devices. If you see any unfamiliar devices, disconnect them immediately.

3. Update Your Smart Devices and Computers: Go to each device's settings and check for software updates. This includes smart cameras, thermostats, TVs, laptops, and phones. Keeping devices updated prevents hackers from exploiting vulnerabilities.

4. Change Your Wi-Fi Password: Use a strong password with at least 12 characters, including letters, numbers, and symbols. Reconnect your devices using the new password.

5. Check Your Security Cameras (If Installed): If you have smart security cameras, review recent recordings to see if they have been accessed unexpectedly. Change their passwords to something strong and unique.

6. Scan Your Computer for Malware: If you use a Windows or Mac computer, run a full antivirus scan to check for infections.

7. Monitor for Further Alerts: If you continue receiving alerts about suspicious network activity, you may need professional help to secure your network.

Final Thoughts

If you follow these steps, your home network will be significantly safer. However, if the suspicious activity continues, it may indicate a deeper security issue requiring expert intervention.
I highly recommend taking these steps immediately to ensure your privacy and safety. If you need any help or have questions, please feel free to reach out.

Stay safe, [Your Name] Cybersecurity Specialist

Figure 1. Example of a cybersecurity alert rewritten by GPT-4o into a detailed, user-friendly notification tailored for non-expert homeowners.

II. Related Work

A. *Smart Home Threat Landscape and Intrusion Detection*

Modern smart homes are equipped with a variety of interconnected devices—ranging from smart TVs and refrigerators to thermostats and lighting systems—that enhance convenience and automation. However, these devices often suffer from inadequate security measures, such as the lack of regular firmware updates, making them attractive targets for cyberattacks [18]. Their interconnected nature means that a compromise in one device can potentially lead to a breach across the entire home network [19]. This risk is further amplified by the fact that many users lack the technical expertise needed to properly configure and secure these devices [20].

To mitigate these risks, considerable research has been directed toward the development of IDS tailored for smart home environments. Anthi et al. [21] introduced a supervised IDS capable of detecting various network-based attacks in IoT (Internet of Things) environments. Sikder et al. [22] developed Aegis+, a context-aware and platform-independent security framework that provides users with detailed, customizable alerts about malicious activity, including the type of event, affected devices, and their physical locations. Similarly, the Dynamic Risk Assessment Framework (DRAF) proposed by Collen and Nijdam [23] dynamically assesses IoT threats and adjusts alerts based on user-defined risk thresholds. Visoottiviseth et al. [24] presented PITI, a hybrid IDS that enhances user awareness by delivering auditory and textual alerts with detailed information about detected attacks and the IP addresses of affected devices.

B. Usable Security Notifications

Security alerts aim to warn users before harm occurs, but their effectiveness often suffers due to misunderstandings, lack of trust, or perceived inconvenience, especially among non-experts [25], [26]. Fear-based messaging, while tempting, has proven ineffective and can erode trust [16], [27].

Instead, effective alerts should use brief, nontechnical language [10], [28], clearly explain the risk [10], the consequences of ignoring it [10], and how the threat could personally affect the user [12], [13]. Alerts should also provide actionable steps for mitigation [10], ideally in a way that aligns with users' mental models [12].

Theories such as Protection Motivation Theory (PMT) [9] and the Communication-Human Information Processing (C-HIP) model [11] support this approach by emphasizing the roles of perceived severity, response efficacy, and cognitive processing in user behavior. Cranor [29] and Zimmermann et al. [30] further advocate for human-centered security, shifting the focus from human error to system support.

C. LLMs for Cybersecurity Communication

LLMs increasingly influence many aspects of cybersecurity [31], one of which is their ability to translate technical outputs—such as IDS alerts and vulnerability reports—into formats understandable by non-experts.

ChatIDS [5], introduced by Jüttner et al., utilizes GPT-3.5-turbo (Generative Pre-trained Transformer) to translate IDS alerts into user-friendly security notifications tailored for non-expert users in smart home environments. Similarly, ChatSEC [6], developed by Hoffmann and Buchmann, employs GPT-4 to transform vulnerability scan results into accessible explanations, supporting university network administrators with limited IT security expertise. HuntGPT [32], introduced by Ali and Kostakos, combines machine learning-based IDS with explainable Artificial Intelligence and GPT-3.5-turbo to provide analysts with actionable threat explanations through a conversational dashboard. SHIELD [33], proposed by Gandhi et al., integrates statistical anomaly detection, graph-based analysis, and LLM reasoning to detect and explain advanced persistent threats, offering interpretable attack narratives to security analysts.

D. Prompt Strategies

Prompt engineering is the practice of designing inputs to LLMs to improve the accuracy and relevance of their outputs. How a task is framed through role assignment, structured instructions, or contextual information can strongly influence model behavior. Common strategies include chain-of-thought prompting, self-reflection, and persona conditioning. For example, assigning the model the role of an expert or breaking down a complex instruction into steps can lead to more coherent and useful responses. These techniques help align model inference with user intent, especially in domains that require clarity for non-expert users [34].

Current state-of-the-art models include DeepSeek R1 [35], OpenAI's GPT-4o and O1 [36], [37], and Grok 3 from xAI [38]. While each model varies in architecture and behavior, their performance is strong in natural language reasoning, code generation, and multimodal inference, according to multiple benchmarks [39], [40].

E. Qualitative Evaluation of LLM Responses

Automated reference-based metrics like BERTScore [41] and MoverScore [42] fall short when applied to open-ended language tasks, where valid responses can vary widely in form. Their limitations in capturing semantic nuance or conversational appropriateness have been well documented [43], motivating a shift toward qualitative evaluation strategies.

To automate evaluation, frameworks such as OpenAI Evals [44] and G-Eval [45] have emerged. OpenAI Evals provides a structured environment for benchmarking across diverse tasks, while G-Eval uses LLMs as evaluators to assess dimensions like correctness, coherence, and helpfulness.

Recent work has further refined the dimensions used in qualitative evaluation. Chang et al. [7] identify key criteria such as factual accuracy, relevance to the prompt, fluency, transparency in reasoning, safety in terms of avoiding harmful or misleading content, and general alignment with human values. In a conversational context, the FED framework [8] introduces similar but dialogue-specific dimensions, focusing on contextual relevance, logical coherence, natural phrasing, factual correctness, and user engagement.

In domain-specific settings like cybersecurity, the SECURE benchmark [46] evaluates LLMs on tasks that require contextual understanding, factual consistency, and reasoning over real-world advisories. Its focus on practical, high-stakes scenarios makes it a valuable reference for qualitative evaluation in specialized domains.

III. Our HCSAEF Approach

We introduce HCSAEF, our Human-Centered Security Alert Evaluation Framework, to evaluate LLM-generated cybersecurity notifications across seven dimensions. We adapted the dimensions *Context*, *Correctness*, and *Intuitiveness* from general LLM evaluation frameworks [7], [8], which focus on accuracy, relevance, and clarity. The remaining dimensions, *Countermeasures*, *Consequences*, *Personalization*, and *Urgency*, were derived from security communication research. In particular, *Countermeasures* and *Consequences* reflect Protection Motivation Theory and the need for actionable, motivating content [9]–[11]. *Personalization* improves relevance to the user [12], [13], while *Urgency* emphasizes timely action without relying on fear appeals [14]–[16].

We rate each dimension on a 5-point Likert scale from 0 to 4, which aligns with common practice in this field. The lowest rating, 0 (*Unsatisfactory*), means that this dimension is not present in the notification. 1 (*Needs Improvement*) suggests that the dimension is present but not adequately worded. 2 (*Satisfactory*) refers to a clearly identifiable dimension. 3 (*Very Good*) indicates a dimension that is well fulfilled. Finally, 4 (*Outstanding*) means that the dimension exceeds expectations. In the following, we explain each dimension in alphabetical order and describe how it is rated.

a) Consequences: The dimension **Consequences** (see Table I) measures whether the consequences of disregarding the particular alert are communicated to the user.

TABLE I
DEFINITION OF THE DIMENSION "CONSEQUENCES".

Scale	*Definition*
0	The notification does not mention consequences.
1	The consequences are mentioned at a superficial level, e.g., "Not acting could result in a loss of data."
2	General consequences are mentioned without details, e.g., "Someone could steal personal data from your devices."
3	Specific consequences for the home network are mentioned, e.g., "This could lead to data theft, financial or legal problems, or even your smart home devices being used for espionage."
4	The notification names specific consequences along with the affected devices, e.g., "An attacker could eavesdrop on your conversations with your Echo Hub or track movement with your Shelly Motion Sensor."

For example, the consequences of disregarding a successful denial-of-service attack on a smart device are typically low. The user could simply wait out the attack until the device is working again. Non-existent, superficial, or generic consequences result in lower ratings. What a user without cybersecurity expertise actually needs is an explanation of the consequences that is specific to their network setup or, even better, specific to their network and the devices present on it.

b) Context: Dimension **Context** (see Table II) reflects how well the cybersecurity threat is explained. The user needs this information to understand what the threat means for the security of their home.

TABLE II
DEFINITION OF THE DIMENSION "CONTEXT".

Scale	*Definition*
0	The notification does not mention the context of the threat.
1	The context is mentioned at a superficial level, e.g., "Malicious software, designed to damage or disrupt systems, could steal data or gain unauthorized access."
2	General contextual information is provided, e.g., "There is traffic inside your network that looks as if it is related to a type of malware called the Harakit botnet."
3	Specific context about the attack mechanism is given, e.g., "Imagine your router as a locked door, and a hacker trying to trick the lock and enter your network uninvited."
4	Detailed information about all concepts needed to understand the cybersecurity threat without reading external sources.

For example, it is important to understand whether a threat is about reconnaissance and preparation for an attack, or an ongoing attack. The scale for this dimension ranges from not mentioning the context (0) to explaining the threat in great detail (4), so that the user does not need external information sources to fully understand the threat.

c) Countermeasures: Dimension **Countermeasures** (see Table III) is about explaining countermeasures that are appropriate to ward off the cybersecurity threat. A countermeasure is satisfactory if it is rather broad and unspecific but generally applicable and mitigates the threat to some extent.

TABLE III
DEFINITION OF THE DIMENSION "COUNTERMEASURES".

Scale	*Definition*
0	The notification does not mention countermeasures.
1	Countermeasures are incomplete or too advanced, e.g., "Browse the system log for indications of an attack."
2	Unspecific but working countermeasures are described, e.g., "Disconnect the router from the network."
3	Specific measures are explained step by step, e.g., "Unplug the router, perform a factory reset, and install a new firmware."
4	Intuitive explanations of specific measures do not leave room for misunderstandings, e.g., describe in detail how to perform a factory reset and install an update on a certain router.

For example, the user could simply turn off the threatened device. Much better countermeasures allow the user to eliminate a device's vulnerability, particularly if the countermeasure is intuitively explained step by step.

d) Correctness: Dimension **Correctness** (see Table IV) considers whether the dimensions of consequences, context, countermeasures, and urgency of the cybersecurity alert are neither missing, flawed, hallucinated, misleading, incorrect, nor described in a way that leaves room for mistakes for a user without cybersecurity expertise.

TABLE IV
DEFINITION OF THE DIMENSION "CORRECTNESS".

Scale	*Definition*
0	Consequences, context, countermeasures, or urgency are either missing, hallucinated, misleading, or incorrect, so that serious cybersecurity risks persist.
1	Consequences, context, countermeasures, or urgency are flawed or misleading, but this can be recognized with some research.
2	Incorrect or inconsistent consequences, context, countermeasures, or urgency can be recognized easily, e.g., if the notification mentions a device that is not in the network.
3	Consequences, context, countermeasures, and urgency are essentially correct, but the wording leaves room for mistakes.
4	Consequences, context, countermeasures, and urgency are correctly and unmistakably described.

The rating of this dimension is based on the impact on cybersecurity. For example, a flawed countermeasure that has such an impact would be to stop warning messages about blocked network connections by disabling the router's firewall. On the other hand, an example of correct urgency is a notification that unmistakably explains how quickly a threat could result in which kind of harm to the home.

e) Intuitiveness: Dimension **Intuitiveness** (see Table V) measures whether the notification uses intuitive wording. This relates to the user's assumed lack of knowledge regarding cybersecurity-specific terms.

TABLE V
DEFINITION OF THE DIMENSION "INTUITIVENESS".

Scale	*Definition*
0	Consequences, context, countermeasures, or urgency are either missing or contain deep cybersecurity technical terms, e.g., "HTTP Response abnormally chunked."
1	Some information related to consequences, context, countermeasures, or urgency is not intuitively understandable, e.g., "ntalkd might have a vulnerability hackers could exploit."
2	Countermeasures and urgency are intuitively understandable, which allows the user to mitigate an attack without understanding it.
3	Context, countermeasures, and urgency are intuitively understandable, which allows the user to assess and mitigate the attack.
4	All parts of the rewritten notification are concise and understandable, without referring to deep cybersecurity terms.

For example, we do not expect the user to be familiar with the names of attack vectors, specific threats, network protocols, Linux daemons, or network services. Intuitiveness and correctness meet at rating 0 (unsatisfactory), because missing information is unintuitive and incorrect at the same time. Our scale reflects that it is less of a problem if users don't understand the attack, as long as they can fix it properly.

f) Personalization: Dimension **Personalization** (see Table VI) considers to what extent the notification is personalized to the user, their use case, and home network.

TABLE VI
DEFINITION OF THE DIMENSION "PERSONALIZATION".

Scale	*Definition*
0	The notification does not refer to the user or the network setup.
1	The notification is less specific and broad, e.g., "Anomalous actions are often first indicators of compromised devices."
2	The notification is tailored to the user and their network, e.g., "The attacker could gain unauthorized access to your Echo Hub, potentially stealing sensitive information or using it to attack other networks."
3	The notification is tailored to the user and their network and also refers to the specific mode of attack, e.g., "The malware Linux.IoTReaper tries to infect your Echo Hub, and could use it to attack others from your network."
4	The notification includes comprehensive information about the user, the devices under attack, and the compromised use case, e.g., "Dear John, Linux.IoTReaper scans networks for vulnerable Linux devices and attempts to log into the devices. After that, the malware installs itself onto the system and begins downloading and executing commands from (...)"

Thus, we assess whether a user can relate a cybersecurity threat to their actual situation. This refers to the network, its connected devices, and how the devices are configured and used. For example, assume a session-hijacking attempt on a smart security camera. By relating this alert to their concrete installation, the user can decide whether this is a threat to this specific camera or not. If the camera is disallowed from connecting to external devices anyway, the alert can be ignored.

g) Urgency: Dimension **Urgency** (see Table VII) determines how well the notification takes into account the urgency of dealing with the cybersecurity threat.

TABLE VII
DEFINITION OF THE DIMENSION "URGENCY".

Scale	*Definition*
0	The notification does not address the urgency of action.
1	The urgency is communicated in unspecific, broad terms, e.g., "It is important to secure the network."
2	A level of urgency is communicated, e.g., "The detected attack does not directly threaten your Echo Hub."
3	Urgency is communicated and explained, e.g., "It's important to take action quickly. Here's why: (...)"
4	Urgency is communicated and explained, and also considered in the writing style of the countermeasures, e.g., "Your Echo Hub is under attack. It is important to quickly disconnect it from the network, before the attacker installs malware."

For example, ongoing attacks may require an immediate response, while an alert about a vulnerability that is not currently being exploited may allow for a certain delay. Outstanding (4) is a notification that not only tells the level of urgency but also uses wording for the entire message that reflects how quickly a response to the alert should be made.

IV. CASE STUDY

In this section, we demonstrate HCSAEF's applicability for multifaceted analyses with three use cases: *"Comparing Different Prompts"* for prompt optimization, *"Comparing Different LLMs"* for explaining cybersecurity issues, and *"Robustness of the Response"* of the LLM.

A. Use Case: Comparing Different Prompts

We exemplarily chose two different prompts, as shown in Table VIII. **Prompt 1** follows a *zero-shot* prompting approach, i.e., it consists of a single prompt without any examples of what the output should look like. The prompt is supplemented by a list of devices in the network that might be under attack. **Prompt 2** uses *impersonation*, *zero-shot chain-of-thought* prompting, and reflection [34], i.e., it tells the LLM to deliver an output according to a certain role, contains contextual information about the general setting, and urges the LLM to reason and reflect on its answer. However, Prompt 2 does not deliver details of the devices on the network to an externally hosted LLM.

To find out with HCSAEF which prompt is better suited for a user without cybersecurity expertise to deal with a potential cyberattack, we replace [ALERT] with the example from the introduction, "HTTP Response abnormal chunked for transfer-encoding". Then, we execute both prompts with ChatGPT 4o [36] and evaluate its output with HCSAEF. Figure 1 exemplarily shows GPT 4o's output for Prompt 2 with the alert

TABLE VIII
PROMPTS

No.	Prompt
1	Explain the cybersecurity alert [ALERT] to a user without cybersecurity expertise. Align your explanation to the following home devices: Blink Surveillance IP Camera, Echo Hub, Smart TV, Game Console, Blink Camera, Shelly Motion Sensor. Provide countermeasures to isolate the attack and mitigate the possible damage. The countermeasures should be easy to follow and only involve tasks that are practicable for users without cybersecurity expertise. Tell the urgency of the issue.
2	Consider a private home network containing various smart home devices. A network monitoring tool has detected suspicious network traffic and generated the alert [ALERT]. You are a cybersecurity expert with years of professional experience in incident response. Your task is to write a message to the homeowner, which informs them about this alert. The homeowner has no prior knowledge in computer science and cybersecurity. Find out if the alert means that the network is currently under attack. Communicate the current threat to which the network is exposed. Explain which devices could be under attack. Explain how urgent it is to deal with the alert, and communicate the consequences of not reacting. Provide a detailed step-by-step plan of measures to mitigate the security threat. Reflect on your message and ensure that it is easy to follow for a user without technical expertise.

TABLE IX
EVALUATING FIGURE 1 WITH HCSAEF.

Dimension	Rating	Rationale
Consequences	3	Consequences are specific and detailed to the extent of the information provided in the prompt.
Context	3	Context is specific but lacks some detail, e.g., what does "sending or receiving data in an abnormal way" mean?
Countermeasures	4	Meaningful countermeasures are provided and explained.
Correctness	4	The rewritten alert carefully explains that abnormally chunked transfer encodings are not an attack as such, but might be an indication that an attacker is trying to find a weak spot on a device.
Intuitiveness	4	The rewritten alert only uses technical terms at an intuitive level.
Personalization	2	Although no devices were mentioned in the prompt, the rewritten alert refers to typical devices that could be at risk.
Urgency	4	The rewritten alert explains in detail that an attack may be underway, which needs to be dealt with urgently.

"*HTTP Response abnormal chunked for transfer-encoding*". Table IX shows the result of this evaluation.

The table indicates that Prompt 2 indeed produces a notification that helps an everyday user secure their home network. However, there is room for improvement regarding the context of the attack, more specific consequences, and personalization. HCSAEF shows that it is worth considering providing the prompt with more details about the network and the user.

Figure 2 compares the output of Prompt 1 and Prompt 2, both generated with GPT 4o. Prompt 1 uses a simpler prompting scheme than Prompt 2 but adds details about the network, as suggested by Table IX. For brevity, we refrain from reproducing the rewritten alert and the rationale for HCSAEF's assessment.

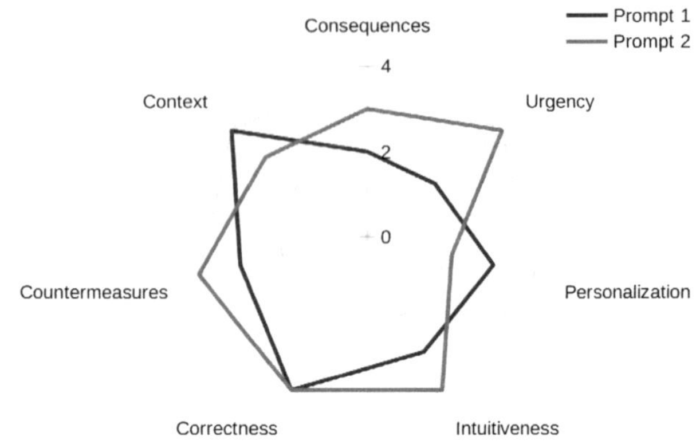

Figure 2. Comparing Prompt 1 and Prompt 2 with HCSAEF.

Figure 2 shows that adding further details indeed increases the ratings for Context and Personalization. However, with a simpler prompting scheme, the LLM produced a coarser output. For example, the LLM did not use the provided details about the devices to explain which cybersecurity risks exist due to the detected irregularities, and where to look for a reset button or firmware updates. With Prompt 1, however, the LLM generated a more general output and just mentioned the devices in an unspecific way. The countermeasures included tasks that require expertise, e.g., "*Disable unused remote access features on your devices.*", resulting in a lower rating for Intuitiveness.

We conclude that HCSAEF indeed provides a differentiated evaluation of security alerts rewritten by an LLM. This helps when tuning the prompts and deciding whether to provide details regarding installed devices and network configurations.

B. Use Case: Comparing Different LLMs

To evaluate how well each LLM explains a cybersecurity alert to everyday users, we ran experiments in March 2025 using the public web interfaces of the respective platforms. We tested Grok3 (grok-3-latest) [38], GPT4o (chatgpt-4o-latest) [36], OpenAI o1 (o1-2024-12-17) [37], and DeepSeekR1 (deepseek-r1:671b) [35] with Prompt 1. All models were used with default settings, without fine-tuning or system modifications. Each received the same zero-shot prompt including the alert and network device details. For brevity, we summarize key output differences without reproducing full responses.

Figure 3 shows the ratings of the LLMs we tested with Prompt 1. Grok3 outperformed all other LLMs, using the devices in the prompt to explain in detail the attack consequences, how to narrow down infected devices, and how to perform a factory reset. It also conveyed the urgency clearly, stating, "*This isn't a drop everything and panic situation, but it's serious enough to act on quickly—think of it like noticing a stranger hanging around your front door.*"

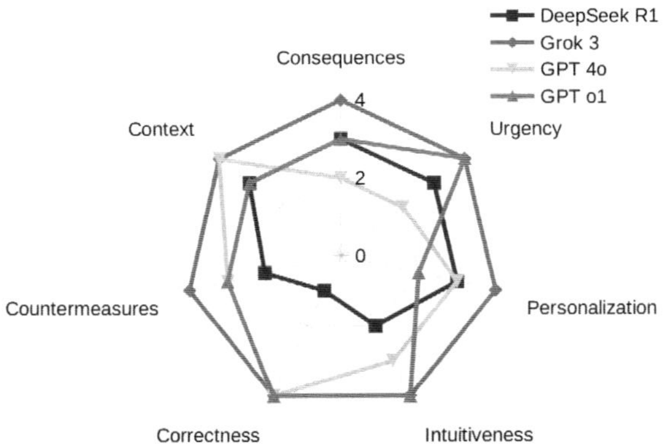

Figure 3. Comparing different LLMs with HCSAEF.

In contrast, DeepSeek R1 generated misleading countermeasures that would provide new vulnerabilities, e.g., suggesting that the password for the security camera should be reset to "*C@meraSunset2024*", which an attacker could brute-force with a dictionary quickly. DeepSeek R1 also delivered superficial and less complete consequences and assumed that any device in the network performs a factory reset by pressing the reset button for 10 seconds.

We already discussed the performance of GPT 4o in the last subsection. GPT o1 performed slightly better. Its extended reasoning provided a more elaborate list of consequences of ignoring the alert. It also did not need technical terms to explain the cybersecurity threat and related countermeasures in precise language. However, GPT o1 did not use the devices given in the prompt to generate a personalized answer. Instead, GPT o1 restricted itself to general (but correct) explanations and countermeasures, such as "*Keep an eye on your devices for unusual behavior—like random reboots, significantly slower performance, or new apps that you never installed on your Smart TV or Game Console. Weird changes often hint at malicious activity.*"

We conclude that HCSAEF generates a well-differentiated picture of the abilities of various LLMs to explain complex cybersecurity alerts. It seems that there are big differences in how the LLMs evaluate the same prompt, and selecting the proper model is an important step.

C. Use Case: Robustness of the Response

To find out how robust the generated responses are, we repeated Prompt 1 with Grok 3 and GPT 4o three times each. We did not modify the default "temperature" parameters. We observed that Grok's answers did not deviate much from one execution to another. Sometimes, the order of the countermeasures changed, and there were variations in the wording. Occasionally, Grok 3 decided to provide emotional support (e.g., "*You don't need to be a tech wizard to handle this!*") or indicate the effort needed (e.g., "Check for Updates (,,,) Time: 10-15 minutes per device (plus update download time)"). All of Grok's responses were rated "Outstanding" in each dimension, with one exception: Once, Grok suggested a weak, dictionary-based password ("*Set a new password (...) like MyDogRocks2025!*").

In contrast, GPT 4o's responses deviated significantly from one execution to another. It sometimes decided to consider the list of devices in the prompt and provided a personalized response, including a detailed step-by-step guide on how to execute a factory reset on each device named in the prompt. Since we executed our case study at different times of the day, we suspect that GPT 4o produces a more sophisticated response at times of lower system load. Figure 4 shows the evaluation of three executions of Prompt 1 with GPT-4o.

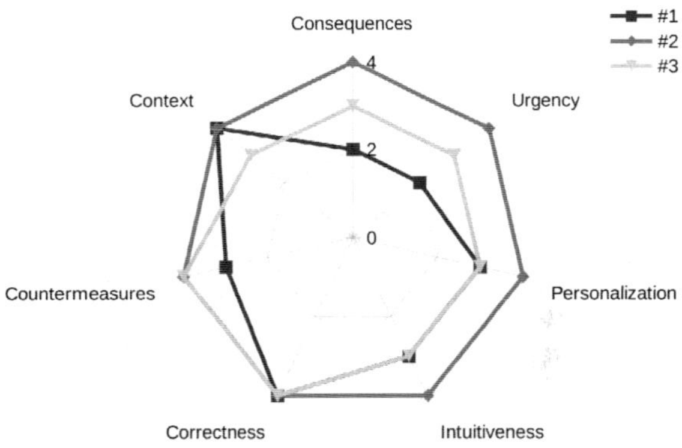

Figure 4. GPT 4o executing Prompt 1 three times.

We conclude that HCSAEF allows us to observe important properties regarding the robustness of the prompt executions, which will foster fine-tuning the model or adjusting the temperature settings. For example, we observed GPT 4o generating heterogeneous responses, but all of them were correct.

V. Conclusion and Future Work

The proliferation of smart devices has made cybersecurity tools like firewalls and IDS relevant to everyday users. LLMs have been proposed to rewrite the technical alerts of security tools into actionable notifications that are intended to help private users secure their homes. This work introduces HCSAEF, which allows for the evaluation of such notifications across seven dimensions. The purpose of HCSAEF is to support multifaceted analyses, such as comparing the capabilities of different LLMs in explaining cybersecurity issues, different prompting strategies, or whether providing more details to the LLM actually leads to better notifications. We have demonstrated HCSAEF's applicability through a case study.

For the time being, we have evaluated HCSAEF's dimensions manually. Our next step will be implementing HCSAEF into a RAG approach, i.e., we will generate a synthetic evaluation data set as a reference and use an LLM-as-a-judge approach to automatically evaluate cybersecurity notifications. Once automated, we will use HCSAEF for large-scale experiments with various rewriting approaches, prompting strategies, and LLMs. Furthermore, we plan to run comparative experiments to determine whether HCSAEF's evaluation is similar to the assessment of a human user, in order to fine-tune the rating and build a ground truth for future evaluations.

ACKNOWLEDGMENT

We sincerely thank Louis Carlos Roth for his invaluable assistance with the evaluation framework and the case studies. The authors acknowledge the financial support by the Federal Ministry of Research, Technology and Space of Germany and by Sächsische Staatsministerium für Wissenschaft, Kultur und Tourismus in the programme Center of Excellence for AI-research "Center for Scalable Data Analytics and Artificial Intelligence Dresden/Leipzig", project identification number: ScaDS.AI

REFERENCES

[1] K. Ingham and S. Forrest, "A history and survey of network firewalls," *University of New Mexico, Tech. Rep*, 2002.

[2] J. Liang and Y. Kim, "Evolution of firewalls: Toward securer network using next generation firewall," in *IEEE 12th Annual Computing and Communication Workshop and Conference*, 2022, pp. 752–759.

[3] A. Tundis, W. Mazurczyk, and M. Mühlhäuser, "A review of network vulnerabilities scanning tools: types, capabilities and functioning," in *Proceedings of the 13th International Conference on Availability, Reliability and Security*, ser. ARES '18. Association for Computing Machinery, 2018.

[4] A. Patel, Q. Qassim, and C. Wills, "A survey of intrusion detection and prevention systems," *Information Management & Computer Security*, vol. 18, no. 4, pp. 277–290, 2010.

[5] V. Jüttner, M. Grimmer, and E. Buchmann, "ChatIDS: Advancing explainable cybersecurity using generative AI," *International Journal On Advances in Security*, vol. 17, no. 1,2, 2024.

[6] M. Hoffmann and E. Buchmann, "Chatsec: Spicing up vulnerability scans with AI for heterogeneous university it - towards enhancing security vulnerability reports for non-experts," in *Proceedings of the Conference on AI-based Systems and Services (AISyS'24)*, 2024.

[7] Y. Chang *et al.*, "A survey on evaluation of large language models," *ACM Trans. Intell. Syst. Technol.*, vol. 15, no. 3, 2024.

[8] S. Mehri and M. Eskenazi, "Unsupervised evaluation of interactive dialog with DialoGPT," in *Proceedings of the 21th Annual Meeting of the Special Interest Group on Discourse and Dialogue*, O. Pietquin *et al.*, Eds. 1st virtual meeting: Association for Computational Linguistics, Jul. 2020, pp. 225–235.

[9] R. W. Rogers, "Cognitive and physiological processes in fear appeals and attitude change: A revised theory of protection motivation," *Social psychology: A source book*, pp. 153–176, 1983.

[10] C. Bravo-Lillo, L. F. Cranor, J. Downs, and S. Komanduri, "Bridging the gap in computer security warnings: A mental model approach," *IEEE Security & Privacy*, vol. 9, pp. 18–26, 2011.

[11] M. S. Wogalter, "Communication-human information processing (c-hip) model," in *Forensic human factors and ergonomics*. CRC Press, 2018.

[12] S. Bartsch, M. Volkamer, H. Theuerling, and F. Karayumak, "Contextualized web warnings, and how they cause distrust," in *Trust and Trustworthy Computing: 6th International Conference*. Springer, 2013, pp. 205–222.

[13] M. Kauer *et al.*, "It is not about the design - it is about the content! making warnings more efficient by communicating risks appropriately," in *SICHERHEIT 2012 – Sicherheit, Schutz und Zuverlässigkeit*, 2012.

[14] C. Conrad, J. Aziz, N. Smith, and A. Newman, "What do users feel? towards affective eeg correlates of cybersecurity notifications," in *Information Systems and Neuroscience*, F. D. Davis, R. Riedl *et al.*, Eds. Cham: Springer International Publishing, 2020, pp. 153–162.

[15] A. Von Preuschen, M. C. Schuhmacher, and V. Zimmermann, "Beyond fear and frustration - towards a holistic understanding of emotions in cybersecurity," in *Proceedings of the Twentieth USENIX Conference on Usable Privacy and Security*. USENIX Association, 2024.

[16] A. Sasse, "Scaring and bullying people into security won't work," *IEEE Security & Privacy*, vol. 13, no. 3, pp. 80–83, 2015.

[17] L. Zheng *et al.*, "Judging LLM-as-a-Judge with MT-Bench and Chatbot Arena," in *Advances in Neural Information Processing Systems*, A. Oh, T. Naumann *et al.*, Eds., vol. 36. Curran Associates, Inc., 2023, pp. 46 595–46 623.

[18] C. Chhetri and V. Motti, "Identifying vulnerabilities in security and privacy of smart home devices," in *National Cyber Summit (NCS) Research Track 2020*, K.-K. R. Choo, T. Morris *et al.*, Eds. Cham: Springer International Publishing, 2021, pp. 211–231.

[19] H. Touqeer *et al.*, "Smart home security: challenges, issues and solutions at different IoT layers," *J. Supercomput.*, vol. 77, no. 12, p. 14053–14089, dec 2021.

[20] N. Pattnaik, S. Li, and J. R. C. Nurse, "A survey of user perspectives on security and privacy in a home networking environment," *ACM Computing Surveys*, vol. 55, pp. 1 – 38, 2022.

[21] E. Anthi, L. Williams, M. Słowińska, G. Theodorakopoulos, and P. Burnap, "A supervised intrusion detection system for smart home IoT devices," *IEEE Internet of Things Journal*, vol. 6, no. 5, pp. 9042–9053, 2019.

[22] A. K. Sikder, L. Babun, and A. S. Uluagac, "Aegis+: A context-aware platform-independent security framework for smart home systems," *Digital Threats*, vol. 2, no. 1, 2021.

[23] A. Collen and N. A. Nijdam, "Can I sleep safely in my smarthome? a novel framework on automating dynamic risk assessment in IoT environments," *Electronics*, vol. 11, no. 7, 2022.

[24] V. Visoottiviseth, G. Chutaporn, S. Kungvanruttana, and J. Paisarnduangjan, "Piti: Protecting internet of things via intrusion detection system on raspberry pi," in *2020 International Conference on Information and Communication Technology Convergence (ICTC)*, 2020, pp. 75–80.

[25] M. Wogalter, "Purposes and scope of warnings," *Handbook of Warnings*, pp. 3–9, 01 2006.

[26] K. S. Jones, N. R. Lodinger, B. P. Widlus, A. Siami Namin, E. Maw, and M. E. Armstrong, "How do non experts think about cyber attack consequences?" *Information & Computer Security*, vol. 30, no. 4, pp. 473–489, 2022.

[27] M. Dupuis, A. Jennings, and K. Renaud, "Scaring people is not enough: An examination of fear appeals within the context of promoting good password hygiene," in *Proceedings of the 22nd Annual Conference on Information Technology Education*. Association for Computing Machinery, 2021, pp. 35–40.

[28] L. Bauer, C. Bravo-Lillo, L. Cranor, and E. Fragkaki, "Warning design guidelines," CyLab, Carnegie Mellon University, Tech. Rep., 2013.

[29] L. F. Cranor, "A framework for reasoning about the human in the loop," in *Proceedings of the Conference on Usability, Psychology, and Security*, ser. UPSEC'08. USA: USENIX Association, 2008.

[30] V. Zimmermann and K. Renaud, "Moving from a 'human-as-problem" to a 'human-as-solution" cybersecurity mindset," *International Journal of Human-Computer Studies*, vol. 131, pp. 169–187, 2019.

[31] J. Zhang *et al.*, "When LLMs meet cybersecurity: a systematic literature review," *Cybersecurity*, vol. 8, no. 1, p. 55, 2025. [Online]. Available: https://doi.org/10.1186/s42400-025-00361-w

[32] T. Ali and P. Kostakos, "Huntgpt: Integrating machine learning-based anomaly detection and explainable AI with Large Language Models (LLMs)," 2023.

[33] P. A. Gandhi, P. N. Wudali, Y. Amaru, Y. Elovici, and A. Shabtai, "Shield: Apt detection and intelligent explanation using LLM," 2025.

[34] S. Schulhoff *et al.*, "The prompt report: A systematic survey of prompt engineering techniques," *arXiv preprint arXiv:2406.06608*, 2024.

[35] DeepSeek, "Deepseek-r1," 2025, accessed: 2025-04-10. [Online]. Available: https://github.com/deepseek-ai/DeepSeek-R1

[36] OpenAI, "Hello gpt-4o," 2024, accessed: 2025-04-10. [Online]. Available: https://openai.com/index/hello-gpt-4o/

[37] ——, "Introducing openai o1-preview," 2024, accessed: 2025-04-10. [Online]. Available: https://openai.com/index/introducing-openai-o1-preview/

[38] xAI, "Grok 3: The next generation of conversational AI," 2024, accessed: 2025-04-10. [Online]. Available: https://x.ai/grok

[39] J. Chavez, "LLM leaderboard," https://llm-stats.com/, 2025, accessed: 2025-04-10.

[40] UC Berkeley SkyLab and LMArena, "Chatbot arena LLM leaderboard: Community-driven evaluation for best LLM and AI chatbots," https://lmarena.ai/, 2025, accessed: 2025-04-10.

[41] T. Zhang, V. Kishore, F. Wu, K. Q. Weinberger, and Y. Artzi, "Bertscore: Evaluating text generation with bert," *arXiv.1904.09675*, 2020.

[42] W. Zhao *et al.*, "MoverScore: Text generation evaluating with contextualized embeddings and earth mover distance," in *9th International Joint Conference on Natural Language Processing (EMNLP-IJCNLP)*, K. Inui, J. Jiang *et al.*, Eds. Association for Computational Linguistics, 2019, pp. 563–578.

[43] C.-W. Liu *et al.*, "How NOT to evaluate your dialogue system: An empirical study of unsupervised evaluation metrics for dialogue response generation," in *Proceedings of the 2016 Conference on Empirical Methods in Natural Language Processing*, J. Su, K. Duh, and X. Carreras, Eds. Association for Computational Linguistics, Nov. 2016, pp. 2122–2132.

[44] OpenAI, "Openai evals: A framework for evaluating LLMs and LLM Systems," 2023, accessed: 2025-03-28. [Online]. Available: https://github.com/openai/evals

[45] Y. Liu, D. Iter, Y. Xu, S. Wang, R. Xu, and C. Zhu, "G-Eval: NLG evaluation using GPT-4 with better human alignment," *arXiv preprint arXiv:2303.16634*, 2023.

[46] D. Bhusal *et al.*, "Secure: Benchmarking generative large language models for cybersecurity advisory," *CoRR*, vol. abs/2405.20441, 2024.

Quantized Rank Reduction: A Communications-Efficient Federated Learning Scheme for Network-Critical Applications

Dimitrios Kritsiolis and Constantine Kotropoulos
Department of Informatics
Aristotle University of Thessaloniki
Thessaloniki 54124, Greece
email: {dkritsi, costas}@csd.auth.gr

***Abstract*—Federated learning is a machine learning approach that enables multiple devices (i.e., agents) to train a shared model cooperatively without exchanging raw data. This technique keeps data localized on user devices, ensuring privacy and security, while each agent trains the model on their own data and only shares model updates. The communication overhead is a significant challenge due to the frequent exchange of model updates between the agents and the central server. In this paper, we propose a communication-efficient federated learning scheme that utilizes low-rank approximation of neural network gradients and quantization to significantly reduce the network load of the decentralized learning process with minimal impact on the model's accuracy.**

Keywords-federated learning; Tucker decomposition; SVD; quantization.

I. INTRODUCTION

As artificial intelligence and machine learning evolve, new computational paradigms are emerging to address the increasing demand for privacy, efficiency, and scalability. One such approach is Federated Learning (FL), a decentralized learning technique that enables model training across multiple devices or agents without requiring direct data sharing [1] [2]. In FL, end devices train their model using local data and send model updates to the server for aggregation rather than sharing raw data. This approach enhances data privacy while allowing the server to refine the global model based on updates from multiple devices. FL is a key enabler of artificial intelligence in mobile devices and the Internet of Things (IoT) [3].

One of the key challenges in FL is the significant communications overhead, which does not scale efficiently as the number of participating devices increases [4]. The just-described issue becomes even more pronounced in deep learning, where models consist of voluminous parameters that must be shared by each client with the server at every training iteration. As a result, the communication bottleneck diminishes the advantage of distributed optimization, slowing the overall training process and reducing the efficiency gains expected from decentralized learning [5] [6]. To address this issue, we aim to compress and quantize the updates sent by clients, thereby mitigating the effects of communication overhead without significantly deteriorating the model's performance.

Before explaining the compression and quantization techniques, we formally introduce the distributed learning problem [7] solved by FL, i.e.,

$$\min_{\boldsymbol{\theta}} f(\boldsymbol{\theta}) = \min_{\boldsymbol{\theta}} \sum_{c \in \mathfrak{C}} f_c(\boldsymbol{\theta}) \quad \text{with} \quad f_c(\boldsymbol{\theta}) := \sum_{n=1}^{N_c} J(\boldsymbol{X}_{c,n}; \boldsymbol{\theta}), \tag{1}$$

where $\boldsymbol{\theta}$ denotes the parameters of the central model being trained, $\mathfrak{C}$ is the set of clients participating in FL with $|\mathfrak{C}| = C$, $\boldsymbol{X}_{c,n}$ is the n-th data point of client c (which can be a feature matrix or generally a feature tensor), N_c is the total number of data points at client c, $J(\boldsymbol{X}_{c,n}, \boldsymbol{\theta})$ is the loss function used in the FL setting and $f_c(\boldsymbol{\theta})$ is the local loss associated with client c and its data. The overall loss function we optimize is $f(\boldsymbol{\theta})$.

Problem (1) is solved using gradient descent. The gradient descent update at iteration $k+1$ is given by

$$\boldsymbol{\theta}^{k+1} = \boldsymbol{\theta}^k - \alpha \sum_{c \in \mathfrak{C}} \nabla f_c(\boldsymbol{\theta}^k), \tag{2}$$

where $\nabla f_c(\boldsymbol{\theta}^k)$ is the local gradient of client c associated with its data, and α is the learning rate. The sum term in (2) is a distributed version of gradient descent, also known as *Federated Averaging* [8]. Equation (2) implies that each client communicates its local gradient to the server at each training iteration. Depending on the quality of the network connection of each client, a significant overhead is introduced to the FL process. This overhead can surpass the computational cost of training a model for the client. To minimize the data transmission overhead on the distributed training process, we propose to compress the gradient of the loss function, which is reshaped to a matrix or tensor, into a more compact form utilizing a low-rank approximation [9] [10] [11] and then quantize the resulting compact form to reduce further the volume of the data to be transmitted at each iteration. The proposed novel scheme leverages the low-rank approximation of neural network gradients and established quantization algorithms.

The outline of the paper is as follows. Section II briefly describes the preliminaries, i.e., gradient compression and quantization. Section III details the proposed Quantized Rank Reduction (QRR) scheme and discusses the experimental results. Conclusions are drawn in Section IV. The code for QRR can be found at [12].

II. PRELIMINARIES

A. Gradient Compression

Neural network gradients are expressed in matrix or vector form [13]. Suppose we have a function $\boldsymbol{f} : \mathbb{R}^n \rightarrow \mathbb{R}^m$ that maps a vector of length n to a vector of length m:

$$\boldsymbol{f}(\boldsymbol{x}) = \begin{bmatrix} f_1(x_1, \ldots, x_n) \\ f_2(x_1, \ldots, x_n) \\ \vdots \\ f_m(x_1, \ldots, x_n) \end{bmatrix}. \tag{3}$$

The partial derivatives of the vector function are stored in the Jacobian matrix $\frac{\partial \boldsymbol{f}}{\partial \boldsymbol{x}}$, with $\left(\frac{\partial \boldsymbol{f}}{\partial \boldsymbol{x}}\right)_{ij} = \frac{\partial f_i}{\partial x_j}$:

$$\frac{\partial \boldsymbol{f}}{\partial \boldsymbol{x}} = \begin{bmatrix} \frac{\partial f_1}{\partial x_1} & \cdots & \frac{\partial f_1}{\partial x_n} \\ \vdots & \ddots & \vdots \\ \frac{\partial f_m}{\partial x_1} & \cdots & \frac{\partial f_m}{\partial x_n} \end{bmatrix}. \tag{4}$$

In the FL context, Jacobian matrices, such as (4), are computed by the clients using the backpropagation algorithm and sent back to the server. The server aggregates them to train the central model via gradient descent. For example, consider the weights of a fully connected layer $\boldsymbol{W} \in \mathbb{R}^{D_{out} \times D_{in}}$ and the bias term $\boldsymbol{b} \in \mathbb{R}^{D_{out} \times 1}$ along with the scalar loss function $J(\cdot)$ used by the neural network, where D_{out} is the size of the fully connected layer output and D_{in} is the size of the input to that layer. After training on its data, each client will derive a gradient reshaped as matrix $\frac{\partial J}{\partial \boldsymbol{W}} \in \mathbb{R}^{D_{out} \times D_{in}}$, as well as the gradient for the bias term $\frac{\partial J}{\partial \boldsymbol{b}} \in \mathbb{R}^{D_{out} \times 1}$. These gradients will be transmitted to the server to train the central model.

Transmitting the gradients to the server can be slow, especially when training a model with many parameters. The biggest communications overhead comes from $\frac{\partial J}{\partial \boldsymbol{W}}$ and not from $\frac{\partial J}{\partial \boldsymbol{b}}$. This is why we seek to compress $\frac{\partial J}{\partial \boldsymbol{W}}$ by applying the truncated Singular Value Decomposition (SVD), transmitting only the SVD components to the server, and reconstructing $\frac{\partial J}{\partial \boldsymbol{W}}$ on the server using the SVD components.

SVD is a matrix factorization technique that decomposes a matrix $\boldsymbol{A} \in \mathbb{R}^{m \times n}$ into three matrices:

$$\boldsymbol{A} = \boldsymbol{U} \, \boldsymbol{\Sigma} \, \boldsymbol{V}^\top, \tag{5}$$

where $\boldsymbol{U}$ is an $m \times m$ orthonormal matrix containing the left singular vectors of $\boldsymbol{A}$ in its columns, $\boldsymbol{\Sigma}$ is an $m \times n$ matrix with the singular values $\sigma_1, \sigma_2, \ldots, \sigma_r$, in descending order as its diagonal entries, for $r \leq \min(m, n)$ being the rank of matrix $\boldsymbol{A}$, and $\boldsymbol{V}$ is a $n \times n$ orthogonal matrix containing the right singular vectors of $\boldsymbol{A}$ in its columns. We can approximate the matrix $\boldsymbol{A}$ by keeping only the ν largest singular values:

$$\boldsymbol{A} \approx \boldsymbol{A}_\nu = \boldsymbol{U}_\nu \, \boldsymbol{\Sigma}_\nu \, \boldsymbol{V}_\nu^\top, \tag{6}$$

where $\boldsymbol{U}_\nu \in \mathbb{R}^{m \times \nu}$, $\boldsymbol{\Sigma}_\nu \in \mathbb{R}^{\nu \times \nu}$ and $\boldsymbol{V}_\nu \in \mathbb{R}^{n \times \nu}$ with $\nu < r$. The approximation error of $\boldsymbol{A}$ by $\boldsymbol{A}_\nu$ is given by

$$||\boldsymbol{A} - \boldsymbol{A}_\nu||_F^2 = \sum_{j=\nu+1}^{r} \sigma_j^2, \tag{7}$$

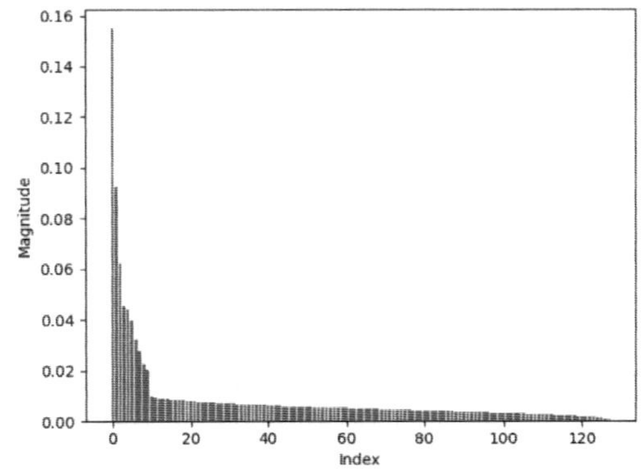

Figure 1. Magnitude of the singular values of the gradient of a fully connected layer.

where $|| \cdot ||_F$ denotes the Frobenius norm and σ_j, $j > \nu$ are the truncated singular values.

The approximation of $\frac{\partial J}{\partial \boldsymbol{W}} \in \mathbb{R}^{D_{out} \times D_{in}}$ with a truncated SVD is justified because such matrices are generally low-rank and have a few dominant singular values [14]. This was experimentally verified by plotting the magnitudes of the singular values of a fully connected layer's gradient in Figure 1, where only a few of the 128 singular values are significantly larger than 0.

Suppose we only transmit $\boldsymbol{U}_\nu$, $\boldsymbol{V}_\nu$, and the diagonal entries of $\boldsymbol{\Sigma}_\nu$. For the truncated SVD to be more communication-efficient than transmitting the full matrix $\frac{\partial J}{\partial \boldsymbol{W}}$, the following inequality must hold:

$$D_{out} \cdot \nu + \nu + D_{in} \cdot \nu < D_{out} \cdot D_{in}. \tag{8}$$

Factorization can also be applied to convolutional layers. In a convolutional layer, the weights are represented by a 4-dimensional tensor $\mathcal{W} \in \mathbb{R}^{C_{out} \times C_{in} \times H \times W}$, where C_{out} is the number of output channels, C_{in} is the number of input channels and $H \times W$ is the size of the convolutional filter. The bias terms are represented as a vector $\boldsymbol{b} \in \mathbb{R}^{C_{out} \times 1}$. To reduce the communications overhead of transmitting the gradient of a convolutional layer $\frac{\partial J}{\partial \mathcal{W}}$ reshaped to a tensor, we factorize the tensor using the Tucker decomposition [15], which has been used for factorization and compression of neural networks [16] [17].

The Tucker decomposition is a higher-order generalization of SVD. It factorizes a tensor $\mathcal{X} \in \mathbb{R}^{I_1 \times I_2 \times \ldots \times I_N}$ into a core tensor $\mathcal{G} \in \mathbb{R}^{r_1 \times r_2 \times \ldots \times r_N}$ and a set of factor matrices $\boldsymbol{F}_i \in \mathbb{R}^{I_i \times r_i}$, $i = 1, \ldots, N$, where $r_i < I_i$ are the reduced ranks on each mode. $\mathcal{X}$ is approximated as [18]:

$$\mathcal{X} \approx \mathcal{G} \times_1 \boldsymbol{F}_1 \times_2 \boldsymbol{F}_2 \times_3 \ldots \times_N \boldsymbol{F}_N, \tag{9}$$

where $\times_n$ denotes the mode-n product of a tensor and matrix. Given a tensor $\mathcal{X} \in \mathbb{R}^{I_1 \times I_2 \times \ldots \times I_N}$ and a matrix $\boldsymbol{F} \in \mathbb{R}^{J \times I_n}$ the mode-n product of $\mathcal{X}$ with $\boldsymbol{F}$ is denoted as $\mathcal{Y} = \mathcal{X} \times_n \boldsymbol{F}$, where $\mathcal{Y} \in \mathbb{R}^{I_1 \times \ldots \times I_{n-1} \times J \times I_{n+1} \ldots \times I_N}$ has elements:

$$\mathcal{Y}_{i_1, \ldots, i_{n-1}, j, i_{n+1}, \ldots, i_N} = \sum_{i_n=1}^{I_n} \mathcal{X}_{i_1, \ldots, i_N} \cdot \boldsymbol{F}_{j, i_n}. \tag{10}$$

When transmitting the gradient of a convolutional layer reshaped to a tensor, $\frac{\partial J}{\partial \mathbf{W}} \in \mathbb{R}^{C_{out} \times C_{in} \times H \times W}$, with reduced ranks for each mode r_1, r_2, r_3, and r_4, we only transmit the core tensor and factor matrices. For the Tucker decomposition to be more communication-efficient, the following inequality must be true:

$$\begin{aligned} r_1 \cdot r_2 \cdot r_3 \cdot r_4 + C_{out} \cdot r_1 + C_{in} \cdot r_2 \\ + H \cdot r_3 + W \cdot r_4 < C_{out} \cdot C_{in} \cdot H \cdot W. \end{aligned} \tag{11}$$

B. Gradient Quantization

To further reduce the communication overhead of the FL setup, in addition to compressing the updates sent by the clients to the server, we also quantize them. Quantizing the gradients of each client leads to a modified version of (2) called Quantized Gradient Descent [19]:

$$\boldsymbol{\theta}^{k+1} = \boldsymbol{\theta}^k - \alpha \sum_{c \in \mathfrak{C}} Q\left(\nabla f_c(\boldsymbol{\theta}^k)\right), \tag{12}$$

where $Q\left(\nabla f_c(\boldsymbol{\theta}^k)\right)$ is the quantized gradient update of client c. Methods employing differential quantization of the gradients have also been proposed [20] [21].

The quantization scheme we use resorts to the Lazily Aggregated Quantized (LAQ) algorithm [22]. Specifically, in LAQ, the gradient descent update is given by

$$\boldsymbol{\theta}^{k+1} = \boldsymbol{\theta}^k - \alpha \nabla^k, \text{ with } \nabla^k = \nabla^{k-1} + \sum_{c \in \mathfrak{C}} \delta Q_c^k, \tag{13}$$

where ∇^k is the aggregated quantized gradient updates at iteration k, and $\delta Q_c^k := Q_c(\boldsymbol{\theta}^k) - Q_c(\boldsymbol{\theta}^{k-1})$ is the difference of the quantized gradient updates of client c at iterations k and $k-1$. The quantized gradient update of client c at iteration k is $Q_c(\boldsymbol{\theta}^k)$, and it is computed using the current gradient update $\nabla f_c(\boldsymbol{\theta}^k)$ and the previous quantized update $Q_c(\boldsymbol{\theta}^{k-1})$:

$$Q_c(\boldsymbol{\theta}^k) = \mathbb{Q}\left(\nabla f_c(\boldsymbol{\theta}^k),\, Q_c(\boldsymbol{\theta}^{k-1})\right), \tag{14}$$

where $\mathbb{Q}$ denotes the quantization operator. The operator $\mathbb{Q}$ entails the following quantization scheme.

The gradient update $\nabla f_c(\boldsymbol{\theta}^k)$ is quantized by projecting each element on an evenly-spaced grid. This grid is centered at $Q_c(\boldsymbol{\theta}^{k-1})$ and has a radius of $R_c^k = ||\nabla f_c(\boldsymbol{\theta}^k) - Q_c(\boldsymbol{\theta}^{k-1})||_\infty$, where $||\boldsymbol{x}||_\infty = \max(|x_1|, \ldots, |x_n|)$ is the max norm. The i-th element of the quantized gradient update of client c at iteration k is mapped to an integer as follows

$$[q_c(\boldsymbol{\theta}^k)]_i = \left\lfloor \frac{[\nabla f_c(\boldsymbol{\theta}^k)]_i - [Q_c(\boldsymbol{\theta}^{k-1})]_i + R_c^k}{2\tau R_c^k} + \frac{1}{2} \right\rfloor, \tag{15}$$

with $\tau := 1/(2^\beta - 1)$ defining the discretization interval. All $[q_c(\boldsymbol{\theta}^k)]_i$ are integers in the range $\{0, 1, \ldots, 2^\beta - 1\}$ and therefore can be encoded by using only β bits. The difference δQ_c^k is computed as

$$\delta Q_c^k = Q_c(\boldsymbol{\theta}^k) - Q_c(\boldsymbol{\theta}^{k-1}) = 2\tau R_c^k\, Q_c(\boldsymbol{\theta}^k) - R_c^k \mathbf{1}, \tag{16}$$

where $\mathbf{1} = [1 \ldots 1]^\top$. This quantity can be transmitted with 32 + βn bits instead of $32n$ bits. That is, 32 bits for R_c^k and β bits for each of the n elements of the gradient update. The computation requires each client to retain a local copy of $Q_c(\boldsymbol{\theta}^{k-1})$. The server can recover the gradient update of client c, assuming it knows the number of bits used for quantization, β, as

$$Q_c(\boldsymbol{\theta}^k) = Q_c(\boldsymbol{\theta}^{k-1}) + \delta Q_c^k. \tag{17}$$

The discretization interval is $2\tau R_c^k$. Therefore, the quantization error cannot be larger than half of the interval

$$||\nabla f_c(\boldsymbol{\theta}^k) - Q_c(\boldsymbol{\theta}^k)||_\infty \leq \tau\, R_c^k. \tag{18}$$

III. PROPOSED SCHEME

A. Quantized Rank Reduction

By combining compression and quantization, we propose a new scheme for communication-efficient FL, namely the QRR. The gradient descent step (2) becomes

$$\begin{aligned} \boldsymbol{\theta}^{k+1} &= \boldsymbol{\theta}^k - \alpha \sum_{c \in \mathfrak{C}} QRR_c\left(\boldsymbol{\theta}^k\right), \\ QRR_c\left(\boldsymbol{\theta}^k\right) &= \mathbb{C}^{-1}\left(\mathbb{Q}\left(\mathbb{C}\left(\nabla f_c(\boldsymbol{\theta}^k)\right), \mathbb{C}\left(\nabla f_c(\boldsymbol{\theta}^{k-1})\right)\right)\right), \end{aligned} \tag{19}$$

where $\mathbb{Q}$ is the quantization operator, $\mathbb{C}$ is the compression operator, and $\mathbb{C}^{-1}$ is the decompression operator. Each client applies the operators $\mathbb{C}$ and $\mathbb{Q}$ to compress and quantize its gradient update, while the server receives the updates and applies $\mathbb{C}^{-1}$ to decompress them and perform gradient descent.

$\mathbb{C}$ entails compressing the gradients using SVD or Tucker decomposition. For the gradient of a fully connected layer of client c at iteration k reshaped to a matrix $\frac{\partial J}{\partial \boldsymbol{W}_c^k} \in \mathbb{R}^{D_{out} \times D_{in}}$ we use a truncated SVD for compression

$$\frac{\partial J}{\partial \boldsymbol{W}_c^k} \approx \boldsymbol{U}_c^k\, \boldsymbol{\Sigma}_c^k\, (\boldsymbol{V}_c^k)^\top, \tag{20}$$

where $\boldsymbol{U}_c^k$, $\boldsymbol{\Sigma}_c^k$ and $\boldsymbol{V}_c^k$ are the SVD components of $\frac{\partial J}{\partial \boldsymbol{W}_c^k}$ retaining only the ν largest singular values.

In case the gradient update is a tensor, such as the gradient of a convolutional layer $\frac{\partial J}{\partial \mathbf{W}_c^k} \in \mathbb{R}^{C_{out} \times C_{in} \times H \times W}$, we compress it using the Tucker decomposition

$$\frac{\partial J}{\partial \mathbf{W}_c^k} \approx \mathcal{G}_c^k \times_1 (\boldsymbol{F}_1)_c^k \times_2 (\boldsymbol{F}_2)_c^k \times_3 (\boldsymbol{F}_3)_c^k \times_4 (\boldsymbol{F}_4)_c^k. \tag{21}$$

The compression is controlled by the parameter p, which represents the percentage of the original rank that is retained. For SVD, the new reduced rank is computed as

$$\nu = \lceil p \cdot \min(D_{out}, D_{in}) \rceil. \tag{22}$$

In the case of the Tucker decomposition, the reduced ranks of the core tensor are computed as

$$\begin{aligned} r_1 &= \lceil p \cdot C_{out} \rceil, & r_2 &= \lceil p \cdot C_{in} \rceil, \\ r_3 &= \lceil p \cdot H \rceil, & r_4 &= \lceil p \cdot W \rceil. \end{aligned} \tag{23}$$

For inequalities (8) and (11) to hold, we typically want p to be small, i.e., $p < 0.5$.

The gradients of the bias terms $\frac{\partial J}{\partial \boldsymbol{b}_c^k} \in \mathbb{R}^{D_{out} \times 1}$ are quantized only without compression.

The operator $\mathbb{Q}$ is described in Section II-B. Each component resulting from the factorization of the gradient update using either SVD or Tucker decomposition is quantized according to this scheme. Client c must store the previous quantized components of its gradient update locally. For each matrix $\frac{\partial J}{\partial \boldsymbol{W}_c^k}$ it has to store $Q(\boldsymbol{U}_c^{k-1})$, $Q(\boldsymbol{\Sigma}_c^{k-1})$ and $Q(\boldsymbol{V}_c^{k-1})$. For each gradient tensor $\frac{\partial J}{\partial \mathcal{W}_c^k}$, it has to store $Q(\mathcal{G}_c^{k-1})$ and $Q((\boldsymbol{F}_1)_c^{k-1}), \ldots, Q((\boldsymbol{F}_4)_c^{k-1})$. For each bias gradient vector $\frac{\partial J}{\partial \boldsymbol{b}_c^k}$ the previous quantized vector $Q(\frac{\partial J}{\partial \boldsymbol{b}_c^{k-1}})$ must also be stored. The parameter β is the number of bits used to encode each element and controls the quantization accuracy.

The server receives each client's gradient updates and computes the current iteration's quantized factor components according to (17). Equation (17) requires that the server also store each client's previously quantized factors. Once the server has the current quantized factors, it applies the operator $\mathbb{C}^{-1}$ to reconstruct the gradient updates of each client. That is, for each client c and each model parameter P in the clients' gradient updates,

- if $P = \boldsymbol{W}_c^k \in \mathbb{R}^{D_{out} \times D_{in}}$:

$$\frac{\partial J}{\partial \boldsymbol{W}_c^k} \approx Q(\boldsymbol{U}_c^k)\, Q(\boldsymbol{\Sigma}_c^k)\, Q(\boldsymbol{V}_c^k)^\top, \tag{24}$$

- if $P = \mathcal{W}_c^k \in \mathbb{R}^{C_{out} \times C_{in} \times H \times W}$:

$$\begin{aligned}\frac{\partial J}{\partial \mathcal{W}_c^k} \approx\ & Q(\mathcal{G}_c^k) \times_1 Q((\boldsymbol{F}_1)_c^k) \times_2 Q((\boldsymbol{F}_2)_c^k) \\ & \times_3 Q((\boldsymbol{F}_3)_c^k) \times_4 Q((\boldsymbol{F}_4)_c^k),\end{aligned} \tag{25}$$

- if $P = \boldsymbol{b}_c^k \in \mathbb{R}^{D_{out} \times 1}$:

$$\frac{\partial J}{\partial \boldsymbol{b}_c^k} \approx Q(\frac{\partial J}{\partial \boldsymbol{b}_c^k}). \tag{26}$$

The server then uses the gradient approximations to perform the distributed gradient descent.

B. Experimental Results

Experiments were conducted to compare the performance of the proposed QRR with stochastic federated averaging, referred to as Stochastic Gradient Descent (SGD), and with the Stochastic LAQ (SLAQ) [22]. To measure the performance of each method, we kept track of the loss and accuracy of the model, as well as the number of bits transmitted by the clients during each iteration. Since the SLAQ algorithm skips uploading the gradient update of some clients based on their magnitude, we also recorded the number of communications. Next, we clarify the terms used in the experiments:

- By **iteration**, we mean a full round of FL, which consists of the server passing the central model's weights to the clients, the clients computing their local mean gradient over a single batch and sending it to the server, and the server aggregating the clients' gradients and updating the central model.
- By **communication**, we refer to the data exchange from the client to the server, i.e., when the client sends its local gradient update to the server.
- By **bits**, we measure only the number of bits of the gradient updates transferred from the clients to the server, since the bits required to transmit the model weights from the server to all the clients are constant and common across all methods.

All the experiments used 10 clients and quantized the compressed gradient updates using $\beta = 8$ bits. The learning rate was $\alpha = 0.001$, and the batch size was equal to 512. For the SLAQ algorithm, the parameters used were $D = 10$, $\xi_1, \ldots, \xi_D = 1/D$, and 8 bits for quantization.

The first experiment utilized the MNIST dataset [23] of 28×28 grayscale images of handwritten digits. A simple Multi-Layer Perceptron (MLP) network was employed, comprising a hidden layer with 200 neurons, a Rectified Linear Unit (ReLU) activation function, and input and output layers of size 784 (28×28) and 10, respectively, with a cross-entropy loss function. 60,000 training samples were randomly selected and equally distributed among the 10 clients. A total of 10,000 test samples were used to evaluate the performance of the central model. The results for 1000 iterations are presented in Table I for various values of p in QRR.

QRR achieves an accuracy of around 1-2% lower than SGD and SLAQ. However, it transmits 3.16-9.43% of the bits transmitted by SGD and 14.8-44.05% of the bits transmitted by SLAQ, depending on the choice of the parameter p. In Figure 2, the loss, the gradient ℓ_2 norm, and the accuracy are plotted against each method's number of iterations and bits. QRR has a slower convergence rate with respect to (wrt) the iteration number than SGD and SLAQ. The smaller p is, the slower the loss convergence, as evidenced in Figure 2(a) since we have less accurate reconstructions of the gradients with smaller p values. However, performance wrt the number of bits transmitted is better, as seen in Figures 2(b), 2(d), and 2(f), i.e., a smaller loss, a smaller gradient ℓ_2 norm, and higher accuracy are measured for a fixed number of bits.

The second experiment used the same setup as the first, with the difference that the MLP network was replaced by a Convolutional Neural Network (CNN). The CNN consisted of 2 convolutional layers using 3×3 filters with 16 and 32 output channels, respectively, a max pooling layer that reduced the input size by half, and 1 fully connected layer. The activation function used after each layer was the ReLU function, and the loss function used was the cross-entropy loss.

Table II summarizes the results using the CNN. Figure 3 displays the evolution of the loss, gradient ℓ_2 norm, and accuracy wrt the number of iterations and bits. The curves for loss and accuracy versus iterations or bits are similar to those of the first experiment. QRR scores 1-3% lower in accuracy but requires 2.75-7.84% of the bits of SGD and 13.52-38.52% of the bits of SLAQ, depending on the choice of p.

In the third experiment, the CIFAR-10 dataset [24] was used with a small, VGG-like [25] CNN consisting of three convolutional blocks with 3x3 convolutions, ReLU activations,

TABLE I. RESULTS OF QRR COMPARED TO SLAQ and SGD FOR AN MLP APPLIED TO THE MNIST DATASET.

Algorithm	# Iterations	# Bits	# Communications	Loss	Accuracy	Gradient ℓ_2 norm
SGD	1000	5.088×10^{10}	10000	0.376	89.92%	2.297
SLAQ	1000	1.089×10^{10}	8559	0.378	89.89%	2.026
QRR($p = 0.3$)	1000	4.798×10^{9}	10000	0.415	89.20%	1.945
QRR($p = 0.2$)	1000	3.205×10^{9}	10000	0.441	88.93%	2.846
QRR($p = 0.1$)	1000	1.612×10^{9}	10000	0.501	88.22%	1.866

TABLE II. RESULTS OF QRR COMPARED TO SLAQ and SGD FOR A CNN APPLIED TO THE MNIST DATASET.

Algorithm	# Iterations	# Bits	# Communications	Loss	Accuracy	Gradient ℓ_2 norm
SGD	1000	1.302×10^{11}	10000	0.263	92.56%	21.154
SLAQ	1000	2.653×10^{10}	8151	0.251	92.70%	9.769
QRR($p = 0.3$)	1000	1.022×10^{10}	10000	0.291	91.49%	19.287
QRR($p = 0.2$)	1000	6.650×10^{9}	10000	0.335	89.91%	42.026
QRR($p = 0.1$)	1000	3.588×10^{9}	10000	0.330	90.48%	30.455

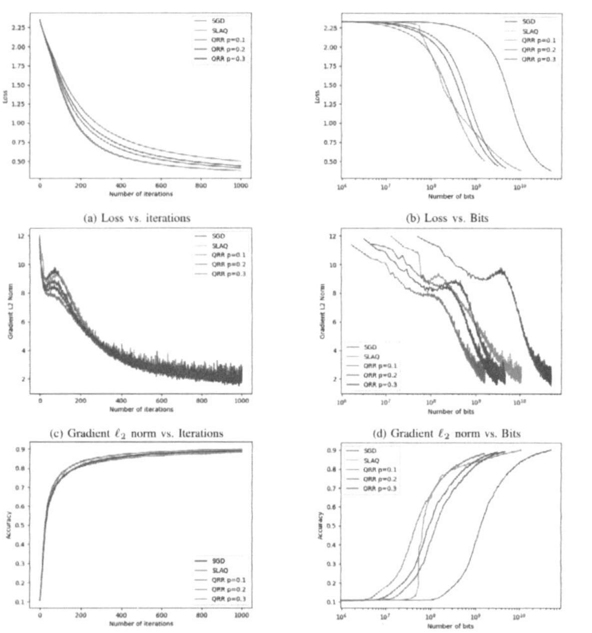

(a) Loss vs. iterations (b) Loss vs. Bits (c) Gradient ℓ_2 norm vs. Iterations (d) Gradient ℓ_2 norm vs. Bits (e) Accuracy vs. Iterations (f) Accuracy vs. Bits

Figure 2. Loss, gradient ℓ_2 norm, and accuracy plotted against the number of iterations and bits for the MLP network and the MNIST dataset.

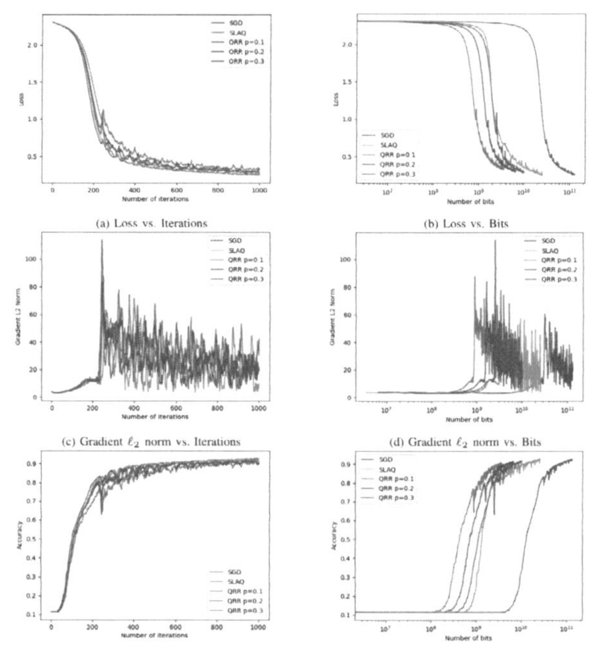

(a) Loss vs. Iterations (b) Loss vs. Bits (c) Gradient ℓ_2 norm vs. Iterations (d) Gradient ℓ_2 norm vs. Bits (e) Accuracy vs. Iterations (f) Accuracy vs. Bits

Figure 3. Loss, gradient ℓ_2 norm, and accuracy plotted against the number of iterations and bits for the CNN and the MNIST dataset.

max pooling, and dropout layers, with the number of filters increasing from 32 to 64 and then to 128. We used different values of p to demonstrate that p can be chosen based on the client's connection speed and the amount of data transmitted from that client. Evenly spaced values in $[0.1, 0.3]$ were assigned to the p parameter of each client. The experiment ran for 2000 iterations, using a learning rate of 0.01 for the first 1000 iterations to accelerate convergence, and then 0.001 for the remaining iterations to ensure stable training.

Table III shows that QRR achieves 8–9% lower accuracy than SGD and SLAQ, while transmitting only 3.34% and 15.26% of the bits transmitted by SGD and SLAQ, respectively. Figure 4 plots the loss, gradient ℓ_2 norm, and accuracy versus iterations or transmitted bits for the VGG-like CNN on CIFAR-10. Although the low-rank approximation of the gradients leads to reduced accuracy on this dataset, which is more complex than MNIST, QRR remains useful for quickly reaching a deployable model state before switching to a more accurate one, compared to less network-efficient methods such as SGD or SLAQ.

Finally, the client-side overhead of QRR was measured in the setup of the last experiment using SGD as a baseline. On average, QRR needed 1.2× more memory and 3.82× more computation time. For comparison, SLAQ required 13× more memory and 1.08× more computation time.

IV. CONCLUSIONS

We have proposed a scheme that leverages the low-rank approximation of neural network gradients and utilizes established quantization algorithms to significantly reduce the amount of data transmitted in an FL setting. The proposed Quantized Rank Reduction scheme has slightly lower accuracy than Federated Averaging or SLAQ, but it transmits only

TABLE III. RESULTS OF QRR COMPARED TO SLAQ and SGD FOR A VGG-LIKE CNN APPLIED TO THE CIFAR-10 DATASET.

Algorithm	# Iterations	# Bits	# Communications	Loss	Accuracy	Gradient ℓ_2 norm
SGD	2000	3.52×10^{11}	20000	1.213	56.72%	6.246
SLAQ	2000	7.72×10^{10}	17548	1.242	55.73%	5.493
QRR	2000	1.17×10^{10}	20000	1.441	47.57%	5.088

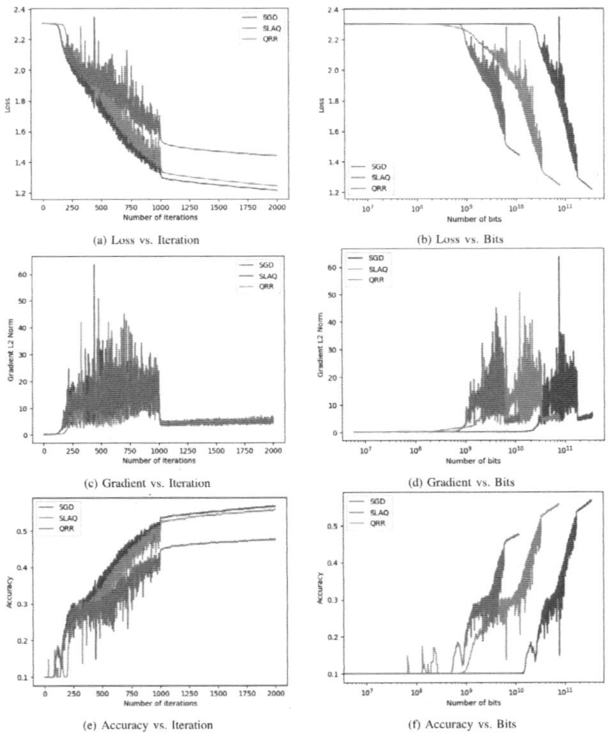

(a) Loss vs. Iteration
(b) Loss vs. Bits
(c) Gradient vs. Iteration
(d) Gradient vs. Bits
(e) Accuracy vs. Iteration
(f) Accuracy vs. Bits

Figure 4. Loss, gradient ℓ_2 norm, and accuracy plotted against the number of iterations and bits for the VGG-like CNN and the CIFAR-10 dataset.

a fraction of the bits required by the other methods. It converges more slowly with the number of iterations, but faster when considering the number of bits transmitted. There is an added computational and memory overhead on both the client and server sides. However, this scheme can prove helpful in network-critical applications, where sensors or devices participating in the distributed learning process are located in remote locations with very slow network connections.

REFERENCES

[1] J. Konečný, H. B. McMahan, F. X. Yu, P. Richtárik, A. T. Suresh, and D. Bacon, "Federated learning: Strategies for improving communication efficiency," 2017. [Online]. Available: https://arxiv.org/abs/1610.05492
[2] C. Zhang *et al.*, "A survey on federated learning," *Knowledge-Based Systems*, vol. 216, p. 106775, 2021.
[3] W. Lim *et al.*, "Federated learning in mobile edge networks: A comprehensive survey," *IEEE Communications Surveys & Tutorials*, vol. 22, no. 3, pp. 2031–2063, 2020.
[4] M. Asad *et al.*, "Limitations and future aspects of communication costs in federated learning: A survey," *Sensors*, vol. 23, no. 17, p. 7358, 2023.
[5] P. Kairouz *et al.*, "Advances and open problems in federated learning," *Foundations and Trends® in Machine Learning*, vol. 14, no. 1-2, pp. 1–210, 2021.
[6] M. Li, D. G. Andersen, A. Smola, and K. Yu, "Communication efficient distributed machine learning with the parameter server," in *Advances in Neural Information Processing Systems*, 2014, vol. 27, pp. 19—-27.
[7] Y. Arjevani and O. Shamir, "Communication complexity of distributed convex learning and optimization," in *Advances in Neural Information Processing Systems*, 2015, vol. 28, pp. 1756—1764.
[8] B. McMahan, E. Moore, D. Ramage, S. Hampson, and B. A. y Arcas, "Communication-efficient learning of deep networks from decentralized data," in *Artificial Intelligence and Statistics*. PMLR, 2017, pp. 1273–1282.
[9] H. Kim, M. U. K. Khan, and C.-M. Kyung, "Efficient neural network compression," in *Proceedings of the IEEE/CVF Conference on Computer Vision and Pattern Recognition*, 2019, pp. 12 569–12 577.
[10] L. Liu and X. Xu, "Marvel: Towards efficient federated learning on IoT devices," *Computer Networks*, vol. 245, p. 110375, 2024.
[11] Y. Liu and M. K. Ng, "Deep neural network compression by Tucker decomposition with nonlinear response," *Knowledge-Based Systems*, vol. 241, p. 108171, 2022.
[12] "Quantized rank reduction: A communications-efficient federated learning scheme for network-critical applications," [retrieved: May 22, 2025]. [Online]. Available: https://github.com/Kritsos/QRR-code
[13] K. Clark, "Computing neural network gradients," Stanford University, August 2018, Notes.
[14] S. Oymak, Z. Fabian, M. Li, and M. Soltanolkotabi, "Generalization guarantees for neural networks via harnessing the low-rank structure of the Jacobian," 2019. [Online]. Available: https://arxiv.org/abs/1906.05392
[15] L. R. Tucker, "Some mathematical notes on three-mode factor analysis," *Psychometrika*, vol. 31, no. 3, pp. 279–311, 1966.
[16] G. G. Calvi, A. Moniri, M. Mahfouz, Q. Zhao, and D. P. Mandic, "Compression and interpretability of deep neural networks via Tucker tensor layer: From first principles to tensor valued back-propagation," 2019. [Online]. Available: https://arxiv.org/abs/1903.06133
[17] J.-T. Chien and Y.-T. Bao, "Tensor-factorized neural networks," *IEEE Transactions on Neural Networks and Learning Systems*, vol. 29, no. 5, pp. 1998–2011, 2017.
[18] L. De Lathauwer, *Signal Processing Based on Multilinear Algebra*. Katholieke Universiteit Leuven, 1997.
[19] D. Alistarh, D. Grubic, J. Li, R. Tomioka, and M. Vojnovic, "QSGD: Communication-efficient SGD via gradient quantization and encoding," in *Advances in Neural Information Processing Systems*, 2017, vol. 30, pp. 1707—1718.
[20] K. Mishchenko, E. Gorbunov, M. Takáč, and P. Richtárik, "Distributed learning with compressed gradient differences," 2023. [Online]. Available: https://arxiv.org/abs/1901.09269
[21] N. Tonellotto, A. Gotta, F. M. Nardini, D. Gadler, and F. Silvestri, "Neural network quantization in federated learning at the edge," *Information Sciences*, vol. 575, pp. 417–436, 2021.
[22] J. Sun, T. Chen, G. B. Giannakis, Q. Yang, and Z. Yang, "Lazily aggregated quantized gradient innovation for communication-efficient federated learning," *IEEE Transactions on Pattern Analysis and Machine Intelligence*, vol. 44, no. 4, pp. 2031–2044, 2020.
[23] L. Deng, "The MNIST database of handwritten digit images for machine learning research," *IEEE Signal Processing Magazine*, vol. 29, no. 6, pp. 141–142, 2012.
[24] A. Krizhevsky, "Learning multiple layers of features from tiny images," University of Toronto, Tech. Rep., 2009. [Online]. Available: https://www.cs.toronto.edu/~kriz/learning-features-2009-TR.pdf
[25] K. Simonyan and A. Zisserman, "Very deep convolutional networks for large-scale image recognition," 2015. [Online]. Available: https://arxiv.org/abs/1409.1556

System Integration of Multi-Modal Sensor for Robotic Inspection of Power Lines

Gustavo Fardo Armênio, João Henrique Campos Soares, Maria Luiza Cenci Stedile, Oswaldo Ramos Neto, Ronnier Frates Rohrich and Andre Schneider de Oliveira
Graduate Program in Electrical and Computer Engineering
Program in Computer Science
Universidade Tecnológica Federal do Paraná
Curitiba, Brazil
e-mail: {gustavofardoarmenio | jsoares.2021 | mstedile | oswaldo}@alunos.utfpr.edu.br
{rohrich | andreoliveira}@utfpr.edu.br

Abstract—**This study aimed to predict current and future issues in high-voltage-transmission lines using an integrated, specially designed multimodal-robotic sensor system for inspection. The system comprises several distinct sensors employed for the analysis of specific spectrums, such as, thermal, acoustic, spatial, visual, spectroradiometric, and referencing. Information obtained from different viewpoints and interfaces at different times are standardized and correlated to obtain composite-inspection data. This sensor (coupled to a cable-driven robotic platform) is intended to execute autonomous inspection of transmission elements by working over the power lines.**

Keywords-inspection; multimodal; robot.

I. Introduction

Power-grid functionality is reliant on electric-transmission-line integrity and reliability. Transmission lines are the backbone of electricity-distribution networks and are susceptible to threats ranging from environmental to human-induced disruptions. Weather-related events alone account for a significant proportion of transmission-line failures, underscoring the need for robust inspection protocols.

Proactive, inspection strategies can enhance the reliability of the power-transmission infrastructure and contribute to cost savings and operational efficiency. Investments in preventive maintenance (including routine transmission-line inspections) yield substantial returns by reducing outage durations, averting system failures, and minimizing associated economic losses. Advanced inspection technologies, such as Unmanned Aerial Vehicle (UAVs) [1]; light detection and ranging (LiDAR) [2]; and thermal imaging [3], facilitate comprehensive assessments of line components and prompt identification of defects and vulnerabilities [4], [5].

Traditionally, these inspections have relied on manual, visual assessments and single-sensor technologies such as infrared cameras or optical sensors. However, recent advancements in sensor technology have facilitated the development of multimodal sensors that can integrate multiple sensing capabilities into a single system—enhancing the effectiveness, accuracy, and efficiency of power-line inspections.

This integration allows for comprehensive data collection from different perspectives, allowing detection of potential issues, with greater accuracy [6]–[8]. For instance, in electrical systems, thermal imaging can detect hotspots (indicating potential overheating or electrical faults), whereas optical cameras provide high-resolution images for the visual inspection of physical damage or anomalies. LiDAR generates three-dimensional (3D) models of power lines and the surrounding vegetation, helping to identify encroachments and structural issues. Acoustic sensors detect partial discharge and other such signals, indicative of electrical malfunctions. By leveraging these diverse, sensing capabilities, multimodal sensors can identify a greater range of defects and conditions relative to single-sensor systems.

The integration of multiple sensing modalities enhances the accuracy and reliability of inspections [9], [10]. Each sensor type has its own strengths and limitations, and combining them mitigates the individual weaknesses. For example, optical cameras may be impeded by poor lighting conditions; however, thermal imaging can still detect issues under low-light conditions. Similarly, LiDAR can penetrate foliage to some extent, providing a clearer view of the power-line surroundings than optical cameras alone. Moreover, the fusion of data from different sensors allows for the cross-verification of findings, reducing false positives and negatives [11]. This redundancy ensures that the detected anomalies are genuine, enabling more reliable, maintenance decisions and actions.

With a multimodal sensor-equipped drone or vehicle, a single pass can gather comprehensive data, reduce inspection times, and reduce labor costs [12], eliminating the need for multiple passes. The high level of detail and accuracy provided by multimodal sensors leads to earlier detection of potential issues, preventing minor problems from escalating into major failures. Proactive-maintenance reduces downtime and repair costs, contributing to cost-effective, power-line management.

Power-line inspection is hazardous and often requires personnel to work at significant heights or close to high-voltage equipment. The use of multimodal sensors that are mounted on drones or robotic systems, reduces the need for human inspectors to operate in dangerous environments [13]–[15] and permits inspections in inaccessible and hazardous areas. The diverse data collected by multimodal sensors are ideal for integration with advanced analytics and machine-learning algorithms. By analyzing both historical and real-time data, these systems can predict potential failures and proactively recommend preventive-maintenance actions, thereby enhancing the overall reliability and resilience of the power grid.

This paper presents a novel, multimodal sensor coupled to an autonomous inspection robot (moving over an electric cable) for transmission-line inspection. The multispectral sensor integrates several perception sources to produce a unique inspection map.

The paper is organized into five sections. Section 2 discusses the concept of *LaRa* autonomous inspection robot. Section 3 discusses the proposed approach for *MultiSpectrum* sensor integration. Section 4 explains the experimentation and evaluation. Finally, Section 5 shows the conclusions.

II. *LaRa*: Autonomous Robot for Multi-Modal Predictive Inspection of High-Voltage Transmission Lines

The mobile robot autonomously performs inspections by traveling directly over the electrical cables. The autonomous robot for the multimodal predictive inspection of high-voltage transmission lines (*LaRa*) is designed to attach to the cable and move with precision, carrying the multimodal inspection system, as shown in Figure 1.

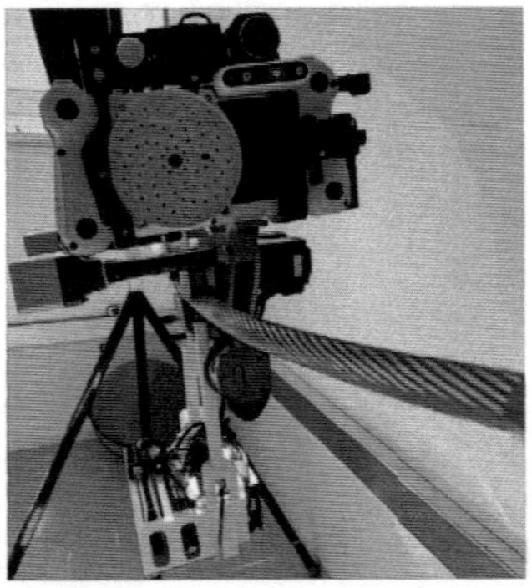

Figure 1. The *LaRa* robot.

Two wheels are used to ensure support on the electrical cable: one wheel is free, and the other is driven by a servomotor. The third wheel is part of a connecting rod–crank system that moves the non-actuated wheel toward the cable, maintaining a clamping pressure similar to that of a robotic claw. This wheel can also move linearly away from the cable, allowing the robot to be removed and perform obstacle suppression maneuvers.

The cable-gripper system is mounted on a structure consisting of two parallel plates separated by fixed spacers, as shown in Figure 2. Between these plates, a connecting rod–crank system moves the fixing wheel at the bottom of the cable. The motors are fixed to the front part of the claw, which interferes with the stabilization of the system on the cable, leading to rotation around the cable and potential falls.

The *LaRa* robot features a lower luggage rack fixed with two articulated arms to ensure that the weight is always directed toward the gravitational force at the center of the cable gripper. The luggage rack houses the electronic control system, motor power, control system, and battery of the robot.

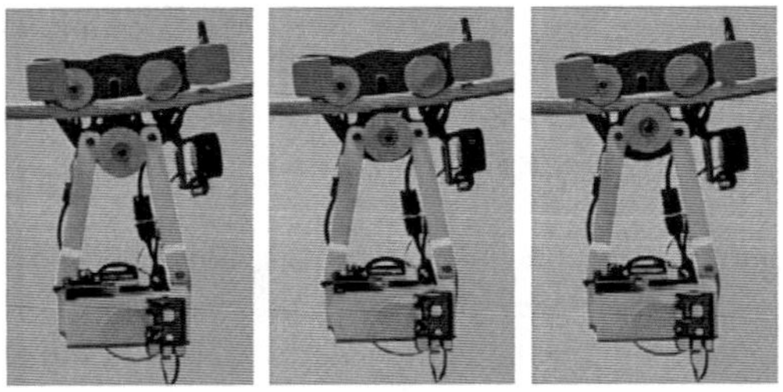

Figure 2. Cable-gripper system in action.

The center of mass of the system is aligned with the cable center, which is achieved by introducing two counterweight arms. One of these arms also serves as a support for the attachment of the multimodal inspection sensor.

III. The Architecture of *MultiSpectrum* Sensor

The *MultiSpectrum* sensor comprised several sensors, specially designed to evaluate electric faults (Figure 3). All the sensors were integrated into a stacked inspection map. This approach was detailed further in an earlier study [16].

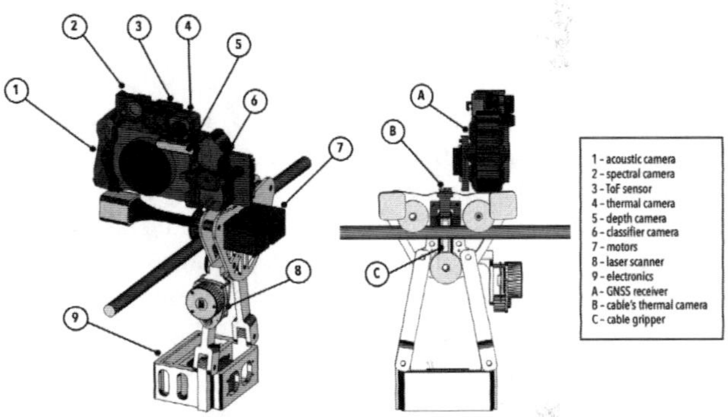

Figure 3. Modules of *LaRa* robot.

Figure 4 illustrates the integration of various sensor modules within the multispectral system designed for robotic inspection of transmission lines. This multimodal-sensor suite comprises several interconnected components, each serving a distinct function to ensure comprehensive monitoring and analysis of transmission line conditions.

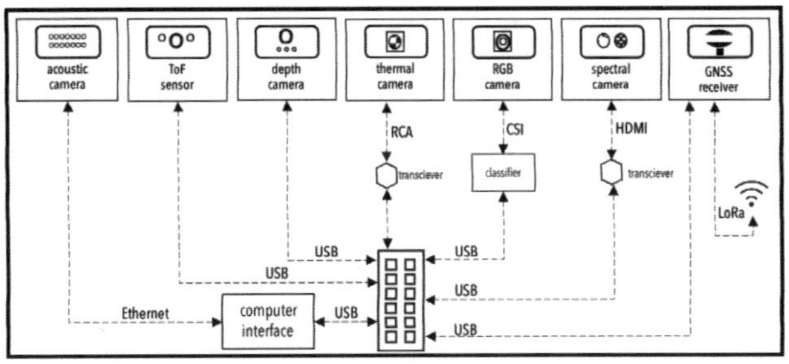

Figure 4. Integration of sensor modules.

The Real-Time Kinematic (RTK) Global Navigation Satellite System (GNSS) receiver provides geospatial data, enabling precise location tracking by robot inspectors. It connects via a Universal Serial Bus (USB) for data transmission and supports LoRa communication for long-range, low-power wireless connectivity aimed at RTK accuracy.

The spectral camera, equipped to capture a wide range of wavelengths, offers a detailed analysis of the material properties of the transmission lines and communicates with the central system through a high-definition multimedia interface to ensure high-quality data transfer; the aim was to analyze the proximity of the electric elements to vegetation.

The Red-Green-Blue (RGB) camera captures standard color images essential for visual inspection. It interfaces with the system using a Camera Serial Interface (CSI), that feeds directly into the Graphics Processing Unit (GPU) classifier for real-time image processing.

The thermal camera detects heat signatures and hotspots and identifies potential overheating issues or faults. It uses an RCA connection coupled with a transceiver to convert and transmit data through USB.

The depth camera provides 3D data, crucial for assessing the spatial relationships and physical conditions of transmission lines and their surrounding environment. It connects using a USB.

A Time-of-Flight (ToF) sensor measures the time required for a light signal to reflect from the object. It provides precise distance measurements and communicates with the system via USB. Sensor calibration and global referencing are crucial.

The acoustic camera captures sound waves to detect anomalies that may not be visible or detectable through other sensors, and is integrated into the system using an Ethernet connection for reliable data transfer.

A. *Multi-modal sensing*

Integrating multimodal sensors involves combining data from various sensors to understand the environment or system comprehensively and accurately. The integration process leverages the strengths of each sensor type, compensating for individual sensor weaknesses and providing a richer dataset. The key to successful multimodal sensor integration lies in effective data fusion. Data-fusion algorithms combine information from different sensors to produce more accurate, reliable, and coherent information. This process often involves synchronizing data streams, spatially and temporally aligning data, and filtering noise.

The challenges in multimodal sensor integration include ensuring interoperability between different sensor types, managing large volumes of data, and maintaining real-time processing capabilities. Ensuring interoperability involves addressing various technical and operational issues because different sensors often have distinct communication protocols, data formats, and sampling rates. To integrate these sensors seamlessly, a common framework or middleware is required to translate and standardize the data from each sensor type.

The Petri net flow for the multispectral sensor system illustrates the comprehensive workflow involved in the multimodal inspection of transmission lines, as shown in Figure 5. The process begins with the system in a ready state (p1), which is initialized and prepared for inspection. Upon starting the inspection (t1), the system waits for inputs from various sensors, including spectral (p2), depth (p3), RGB (p4), thermal (p5), distance (p6), ToF (p7), GNSS (p8), and acoustic (p13) data.

Each type of sensor input underwent specific acquisition and processing steps. The spectral images were filtered (t9) and registered (t15) to align them accurately, resulting in a filtered spectral image (p9) and registered spectral image (p16). The depth images were resized (t10) and warped (t16) to correct any distortions, producing a resized depth image (p10) and depth layer (p17). The RGB images were classified (t11) to identify relevant features, resulting in a classified RGB image (p11). The thermal images were resized (t12), decomposed into component parts (t17), and registered (t20) to align with the other sensor data, resulting in a resized thermal image (p12), decomposed thermal image (p18), and registered thermal image (p22). The acoustic images were resized (t18), filtered to remove noise (t21), and registered (t23) for accurate alignment, resulting in an adjusted acoustic image (p19) and a filtered acoustic image (p23).

After initial processing, the system combined and adjusted the data layers. Spectral images were warped (t19) and integrated into a spectral layer (p21), thermal images that underwent thermal warping (t22) were integrated into a thermal layer (p24), and acoustic images were warped (t24) and integrated into an acoustic layer (t26). These processed layers were stacked to form a comprehensive inspection map (p25).

The inspection map was further refined through georeferencing (p27) to ensure that the data were accurately mapped to real-world coordinates. The final outputs of this process included detailed inspection maps (p28) that provided a thorough overview of the inspection results and geospatially contextualized data, indicating the precise locations of the inspected areas (p29).

B. *Global localization of multi-modal inspection*

The multispectral sensor employs an RTK-GNSS to ensure the correct localization of electric components and to allow correlation between different inspections. The RTK GNSS employs a stationary base station and *LaRa* robot (i.e., rover) to obtain highly accurate positioning data with centimeter-level accuracy. The base station measures signals from the GNSS satellites and calculates the errors caused by atmospheric conditions, satellite-orbit inaccuracies, and other factors. These corrections are sent to the *LaRa* robot in real-time, through a communication link (LoRa), allowing it to adjust its calculations and achieve higher accuracy. The *LaRa* robot then applies these corrections to improve positional accuracy, as illustrated in Figure 6.

Figure 7 illustrates the process of integrating sensor data for locating the nearest power pole on a transmission line. The process begins by measuring distances using ToF and depth sensors to accurately measure nearby objects. The system then computes the nearest point relative to the sensor. The

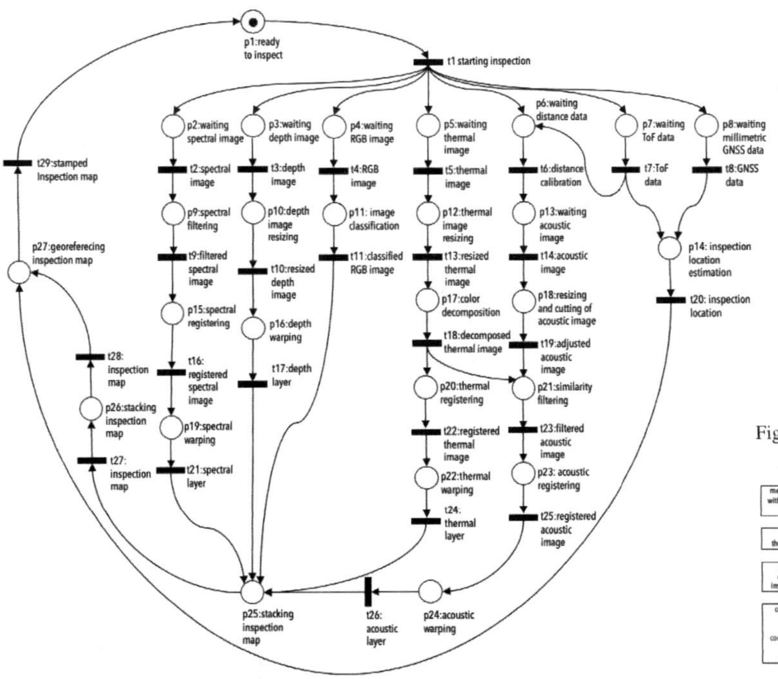

Figure 5. Petri-Net of of Multi-modal sensing of MultiSpectrum sensor.

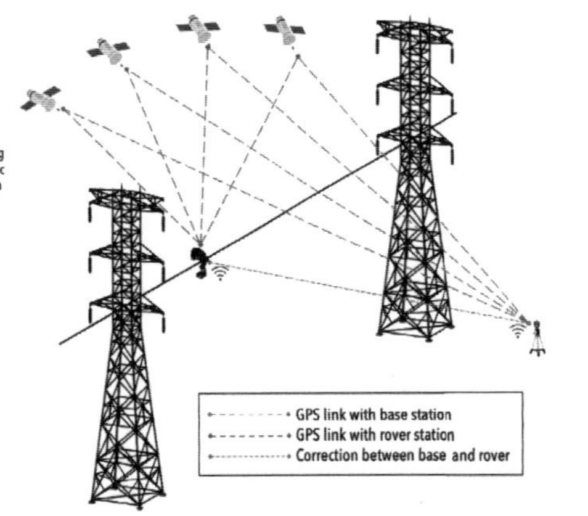

Figure 6. Scheme of global localization through RTK GNSS.

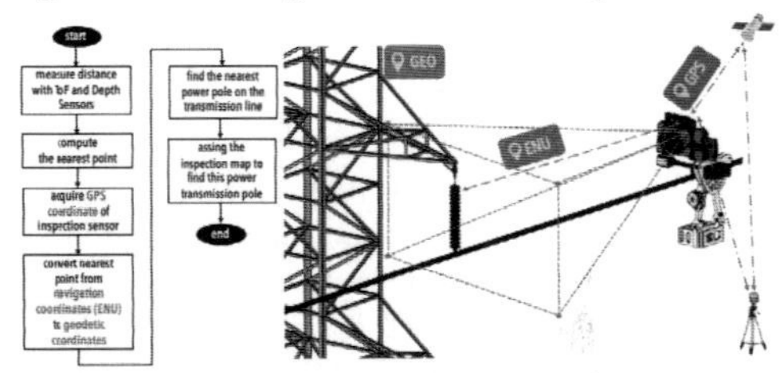

Figure 7. Transformation from local to global coordinates.

RTK-GNSS coordinates of the inspection sensor are acquired, providing its geographic position.

The nearest point, initially in the East-North-Up (ENU) coordinates (a local Cartesian coordinate system), was converted to geodetic coordinates (latitude, longitude, and altitude). The system identified the nearest power pole on the transmission line by matching it to a map or a database of pole locations. Finally, an inspection map was assigned to the identified power-transmission pole, which linked the sensor data to a specific location in the transmission infrastructure.

This process effectively integrates local measurements and global positioning to precisely locate power poles for inspection and correlates them with previous inspections, allowing for the prediction of future behaviors.

C. Object classification and recognition

Here, the objective was to develop a device capable of detecting key elements (such as insulators, transmission towers, and dampers) along transmission lines, in real-time, utilizing local processing with energy consumption compatible with battery-usage. Initially, the primary component of the device was defined as a tool capable of detecting objects in an image with high reliability. The eighth (state-of-the-art) version of the YOLO (You Only Look Once) neural-network architecture (YOLOv8) was selected owing to its optimization ease and flexibility of application. YOLOv8 is provided through an SDK maintained in the Ultralytics library and features a simple Python interface that facilitates the configuration of network parameters and training procedures [17].

To enable the near-real-time processing of a neural network such as YOLO, it is necessary to have hardware, capable of supporting the parallel processing of the network layers. An NVIDIA Jetson Nano B01 with 4GB of random-access memory was selected because of its compact size, low-energy consumption, and graphical-acceleration capabilities. Their applications are further supported by multiple interfaces with other devices and peripherals. By utilizing the MIPI CSI input, it is possible to attach a Raspberry Pi V2 camera designed for embedded systems (with reduced energy consumption and weight) for environmental image capture. Additionally, the UART TTL serial-interface pins enabled communication between the detection device and other computers using an FT232 Serial-USB converter. For training, approximately 540 images were selected from photos and videos of transmission-line, drone inspections. The images were labeled with rectangular annotations. The classes were named after the key elements: Transmission Tower, Insulator, Damper, and Transformer. The training was performed using 200 epochs, a batch size of 16 samples, and an image size of 640 × 640 pixels.

The training results were visualized in a confusion matrix (shown in Figure 8). A high accuracy for transmission towers and isolators, with true-positive rates of 90% and 88%, respectively, can be seen. The Damper class had a lower true positive rate of 64%, and the Transformers were correctly classified at 85%.

The training was also evaluated using a bar chart (Figure 9), which illustrates the distribution of instances for four classes: Damper, Isolator, Transmission Tower, and Transformer. The Damper class had the fewest instances, with fewer

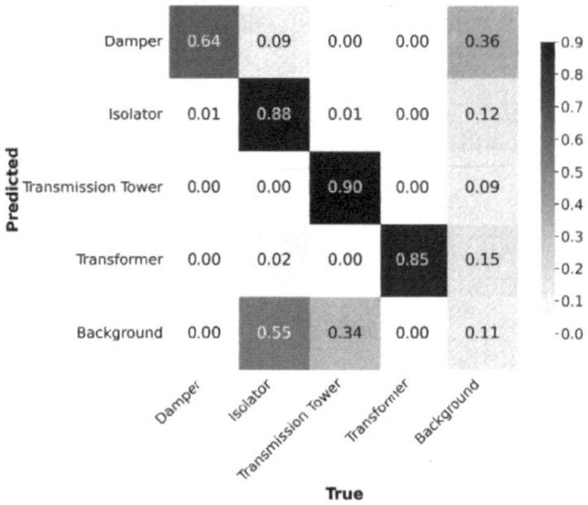

Figure 8. Confusion matrix of training.

than 500 examples, indicating that this class was relatively underrepresented in the dataset. In contrast, the Isolator class had the highest number of instances, with approximately 3000 examples, suggesting that the model had more data to learn from for this class, potentially leading to higher prediction accuracy. The Transmission Tower class had a moderate number of instances, approximately 1500, providing a balanced amount of data for model training compared with the others. The Transformer class had the fewest instances after the damper, with fewer than 500 examples, which, like the Damper class, might have affected the ability of the model to accurately predict this class.

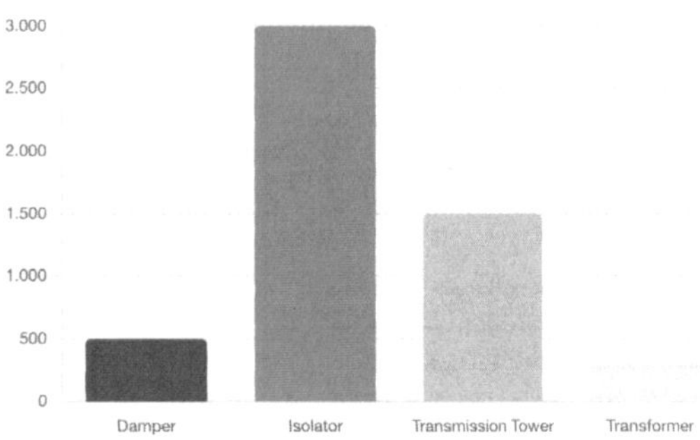

Figure 9. Instances of training.

Figure 10 presents two graphs tracking the mean average precision at IoU = 0.50 (mAP50) and mAP at IoU = 0.95 (mAP95) metrics over 200 training epochs. The mAP50 graph demonstrated rapid initial improvement from around 0.30 to approximately 0.83, indicating that the model quickly learns to detect objects with moderate IoU thresholds. The curve then showed a more gradual increase as the training progressed, stabilizing at approximately 0.83. This suggests that the model achieved high precision for easier detection and maintained consistent performance towards the end of the training period.

The mean Average Precision (mAP) in the range 0.50 < Intersection over Union (IoU) < 0.95 (mAP50-95) graph starts lower, around 0.20, but steadily increases throughout the training process, reaching approximately 0.56. This reflected

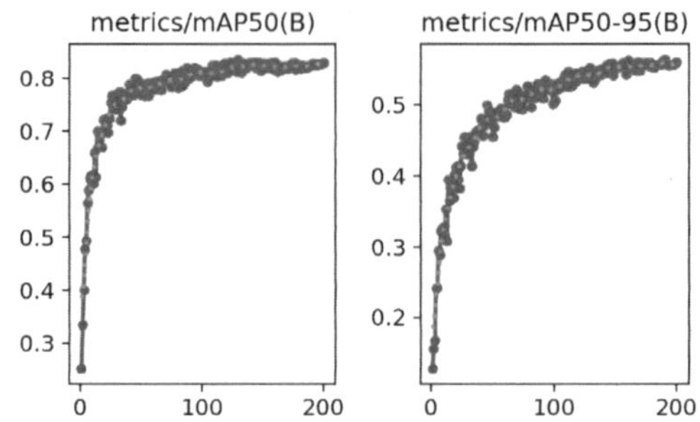

Figure 10. Training accuracy analysis.

the growing ability of the model to handle more challenging detection scenarios, although with a slower improvement compared with the mAP50 metric. The gradual rise and final values indicated that while the model performed well, its precision decreased as the IoU threshold increased. The output of evaluation of object classification can be seen in Figure 11.

Figure 11. Evaluation of object classification.

IV. Multi-Modal Inspection

Multi-modal inspection is consolidated into a comprehensive multi-layer inspection map with global referencing for a specific transmission tower. Each layer of the map represents a distinct spectrum of analysis for the transmission line elements, as illustrated in Figure 12.

The first layer utilizes visual analysis to identify visible faults in high resolution and recognize power line elements. This identification is performed using object classification and recognition methods and serves as a foundation for subsequent layers. The second layer employs depth spectrum analysis, enabling volumetric inspection of elements and spatial correlation. The third layer is dedicated to thermal analysis, detecting anomalies in thermal profiles and identifying hotspots. The fourth layer focuses on acoustic spectrum analysis, examining distortions in the acoustic response of elements to diagnose malfunctions such as breaks, wear, and the corona effect. The fifth layer analyzes the vegetation spectrum, evaluating the proximity of vegetation to the elements and its potential to cause electrical arcs.

V. Conclusions

This paper presents a multispectral-sensor system for the multimodal-robotic inspection of high-voltage-transmission

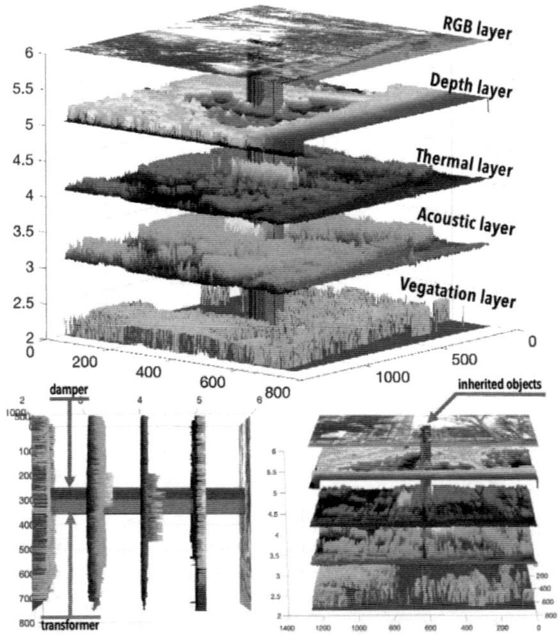

Figure 12. Multi-Modal inspection map.

lines. The system integrates various sensors — thermal, acoustic, spatial, visual, spectroradiometer, and referencing — to enable the accurate prediction of current and future issues. Standardizing and correlating data from these sensors provides comprehensive inspection results, enhancing the accuracy and reliability of power-line maintenance.

A key feature of the multispectral sensor is the RTK-GNSS, which ensures precise localization with centimeter-level accuracy and is crucial for correlating data from different inspections. The system employs a stationary base station and *LaRa* robot to provide real-time corrections, thereby improving the positional accuracy of the electric components along the transmission lines. Additionally, the device uses the YOLOv8 neural network for the real-time detection of elements such as insulators, transmission towers, and dampers, chosen for its high reliability and ease of application. The training and evaluation of the YOLOv8 model highlighted potential accuracy variations based on the class representation. Overall, the multispectral-sensor system, with its advanced integration of RTK-GNSS and YOLOv8, offers a state-of-the-art solution for the autonomous and efficient predictive inspection of power lines.

ACKNOWLEDGMENT

The project is supported by the National Council for Scientific and Technological Development (CNPq) under grant number 407984/2022-4; the Fund for Scientific and Technological Development (FNDCT); the Ministry of Science, Technology and Innovations (MCTI) of Brazil; the Araucaria Foundation; the General Superintendence of Science, Technology and Higher Education (SETI); and NAPI Robotics.

REFERENCES

[1] Z. Wang, Q. Gao, J. Xu, and D. Li, "A review of uav power line inspection", in *Advances in Guidance, Navigation and Control: Proceedings of 2020 International Conference on Guidance, Navigation and Control, ICGNC 2020, Tianjin, China, October 23–25, 2020*, Springer, 2022, pp. 3147–3159.

[2] N. Munir, M. Awrangjeb, and B. Stantic, "Power line extraction and reconstruction methods from laser scanning data: A literature review", *Remote Sensing*, vol. 15, no. 4, p. 973, 2023.

[3] F. Shams *et al.*, "Thermal imaging of utility power lines: A review", in *2022 International Conference on Engineering and Emerging Technologies (ICEET)*, IEEE, 2022, pp. 1–4.

[4] L. Yang *et al.*, "A review on state-of-the-art power line inspection techniques", *IEEE Transactions on Instrumentation and Measurement*, vol. 69, no. 12, pp. 9350–9365, 2020.

[5] A. Sriram and T. Sudhakar, "Technology revolution in the inspection of power transmission lines-a literature review", in *2021 7th International Conference on Electrical Energy Systems (ICEES)*, IEEE, 2021, pp. 256–262.

[6] O. Kullu and E. Cinar, "A deep-learning-based multi-modal sensor fusion approach for detection of equipment faults", *Machines*, vol. 10, no. 11, p. 1105, 2022.

[7] O. Kähler, S. Hochstöger, G. Kemper, and J. Birchbauer, "Automating powerline inspection: A novel multisensor system for data analysis using deep learning", *The International Archives of the Photogrammetry, Remote Sensing and Spatial Information Sciences*, vol. 43, pp. 747–754, 2020.

[8] F. Najar, M. Ghommem, S. Kocer, A. Elhady, and E. M. Abdel-Rahman, "Detection methods for multi-modal inertial gas sensors", *Sensors*, vol. 22, no. 24, p. 9688, 2022.

[9] J. Petrich, Z. Snow, D. Corbin, and E. W. Reutzel, "Multi-modal sensor fusion with machine learning for data-driven process monitoring for additive manufacturing", *Additive Manufacturing*, vol. 48, p. 102 364, 2021.

[10] C. Martin, E. Schaffernicht, A. Scheidig, and H.-M. Gross, "Multi-modal sensor fusion using a probabilistic aggregation scheme for people detection and tracking", *Robotics and Autonomous Systems*, vol. 54, no. 9, pp. 721–728, 2006.

[11] P. Karle, F. Fent, S. Huch, F. Sauerbeck, and M. Lienkamp, "Multi-modal sensor fusion and object tracking for autonomous racing", *IEEE Transactions on Intelligent Vehicles*, vol. 8, no. 7, pp. 3871–3883, 2023.

[12] P. Nooralishahi, F. López, and X. P. Maldague, "Drone-enabled multimodal platform for inspection of industrial components", *IEEE Access*, vol. 10, pp. 41 429–41 443, 2022.

[13] M. Jeon, J. Moon, S. Jeong, and K.-Y. Oh, "Autonomous flight strategy of an unmanned aerial vehicle with multimodal information for autonomous inspection of overhead transmission facilities", *Computer-Aided Civil and Infrastructure Engineering*, 2024.

[14] B. Jalil, D. Moroni, M. Pascali, and O. Salvetti, "Multimodal image analysis for power line inspection", in *Proceedings of the International Conference on Pattern Recognition and Artificial Intelligence, Montreal, QC, Canada*, 2018, pp. 13–17.

[15] S. Cao *et al.*, "Multi-sensor fusion and data analysis for operating conditions of low power transmission lines", *Measurement*, vol. 190, p. 110 586, 2022.

[16] R. F. Rohrich and A. S. de Oliveira, "Multispectrum inspection of overhead power lines.", in *20th International Conference on Informatics in Control, Automation and Robotics*, 2023, pp. 119–126.

[17] G. Jocher and Ultralytics, *Yolo by ultralytics*, https://github.com/ultralytics/yolov8, Accessed: 2024-07-09, 2023.

A Novel Robotic Mechanism for Efficient Inspection of High-Voltage Transmission Lines

Oswaldo Ramos Neto, José Mário Nishihara, Davi Riiti Goto do Valle, Alexandre Domingues, Ronnier Frates Rohrich and André Schneider de Oliveira
e-mail: {oswaldo | josalb | daviriit | alexandredomingues}@alunos.utfpr.edu.br
{rohrich | andreoliveira}@utfpr.edu.br

Abstract—**High-voltage transmission line inspections have traditionally been performed using helicopters and human operators, making it a hazardous and costly task. This paper presents a novel robotic system designed to autonomously navigate transmission lines and overcome obstacles such as vibration dampers. The proposed system incorporates a movement mechanism that utilizes stepper motors and a gear-driven pivoting system, allowing the robot to navigate obstacles efficiently while maintaining stability. The structure, developed using aluminum profiles for modularity, ensures adaptability for future enhancements. Experimental results demonstrate the effectiveness of the design in maintaining safe and continuous movement along power lines, offering a promising alternative for autonomous power line inspection.**

Keywords-Inspection; Robots; Power cables; Safety; Power system reliability; Wheels.

I. INTRODUCTION

High-voltage power line inspection is traditionally performed by helicopters and human operators, with significant safety concerns. This issue has led to the development of autonomous robotic solutions that can perform inspections, improving safety and efficiency. However, the main difficulty is designing a system capable of overcoming the environmental and structural obstacles inherent in power lines.

The challenge is ensuring that robotic systems can navigate these obstacles while maintaining balance and operational efficiency. This paper discusses a novel mechanism capable of autonomous, safe, and reliable power line inspections, which overcomes the elements of the power line.

The rest of the paper is structured as follows. Section II provides a review of the related literature. Section III introduces the design and development of the autonomous cable-line crawling robot. Section IV details the mechanism proposed for overcoming obstacles on power line components. Finally, Section V presents the conclusions, including key findings and recommendations for future research.

II. RELATED WORK

Some strategies have been developed to assist inspection robots in overcoming obstacles on power transmission lines. One interesting approach involves employing a sophisticated movement strategy wherein the robot secures itself at a stable point and maneuvers its support and movement segments over an obstacle, as discussed in [1]. This method, however, can be complex to implement and may require precise coordination, posing a challenge in highly variable environmental conditions.

Another approach focuses on designing robots that can actively adjust their center of mass, inspired by how monkeys navigate branches, as in [2]. This approach has shown effectiveness in obstacle avoidance by allowing the robot's structure to shift dynamically. Despite its promise, constant rebalancing during operation presents a challenge, particularly under conditions of instability like gusty winds.

Research efforts have also concentrated on enhancing robot stability during transit across the line's components [3]. These methods ensure the robot maintains balance while moving, although they may limit the system's agility and responsiveness. These limitations emphasize the need for solutions that balance stability, agility, and environmental adaptability.

This paper addresses these gaps by proposing a mechanism that combines the overcoming of power line elements (such as dampers, wire markers, and insulators) with stability, aiming to improve the efficiency and safety of autonomous line inspections, same in adverse weather conditions.

III. THE ROBOTIC MECHANISM

In this type of robot, the center of gravity is crucial: the lower it is positioned, the greater the stability. Based on this principle, the structure was designed using SOLIDWORKS mechanical modeling and analysis software to achieve optimal mass distribution. The objective was to ensure that the center of gravity was centrally located and positioned below the support point, as presented in Figure 1.

Figure 1. Robotic Mechanism for Inspection of High-Voltage Transmission Lines.

The structure was built using aluminum profiles, allowing for easy assembly and the potential for adding new modules. Steel plates were also used to cover the front of the robot, which not only protect the control systems from external elements but also serve as counterweights. The structure can

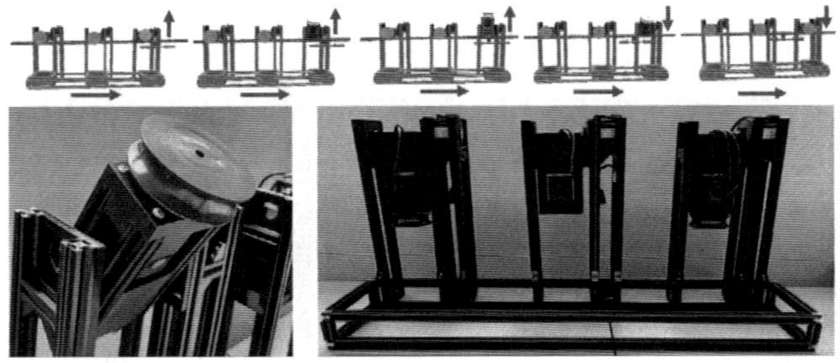

Figure 2. Demonstration of actuation and obstacle avoidance.

be divided into four parts: the main section, which houses the 24-volt batteries and controllers, and three vertical structures that accommodate the motors and actuators, as depicted in Figure 3.

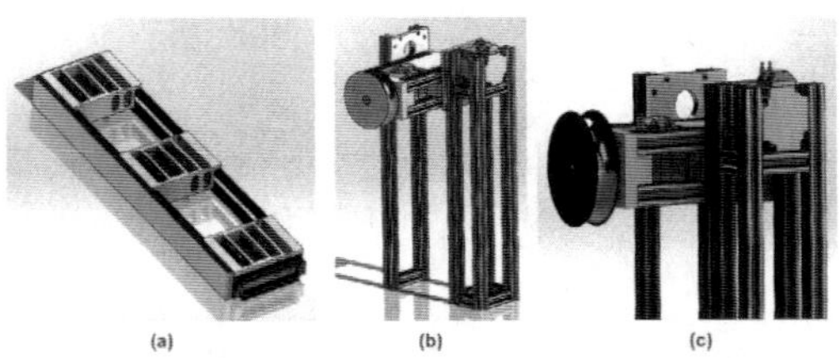

Figure 3. Robot elements.

IV. Actuation and Obstacle Avoidance

A mechanism was developed that uses three stepper motors, each equipped with a steel pulley with a one-inch gap to allow the robot to move along the transmission cables. As the pulleys rotate, they provide linear motion along the steel cable, ensuring stable and precise movement, as seen in Figure 2.

A pivoting mechanism was designed for the movement system to enable the robot to overcome obstacles fixed to the transmission line. This mechanism employs three stepper motors, one for each pulley—mounted on the sides of the supports. Through a gear transmission system with a 2.75:1 reduction ratio, each pulley support is sequentially rotated clockwise until it reaches a 90 degree angle, as shown in Figure 4, effectively moving the pulleys away from the obstacle. Once the obstacle is cleared, the pulleys are returned counterclockwise to their original position on the transmission line.

Additionally, a locking system was implemented using solenoid actuators. When the pulley support system is correctly positioned, these actuators engage to prevent excessive load on the movement system, thereby protecting the motors from overload. This mechanism serves as a mechanical safety lock ensuring that the robot remains securely suspended on the transmission cables.

V. Conclusion

This paper presents a novel cable-line crawling robot to overcome the obstacles commonly found on power lines.

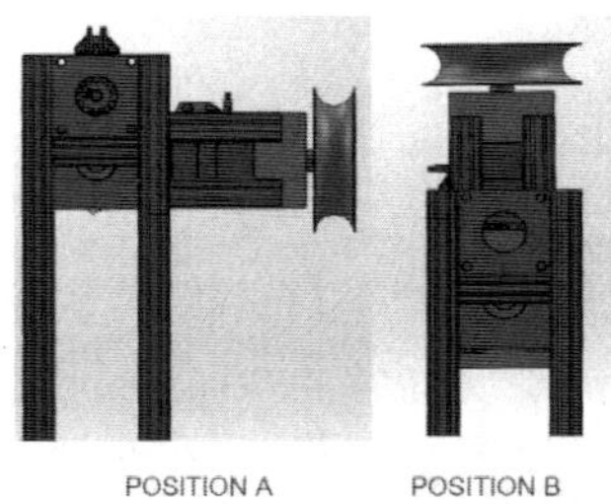

Figure 4. Pulley Positions.

The proposed solution successfully navigates power lines and bypasses obstacles such as dampers, wire markers, and insulators, maintaining stability to perform integrity inspections. The modular design of the inspection robot, using aluminum profiles, allows it to be adapted to various power line configurations by adjusting its length and incorporating additional robotic arms.

Future research will focus on improve control systems, integrating advanced sensors like LIDAR, and enhancing autonomous decision-making capabilities. Optimization of energy efficiency and mobility will also be a priority. These improvements aim to create a fully autonomous and reliable inspection robot for power line maintenance.

Acknowledgment

The project is supported by the National Council for Scientific and Technological Development (CNPq) under grant number 407984/2022-4; the Fund for Scientific and Technological Development (FNDCT); the Ministry of Science, Technology and Innovations (MCTI) of Brazil; the Araucaria Foundation; the General Superintendence of Science, Technology and Higher Education (SETI); and NAPI Robotics.

References

[1] N. Pouliot, P.-L. Richard, and S. Montambault, "Linescout technology opens the way to robotic inspection and maintenance of high-voltage power lines," *IEEE Power and Energy Technology Systems Journal*, vol. 2, no. 1, pp. 1–11, 2015.

[2] X. Yue, H. Wang, and Y. Jiang, "A novel 110 kv power line inspection robot and its climbing ability analysis," *International Journal of Advanced Robotic Systems*, vol. 14, Jun. 2017.

[3] J. M. N. de Albuquerque *et al.*, "A novel method for multimodal predictive inspection of power lines," *IEEE Access*, vol. 12, pp. 184 680–184 691, 2024.

Optimizing Neural Networks for Activity Recognition in Daily Living

A Case Study Using Signal Processing and Smartwatch Sensors

Klemens Waldhör
FOM University
Nuremberg, Germany
Email: klemens.waldhoer@fom.de

Philipp Müller
Business Information Systems, FOM University
Nuremberg, Germany
Email: muellerphilipp17.08@gmail.com

Abstract— **This study explores the impact of various signal processing techniques on neural network performance for activity recognition using smartwatch sensor data. Four common Activities of Daily Living (ADLs) including drinking, tumbling, teeth brushing, and walking, are evaluated. Signal processing methods, Gaussian filtering, Principal Component Analysis (PCA), Fourier Transform (FT), Empirical Mode Decomposition (EMD), and Hilbert-Huang Transform (HHT), are systematically assessed for their effectiveness in improving neural network classification accuracy. Multiple deep learning architectures, including Recurrent Neural Networks (RNN), Long Short-Term Memory (LSTM), Gated Recurrent Units (GRU), and Convolutional Neural Networks (CNN), are implemented and compared. Results reveal that signal processing techniques significantly enhance the performance of RNN models, whereas other architectures (LSTM, GRU, CNN) achieve high accuracy (>99%) without additional signal preprocessing. Additionally, a hybrid CNN-LSTM model was successfully deployed on a Samsung Galaxy Watch 6, to classify ADLs within a smartwatch. However, practical implementation challenges, such as battery consumption and the necessity for on-device learning capabilities, are identified. This research provides valuable insights into optimizing neural network performance for wearable computing in resource-constrained environments.**

Keywords*— *Activity Recognition; Signal Processing; Neural Networks; Wearable Computing; Smartwatch Sensors.

I. INTRODUCTION

Germany is undergoing a pronounced demographic transition marked by an increasingly elderly population and persistently low birth rates [1]. By 2049, estimates suggest Germany will require between 280 000 and 690 000 additional care professionals to meet the needs of its aging citizens [2]. To bridge this gap, healthcare systems must turn to technological innovations that streamline patient monitoring and support clinical decision-making.

In this context, wearable devices, most notably smartwatches, have shown considerable promise. Equipped with accelerometers, gyroscopes and heart-rate sensors, they offer continuous, non-invasive tracking of Activities of Daily Living (ADLs), potentially enhancing diagnostic anamnesis and enabling rapid emergency response to events such as falls or acute cardiac episodes [3]-[5].

Yet, deploying advanced neural-network models directly on smartwatches introduces significant challenges: limited processing power, constrained memory, and the need to preserve battery life [6]-[9]. Effective real-time classification of complex movements therefore hinges on balancing model accuracy with resource efficiency.

This study investigates whether neural networks trained on raw smartwatch sensor data can accurately distinguish between a wide range of human movements, whether incorporating signal-processing techniques such as Fourier or wavelet transforms can boost classification performance, and how different time-series encoding methods affect the classification accuracy of these models in multi-class activity recognition.

The rest of the paper is structured as follows. Section II presents the related work. Section III describes the methodology, and Section IV the results. We conclude the work in Section V.

II. RELATED WORK

Time series classification represents one of ten challenging problems in data mining research [10]. The noise in time series data poses a particular challenge that requires sophisticated approaches to address effectively. Previous research by Waldhör and Lutze has successfully demonstrated the real-time recognition of drinking activities using smartwatches [11][12], establishing the feasibility of ADL detection in wearable devices.

The development of RNNs can be traced back to the early 1980s with Hopfield networks [13], designed as content-addressable memory systems. Significant progress was achieved in the 1990s with the introduction of fully connected RNN architectures by researchers like Jeffrey Elman and Michael I. Jordan [14]. However, these networks struggled with the vanishing gradient problem, formally analyzed by Hochreiter [15] and later by Bengio et al. [16].

LSTM networks, introduced by Hochreiter and Schmidhuber [17], addressed these limitations through their innovative cell state architecture. GRU networks, proposed by Cho et al. [18], later offered a simplified alternative to LSTM. CNNs, originally conceived by Kunihiko Fukushima as the Neocognitron [19], have evolved to become powerful tools for pattern recognition and feature extraction.

Recent studies have highlighted the importance of sensor data quality and processing in wearable applications. The integration of smartwatches into Internet of Things (IoT) frameworks, as discussed by Takiddeen and Zualkernan [7], presents both opportunities and challenges for real-time monitoring systems. However, as noted by

Lane et al. [9], deploying deep learning models on mobile and embedded devices remains challenging due to computational and power constraints.

III. METHODOLOGY

A. Data Collection and Processing

Initial training data was sourced from previous research [20][21], providing a foundation for model development. This was supplemented with new data collected using a Samsung Galaxy Watch 6 equipped with an LSM6DSO 6-axis IMU sensor. Following the methodology established by Windler et al. [22], a consistent sampling rate of 10 Hz is maintained across all data sources to ensure compatibility between training and deployment environments.

Signal quality was enhanced through multiple preprocessing steps:

- Nearest neighbor interpolation for consistent sampling, addressing the challenge of variable sensor sampling rates identified in [23]
- DC offset removal by subtracting the average value of each axis over time.
- Gaussian filtering for noise reduction, implemented using one dimensional gaussian filter provided within the SciPy python package, with default sigma values [24]
- Standard scaling for normalization, ensuring consistent feature ranges ($\mu = 0$; $\sigma = 1$) across different sensor axes.

To address demographic variations in movement patterns, we incorporated data gathered from [25] regarding the simulation of older adult movement patterns during data collection. This approach helps ensure the model's applicability across different age groups.

B. Signal Processing Techniques

To extract and enhance salient features from the raw sensor data, different Signal Processing techniques are applied, each of the following.

Principal Component Analysis (PCA) was implemented following the methodology described by Wold et al. [26], aiming to reduce dimensionality while retaining maximum variability within the data. This method is notably effective for handling correlated variables [27].

The Fourier Transform (FT) was implemented using the Fast Fourier Transform algorithm to leverage computational efficiency. FT enables frequency-domain analysis of periodic signals [28], making it especially suitable for the identification of repetitive activities such as walking.

Empirical Mode Decomposition (EMD) was executed according to the original procedure by Huang et al. [29]. EMD decomposes complex signals into Intrinsic Mode Functions (IMFs), which facilitates the analysis of non-linear and non-stationary signals [30].

The Hilbert-Huang Transform (HHT) integrates Empirical Mode Decomposition with the Hilbert spectral analysis, providing detailed time-frequency representation of signals [31]. This technique effectively captures dynamic and varying characteristics in signal behavior [31].

Each transformation method can be sequentially evaluated for its effectiveness in extracting meaningful features, improving classification accuracy, and maintaining computational efficiency, reflecting considerations critical due to resource limitations inherent in smartwatch deployments [9].

C. Neural Network Architectures

To benchmark model families under truly comparable conditions, we wrapped every network in an agent class that exposes the same fit-evaluate-save interface and inherits a common training configuration: 100-step sequences, batch size 64, Adam (lr = 1×10^{-3}), categorical cross-entropy, and early stopping with a patience of 10–20 epochs. The five agents differ only in the layers that transform the input stream.

- RNN agent: three SimpleRNN layers (256 → 512 → 256 units, tanh, 0.3 dropout) capture temporal context, followed by two dense layers (128 → 64, tanh) and a soft-max output.
- LSTM agent: identical topology but with LSTM cells (128 → 256 → 128 units) that retain long-range dependencies while mitigating vanishing gradients.
- GRU agent: a lighter three-layer GRU stack (64 → 128 → 64 units, 0.2 dropout) with dense layers (32 → 16, tanh), trading a smaller footprint for faster convergence.
- CNN agent: three Conv2D blocks (32, 64, 128 filters; 3 × 3 kernels; ReLU) each followed by 2 × 1 max-pooling compress the spectro-temporal representation; a 128-unit dense layer and soft-max complete the classifier.
- CNN - LSTM agent: convolutional features are flattened via TimeDistributed and streamed into two LSTM layers (64 → 32 units, 0.3 dropout) before a 32-unit dense layer and soft-max. This hybrid marries local pattern extraction with sequence modelling.

Because all hyper-parameters outside the feature extractor are shared, performance differences can be attributed purely to the architectures themselves rather than to training-regime artefacts.

IV. RESULTS

A. Model Performance

All architectures except RNN achieved high accuracy When evaluated on raw inertial signals (Table 1), the convolutional (CNN), long short-term memory (LSTM), gated recurrent unit (GRU), and hybrid CNN–LSTM architectures all achieved near-perfect classification accuracies (0.9998–0.9999), whereas the vanilla recurrent network (RNN) yielded a markedly lower accuracy of 0.5747. Applying principal component analysis (PCA) produced only marginal improvement for the RNN, while elevating the CNN to perfect performance and slightly enhancing the hybrid model. Empirical Mode Decomposition (EMD) had the most uniformly positive effect on the RNN, boosting its accuracy to 0.9783, and it maintained or slightly improved the performance of all other models (CNN = 0.9999; LSTM/GRU = 1.0000; CNN–LSTM = 0.9998). The Hilbert–Huang Transform (HHT) exhibited a similar pattern: the RNN rose to 0.9617, the CNN slightly decreased to 0.9988. These results underscore that while empirical decompositions (EMD, HHT) effectively condition data for recurrent architectures, pure spectral filtering (Fourier) may inadvertently disrupt the feature hierarchies learned by convolutional and hybrid models (see Table 1).

TABLE I. MODEL PERFORMANCE

Transfor-mation	Tested model					
	Evaluation Metrics	*CNN*	*RNN*	*LSTM*	*GRU*	*CNN-LSTM*
Raw	Accuracy	0.9999	0.5747	0.9999	0.9999	0.9998
	Precision	0.9999	0.5255	0.9999	0.9999	0.9998
	Recall	0.9999	0.5747	0.9999	0.9999	0.9998
PCA	Accuracy	1.0000	0.6008	0.9999	0.9999	0.9999
	Precision	1.0000	0.5361	0.9999	0.9999	0.9999
	Recall	1.0000	0.6008	0.9999	0.9999	0.9999
Fourier	Accuracy	0.9661	0.5497	0.9977	0.9999	0.5497
	Precision	0.9490	0.3022	0.9977	0.9999	0.3022
	Recall	0.9661	0.5497	0.9977	0.9999	0.5497
EMD	Accuracy	0.9999	0.9783	1.0000	1.0000	0.9998
	Precision	0.9999	0.9781	1.0000	1.0000	0.9998
	Recall	0.9999	0.9783	1.0000	1.0000	0.9998
HHT	Accuracy	0.9988	0.9617	1.0000	1.0000	0.5497
	Precision	0.9988	0.9626	1.0000	1.0000	0.3022
	Recall	0.9988	0.9617	1.0000	1.0000	0.5497

a.

B. Smartwatch Application

An Android Wear application, developed in Kotlin, continuously acquires tri-axial accelerometer and gyroscope signals to enable on-device, real-time activity classification. As shown in Figure 1, the user interface displays a dynamic bar chart of model-predicted confidence scores and incorporates an opt-in toggle for asynchronous data streaming to a remote server. To meet the stringent CPU, memory, and power budgets of a smartwatch, we convert our neural network to a TensorFlow Lite (TFLite) format, achieving a significant reduction in binary size and inference latency without compromising classification accuracy. This architecture demonstrates that sophisticated convolutional–recurrent pipelines can be effectively deployed on resource-limited wearable platforms, paving the way for continuous, unobtrusive monitoring of activities of daily living.

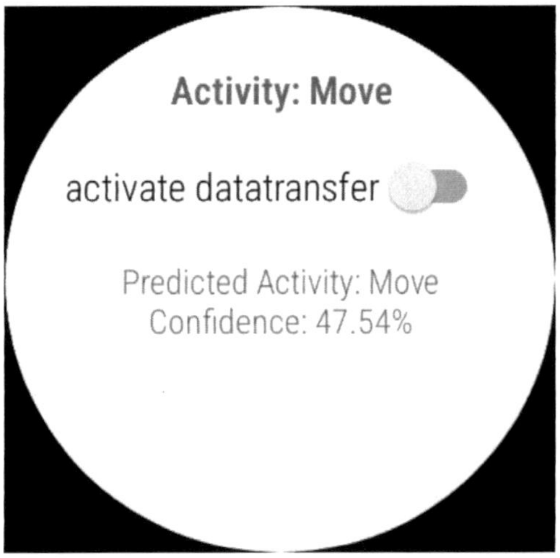

Figure 1. Smartwatch application interface for real-time activity recognition, displaying the predicted activity, confidence scores, and data transfer toggle.

C. Discussion

The deployment of the developed machine learning models on smartwatches highlighted several critical challenges that must be addressed to facilitate effective and continuous real-world use. Key challenges encountered during deployment included battery optimization, real-time processing constraints, the necessity for personalization, and variability in sensor data quality. Specifically, battery optimization emerged as a significant issue, as continuous model inference and sensor activity led to accelerated battery depletion, limiting the device's operational duration. Real-time processing constraints were observed due to the limited computational resources inherent to smartwatches, impacting the responsiveness and efficiency of the classification tasks. The need for personalization became apparent as performance variations were observed across different users and devices, highlighting that static, pre-trained models may not generalize well across diverse real-world conditions. Additionally, variable sensor data quality introduced inconsistencies, influencing the model's accuracy and reliability.

To overcome these limitations and enhance the deployment feasibility of activity classification models on wearable devices, several avenues for future research are recommended, as follows.

1) Development of efficient on-device learning mechanisms: Research should focus on implementing lightweight and computationally efficient on-device learning algorithms capable of continuous adaptation to individual user patterns, thereby enhancing personalization and mitigating performance degradation.
2) Battery consumption optimization: Further research is needed into advanced power management strategies, sensor management optimizations, and computational reductions (e.g., pruning, quantization) to extend battery life without compromising model accuracy.
3) Investigation of transfer learning approaches: Exploring transfer learning could facilitate more rapid personalization by leveraging pre-trained models adapted efficiently to new users with minimal data collection, addressing variability in user behavior and sensor conditions.
4) Integration with eldercare systems: Future studies should consider the integration of activity recognition systems with broader eldercare management platforms to improve the practicality and applicability of these models in monitoring daily activities, supporting elderly users, and enhancing their overall quality of life.

A pivotal evolutionary step to address the observed high variance in individual movement patterns would be to train user-specific models directly on the smartwatch. This approach would significantly enhance the adaptability and precision of activity recognition systems, thus improving their robustness and reliability in personalized, real-world scenarios.

V. Conclusion

This study confirms the viability of accurate human activity recognition using smartwatch sensor data and deep learning models. While advanced neural network architectures such as CNNs and LSTMs achieve high performance with minimal benefit from traditional signal processing techniques, these methods still hold value in enhancing simpler models or improving model efficiency. Importantly, the work underscores the practical constraints of deploying such models on resource-constrained wearable devices. Future research should prioritize energy-efficient inference, explore lightweight architectures, and investigate on-device learning strategies to enable adaptive, real-time activity recognition within the limited computational and power budgets of smartwatches.

References

[1] Statistisches Bundeamt [Statistical Bureau], "Germany's Population by 2060", Accessed: Sep. 23, 2024. [Online]. Available: www.destatis.de.

[2] Deutscher Pflegerat [German Nursing Council], "Alle Hebel zur Bewältigung der Pflegekrise umstellen | Deutscher Pflegerat [Change all levers to tackle the nursing crisis | German Nursing Council]" Accessed: Jun. 15, 2024. [Online]. Available: https://deutscher-pflegerat.de/profession-staerken/pressemitteilungen/loesung-der-pflegekrise-benoetigt-weit-mehr-als-350.000-pflegekraefte-innerhalb-der-naechsten-zehn-jahre

[3] WHO, "mHealth: new horizons for health through mobile technologies: second global survey on eHealth," 2011, Accessed: Sep. 23, 2024. [Online]. Available: https://iris.who.int/handle/10665/44607

[4] M. Mubashir, L. Shao, and L. Seed, "A survey on fall detection: Principles and approaches," 2012, doi: 10.1016/j.neucom.2011.09.037.

[5] S. Patel, H. Park, P. Bonato, L. Chan, and M. Rodgers, "A review of wearable sensors and systems with application in rehabilitation," J Neuroeng Rehabil, vol. 9, p. 21, 2012, doi: 10.1186/1743-0003-9-21.

[6] S. G. G. Selen, N. A. A. Rahman, and K. S. Harun, "A study of wearable IoT device (smartwatch) advantages, vulnerabilities and protection," AIP Conf Proc, vol. 2802, no. 1, Jan. 2024, doi: 10.1063/5.0183094/3126760.

[7] N. Takiddeen and I. Zualkernan, "Smartwatches as IoT edge devices: A framework and survey," 2019 4th International Conference on Fog and Mobile Edge Computing, FMEC 2019, pp. 216–222, Jun. 2019, doi: 10.1109/FMEC.2019.8795338.

[8] F. Stradolini, E. Lavalle, G. De Micheli, P. Motto Ros, D. Demarchi, and S. Carrara, "Paradigm-Shifting Players for IoT: Smart-Watches for Intensive Care Monitoring", 2017, doi: 10.1007/978-3-319-58877-3_9.

[9] N. D. Lane, S. Bhattacharya, A. Mathur, P. Georgiev, C. Forlivesi, and F. Kawsar, "Squeezing Deep Learning into Mobile and Embedded Devices," Pervasive Computing, 2017, doi: 10.1109/ISCA.2016.11.

[10] Q. Yang et al., "10 Challenging Problems in Data Mining Research," Int J Inf Technol Decis Mak, vol. 5, no. 4, pp. 597–604, 2006.

[11] R. Lutze and K. Waldhör, "Smartwatch based tumble recognition — A data mining model comparision study." 2016, IEEE 18th International Conference on e-Health Networking, Applications and Services (Healthcom 2016),) took place 14-17 September 2016 in Munich, Germany, J. J. P. C. Rodrigues, Ed. IEEE, Piscataway, NJ, 1–6.

[12] K. Waldhör and R. Baldauf, "Recognizing Drinking ADLs in Real Time using Smartwatches and Data Mining," Proceedings of the RapidMiner Wisdom Europe, S. Fischer, I. Mierswa and G. Schäfer, Eds. Shaker, Aachen, 1–18, 2015.

[13] J. J. Hopfield, "Neural networks and physical systems with emergent collective computational abilities (associative memory/parallel processing/categorization/content-addressable memory/fail-soft devices)," Proc. NatL Acad. Sci. USA, vol. 79, pp. 2554–2558, 1982, Accessed: Sep. 21, 2024. [Online]. Available: https://www.pnas.org

[14] J. L. Elman, "Finding Structure in Time," Cogn Sci, vol. 14, pp. 179–200, doi: 10.1207/s15516709cog1402_1.

[15] S. Hochreiter, "Untersuchungen zu dynamischen neuronalen Netzen [Investigations into dynamic neural networks]" Diploma, Technische Universität München, vol. 91, no. 1, p. 31, 1991.

[16] Y. Bengio, P. Simard, and P. Frasconi, "Learning Long-Term Dependencies with Gradient Descent is Difficult," IEEE

Trans Neural Netw, vol. 5, no. 2, pp. 157–166, 1994, doi: 10.1109/72.279181.

[17] S. Hochreiter, "Long Short-term Memory," Neural Computation MIT-Press, 1997.

[18] K. Cho et al., "Learning Phrase Representations using RNN Encoder-Decoder for Statistical Machine Translation," pp. 1724–1734, Oct. 2014, doi: 10.3115/v1/D14-1179.

[19] K. Fukushima, "Neocognitron: A self-organizing neural network model for a mechanism of pattern recognition unaffected by shift in position," Biol Cybern, vol. 36, no. 4, pp. 193–202, Apr. 1980, doi: 10.1007/BF00344251/METRICS.

[20] K. Waldhör and R. Lutze, "ADL Detection Challenge at IEEE Healthcom 2016 Conference - Wearables at work.," ADL Detection Challenge at IEEE Healthcom 2016 Conference - Wearables at work, 2016.

[21] F. Full, "Methoden zur Generierung und Klassifizierung von Sensordatan für die ADL-Erkennung," Aug. 2019.

[22] T. Windler, J. Ahmed Ghauri, M. Usman Syed, T. Belostotskaya, V. Chikukwa, and R. Rêgo Drumond, "End-to-End Motion Classification Using Smartwatch Sensor Data", 2020, doi: 10.5445/KSP/1000098011/12.

[23] F. Gu, M. H. Chung, M. Chignell, S. Valaee, B. Zhou, and X. Liu, "A Survey on Deep Learning for Human Activity Recognition," ACM Comput Surv, vol. 54, no. 8, Nov. 2022, doi: 10.1145/3472290.

[24] SciPy, "gaussian_filter1d — SciPy v1.14.1 Manual." Accessed: Oct. 19, 2024. [Online]. Available: https://docs.scipy.org/doc/scipy/reference/generated/scipy.ndimage.gaussian_filter1d.html

[25] K. Waldhör, "Maschinelles Lernen und Smartwatches zur Unterstützung eines selbstbestimmten Lebens älterer Personen [Machine learning and smartwatches to support independent living for older people]" in Künstliche Intelligenz in Wirtschaft & Gesellschaft: Auswirkungen, Herausforderungen & Handlungsempfehlungen [Artificial Intelligence in Business & Society: Impacts, Challenges & Recommendations for Action], T. and K. O. Buchkremer Rüdiger and Heupel, Ed., Wiesbaden: Springer Fachmedien Wiesbaden, 2020, pp. 347–367. doi: 10.1007/978-3-658-29550-9_19.

[26] S. Wold, K. Esbensen, and P. Geladi, "Principal Component Analysis". 1987, Chemometrics and Intelligent Laboratory Systems 2, 1-3, 37–52, Doi: 10.1016/0169-7439(87)80084-9.

[27] I. T. Jolliffe and J. Cadima, "Principal component analysis: a review and recent developments," Philosophical Transactions of the Royal Society A: Mathematical, Physical and Engineering Sciences, vol. 374, no. 2065, p. 20150202, Apr. 2016, doi: 10.1098/rsta.2015.0202.

[28] E. J. Haugstvedt, "On the Potential of Utilizing Laboratory-Scale Experimental Setup as Proxy For Real-Life Applications: Time Series Analysis and Prediction for Hole Cleaning," 2023.

[29] N. Huang et al., "The empirical mode decomposition and the Hilbert spectrum for nonlinear and non-stationary time series analysis," Proceedings of the Royal Society A: Mathematical, Physical and Engineering Sciences, pp. 903–995, 1998, doi: 10.1098/rspa.1998.0193ï.

[30] G. Rilling, P. Flandrin, and P. Gonçalvès, "On empirical mode decomposition and its algorithms", 2025, Accessed: June 19, 2025. [Online]. Available: https://inria.hal.science/inria-00570628/en/.

[31] S. Kizhner, T. P. Flatley, N. E. Huang, K. Blank, E. Conwell, and D. Smith, "On the Hilbert-Huang Transform Data Processing System Development", Accessed: June 19, 2024. [Online]. Available: https://ieeexplore.ieee.org/document/1367979.

Early Response Prediction for H_2 Sensors

Raduan Sarif
Bundesanstalt für Materialforschung und -prüfung (BAM)
Berlin, Germany
e-mail: raduan.sarif@bam.de

Carlo Tiebe
Bundesanstalt für Materialforschung und -prüfung (BAM)
Berlin, Germany
e-mail: carlo.tiebe@bam.de

Christian Herglotz
Brandenburgische Technische Universität Cottbus-Senftenberg
Cottbus, Germany
e-mail: christian.herglotz@b-tu.de

***Abstract*—Green hydrogen (H_2) is essential for the global transition to clean energy; it will significantly reduce emissions from heavy industry and the long-distance transport system. H_2 can be used as fuel in fuel cells, storing surplus renewable energy, and as a feedstock in industrial processes. However, H_2 faces significant safety challenges during storage and transportation. Accidents due to H_2 leakage and explosions raise serious concerns due to its high flammability, rapid diffusion in air, and extremely low ignition energy. To mitigate risks associated with H_2 leakages, reliable and automated H_2 safety systems are essential for emergency repairs or shutdown. An early response from H_2 sensors is crucial for early warning in accidents. The earlier response time of H_2 sensors is often constrained by their sensor principle, which is heavily influenced by the sensor material's properties. This study explores methods for earlier sensor response through predictive algorithms. Specifically, we investigate transient response predictions using a First-Order (FO) model and propose improvements through the First-Order with early response and the First-Order with adapted early response model. Both models can predict the stable value of the H_2 sensor response from a small time window, which is 70.89% and 83.72% earlier, respectively, than the time required for the sensor hardware to reach it physically. The model's performance is evaluated by calculating the fitting error with a 2 % threshold. Our current research lays the groundwork for future advancements in real-time sensor response predictions for hydrogen leakage.**

Keywords-H_2 Safety; H_2 Leakage Detection; H_2 Sensor Data Analysis; H_2 Sensor Response Predictions; First-Order (FO) Model.

I. Introduction

Hydrogen is crucial for clean energy [1], but storage and transportation are complicated and costly. Two common issues during hydrogen storage and transport are leakage and permeation. Leakage occurs when hydrogen escapes from a container, system, or pipeline due to flaws, holes, or cracks, where the lower flammability limit is a concentration of 4 volume fractions in Vol-% [2]. On the other hand, permeation refers to hydrogen's diffusion through the material walls or interstices of containers, piping, or interface materials [3]. According to [4], the recommended allowable hydrogen permeation rate for new containers tested at 15°C is 6.0 mL/hr/L for passenger cars and 3.7 mL/hr/L for city buses. Based on the permissible permeation rate for passenger cars, the hydrogen permeation from a 5-liter cylinder would correspond to 0.6 Vol% per hour.

The safety concerns associated with hydrogen are due to the molecule's small size, which makes it particularly prone to leakage [5]. High-pressure hydrogen storage exacerbates the consequences of leakage, leading to higher release flow rates and easier ignition. Notably, hydrogen-related accidents have occurred in various industrial areas. Significant incidents, such as a 2022 refinery fire caused by a hydrogen leak, are of concern for critical safety issues [6]. Thus, intelligent sensor systems are essential for early-stage leakage detection to prevent H_2 related accidents.

Exploiting signal processing methods for sensor responses enables fast and accurate H_2 leakage identification, leveraging transient signals to ensure early response [7]. Although the internal structure of the sensor imposes limitations on its performance, advanced algorithms can significantly improve accuracy and response time. Predicting stable sensor responses from early response accelerates monitoring, reducing the time to detect leaks and improving H_2 safety. Various studies discuss algorithm developments for predicting hydrogen response, such as Osorio-Arrieta et al. [8], applying the Gauss-Newton method to shorten measurement time by fitting the transient response curve. Hübert et al. [9] measured the sensor t_{90} value based on a mathematical model. Shi et al. [10] use SnO_2-based sensor response prediction for hydrogen detection by artificial intelligence techniques. After reviewing the above studies, we found that most approaches only approximate the entire sensor response from the sensor's entire response. Additionally, few studies have shown the potential to predict H_2 stable concentration from a small time window of the early response [11]–[13]. Our study explores the H_2 stable concentration and the entire H_2 sensor response using a small time window from the early sensor signal. We also tested the model with different ranges of small time window values, rather than only a specific early sensor response signal. Our current research explores the mathematical feasibility of predicting sensor stable response and t_{90} values from the early response small time window.

This paper presents a novel method to obtain stable sensor response predictions using an approximation algorithm. Our proposed models use a small time window from the early response of the sensor to predict the entire H_2 sensor response. The structure of this paper is as follows: Section II discusses the H_2 sensor response dynamics and provides a mathematical explanation of the sensor behavior. Section III describes the experimental setup. Section IV presents the proposed methods, while Section V focuses on the evaluation. Section VI covers the validation, and Section VII provides a detailed discussion. Finally, Section VIII concludes the paper and includes references.

II. Sensor Response Dynamics

H_2 sensors are essential to ensure H_2 safety, leak detections, and control and monitoring of H_2 systems. Various H_2 sensors are commercially available [14], exploiting different detection principles such as catalytic combustion, electrochemical reactions, thermal conductivity, and changes in electrical resistivity. Key sensor selection criteria for H_2 safety and monitoring include sensitivity and quick response time [15]. The sensor detection principle, along with the H_2 flow rate and the chamber size, can significantly affect and disrupt the response time.

Boon-Brett et al. [16] discuss the different methods and setups that affect response time. Sensor response dynamics can be categorized as extrinsic or intrinsic. The extrinsic response time involves gas delivery dynamics influenced by measurement chamber volume and the H_2 flow rates. The intrinsic response time is related to the physical properties of the sensor, reflecting the delay between the exposure of H_2 to the sensing element and the first detection of the signal, known as deadtime θ (seconds).

A graphical representation of an exemplary H_2 concentration (volume fraction in Vol-%) in a chamber is shown in Figure 1. The green curve represents an exponential sensor response with both H_2 increasing and decreasing concentrations for 9600 seconds. With a First Order (FO) model, we can approximate the idealized sensor's response (red curve) for 7200 seconds. Also, the step function (blue curve) defines the release of H_2 flow. H_2 was released at -200 seconds, but the sensor began responding at 0 seconds, which is defined as the deadtime. The maximum sensor response is 0.8 volume fraction in Vol-%. t_{90} represents the time at which the sensor's output reaches 90% of its stable value. In this case, t_{90} is 775 seconds for a concentration of 0.72 Vol-%.

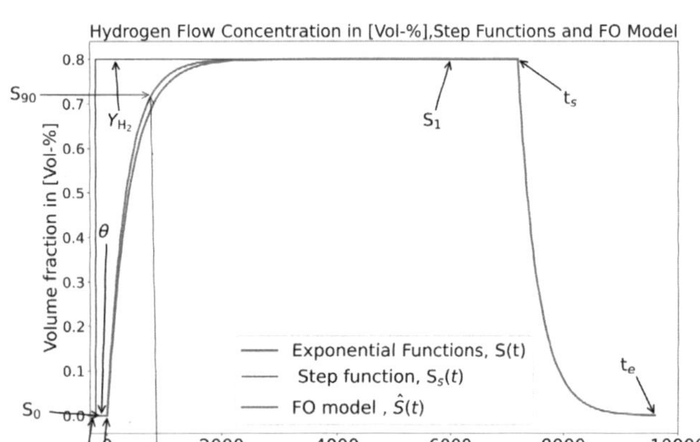

Figure 1: Visualization of exponential functions, step function and FO model for H_2 flow concentration (Vol-%).

As stated in the literature [17], the sensor element transfer function and the transient gas sensor response signal can be modeled as an exponential function. This approach allows determining the transient response curve of the hydrogen sensor for a specified concentration (volume fraction in Vol %) [17]. With changing H_2 concentration, exponential functions can describe both the increase and decrease of the H_2 sensor response.

The sensor response can be idealized by using exponential functions. Equation (1) describes the ideal response $S(t)$, which consists of three exponential functions for changing concentrations over time t (seconds). The time state t_i (seconds) indicates the H_2 concentration release time and also the time of the first recorded measured sample. t_0 (seconds) denotes the moment when the sensor starts to react in H_2 flow changing. The time t_s (seconds) is assumed to be the time at which the sensor reaches its maximum stable response, while t_e (seconds) represents the time at which the sensor reaches its lowest stable response. Three distinct cases are described below:

1) **No Reaction (Deadtime)**: No sensor reaction over H_2 flow changes for the period of $t_i \leq t < t_0$. This duration is called deadtime θ, where the sensor does not yet detect the presence of H_2. After this delay, the sensor begins to register its first response.
2) **Transient Increasing Response**: During $t_0 \leq t \leq t_s$, the sensor starts to react to the presence of H_2 concentration. The response increases as the sensor detects and records the H_2 concentration. We assume that the sensor reaches a maximum stable response at t_s seconds, where we stop the H_2 release.
3) **Transient Decreasing Response**: In the final phase, for $t_s \leq t < t_e$, the sensor response decreases as the H_2 concentration decreases inside the chamber. The decreasing response is recorded until it reaches the lowest stable sensor value, which we assume occurs at t_e seconds.

$$S(t) = \begin{cases} S_0, & t_i \leq t < t_0 \\ S_1 \cdot \left(1 - e^{\left(\frac{-t}{\tau}\right)}\right), & t_0 \leq t \leq t_s \\ S_1 \cdot e^{\left(-\frac{(t-t_s)}{\tau}\right)}, & t_s \leq t < t_e \end{cases} \quad (1)$$

Summarizing, the entire sensor response can be described by $S(t)$, where S_0 is a constant representing the sensor response before H_2 release, whose value should be zero. S_1 is the stable sensor response signal after H_2 flow change. Time constant τ is defined as the ratio of the chamber volume V in the unit liter (L) to the hydrogen flow rate $\dot{V}_{H_2}$ in the unit liter per minute (L/min) in (2).

$$\tau = \frac{V}{\dot{V}_{H_2}} \quad (2)$$

Equation (3) presents the step functions $S_s(t)$ for H_2 flow Y_{H_2} changes. Before time t_i, there is a 0% H_2 flow, after t_i, there is a H_2 flow Y_{H_2} upto time t_s.

$$S_s(t) = \begin{cases} 0, & t \le t_i \\ Y_{H_2}, & t_i \le t \le t_s \end{cases} \tag{3}$$

The sensor's increasing and decreasing response characteristics, including response time and the t_{90} time, are essential for ensuring H_2 safety. ISO 26142 defines response time as the interval from H_2 exposure until the sensor reaches a stable output, which corresponds to the duration of $t_0 \le t \le t_s$ in (1). The t_{90} time is the time for the sensor value to reach 90% of maximum stable response [18]. The t_{90} time is crucial for early leak detection and should be minimized to prevent accidents.

Equation (4) calculates the theoretical t_{90} (seconds) time for H_2 sensors. The sensor response value should match the t_{90} time derived from (4) to be considered a stable response, which is the inverse function of (1) case 2.

$$t_{90} = -\ln\left(1 - \frac{S_{90}}{S_1}\right)\tau \tag{4}$$

In the previous parts, we provided the theoretical background of ideal sensor responses, which can be approximated using various mathematical process modeling approaches. Among them, the First Order Plus Dead Time (FOPDT) model is widely used for simplifying process dynamics, particularly in feedback control loop design [19]. This model is the baseline to construct our simplification, where we focus on the sensor response increasing curve,t, in the range $t_0 \le t \le t_s$. Furthermore, we simplify the FOPDT to the First Order (FO) model, considering the deadtime θ equal to zero. Equation (5) presents the FOPDT model from [20] and FO model in (6), where $\hat{S}$ represents the estimated sensor response.

$$\tau\frac{\mathrm{d}\hat{S}}{\mathrm{d}t} + \hat{S}(t) = K \cdot S_s(t-\theta) \tag{5}$$

$$\tau\frac{\mathrm{d}\hat{S}}{\mathrm{d}t} + \hat{S}(t) = K \cdot S_s(t) \tag{6}$$

The steady-state gain (K) is the ratio of the sensor's response signal corresponding to a step input, as defined in (7).

$$K = \frac{S_1}{Y_{H_2}} \tag{7}$$

Equation (6) replaces the value of (K) and $S_s(t)$ from (7) and (3). The revised model is presented in (8).

$$\tau\frac{\mathrm{d}\hat{S}}{\mathrm{d}t} + \hat{S}(t) = S_1 \tag{8}$$

In addition, the transfer function of the FO (Laplace transformation of (6)) is described by (9), which is commonly used to approximate processes. This study will use this equation to predict the H_2 sensor response based on a small time window from the early response of the sensor.

$$\hat{S}(t) = S_1 \cdot \left(1 - e^{-\frac{t}{\tau}}\right) \tag{9}$$

III. Experimental Setup

This experiment used the NEO983 sensor with a H_2 detection threshold of less than 0.15 volume fraction in Vol-% and a response time of under 3 seconds and t_{90} time of less than 5 seconds. The sensor was tested in a measurement chamber using a double cross-piece DN 160 ISO-K chamber [21]. H_2 was mixed with air during the experiment to create the desired concentration, where airflow volume fractions were 99.2 volume fraction in Vol-%, and H_2 volume fraction was 0.8 volume fraction in Vol-%. The airflow rate was 992 mL/min, and the H_2 flow rate was adjusted to 8 mL/min. Therefore, with a gas flow rate of 1000 mL/min and a chamber volume of 5.8 L. Based on (2), the time constant (τ) is 348 seconds, resulting in a calculated t_{90} time of 801 seconds based on (4).

This setup provided a stable and well-mixed environment for evaluating the sensor's performance under specific H_2 concentrations. The experiment was conducted over two hours following the release of H_2. Once the sensor recorded a stable response, the H_2 release was stopped; after that, the sensor response was monitored until it declined to zero. The NE0983 sensor detected a maximum H_2 concentration of 0.75 volume fraction in Vol-%, compared to the released concentration of 0.8 volume fraction in Vol-%. Figure 2 illustrates the Piping and Instrumentation Diagram (P&ID), a detailed schematic that illustrates the experimental process's piping, equipment, and instrumentation, showing how components are interconnected and controlled. The overall gas flow setup includes a control valve, Mass Flow Controller (MFC), and gas mixer to accurately regulate, measure, and mix H_2 gases.

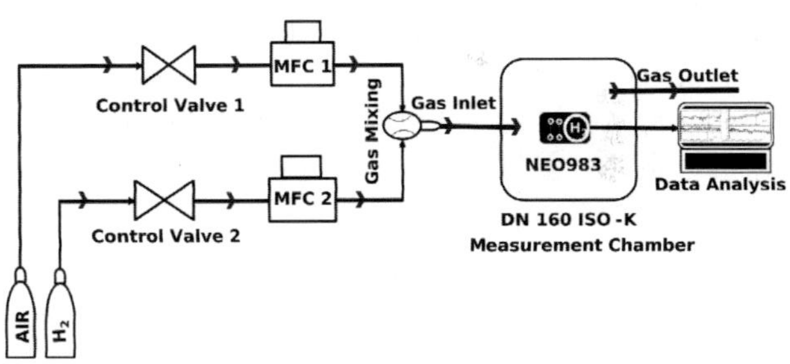

Figure 2: Experiment Pipe & Instrumentation Design.

An additional experiment was conducted as reported in [22], using H_2 concentrations of 0.5, 1.0, 1.5, 2.0, 2.5, 3.0, 3.5, and 4.0 Vol-%. Using the same chamber volume, the gas flow rate is 4643 mL/min with a flow uncertainty of ± 65.8 mL/min. In this case, the time constant (τ) is 75 seconds based on (2), and according to (4), the corresponding calculated t_{90} time is 173 seconds. The sensor response for each concentration was recorded over two hours to observe stable values. These datasets are used for validation in our study. Data analysis and model predictions were performed using the Python programming language within the Jupyter Notebook environment [23].

IV. Methods

In this research, our goal is to rapidly estimate the H_2 sensor response using a small time window from the early response of the sensor. We aim to minimize the prediction time $\hat{t}$, which is passed until a reliable estimate of the sensor response is available, while ensuring a low fitting error in the predicted response $\hat{S}(t)$.

We propose three approaches based on the First-Order (FO) model to achieve the research objective. First, we use the real sensor response data to approximate the entire sensor response. Here, $S_r(t)$ is the time series from a real sensor response, and the variable t is used as a discrete-time index. Next, we define a small time window value $S_w(t)$ to predict the sensor response. $S_w(t)$ begins at the time index corresponding to a threshold value $S_{th} > 0$ Vol-% and ends at time instance t_w. In the last step, we adapt the S_{th} values to improve performance. Finally, the total prediction time $\hat{t}$ is obtained by summing t_w and the model processing time t_m, as shown in (10). The model processing time t_m, represents the calculation time to predict $\hat{S}(t)$ from small time window value $S_w(t)$.

$$\hat{t} = t_m + t_w \tag{10}$$

All three models' outcomes, corresponding fitting errors, and model time-saving efficiency are presented in Section V.

A. FO with Baseline (FOB)

FOB is the baseline model in this study to predict the sensor response $\hat{S}(t)$ from the real sensor response $S_r(t)$. This FOB model took $S_r(t)$ within time range $t_0 \leq t \leq t_s$ as an input to predict the $\hat{S}(t)$. Figure 3 illustrates the sensor response $S_r(t)$ (green curve) with time on the x-axis (in seconds) and H_2 concentration (volume fraction in Vol-%) on the y-axis. The sensor response stable value was 0.75 volume fraction in Vol-%, t_{90} recorded at 1131 seconds with the S_{90} of 0.68 volume fraction in Vol-%. Finally, the sensor response was approximated using the FOB (red curve), where $\hat{S}(t)$ has a stable value of 0.75 Vol-%.

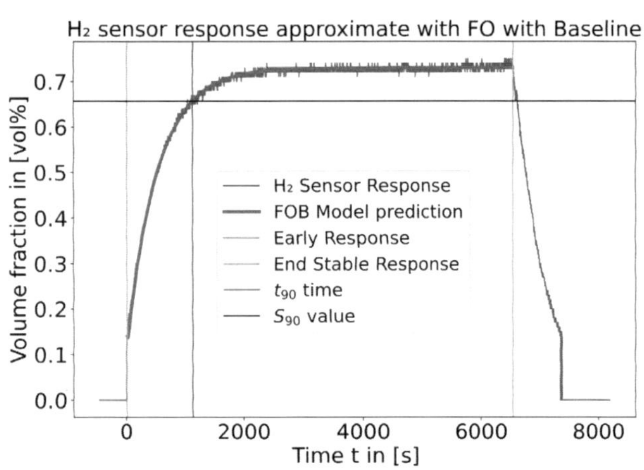

Figure 3: Sensor measure value (green) fitted with FO in Baseline (red).

B. FO with Early Response (FOER)

In FOER, we aim to fit the model to predict the sensor response $\hat{S}(t)$ from a small time window value $S_w(t)$. $S_w(t)$ starts from the time when the sensor response is greater than 0 Vol-% and continues until time t_w. Therefore, the FOER model sets the threshold $S_{th} > 0$ Vol-%. Figure 4 illustrates the $S_w(t)$ (blue curve), where the time window $t_w = 535s$. The predicted sensor response $\hat{S}(t)$ is the red curve with the stable value of 0.75 Vol-%, while the real sensor response $S_r(t)$ is in green curve with the stable value of 0.75 Vol-%. As t_m is $1s$, based on (10) the estimation time $\hat{t}$ is 536 seconds.

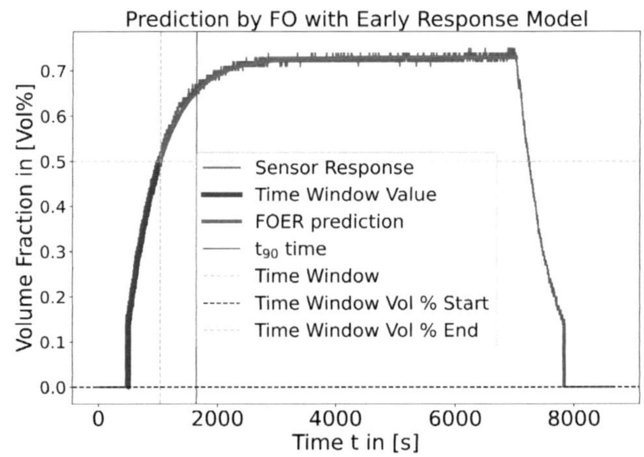

Figure 4: Prediction by FO with early response model.

C. FO with Adapted Early Response (FOAER)

In FOAER, an adapted early response method predicts $\hat{S}(t)$ from $S_w(t)$ by considering a higher S_{th} rather than 0 Vol-%. As a result, we expect that FOAER requires a smaller time window because the impact of the step when the sensor first reacts to the H_2 is mitigated.

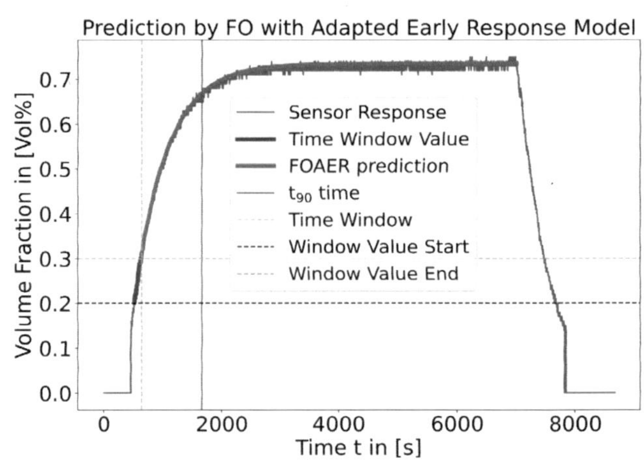

Figure 5: Prediction by FO with adapted early response.

With a threshold of $S_{th} = 0.20$ Vol-%, the model predicts a stable response value of $\hat{S}(t) = 0.74$ Vol-% (red curve), where real sensor's stable value of $S_r(t) = 0.75$ Vol-% (green curve), as shown in Figure 5. Also, Figure 5 depicts $S_w(t)$ in blue curve, where the time window ends at $t_w = 121$ seconds. Based on (10), $\hat{t} = 122$ seconds, where $t_m = 1$s.

V. Evaluation

We evaluate the overall fitting accuracy by calculating the relative fitting error ε in (11). The error is computed between the real sensor response $S_r(t)$ and the model estimation $\hat{S}(t)$. The error is computed over discrete time indices t_i, where $t_0 \leq t_i \leq t_s$, and the total number of index samples is N. The final ε is calculated by summing the errors of N samples and dividing by the number of samples N.

$$\varepsilon = \frac{1}{N} \sum_{i=1}^{N} \left(\frac{|S_r(t_i) - \hat{S}(t_i)|}{S_r(t_i)} \right) \times 100\% \quad (11)$$

Figure 6 illustrates the relationship between the fitting error (ε) and estimated time $\hat{t}$ for the FOER (blue) and the FOAER (orange). The minimum fitting error (ε) over $\hat{t}$ is 0.74% for the FOER and 0.76% for the FOAER. By considering the dynamic behavior of the sensor, this research considers a model error threshold ≤ 2 % as an acceptable and sufficiently good fit. For both our models, fitting error (ε) was below the threshold of ≤ 2 %.

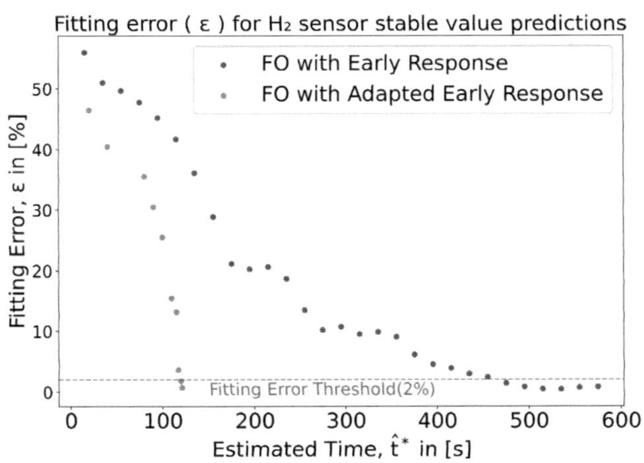

Figure 6: Fitting error (%) for FOER and FOAER.

The main objective of this research is to estimate stable values as quickly as possible. To evaluate this, we calculate the relative time savings η_s by comparing models' estimation time ($\hat{t}^*$) with the sensor's response (t_{90}) defined in (12). The $\hat{t}^*$ is the estimation time corresponding to the minimum fitting error, when the error remains below the 2% threshold. The t_{90} is crucial because it is a common metric to indicate the detection time in the literature [17]. In this study, the sensor response (t_{90}) time was obtained through graphical analysis. If the value η_s is higher, this indicates that the model's prediction efficiency is good and requires less time to predict stable values.

$$\eta_s = \left(\frac{t_{90} - \hat{t}^*}{t_{90}} \right) \times 100\% \quad (12)$$

For estimation time $\hat{t}^*$ the FOER model, η_s is 70.89%, while for the FOAER model, it is 84.50%. Hence, using the FOAER model, we can predict the stable value 13.51% faster than the FOER model.

VI. Validation

In Figure 7 (for FOER) and Figure 8 (for FOAER), we have presented the scatter plots of the fitting errors (ε) over estimations time $\hat{t}^*$, which include H_2 concentrations of 0.5 (blue), 1.0 (orange), 1.5 (green), 2.0 (red), 2.5 (purple), 3.0 (brown), 3.5 (pink), and 4.0 (gray) Vol%. For each concentration, we have considered individual estimation times $\hat{t}^*$ corresponding to the minimum fitting error (ε).

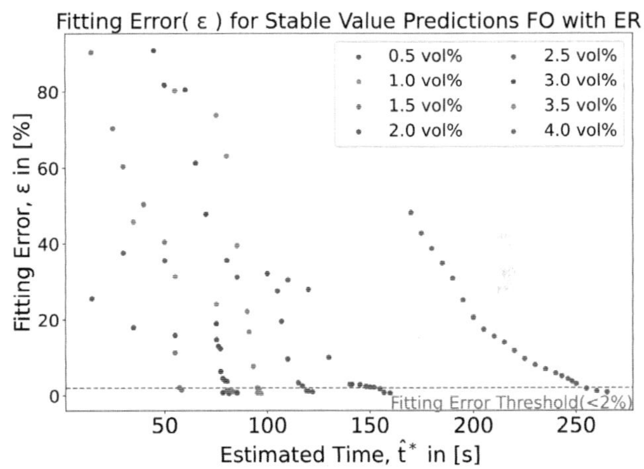

Figure 7: Fitting error (ε) for FOER.

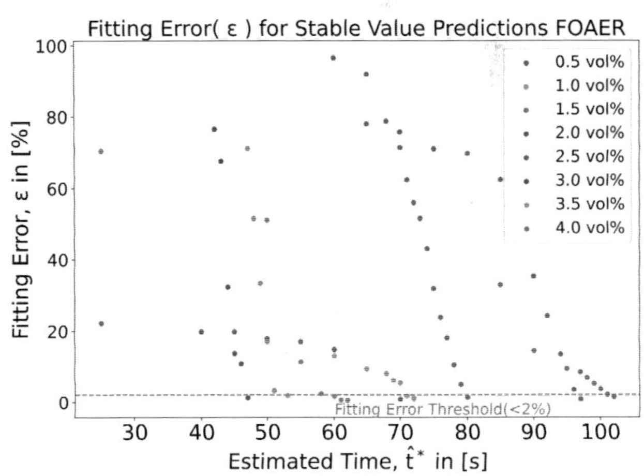

Figure 8: Fitting error (ε) for FOAER.

Table I and Table II present a summary of the H_2 concentration flow, sensor response, and prediction results for the FOER and FOAER models, respectively. Both tables' values in the first and second columns show the target H_2 concentration (Vol%) starting and ending values, which are defined as Q_s and Q_e. The third column shows the sensor's t_{90} response time, followed by the model's estimated time in the fourth column.

The fifth column presents the calculated relative time saved by the model compared to the sensor's t_{90} time. The sixth and seventh columns list the real stable sensor response and the model-predicted stable value, respectively. Finally, the seventh column reports the fitting error between the model and the real sensor stable values. The FOAER models included the adaptive threshold values in the last column of the table.

TABLE I: FOER MODEL SUMMARY: Q_s, Q_e – START/END H_2 CONCENTRATIONS (VOL-%); t_{90}, $\hat{t}^*$ – SENSOR/MODEL TIMES (S); η_s, ε – TIME SAVING/ERROR (%); $S_r(t)$, $\hat{S}(t)$ – REAL/PREDICTED RESPONSES (VOL-%); μ – MEAN.

Q_s	Q_e	t_{90}	$\hat{t}^*$	η_s	$S_r(t)$	$\hat{S}(t)$	ε
0.0	0.8	1131	536	73.20	0.75	0.75	0.74
0.0	0.5	396	82	79.04	0.46	0.46	0.52
0.5	1.0	434	98	77.42	0.95	0.95	0.56
1.0	1.5	436	86	80.28	1.45	1.45	0.85
1.5	2.0	435	161	62.99	1.95	1.95	0.63
2.0	2.5	431	123	71.93	2.45	2.45	0.96
2.5	3.0	418	86	79.43	2.92	2.92	0.64
3.0	3.5	411	96	76.64	3.42	3.42	0.76
3.5	4.0	423	266	37.12	3.93	3.93	0.87
μ	-	-	170.44	70.89	-	-	0.73

TABLE II: OVERVIEW OF FOAER: Q_s, Q_e – START/END H_2 CONCENTRATIONS (VOL-%); t_{90}, $\hat{t}^*$ – SENSOR/MODEL TIMES (S); η_s, ε – TIME SAVING/ERROR (%); $S_r(t)$, $\hat{S}(t)$, S_{th} – RESPONSES/THRESHOLD (VOL-%); μ – MEAN.

Q_s	Q_e	t_{90}	$\hat{t}^*$	η_s	$S_r(t)$	$\hat{S}(t)$	ε	S_{th}
0.0	0.8	1131	122	84.50	0.75	0.75	0.76	0.20
0.0	0.5	396	71	82.07	0.46	0.46	0.84	0.10
0.5	1.0	434	72	83.41	0.95	0.95	1.00	0.24
1.0	1.5	436	63	85.55	1.45	1.45	0.56	0.10
1.5	2.0	435	98	77.47	1.95	1.94	0.87	0.29
2.0	2.5	431	82	80.97	2.45	2.44	1.29	0.35
2.5	3.0	418	81	88.04	2.92	2.91	1.22	0.40
3.0	3.5	411	54	86.86	3.42	3.43	1.83	0.43
3.5	4.0	423	104	75.41	3.93	3.94	1.45	0.55
μ	-	-	79.33	83.72	-	-	1.09	0.30

In the tables above, the mean (μ) for all samples was calculated using (13), where y_i denotes each sample value and n is the total number of samples:

$$\mu = \frac{1}{n}\sum_{i=1}^{n} y_i \tag{13}$$

The computed mean values for estimation time, fitting error, relative time saving, and adaptive threshold are shown in the last row of both tables.

VII. Discussion

We performed a two-sample t-test [24] to statistically evaluate the similarity in the estimation times $\hat{t}^*$ of the FOER and FOAER models. The test provides a t-value, which determines the difference in the variability in the data, and a p-value, which indicates the probability that the observed difference occurred by chance. If the critical t-value 2.306 for $p = 0.05$, as listed in the t-distribution tables [25] is greater than the calculated t-value, the result is considered not statistically significant, indicating that no strong evidence exists to conclude a significant difference between the models.

The model estimation times $\hat{t}^*$ cannot be directly compared because the experiments were conducted under two different time constants (τ). To enable a meaningful comparison and perform a t-test, the estimation time at 0.8 vol% was compensated to align with the conditions used for concentrations from 0.5 to 4.0 vol%, based on (14). Here, $\hat{t}_1^*$ represents the model estimation time obtained at 0.8 vol% with a time constant of $\tau_1 = 348$ seconds, and it is adjusted to $\hat{t}_2^*$, corresponding to $\tau_2 = 75$ seconds, which was used for the concentrations 0.5 to 4.0 vol%. As a result, for 0.8 vol% the compensated estimation times are $\hat{t}_2^* = 118$ s for the FOER model and $\hat{t}_2^* = 26.84$ s for the FOAER model.

$$\hat{t}_2^* = \hat{t}_1^* \cdot \frac{\tau_2}{\tau_1} \tag{14}$$

As shown in Table I and Table II, the estimation time ($\hat{t}^*$) for the FOER model has a mean of 170.44 seconds, while the FOAER model has a mean of 79.33 seconds. After compensating 0.8 vol% estimation time ($\hat{t}^*$), the FOER model has a mean of 123.67 s with a standard deviation of 54.83 s, while the FOAER model has a mean of 68.92 s and a standard deviation of 22.38 s. Based on a two-sample t-test, the calculated t-value is 2.59, which is greater than the critical t-value of 2.306 at a significance level of $p = 0.05$, as referenced in the t-distribution tables [25]. Since the calculated t-value is greater than the critical threshold, we conclude that there is a statistically significant difference between the estimation times of the FOER and FOAER models. However, when excluding the values corresponding to 0.8 vol%, the t-value drops to 2.18, below the critical t-value. This indicates no statistically significant difference between the estimation times of the two models. The t-test results suggest that both models predict the sensor response independently, but their prediction performance is strongly correlated with the time constant (τ) and the extrinsic response time.

Overall, the FOER model achieves an average time-saving efficiency of 70.89% with a fitting error of 0.73%, using a fixed threshold $S_{th} > 0$. In comparison, the FOAER model shows an average higher time-saving efficiency of 83.72% and a fitting error of 1.09%, with the mean threshold of $S_{th} = 0.30$ Vol%. Both models can predict the sensor response using data from a small time window; however, the FOAER model is more appropriate for H_2 leakage detection.

VIII. Conclusion

The study aims to predict the sensor response from a small time window of the sensor's early response without waiting for the sensor values to converge. By leveraging sensor data from various H_2 concentration responses, two FO model approaches are used to make accurate predictions. The evaluation of the models was calculated by the average fitting error (%) with a < 2% threshold and model prediction efficiency. We find that the stable value of the sensor can be predicted in the transient phase of the sensor response with an average fitting error of 0.73%

(for FOER) and 1.09% (for FOAER). This approach allows the detection rate of dangerous concentrations of H_2 70.89 % and 83.72 % earlier than naive methods using unprocessed sensor data. The advantage of the FO model is that it captures systems with exponential response behavior and offers a simple, interpretable framework that requires minimal data, making it well-suited for processes with known dynamics. But on the other hand, data-driven models—such as neural networks or regression techniques—learn input-output relationships from large datasets without relying on a physical model, enabling them to predict sensor responses independently of system-specific dynamics. While this study focused on a single sensor with a deterministic response using the FO model, future work will expand the experimental setup to include multiple sensors and environmental factors, such as temperature and pressure. This will allow the application of data-driven models to capture the system's complexity and variability. Additionally, uncertainties in sensor responses will be addressed to generate large-scale datasets for training robust multivariate data analysis models that can accurately predict sensor stable responses.

Finally, to integrate our approach into embedded sensor systems or edge computing environments, we will develop software that incorporates the trained prediction model and interfaces with the sensor system. In practical applications, this software will capture the H_2 sensor's early response signal immediately after gas exposure, within a defined time window. The model will then analyze this early response to estimate the sensor's stable output value, enabling the system to make rapid decisions or transmit the predicted concentration to a user interface or cloud platform. This approach supports real-time predicting potentially explosive H_2 leaks in critical environments such as hydrogen refueling stations or pipelines. The predicted value will be continuously compared against a predefined explosion threshold to trigger timely warnings, activate alarms, or initiate automatic safety shutdowns when necessary.

References

[1] Q. Hassan, S. Algburi, A. Z. Sameen, H. M. Salman, and M. Jaszczur, "Green hydrogen: A pathway to a sustainable energy future", *International Journal of Hydrogen Energy*, vol. 50, pp. 310–333, 2024.

[2] M. Molnarne and V. Schroeder, "Hazardous properties of hydrogen and hydrogen containing fuel gases", *Process Safety and Environmental Protection*, vol. 130, pp. 1–5, 2019.

[3] W. Umrath, *Fundamentals of Vacuum Technology*. Leybold GmbH, Cologne, 2016, Accessed: July, 01, 2025.

[4] P. Adams, A. Bengaouer, B. Cariteau, V. Molkov, and A. Venetsanos, "Allowable hydrogen permeation rate from road vehicles", *International Journal of Hydrogen Energy*, vol. 36, no. 3, pp. 2742–2749, 2011.

[5] L. Guo *et al.*, "Hydrogen safety: An obstacle that must be overcome on the road towards future hydrogen economy", *International Journal of Hydrogen Energy*, vol. 51, pp. 1055–1078, 2024.

[6] J. X. Wen *et al.*, "Statistics, lessons learned and recommendations from analysis of hiad 2.0 database", *International journal of hydrogen energy*, vol. 47, no. 38, pp. 17 082–17 096, 2022.

[7] R. R. Patil, R. K. Calay, M. Y. Mustafa, and S. Thakur, "Artificial intelligence-driven innovations in hydrogen safety", *Hydrogen*, vol. 5, no. 2, pp. 312–326, 2024.

[8] D. L. Osorio-Arrieta *et al.*, "Reduction of the measurement time by the prediction of the steady-state response for quartz crystal microbalance gas sensors", *Sensors*, vol. 18, no. 8, p. 2475, 2018.

[9] T. Hübert, J. Majewski, U. Banach, M. Detjens, and C. Tiebe, "Response time measurement of hydrogen sensors", *Hydrogen Knowledge Centre*, 2017.

[10] C. Shi, W. Pei, C. Jin, A. Alizadeh, and A. Ghanbari, "Prediction of the sno2-based sensor response for hydrogen detection by artificial intelligence techniques", *International Journal of Hydrogen Energy*, vol. 48, no. 52, pp. 19 834–19 845, 2023.

[11] Y. Shi, S. Ye, and Y. Zheng, "Rapid forecasting of hydrogen concentration based on a multilayer cnn-lstm network", *Measurement Science and Technology*, vol. 34, no. 6, p. 065 101, 2023. DOI: 10.1088/1361-6501/acbdb5.

[12] V. Martvall *et al.*, "Accelerating plasmonic hydrogen sensors for inert gas environments by transformer-based deep learning", *ACS sensors*, 2025.

[13] R. Yang *et al.*, "Ultrafast hydrogen detection system using vertical thermal conduction structure and neural network prediction algorithm based on sensor response process", *ACS sensors*, vol. 10, no. 3, pp. 2181–2190, 2025.

[14] European Commission, *bibleothek – A Bible-based Cultural Network*, https://cordis.europa.eu/project/id/325326, Project No. 325326, CORDIS: EU Research Results, 2016.

[15] W. J. Buttner, M. B. Post, R. Burgess, and C. Rivkin, "An overview of hydrogen safety sensors and requirements", *International Journal of Hydrogen Energy*, vol. 36, no. 3, pp. 2462–2470, 2011.

[16] L. Boon-Brett *et al.*, "Identifying performance gaps in hydrogen safety sensor technology for automotive and stationary applications", *International Journal of Hydrogen Energy*, vol. 35, no. 1, pp. 373–384, 2010.

[17] T. Hübert and U. Banach, "Response time of hydrogen sensors", in *Proceedings of the Fifth International Conference on Hydrogen Safety*, 2013, pp. 9–11.

[18] *ISO 26142:2010: Hydrogen detection apparatus – Stationary applications*, Standard, International Organization for Standardization, 2010.

[19] C. I. Muresan and C. M. Ionescu, "Generalization of the fopdt model for identification and control purposes", *Processes*, vol. 8, no. 6, p. 682, 2020.

[20] C. Cox, J. Tindle, and K. Burn, "A comparison of software-based approaches to identifying fopdt and sopdt model parameters from process step response data", *Applied Mathematical Modelling*, vol. 40, no. 1, pp. 100–114, 2016.

[21] Pfeiffer Vacuum GmbH, *Right angle valve, 320rkd160*, https://www.pfeiffer-vacuum.com/global/en/shop/products/320RKD160, Accessed: May 30, 2025.

[22] M. Bayat and C. Tiebe, *Measurement and Testing Methods for Sensors in Hydrogen Technologies*, BAM TF Tag Energie, 2024.

[23] R. Sarif, "Fopdt model h2 response prediction code", Accessed: July 01, 2025, 2025, [Online]. Available: https://github.com/Raduan01/H2-Response/blob/main/FOPDT%20model%20H2%20Response%20Prediction%20code.py.

[24] NIST/SEMATECH, *1.3.5.2. Confidence Limits for the Mean*, https://www.itl.nist.gov/div898/handbook/eda/section3/eda352.htm, NIST/SEMATECH Engineering Statistics Handbook 2012, Accessed: 2025-07-02.

[25] NIST/SEMATECH, *Engineering statistics handbook 2012-3.6.7.2. paired t-test*, https://www.itl.nist.gov/div898/handbook/eda/section3/eda3672.htm, Accessed: May 30, 2025.

Progressively Overcoming Catastrophic Forgetting in Kolmogorov–Arnold Networks

Evgenii Ostanin
Toronto Metropolitan University
Toronto, Canada
email: eostanin@torontomu.ca

Nebojsa Djosic
Toronto Metropolitan University
Toronto, Canada
email: nebojsa.djosic@torontomu.ca

Fatima Hussain
Toronto Metropolitan University
Toronto, Canada
email: fatima.hussain@torontomu.ca

Salah Sharieh
Toronto Metropolitan University
Toronto, Canada
email: salah.sharieh@torontomu.ca

Alexander Ferworn
Toronto Metropolitan University
Toronto, Canada
email: aferworn@torontomu.ca

Malek Sharieh
Holy Trinity School
Richmond Hill, Canada
email: malek.sharieh@hts.on.ca

Abstract—**Catastrophic forgetting remains a major challenge in continuous learning, particularly for architectures not explicitly designed for knowledge retention. This paper explores Kolmogorov–Arnold networks as an alternative to multilayer perceptrons in such settings. We introduce two freezing strategies: tensor-level spline freezing and point-level control freezing, that exploit the spline-based structure of Kolmogorov–Arnold networks to preserve knowledge from earlier tasks. Experiments on Modified National Institute of Standards and Technology (MNIST) handwritten digit dataset show that both methods yield modest but consistent improvements when paired with replay techniques. The best configurations improve total accuracy by up to 2.2% and reduce forgetting by 5.4% over the no-freeze baseline. These findings reveal a new direction for mitigating forgetting through the selective control of spline parameters specific for the Kolmogorov-Arnold networks. Future work will explore a deeper integration with regularization and expansion methods to further enhance knowledge retention in continual learning.**

Keywords-Continual Learning; Catastrophic Forgetting; Kolmogorov–Arnold Networks; KAN; Spline Freezing; Memory Retention; Experience Replay; Progressive Freezing.

I. Introduction

Continual learning remains a central challenge in modern Machine Learning (ML), particularly in contexts where models must incrementally adapt to new information without catastrophic degradation of previously acquired knowledge [1]. Traditional deep learning models, including Multi-Layer Perceptrons (MLPs), often suffer from *catastrophic forgetting* [2], where performance on earlier tasks deteriorates as new data is introduced. While various techniques such as regularization, dynamic expansion, and rehearsal have been proposed to address this problem [3]–[6], the search for architectures that naturally lend themselves to incremental learning continues.

Kolmogorov–Arnold Networks (KANs), a recent innovation based on the Kolmogorov–Arnold representation theorem [7], have been proposed as interpretable and adaptable neural networks that may address some limitations of fixed-activation architectures. In KANs, traditional scalar weights are replaced by univariate, learnable activation functions (typically splines), enabling fine-grained, input-dependent transformations. Each spline activation has its own parameter set, so during sequential training, only the splines relevant to a new task are updated while the others remain fixed, thus naturally preserving previously acquired knowledge.

In this paper, we evaluate the suitability of KAN for continual learning by comparing their retention capabilities to MLPs under task-incremental training scenarios. Specifically, we adopt the *Split-MNIST* protocol [8] which partitions the MNIST [9] (Modified National Institute of Standards and Technology) handwritten-digit dataset into two sequential training tasks on digits 0–4 and 5–9.

Building on our previous analysis of KANs under adversarial threats [11], [12], this study extends the evaluation to continual learning scenarios, introducing a broader set of robustness indicators. We compare results across architectures and freezing strategies, focusing on metrics of **accuracy**, **retention**, and **forgetting**. Notably, we observe that freezing improves knowledge retention in settings with conventional replay but does not provide consistent benefits when replay is class-balanced. These findings highlight the nuanced interactions between architecture, training dynamics, and memory retention, opening new directions for lifelong learning research.

Main Contributions:

- A comprehensive comparison of KANs and MLP in continual learning using the Split-MNIST benchmark.
- Systematic testing of replay and balanced replay buffer strategies for mitigating forgetting in both model types, using such methods as experience replay (random sampling) and stratified (class-balanced) replay respectively.
- Introduction and evaluation of two novel KAN-specific freezing techniques, targeting spline control points and entire spline tensors.
- Empirical findings showing that KANs benefit from freezing strategies primarily when used in conjunction with naive replay mechanisms.

The remainder of this paper is organized as follows: Section II reviews related work on continual learning and memory retention in neural networks. Section III details the experimental design, including dataset splits, architecture configurations, and freezing protocols. Section IV presents the results of our evaluations, with a comparative analysis of accuracy and forgetting. Section V discusses conclusions and future work directions.

II. Related Work

A. Continual and Lifelong Learning

Continual learning, also referred to as lifelong or incremental learning [1], focuses on enabling models to learn from a stream of tasks without suffering from catastrophic forgetting. This challenge arises when models trained on new data overwrite previously learned information, leading to severe performance drops on older tasks [2], [3]. To systematically evaluate continual learning capabilities, benchmarks such as Split-MNIST [8], [9], [13] are widely adopted. These benchmarks divide a dataset into separate subsets of classes forcing the model to incrementally adapt without access to previous task data during training.

While much of the foundational work in this area has focused on regularization-based methods (e.g., Elastic Weight Consolidation [14]) and architectural adaptation (e.g, dynamically growing networks [15]), rehearsal-based strategies have recently gained prominence for their effectiveness and simplicity. However, many of these techniques are designed around conventional neural architectures, such as MLPs, and their applicability to novel, more interpretable models remains largely unexplored. This paper contributes to bridging this gap by evaluating continual learning in KANs.

B. Replay and Balanced Replay

Replay mechanism attempt to alleviate forgetting by introducing a rehearsal buffer that store and replays a subset of previously encountered samples. The simplest approach, *experience replay*, samples examples uniformly at random from a memory buffer [16], while *balanced replay* aims to ensure class-wise uniformity, especially critical when data from previous tasks are imbalanced or limited [6], [10]. These methods are often paired with online learning or streaming data scenarios, where maintaining compact yet representative memory is crucial.

Despite their widespread adoption in conventional deep learning, replay-based techniques have not been systematically evaluated in emerging network paradigms such as KANs. Given KANs' fundamentally different parameterization, where edge functions are learnable instead of weights alone, it is not immediately clear, whether replay would behave similarly. Our study investigates this open question and quantifies the impact of replay versus balanced replay in KAN training regimes.

C. Kolmogorov-Arnold Networks and Interpretability

KANs [7] represent a significant shift in neural network architecture. Originally proposed by Andrey Kolmogorov in 1957 and later extended by Vladimir Arnold in 1963, the Kolmogorov–Arnold Representation Theorem, also known as the superposition theorem, states that any continuous multivariate function $f(x_1, ..., x_n)$ defined on a bounded domain can be expressed as a finite composition of continuous univariate functions, typically formulated as:

$$f(x) = f(x_1, \ldots, x_n) = \sum_{q=1}^{2n+1} \Phi_q \left(\sum_{p=1}^{n} \phi_{q,p}(x_p) \right) \quad (1)$$

In (1) $\phi_{q,p} : [0,1] \to \mathbb{R}$ are continuous inner functions, and $\Phi_q : \mathbb{R} \to \mathbb{R}$ represent continuous outer functions.

Inspired by the Kolmogorov–Arnold representation theorem, KANs replace scalar edge weights with univariate, learnable spline functions. In KANs each connection from neuron p to q now applies its own spline function $\phi_{q,p}(x_p)$ to the incoming activation x_p, rather than simply multiplying by a constant weight as in MLPs. This change enables each connection to perform a data-driven, nonlinear transformation, offering both functional richness and a degree of interpretability rarely found in traditional models. Rather than stacking fixed nonlinearities at the nodes as in MLPs, KANs achieve expressivity through these adaptable spline-based edge functions.

Although KANs are relatively new, their potential has already sparked interest across many domains. Prior studies have explored their application to time series [17], [18], robustness under adversarial attacks [11], [12], [19], [20], and noise resilience [21], [22]. For instance, [7] demonstrated that KANs can approximate complex mappings with far fewer parameters while retaining interpretability via their control-point structures. However, continual learning in KANs remains underexplored. No prior work has directly evaluated their memory retention across tasks or how spline parameterization interacts with long-term adaptation.

Our study positions itself as one of the first to investigate KANs in a continual learning context, motivated by their spline-based design, which naturally partitions the model into independent, learnable components, and by the opportunity this provides for targeted freezing mechanisms. Figures 1 and 2 highlight the architectural distinction between KAN and MLP, which motivates the design of two freezing strategies: control point-level freezing and tensor-level spline freezing. These mechanisms exploit the hierarchical structure of spline parameters and enable selective locking of the model's knowledge, a novel direction for lifelong learning research.

D. Freezing Mechanisms in Incremental Learning

Weight freezing has been used historically to preserve important parameters while learning new tasks. Techniques like Learning without Forgetting (LwF) [23] and PackNet [24] selectively retain task-specific neurons or weights to reduce interference. More recently, methods such as Progressive Neural Networks [25] have explored architectural partitioning where frozen components are reused or extended.

In the context of KANs, we introduce two distinct types of freezing. First, control **point-level freezing** targets high-importance spline parameters based on magnitude or gradient scores. Second, **tensor-level spline freezing** locks entire univariate transformation functions. These techniques take advantage of the KAN flexible design, where splines are modular and easy to adjust in a detailed way. Our experiments demonstrated that spline-level freezing in KANs offers a new dimension of control not available in traditional ML models, and its interaction with replay dynamics presents novel trade-offs between plasticity and stability.

III. Methodology

A. Architectures

To compare robustness under continual learning, we consider two types of models: a standard MLP and a KAN. The MLP serves as a baseline, while the KAN explores the performance of spline-based representations in a task-incremental settings.

The MLP consists of two linear layers with a Rectified Linear Unit (ReLU) activation in between. The first linear layer maps a flattened 28×28 MNIST image (784-dimensional input) to a 128-dimensional hidden layer. The second (output) layer produces a 10-dimensional output corresponding to the MNIST class logits. Figure 1 demonstrates the MLP architecture used in the experiments.

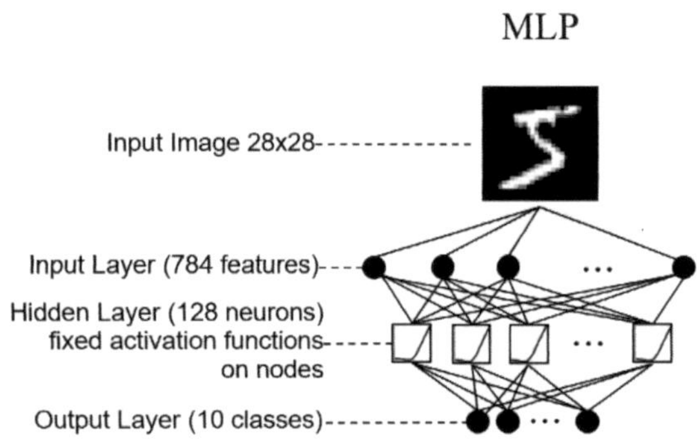

Figure 1. MLP Architecture.

The KAN has a similar structure, with a linear layer projecting inputs to a 128-dimensional hidden space, followed by another linear layer to predict class logits. However, between the input and hidden layers, KAN includes a matrix of learnable spline control weights (128×784), which are not used for direct computation but are integrated into the computation graph. These spline weights can be interpreted as representing local functional transformations and can be subjected to regularization or freezing. KAN architecture is shown in Figure 2.

B. Continual Learning Setup

To simulate continual learning under the Split-MNIST protocol [8], [9], we split the MNIST dataset into two tasks: Task A, containing digits 0 through 4, and Task B, containing digits 5 through 9. The model is first trained on Task A for three epochs, then trained on Task B for three more epochs. Catastrophic forgetting is quantified as the drop in Task A accuracy after Task B training. All experiments use the AdamW optimizer with learning rate 1×10^{-3}, cross-entropy loss, and batch size of 64 images per mini-batch.

C. Replay and Balanced Replay

To mitigate forgetting, we implement two forms of experience replay. In both, we store a subset of Task A examples and mix them into the mini-batches during Task B training.

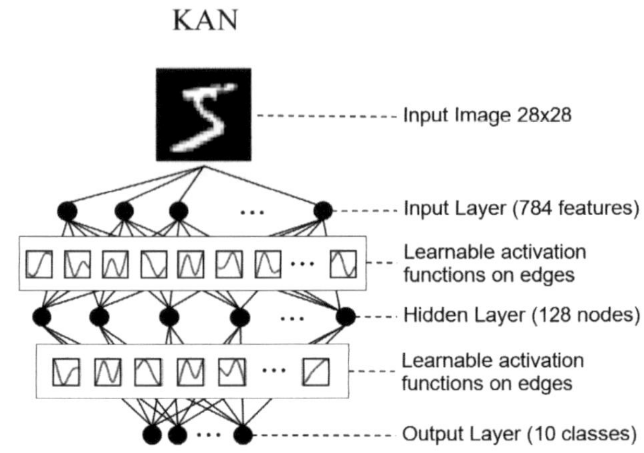

Figure 2. KAN Architecture.

In the first variant, **replay**, we randomly sample a buffer of Task A examples. In the second, **balanced replay**, we sample the replay buffer in a stratified fashion to ensure class balance across the five Task A classes. To avoid confusion with Task B and for brevity, we will refer to balanced replay as stratified replay (s-replay) throughout the paper.

We tested replay buffer sizes of 50, 100, and 500, where the buffer size denotes the number of data samples retained for the next training round. We chose buffer sizes to represent low, medium, and high replay capacities, so we could observe how freezing performs under different conditions. As expected, larger buffers led to better retention. Replay with 50 examples provided moderate improvements, while 500 nearly eliminated forgetting. However, our objective is to explore whether spline freezing can further improve retention. Thus, we selected buffer size 100 for all subsequent experiments. This setting provides a middle ground. It significantly improves performance over the baseline, but leaves room for further gains. Using 50 samples could underestimate the impact of freezing, while 500 would saturate the model's retention capacity, potentially masking the effects of freezing mechanisms.

D. Spline Freezing Strategies

A unique feature of KANs is the presence of interpretable and modular spline parameters. Building on parameter-isolation and architectural-partitioning approaches [24], [25], we evaluate two types of freezing techniques to investigate their effect on continual learning:

(1) Tensor-level (entire spline) freezing: In this strategy, we compute a score for each of the 128 spline rows (or neurons) and freeze the top $k\%$ rows. Three scoring methods are evaluated using such approaches as :

- **weight**: mean absolute value of the weights in each row
- **grad**: mean absolute gradient magnitude per row (requires a gradient pass)
- **weight_grad**: a combination of both (with $\alpha = 0.5$)

(2) Point-level (individual control point) freezing: Here, the same scoring methods are applied to individual elements (control points) in the spline weight matrix. The top $k\%$ of all elements are then frozen, regardless of their row or neuron association.

For both strategies, we test $k \in \{0.05, 0.1, 0.25, 0.5, 0.75\}$, spanning from minimal to aggressive freezing intensities. This range lets us assess how varying degrees of parameter k affect retention under both replay=100 and s_replay=100, yielding 30 experiments per technique. These strategies are visualized in Figure 3. In each case, frozen parameters are excluded from optimization updates by masking their gradients before applying the optimizer step.

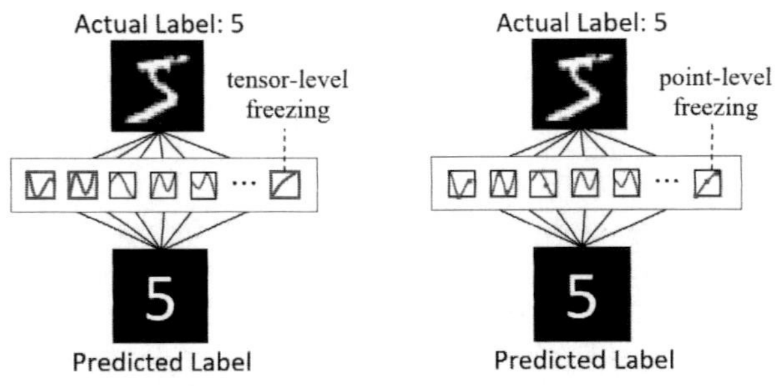

Figure 3. Tensor-level (left) and Point-level (right) freezing strategy.

E. Experimental Pipeline

Each experiment proceeds as follows. The model is initialized and trained on Task A. After evaluating and recording the initial accuracy, the freezing mechanism (if any) is applied using a single gradient pass (when necessary). The model is then trained on Task B, incorporating replayed samples into each batch, as specified. After training, we compute and report the accuracy on Task B (new task), accuracy on Task A (after forgetting), and total accuracy across both tasks. We also compute forgetting as the drop in Task A accuracy before and after Task B training.

The following section presents the experimental results. We first validate the replay strategies across different buffer size and architectures, then evaluate the impact of spline freezing techniques. The aim is to determine whether freezing entire spline or individual components can improve retention in continual learning settings, and whether the choice of scoring strategy or replay method impacts this effect.

IV. Results

A. Baseline Performance and Forgetting

Figure 4 and Table I summarize the performance of MLP and KAN under different training scenarios. The clean setting refers to training on all MNIST classes simultaneously, serving as an upper-bound reference. Both models achieve high accuracy on the full MNIST task (88.8% and 88.6%, respectively), but suffer from severe catastrophic forgetting when trained sequentially on separated tasks. The baseline reflects continual training without any mitigation, revealing the severity of catastrophic forgetting and establishing a comparison point for subsequent interventions. Figure 4 also shows the improvements achieved through replay and s-replay (stratified replay) before any spline or tensor freezing techniques are applied. Table I additionally reports the forgetting metric, which quantifies the reduction in accuracy on Task A after training on Task B. The reported accuracy corresponds to the model's total accuracy after both training phases. For example, in the baseline scenario, Task A accuracy drops by nearly 96%, resulting in an overall accuracy of just 43.4% for MLP and 43.3% for KAN, underscoring the impact of forgetting in continual learning.

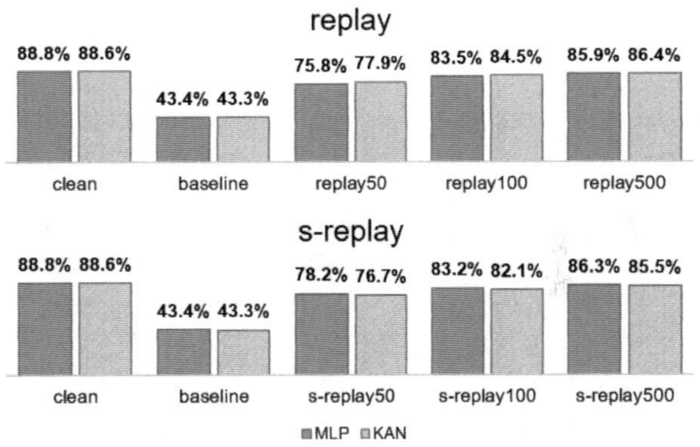

Figure 4. Baseline accuracy and replay effectiveness for MLP and KAN.

TABLE I
BASELINE ACCURACY AND FORGETTING FOR MLP AND KAN.

Scenario	MLP Acc.	KAN Acc.	MLP Forget.	KAN Forget.
Clean	0.888	0.886	-	-
Baseline	0.434	0.433	0.958	0.964
Replay 50	0.758	0.779	0.322	0.275
Replay 100	0.835	0.845	0.149	0.137
Replay 500	0.859	0.864	0.075	0.071
s-Replay 50	0.782	0.767	0.261	0.305
s-Replay 100	0.832	0.821	0.147	0.187
s-Replay 500	0.863	0.855	0.068	0.077

B. Replay and Stratified (Balanced) Replay

We evaluated replay-based strategies with varying buffer sizes. Standard replay (random) and s-replay both improve accuracy and retention, as seen in Figure 4. With replay buffer size 100, MLP and KAN reach 83.5% and 84.5% accuracy, respectively, while s-replay achieves 83.2% for MLP and 82.1% for KAN.

These configurations reduce forgetting substantially, as seen in Table I. The choice of buffer size 100 offers a middle ground between replay_50, which yielded lower gains, and replay_500, which almost eliminated forgetting. We selected 100 for subsequent experiments, as it maintained measurable room for improvement while ensuring sufficient retention to validate the impact of freezing methods.

C. Point-Level Freezing

Point-Freezing (pf) methods, shown in Figure 5, Table II, and Table III, freeze the top-$k\%$ of control points using heuristics based on weights (w), gradients (g), or a weighted average (wg). For s-replay, the best configuration is `pf_g_s-replay100` at $k = 25\%$, which achieved 84.3% accuracy and reduced forgetting to 0.133, outperforming the no-freeze baseline of 82.1% (+2.2%) accuracy and 18.7% (-5.4%) forgetting. In the replay setup, the best pf result was `pf_wg_replay100` at $k = 25\%$, with 84.2% accuracy and 0.133 forgetting.

Across all experiments, s-replay consistently outperformed standard replay in both baseline accuracy and forgetting, even before freezing was applied. Moreover, pf under s-replay remained effective across multiple k values, with most configurations improving over the no-freeze baseline.

These results suggest that s-replay provides a stronger foundation for knowledge retention, likely due to its class-balanced sampling, which ensures more uniform coverage of prior task classes during rehearsal. When combined with pf, this structure appears to help selectively consolidate important spline parameters, leading to synergistic gains in both accuracy and forgetting. The consistent effectiveness of point-level freezing under s-replay highlights its value as a complementary mechanism for continual learning with KANs. Despite these gains, the best s-replay + pf configuration still incurs a 13.3% forgetting rate, underscoring the need to explore additional forgetting mitigation strategies in future work.

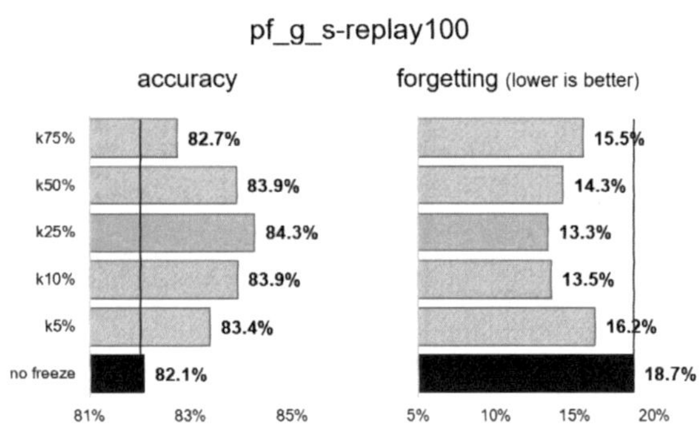

Figure 5. Best KAN scenario with Point-Level Freezing (pf).

D. Tensor-Level Freezing

Tensor-Level Freezing (tf), shown in Figure 6, Table II, and Table III, disables entire spline rows and can yield strong improvements, though it introduces more variance compared to point-level freezing. The best replay configuration is `tf_wg_replay100` at $k = 75\%$, which achieved 85.2% accuracy (+0.7%) and reduced forgetting to 0.101 (-3.6%). For s-replay, the best result is `tf_g_s-replay100` at $k = 75\%$, with 84.3% accuracy and 0.127 forgetting.

Although some configurations (e.g., $k = 10\%$ for `tf_w_replay100`) resulted in noticeable performance drops, the top-performing setups confirm that tensor-freezing can outperform point-freezing in certain cases when appropriately tuned. These gains are most evident at higher freezing thresholds ($k = 50\%$–75%), suggesting that the disabling of larger sets of spline transformations can help stabilize representations after task shifts, particularly when combined with structured replay. However, the broader range of outcomes highlights that tensor freezing is more sensitive to the choice of k and scoring strategy, reinforcing the need for careful calibration.

TABLE II
KAN ACCURACY UNDER REPLAY AND S-REPLAY FOR TENSOR (TF) AND POINT (PF) FREEZING.

Method	no freeze	k5%	k10%	k25%	k50%	k75%
pf_w_replay100	0.845	0.817	0.841	0.830	0.837	0.816
pf_g_replay100	0.845	0.833	0.835	0.822	0.845	0.824
pf_wg_replay100	0.845	0.838	0.832	0.842	0.824	0.844
pf_w_s-replay100	0.821	0.816	0.828	0.831	0.833	0.829
pf_g_s-replay100	0.821	0.834	0.839	0.843	0.839	0.827
pf_wg_s-replay100	0.821	0.825	0.838	0.840	0.838	0.829
tf_w_replay100	0.845	0.851	0.813	0.834	0.844	0.821
tf_g_replay100	0.845	0.840	0.846	0.830	0.834	0.843
tf_wg_replay100	0.845	0.818	0.834	0.833	0.832	0.852
tf_w_s-replay100	0.821	0.837	0.826	0.826	0.835	0.829
tf_g_s-replay100	0.821	0.831	0.832	0.834	0.842	0.843
tf_wg_s-replay100	0.821	0.851	0.841	0.841	0.841	0.837

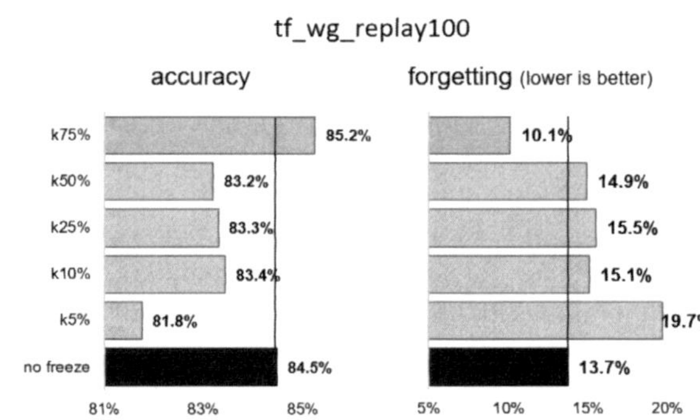

Figure 6. Best KAN scenario with tensor-level freezing (tf).

TABLE III
KAN FORGETTING UNDER REPLAY AND S-REPLAY FOR TENSOR (TF) AND POINT (PF) FREEZING.

Method	no freeze	k5%	k10%	k25%	k50%	k75%
pf_w_replay100	0.137	0.185	0.133	0.154	0.137	0.178
pf_g_replay100	0.137	0.166	0.153	0.178	0.123	0.157
pf_wg_replay100	0.137	0.141	0.144	0.133	0.166	0.112
pf_w_s-replay100	0.187	0.182	0.166	0.160	0.155	0.157
pf_g_s-replay100	0.187	0.162	0.135	0.133	0.143	0.155
pf_wg_s-replay100	0.187	0.173	0.135	0.148	0.130	0.152
tf_w_replay100	0.137	0.116	0.200	0.153	0.133	0.163
tf_g_replay100	0.137	0.121	0.133	0.165	0.158	0.116
tf_wg_replay100	0.137	0.197	0.151	0.155	0.149	0.101
tf_w_s-replay100	0.187	0.141	0.168	0.174	0.130	0.152
tf_g_s-replay100	0.187	0.143	0.164	0.152	0.137	0.127
tf_wg_s-replay100	0.187	0.123	0.134	0.132	0.137	0.136

E. Freezing Strategies: Comparative Effectiveness

Our evaluation of spline freezing strategies shows that both tf and pf methods improve continual learning when paired with replay mechanisms. While both enhance accuracy and retention, their effectiveness depends on the configuration.

pf offers consistent gains, especially under s-replay. Most k values outperform the no-freeze baseline, with the best configuration (`pf_g_s-replay100` at $k = 25\%$) improving accuracy by +2.2% and reducing forgetting by 5.4%. This suggests that fine-grained control over spline weights helps preserve prior task knowledge without impairing new learning.

tf, which locks full spline rows, shows greater variability but also higher potential. The best configuration (`tf_wg_replay100` at $k = 75\%$) yielded the top accuracy overall (+1.0% vs no-freeze) and reduced forgetting by 3.6%. However, tf performance is more sensitive to k and the scoring strategy, and can degrade if freezing is too aggressive.

Figures 5 and 6 summarize the top-performing pf and tf setups. While pf freezing is more robust across scenarios, tf freezing offers a higher ceiling when properly tuned. These complementary traits highlight the adaptability of KANs for continual learning applications.

V. Conclusion and Future Work

This paper investigated KANs in continual learning, demonstrating that both tensor-level and point-level spline freezing consistently improve retention in Split-MNIST when paired with simple replay (up to +2.2 % overall accuracy and a 5.4 % reduction in forgetting). While the absolute improvements are moderate, these KAN-specific freezing strategies leverage the spline structure to preserve prior task knowledge without impeding new learning, opening a promising direction for more targeted retention strategies.

Future work will explore freezing in deeper KANs, integration with regularization and dynamic expansion methods, and testing on more complex benchmarks beyond MNIST. Additionally, we aim to develop adaptive freezing and unfreezing strategies, drawing inspiration from biological learning and synaptic plasticity. With these enhancements, we expect to achieve higher retention and greater robustness in continual learning tasks, further unlocking the potential of KANs for long-term knowledge consolidation.

Acknowledgment

We acknowledge the use of various general-purpose online and cloud-based tools, including those with AI-driven features, during the preparation of this work.

References

[1] B. Liu, "Lifelong machine learning: A paradigm for continuous learning", Frontiers of Computer Science, vol. 11, no. 3, pp. 359–361, 2017.

[2] G. I. Parisi, R. Kemker, J. L. Part, C. Kanan, and S. Wermter, "Continual lifelong learning with neural networks: A review", Neural Networks, vol. 113, pp. 54–71, 2019, [Online]. Available: https://doi.org/10.1016/j.neunet.2019.01.012. Accessed: 14 May 2025.

[3] M. Delange et al., "A continual learning survey: Defying forgetting in classification tasks", IEEE Transactions on Pattern Analysis and Machine Intelligence, pp. 1–1, 2021.

[4] J. Zhang, Y. Fu, Z. Peng, D. Yao, and K. He, "CORE: Mitigating catastrophic forgetting in continual learning through cognitive replay", 2024. [Online]. Available: https://arxiv.org/abs/2402.01348. Accessed: 14 May 2025.

[5] A. Krawczyk and A. Gepperth, "An analysis of best-practice strategies for replay and rehearsal in continual learning", in Proceedings of the IEEE/CVF Conference on Computer Vision and Pattern Recognition, 2024, pp. 4196–4204.

[6] L. Liu, L. Liu, and Y. Cui, "Prior-free balanced replay: Uncertainty-guided reservoir sampling for long-tailed continual learning", 2024. [Online]. Available: https://arxiv.org/abs/2408.14976. Accessed: 14 May 2025.

[7] Z. Liu et al., "KAN: Kolmogorov-Arnold networks", Apr. 2024, [Online]. Available: http://arxiv.org/abs/2404.19756. Accessed: 14 May 2025.

[8] F. Zenke, B. Poole, and S. Ganguli, "Continual learning through synaptic intelligence", 2017. [Online]. Available: https://arxiv.org/abs/1703.04200. Accessed: 14 May 2025.

[9] L. Deng, "The MNIST database of handwritten digit images for machine learning research", IEEE Signal Processing Magazine, vol. 29, pp. 141–142, Jun. 2012.

[10] A. Chaudhry et al., "On tiny episodic memories in continual learning", 2019. [Online]. Available: https://arxiv.org/abs/1902.10486. Accessed: 14 May 2025.

[11] E. Ostanin, N. Djosic, F. Hussain, S. Sharieh, and A. Ferworn, "Evaluating the robustness of Kolmogorov-Arnold networks against noise and adversarial attacks", in Proceedings of the SECURWARE 2024, The Eighteenth International Conference on Emerging Security Information, Systems and Technologies, Nov. 2024, pp. 11–16.

[12] N. Djosic, E. Ostanin, F. Hussain, S. Sharieh, and A. Ferworn, "KAN vs KAN: Examining Kolmogorov-Arnold networks (KAN) performance under adversarial attacks", in Proceedings of the SECURWARE 2024, The Eighteenth International Conference on Emerging Security Information, Systems and Technologies, Nov. 2024, pp. 17–22.

[13] M. Farajtabar, N. Azizan, A. Mott, and A. Li, "Orthogonal gradient descent for continual learning", 2019. [Online]. Available: https://arxiv.org/abs/1910.07104. Accessed: 14 May 2025.

[14] J. Kirkpatrick et al., "Overcoming catastrophic forgetting in neural networks", Proceedings of the National Academy of Sciences, vol. 114, no. 13, pp. 3521–3526, Mar. 2017. [Online]. Available: http://dx.doi.org/10.1073/pnas.1611835114. Accessed: 14 May 2025.

[15] J. Yoon, E. Yang, J. Lee, and S. J. Hwang, "Lifelong learning with dynamically expandable networks", 2018. [Online]. Available: https://arxiv.org/abs/1708.01547. Accessed: 14 May 2025.

[16] D. Rolnick, A. Ahuja, J. Schwarz, T. P. Lillicrap, and G. Wayne, "Experience replay for continual learning", 2019. [Online]. Available: https://arxiv.org/abs/1811.11682. Accessed: 14 May 2025.

[17] K. Xu, L. Chen, and S. Wang, "Kolmogorov-Arnold networks for time series: Bridging predictive power and interpretability", Jun. 2024, [Online]. Available: http://arxiv.org/abs/2406.02496. Accessed: 14 May 2025.

[18] C. J. Vaca-Rubio, L. Blanco, R. Pereira, and M. Caus, "Kolmogorov-Arnold networks (KANs) for time series analysis", May 2024, [Online]. Available: http://arxiv.org/abs/2405.08790. Accessed: 14 May 2025.

[19] A. D. M. Ibrahum, Z. Shang, and J.- E. Hong, "How resilient are Kolmogorov–Arnold networks in classification tasks? A robustness investigation", Applied Sciences, vol. 14, no. 22, 2024

[20] T. Alter, R. Lapid, and M. Sipper, "On the robustness of Kolmogorov-Arnold networks: An adversarial perspective", 2024. [Online]. Available: https://arxiv.org/abs/2408.13809. Accessed: 14 May 2025.

[21] C. Zeng, J. Wang, H. Shen, and Q. Wang, "KAN versus MLP on irregular or noisy functions", 2024, [Online]. Available: https://arxiv.org/abs/2408.07906. Accessed: 14 May 2025.

[22] H. Shen, C. Zeng, J. Wang, and Q. Wang, "Reduced effective-ness of Kolmogorov-Arnold networks on functions with noise", Jul. 2024, [Online]. Available: http://arxiv.org/abs/2407.14882. Accessed: 14 May 2025.

[23] Z. Li and D. Hoiem, "Learning without forgetting", 2017. [Online]. Available: https://arxiv.org/abs/1606.09282. Accessed: 14 May 2025.

[24] A. Mallya, D. Davis, and S. Lazebnik, "Piggyback: Adapting a single network to multiple tasks by learning to mask weights", 2018. [Online]. Available: https://arxiv.org/abs/1801.06519. Accessed: 14 May 2025.

[25] A. A. Rusu et al., "Progressive neural networks", 2022. [Online]. Available: https://arxiv.org/abs/1606.04671. Accessed: 14 May 2025.

Redefining Leadership: AI Literacy is a Strategic Imperative for 21st Century Leaders

Claudette McGowan
Toronto Metropolitan University
Toronto, Canada
email: cmcgowan@torontomu.ca

Salah Sharieh
Toronto Metropolitan University
Toronto, Canada
email: salah.sharieh@torontomu.ca

Alexander Ferworn
Toronto Metropolitan University
Toronto, Canada
email: aferworn@torontomu.ca

***Abstract*—Artificial Intelligence (AI) is reshaping leadership by necessitating a blend of technological proficiency and ethical insight. This paper examines the imperative for leaders to attain AI literacy to effectively integrate AI into strategic decision-making and organizational resilience. It discusses varying levels of AI proficiency, identifies barriers to adoption, and underscores the importance of aligning leadership practices with emerging policy frameworks. By embracing AI literacy, leaders can navigate the complexities of the digital era, ensuring their organizations remain competitive and ethically grounded.**

Keywords-Artificial Intelligence; Leadership; AI Literacy; Organizational Resilience; Ethical Governance; Strategic Decision Making; AI Integration; Policy Frameworks.

I. INTRODUCTION

Artificial Intelligence (AI) has entered a new age. Historically, intuition, experience, and straightforward cause-and-effect thinking has anchored leaders. AI, Machine Learning (ML), neural networks, challenge the paradigm of what makes an exceptional leader in the 21st century. The value of aggregating data and tapping into deep learning has enhanced the capabilities of machines to extract insights from data [1]. Next, [2] extended this trajectory and demonstrated that unsupervised learning at scale, in their case, producing the first generation of GPT language models, could deliver emergent behaviors previously exclusive to humans. These technical benchmarks force executives to reassess, in an AI-driven environment, how knowledge is acquired, how judgments are justified, and what exactly defines competence.

Leaders especially must understand what AI is and is not. [3] define AI as a system's ability to interpret external data correctly, learn from such data, and use those learnings to achieve specific goals and tasks through flexible adaptation. This description highlights how, instead of only running on hard-coded instructions, AI systems independently grow and evolve through experience. [4] argue that, from a commercial standpoint, like prior inventions such as the steam engine and electricity, AI, especially ML, has become the most significant general-purpose technology of our time. They point out that ML unlocks productivity benefits by automating simple and complex tasks.

AI literacy goes beyond mere technological knowledge. It requires understanding the fundamental concepts behind how AI systems make decisions and learn. Leaders should be aware of the differences between supervised, unsupervised, and reinforcement learning, comprehend what it means when a model overfits or why an algorithm could be biased, and appreciate the constraints of AI. Large language models, for example, can create confident-sounding responses but lack actual comprehension. [5] warn, even powerful AI, such as the generative models of today, often lacks a genuine understanding of the material it generates. An AI-literate leader would understand the current limitations of AI and apply checks and balances when using such AI platforms.

Additional background information is drawn from the body of research on digital and information literacy [6]. It is worth noting that information overload has become a significant issue in the digital era. The flood of statistics and analytics can overwhelm decision-makers, causing uncertainty rather than insight. Big data-loving AI systems can either exacerbate or aid in controlling this overload, depending on their application. AI literacy enables leaders to utilize AI to distinguish between signal and noise, thereby reducing the noise level rather than adding to it. Fundamentally, Chief Executive Officers (CEOs) equipped with a knowledge of how algorithms function are better positioned to direct their companies in an era of data driven complexity.

II. AI AS A LEADERSHIP IMPERATIVE

Unlike earlier developments, AI continually evolves through feedback loops, transfer learning, and reinforcement, therefore, leadership in this field is not fixed but rather must be iterative, experimental, and ethical. Strategic leaders must be able to distinguish between accurate signals and hype, as well as between deployable solutions and speculative prototypes. They must assess not only what an AI system can achieve, but also what it should do, considering social values and organizational objectives. Practically, this means that leaders must be willing to challenge model outputs and forecast secondary impacts of AI deployment. As [4] underline, the transformational power of AI is limited by *what it cannot do* for a company. In ethical decision-making, creative vision, or knowledge of stakeholder environments, leaders must choose where human judgment and domain expertise remain indispensable.

The changing nature of technology feeds leadership mandates surrounding AI. New AI systems are more than just tools; in some circumstances, they operate as autonomous agents that learn and make decisions independently. [7] explain how a new generation of AI systems are actors in and of themselves, making crucial decisions and changing results without direct human guidance. This blurs the boundaries separating the tool from collaborator. Leaders must learn how to collaborate with AI, guiding these systems through well-defined goals and governance, while also trusting them to operate in areas where they excel. Finding the balance is of great importance as too little control and the AI can drift, too much micromanagement and the leader loses the advantage of AI. Leading AI literacy promotes the concept of epistemic humility, acknowledging that in certain situations, an algorithm's superior pattern-spotting capabilities can be complemented by the wisdom to recognize when human supervision should replace algorithmic guidance.

The business literature increasingly presents AI literacy as a fundamental leadership ability. Leading in an AI-powered environment requires redefining cooperation between humans and intelligent technology, according to a Harvard Business Review study [7]. Whether via shadowing data science teams or prototyping with no-code ML tools, leaders who interact with AI tools personally develop an instinct of what drives system performance. Such involvement dispels the myth of AI as a black box. The idea of mystery can discourage executive participation. Although the technical specifics of deep learning may be challenging, non-engineers can gain a good understanding of the concepts and underpinnings, such as training data quality, model bias, or overfitting.

An alarming statistic comes from a survey by the McKinsey Global Institute [8], which revealed that almost 50% of board directors claim AI is not currently on their agenda. Reflecting a gap in top-down participation, many executives have yet to address AI strategy in the boardroom. According to McKinsey Global Institute [8] research, only 1% of executives believe their company has reached AI maturity, where AI is integrated into most processes, despite almost all organizations investing in AI. Leaders are not moving fast enough to develop AI at scale. Many companies lack qualified leadership to support and guide AI initiatives and acquiring tools without a capable workforce is not a fast path to success. Human intelligence coupled with AI is a prerequisite for business leadership. Like those who neglected the internet, mobile and social media revolutions, leaders who fail to adapt will progressively find their companies at a competitive disadvantage.

Engaging the hearts and minds of the workforce is necessary to build trust, a sometimes-undervalued component of the AI leadership mandate. If employees and consumers are skeptical about the intentions and competency of the organizations/leaders using AI solutions, they will not entirely welcome them. According to a recent article in Harvard Business Review [7], workers will not trust AI if they doubt the judgment and openness of their executives regarding AI applications. Building trust requires leaders to clearly explain how AI is applied, address concerns about job displacement, and provide an ethical, human-centered example of how to integrate AI effectively.

III. ORGANIZATIONAL RESILIENCE AND AI INTEGRATION

Organizational resilience in the era of AI is about *adaptive intelligence*. AI is becoming a significant enabler of resilient businesses' capacity to notice and react to changes in their environment more quickly and efficiently. Particularly with real-time data, modern AI systems can predict disturbances, spot weak signals, and replicate events. Those who understand the principles and framework of these models are more suited to calibrate them as tools for resilience. An operations CEO who is AI-literate, for instance, may stress-test supply chain weaknesses using ML models or project changes in customer demand, and then adjust their strategy.

Companies that utilize AI for predictive decision-making and scenario planning outperform their competitors by up to 20% in operational efficiency, according to the McKinsey Global Institute [8]. Typically, this efficiency leads to improved handling of disturbances. For instance, during the COVID19 pandemic, companies with sophisticated AI analytics were able to adjust their business models rapidly. One prominent example is Airbnb, whose leadership utilized AI-driven analytics to identify an increase in demand for longer-term rentals and local stays when global travel came to a halt. They quickly turned their attention to assist work-from-anywhere accommodations. Airbnb's decision to couple data and innovative ideas about new consumer categories with trust in algorithms and data, helped them steer a significant turnaround. Deloitte Insights [9] emphasizes that for companies driven by AI, adaptability is a vital survival trait. The most resilient companies are those whose cultures and leadership can adapt to signals driven by AI.

Resilience is also about growing from mistakes and AI systems will occasionally make mistakes. A CEO knowledgeable in AI can view these events as opportunities for the algorithm to be retrained or updated, and for the company to enhance its operations. If an AI model in a healthcare system misses an anomaly related to a patient case, for instance, an AI-literate Chief Medical Officer would examine whether the training data lacked such cases and then either enhance the data or adjust the thresholds, rather than merely blaming the black box AI. This reflects a more general truth: human resilience and system resilience are intertwined. By managing complexity and scale beyond human capacity, AI can help a company become more resilient.

Resilient companies utilize AI not only to address issues but also to drive constant innovation. Resilient businesses can investigate what if scenarios, such as what if a new competitor emerges. This is an opportunity to get better prepared with strategic options that incorporate AI into their scenario planning. This drives the company from passive shock to active future shaping. According to [4], companies that fully absorb AI's potential will be the ones to create entirely new business models in the face of change. In this sense, strategic resilience, the capacity to not only survive but also seize opportunities, becomes dependent on AI literacy among executives.

IV. DEGREES OF AI PROFICIENCY FOR LEADERS

AI competency ranges from basic literacy to strategic fluency and, for ultimately, technical depth - it is not homogeneous. Although every leader should have a basic understanding of how AI operates and its consequences, not every leader needs to be an AI specialist. Three escalating tiers of AI competency for leaders allow us to:

1) Foundational Reading

Leaders at this level understand basic concepts and terms. They are familiar with essential metrics, such as accuracy and error levels, and understand the mechanism a learning algorithm employs, for example, pattern matching in historical data. Additionally, they comprehend the difference between supervised and unsupervised learning. They also understand concepts such as overfitting, model bias, and the need for high-quality training data. They may not build models, but a leader with basic AI literacy can keep pace and ask good questions. For example, they might ask, has this recommender system been evaluated for differential fairness across customer segments or how confident are we in the predictions, and what is the basis for that confidence?

2) Strategic Fluency

Incorporating AI within organizational strategy and cross functional collaboration is a sign of strategic fluency. They are more concerned with the broader implications of AI, including its ethical, legal, and competitive aspects. For example, at this level, a leader understands the importance of algorithmic fairness and can evaluate where and how an AI system impacts stakeholders. From a model report, they might be able to determine where the model performs well and where it fails.

Strategic fluency also encompasses awareness of developing AI rules and standards, such as the EU's proposed AI Act or Canada's AIDA [10], and the ability to foresee how these will affect the company's operations. At this level, a leader could spearhead an AI governance group or help to define an AI strategy. They can convert corporate needs into directions for AI teams; technical complexities into language that the C-suite and board can comprehend. Essentially, they serve as a bridge between technical professionals and the broader organization, ensuring that AI initiatives align with corporate strategy and values.

3) Technical Depth & Expertise

Although this is more common for Chief Technology Officers or Chief Data Scientists than CEOs, some leaders may delve deeper technically into AI. Still, some tech-savvy leaders interact directly with code or model development. At this level, a leader may possess a strong understanding of AI architecture and techniques, or personally experiment with ML models, perhaps using autoML tools or Python notebooks. By advocating new AI uses, they can rigorously question presumptions, challenge AI system design, and inspire innovation.

Although not every company will have a CEO capable of programming an algorithm, having some top executives or advisers with this knowledge can be highly beneficial. These individuals ensure the business stays at the forefront and can guide others in the C-suite on AI issues. Crucially, even technically skilled leaders must also excel in the human and strategic aspects; sheer technical knowledge without strategic vision or ethical foundation can lead to solutions in search of problems or, worse, to reckless deployments.

At any point on the spectrum above, AI-proficient leaders ultimately act as interpreters and guides, tailored to their position. They convert corporate priorities into AI development roadmaps and translate the promise of AI into commercial prospects. They help their companies create teams and cultures prepared for AI. They might initiate training initiatives to increase AI literacy among the managers, for instance, [11] demand for a system of lifetime learning in the workforce to accommodate AI-driven change. Indeed, [11] contends that society and businesses must reorganize around lifelong learning to keep pace with automation and AI a concept that holds as much relevance for executives as for front-line workers overall, developing different levels of AI competency in leadership results in a common language and understanding that helps the entire company navigate the AI era more successfully.

Leadership that is both AI-literate and emotionally savvy about change management makes a significant difference, as evidenced by these case studies across banking, energy, healthcare, and manufacturing. In every case, even if the technology itself was advanced, its effectiveness depended on human leaders who understood it and could include it into organizational processes and culture; it was not a magic bullet. Those executives who were AI-literate were able to ask important questions, create suitable guardrails, engage the correct stakeholders, and ultimately convert AI capability into real-world business value. As a result, those companies not only made effective use of AI but also developed new capabilities that made them more resilient and innovative.

V. BARRIERS TO ADOPTION AND LITERACY

When business objectives and risk frameworks are misaligned, IT teams may struggle to interpret strategic priorities. Data scientists and engineers, on the other hand, speak a language like mathematical models, codes, and APIs, which corporate managers often find beyond their level of understanding. This mismatch can hinder communication and result in either neglected AI solutions, or AI solutions that fail to address the actual problem.

Another factor that can impede the embracing of AI literacy are psychological and cultural elements. Time constraints are often mentioned; senior executives may not prioritize learning AI principles when they are busy running the company. Obsolescence is a concern among experienced executives that the world is advancing faster than their capacity to learn, which can also lead to a resistance to new technological change. The lack of organized learning paths for leaders aggravates this. Employees may receive training courses, but who guides directors and CEOs on the use of AI? Although this is beginning to change, few MBA programs or executive education courses have recently extensively incorporated AI and data science into their core curriculum. [11] notes that leaders run the risk of lagging behind and then opposing what they do not comprehend if they reject ongoing education.

Other obstacles are pragmatic problems such as a lack of data infrastructure needed for significant AI integration given data is locked in silos, of poor quality, or not readily available in real time. Early AI experiments that fail or underperform can poison leadership on further investment. If not correctly framed, such failures could support a narrative that AI did not work for us.

The quantity of data and the hype surrounding AI pose another obstacle. Paradoxically, too much noise is a problem even if ignorance is a challenge. Extreme media hype cycles accompany the fast-moving AI industry. The topic is AI defeating humans in a game one week, and the following week it will be a chatbot producing poetry. This firehose of information can destabilize a busy leader, causing uncertainty about what truly matters for their company. According to [6], information overload is a condition characterized by an overwhelming amount of relevant and semi-relevant information that becomes a burden rather than a benefit. Leaders in the AI space must contend with an excess of jargon, vendor presentations, and anecdotal success tales. Differentiating signal from noise itself requires some degree of AI literacy to understand, for instance, that success in beating human gamers does not automatically translate into a breakthrough in one's sector.

It is crucial to create translators or champions of cross functional AI that span different departments. These could be rising leaders with adequate technical knowledge and commercial sense to act as middlemen. They can help translate needs and findings and support company executives in meetings with data teams. Some companies have even established the position of Chief AI Officer or expanded the Chief Information Officer (CIO) role to address AI strategy and education throughout the company specifically.

The road to universal AI literacy in leadership is impacted by communication gaps, fear and inertia, cultural opposition, infrastructure barriers, and other trials. Not one of these challenges is insurmountable. Through deliberate approaches such as education, translation roles, cultural change, and opportunities to learn/practice, organizations can begin to close the AI literacy gap. The outcome will be leaders who actively utilize AI, rather than simply having passive awareness of it, and teams that are enabled to grow with AI, rather than being limited by inadequate communication.

VI. POLICY ADVICE AND FRAMEWORK OF GOVERNMENT

As companies strive to achieve, matching efforts aimed at embedding AI literacy into leadership and operations with newly proposed rules and governance frameworks at national and international levels is equally crucial. Governments, business agencies, and multi-stakeholder groups are driven by the rapid evolution of AI to establish norms and parameters that ensure responsible research and the development of beneficial applications. Along with their layers of technology and strategy, leaders must also be well-versed in the state of the policy landscape surrounding AI. It equips them to shape future-ready business strategy, while driving proactive industry governance standards and regulation compliance.

The recent OECD AI Principles [12] have attracted interest as they are among the highest-level global guidelines offered for what constitutes trustworthy AI. The OECD's five fundamental pillars of AI governance [12] are: inclusive growth, sustainable development, and well-being; respect for the rule of law, human rights, and democratic values; transparency and explainability; robustness, security, and safety; and responsibility. They insist that AI be human-centric and incorporate safeguards for the design and implementation of AI systems. According to the transparency principle, for example, people should be aware when interacting with an AI system and understand how it makes decisions that affect their lives. Effective control and redress mechanisms will enable businesses to take responsibility for the outcomes of their AI systems.

Implementing such ideas within a company could involve establishing an internal review board for high-impact AI projects, implementing an AI ethics policy, or conducting algorithm bias tests. Addressing this requirement to put abstract ideas into practical use, one of the suggestions in our initial study was to translate OECD and UNESCO principles into actionable scorecards linked to Key Performance Indicators (KPIs). For their initiatives, several businesses have begun creating AI ethics scorecards, which compare them against standards such as fairness or openness. Not leaving these projects entirely to IT or compliance departments to lead the way but instead engaging forward-looking leaders is an optimal path forward.

Additionally, national policies are being formulated, as seen in the case of Canada. The proposed Artificial Intelligence and Data Act (AIDA) in Bill C-27 [10] is one of the first moves in North America to regulate private sector AI systems. Aiming to identify key AI systems that can have a negative impact on health, safety, or rights, AIDA employs a risk-based approach, as reported in [10]. Under the Act, businesses would be required to assess their potential risks and biases associated with AI. It provides basic ideas for systems needing human supervision, explainability, justice, non-discrimination, safety, security, and responsibility, as well as elements for evaluating high-risk AI, including the possibility for harm and the scope of usage.

Regulatory organizations in sectors such as healthcare, banking, and transportation are closely monitoring the development of AI. For instance, financial authorities are examining algorithmic trading and lending algorithms, while the U.S. FDA is creating rules on AI and ML in medical devices. Leaders in organizations in these fields must stay current with such changes. For example, an executive at an insurance company should be aware of any rules from insurance authorities regarding the use of AI in underwriting or claims, which typically emphasize fairness and transparency to consumers.

Research companies and consulting firms have contributed to the discussion with thorough ideas on the governance of AI. Deloitte [9], McKinsey [8], and PwC [13] have offered analysis on how companies might navigate the AI revolution. For example, Deloitte has emphasized the need for enhanced board oversight of AI. A poll by Deloitte Global [9] revealed a governance gap, with almost half of company boards not discussing AI at the board level. Boards should regard AI as a boardroom issue, according to [9], thereby ensuring that issues of AI risk and strategy receive the highest level of attention and consideration.

Through its Global Institute and industry research, McKinsey has emphasized the importance of aligning AI strategy with corporate value and workforce growth. Investing in reskilling the workforce alongside AI deployment is a key proposal [8] that will enable employees to work effectively with new systems, rather than being replaced or disenchanted. These initiatives demystify AI for the entire workforce, thereby fostering an AI-ready culture that aligns with the leadership literacy.

Similarly, as underlined in [13], there is a need to develop trust and responsible AI techniques. According to [13], companies that excel in AI adoption often also lead in creating systems for AI governance and ethics. PwC's research [13] reveals that organizations achieving a noteworthy return on investment from AI are those that prioritize data security and model interpretability from the outset. One often referenced PwC statistic is their projection of AI's potential $15.7 trillion impact on the global economy by 2030, which serves as a wake-up call, emphasizing the enormous risks. [13] advises CEOs to ensure that AI has a seat at the table in business planning conversations and incorporates AI into top-level company strategy.

In the realm of public policy, leaders have the opportunity and obligation to help shape sound AI governance by lobbying and setting a good example. By volunteering in industry consortia or government advisory groups on AI, business leaders can lend their expertise toward creating effective yet not innovation-stifling rules. In a few cases, banks and tech firms have collaborated with authorities to establish sandboxes for the controlled testing of AI systems, thereby advancing the collective understanding of governance and innovation. When leaders and companies convert all of these frameworks and concepts, a few concrete actions emerge.

1) Create AI governance systems

Establish official systems, such as AI monitoring boards or assigned accountable AI agents. These systems should align with external values [12] and ensure continuous adherence to evolving rules such as AIDA [10] or others. They also indicate internally that AI should be managed with the same level of strictness as other significant corporate hazards.

Create explicit rules and guidelines for the advancement and application of AI. An AI ethics guideline document, for instance, states that all project teams must abide by it and could cover acquiring appropriate consent for data usage, avoiding certain sensitive features such as not using protected attributes in models, and requirements for explainability when decisions impact consumers. Escalation procedures when an AI system encounters scenarios it is not confident about.

2) Invest in Training and Awareness (Policy Literacy)

Policy literacy on AI is much needed, much as we discuss AI literacy. Leaders should ensure that their teams, especially those involved in AI, are aware of the ethical and regulatory requirements they are expected to fulfill. This may require bringing in legal experts to brief the technical teams or hosting seminars on forthcoming rules. On the other hand, it entails educating legal teams and compliance agents in the knowledge of AI sufficient to manage it effectively. The two-way learning reflects the need for a multidisciplinary approach.

3) Transparency and Stakeholder Communication

Establish a policy of open communication regarding AI applications. This can include releasing AI transparency reports, which some businesses have begun doing, revealing where and how they apply AI, much like privacy transparency reports. Along with ways for consumers to request human review, as some laws, such as the European Union's GDPR, require, it can also involve interacting with them, for example, by sending a notification when AI is employed in making a significant judgment concerning them. Leaders should frame transparency as an opportunity to create trust rather than a compliance burden.

REFERENCES

[1] G. E. Hinton, S. Osindero, and Y.-W. Teh, "A fast learning algorithm for deep belief nets", Neural Computation, vol. 18, no. 7, pp. 1527–1554, 2006.

[2] A. Radford et al., "Improving language understanding by generative pre-training", OpenAI, San Francisco, CA, 2018.

[3] A. Kaplan and M. Haenlein, "Siri, Siri, in my hand: Who's the fairest in the land? On the interpretations, illustrations, and implications of artificial intelligence", Business Horizons, vol. 62, no. 1, pp. 15–25, 2019.

[4] E. Brynjolfsson and A. McAfee, "The business of artificial intelligence: What it can and cannot do for your organization", Harvard Business Review, vol. 7, no. 1, pp. 1–2, 2017.

[5] G. Marcus and E. Davis, "Rebooting AI: Building artificial intelligence we can trust", Vintage, 2019.

[6] D. Bawden and L. Robinson, "Information overload: An introduction", in Oxford Research Encyclopedia of Politics, 2020.

[7] J. Heimans and H. Timms, "Leading in a world where AI wields power of its own", Harvard Business Review, vol. 102, no. 1–2, pp. 71–79, 2024.

[8] M. Chui, L. Yee, B. Hall, and A. Singla, "The state of AI in 2023: Generative AI's breakout year", McKinsey & Company, 2023.

[9] Deloitte Insights, "Leadership in the age of AI: Adaptability as a critical survival skill", Deloitte Insights Report, 2023.

[10] Canada Gazette, "Artificial Intelligence and Data Act (AIDA) – proposed legislation in bill c-27", Canada Gazette, Part I, vol. 157, no. 27, 2023.

[11] D. M. West, "The future of work: Robots, AI, and automation", Brookings Institution Press, 2018.

[12] OECD, "OECD principles on artificial intelligence", OECD, Paris, France, 2019.

[13] PwC, "AI Predictions 2022: Thriving in the era of AI", PwC Report, 2022.

Inducing and Detecting Anchoring Bias via Game-Play in Time-extended Decision-Making Tasks

Prithviraj Dasgupta, John Kliem, Mark A. Livingston, and Jonathan W. Decker
Information and Decision Sciences Branch
Naval Research Laboratory, Washington, DC, USA
e-mail: {prithviraj.dasgupta.civ | john.kliem3.civ}@us.navy.mil
e-mail: {mark.a.livingston18.civ | jonathan.w.decker4.civ}@us.navy.mil

Abstract—**We consider the problem of detecting anchoring bias in problems where a decision maker has to make multiple, correlated decisions over time. The main research question we investigate is whether the problem's solution from working on the problem multiple times has an anchoring effect on the decisions made to solve the problem in the future. To address this question, we propose a computer-based navigation game where an autonomous agent dynamically adapts initially hidden information that is required by human players to solve the game, in successive iterations of the game. We use the navigation decisions made by human players while playing the game, as the game information gets incrementally revealed, to infer the presence of anchoring bias in the player's decisions. Our results with game-playing data collected from 74 human subjects comprising Navy and Marine trainee personnel show a strong evidence of anchoring bias, although the bias diminishes rapidly after the player is exposed to information that contradicts the information in the anchor. We have also validated our results using an anchoring bias model from literature to show that our results conform to the model in 77-80 percent of game-play instances.**

Keywords-anchoring bias; decision-making; human participant user study.

I. INTRODUCTION

Cognitive biases in human decision-making while solving a problem are known to affect the problem's outcome [1]. These biases usually degrade the outcome's value to the decision maker and to others that are affected by the problem's outcome. Researchers have proposed several techniques to detect and analyze cognitive biases in decision making. In this paper, we analyze a commonly encountered cognitive bias called the anchoring bias [2] while focusing on problems that involve time-extended or sequential decision-making. Time-extended decision-making instances abound in daily living tasks as well as longer term decision problems.

Recently, researchers [3,4] have reported the presence of anchoring bias in decision making for time-extended tasks. However, in these research studies, while making the decision for the current task the decision maker had access to the features of the current task, in addition to their experience from past decisions on similar tasks stored in their memories. In contrast, if access to the current task's features while making the decision for the task were to be taken away, and the decision maker had to rely solely on experiences from memory from similar tasks to make decisions, is anchoring bias still present? This question does not seem to have been investigated reasonably well in existing anchoring bias research.

To address this research gap, we design a study where an autonomous agent dynamically adapts the current tasks' features, which are then incrementally revealed to the decision maker via the decisions made by the decision maker. The decisions made by the decision maker are then analyzed for anchoring bias. Figure 1 illustrates our design idea. The conventional sequential decision making process, where the history of decision outcomes – as well as the current task features – affect the decision on the current task, is shown in Figure 1(a). In contrast, the decision-making process we investigate in this paper is shown in Figure 1(b), where the current task's values are invisible or masked and the current task's decision is based only on past decision outcomes. We employed a game to enable human subjects make successive time-extended decisions and developed algorithms to analyze the presence of anchoring bias in the decisions as well as predict the propensity of displaying anchoring bias based on past decisions. Our results, performed with a group of 74 human subjects, show strong evidence of anchoring bias across 90% of the subjects, while our anchoring bias prediction model shows accuracy in the range of 77–80%. These results support the correctness of our study and the anchoring bias prediction model. Our results also show that anchoring often persisted beyond the first trial, although the prediction model's accuracy beyond the first trial diminished substantially.

The remainder of the paper is organized as follows: In Section II, we review related work. In Section III, we introduce our game designed to elicit anchoring bias in sequential decision-making. In Section IV, we describe the human user study we conducted and our analysis of the resulting data. In Section V, we discuss our study and the lessons we believe we can learn from it. Section VI offers some concluding remarks and directions for future work.

II. RELATED WORK

Anchoring bias [2] causes humans to rely heavily on an initial piece of information, called an *anchor*. Because of this, humans tend to overlook information that would lead to better choices in subsequent decisions, and, instead, gravitate towards choices that align with the anchor. Initial research on analyzing anchoring biases focused on single-point decision problems. The main experimental roundup used for anchoring bias in such single-point decisions is the following: first, a decision maker is exposed to a certain piece of information, called the

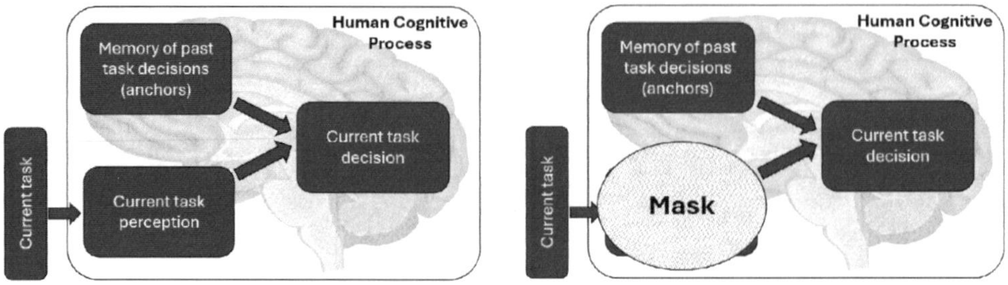

(a) (b)

Figure 1. (a) Conventional decision-making process based on perception of current task's features and memory of past decision outcomes, (b) Masked decision-making process where current task features are not available; decisions are based on memory of past decisions.

anchor, about the likely outcome of a decision. Thereafter, the decision maker is asked to make the same or a very similar decision. Anchoring bias is claimed to affect the latter decision if the latter decision's outcome is similar to the initial decision outcome. A canonical example is to anchor the decision maker to a price point, e.g., 100 for a certain piece of clothing. Subsequently, the decision maker is shown a similar piece of clothing that is priced well-below (or well-above) 100, without revealing the price, and asked its worth. If the decision maker says that the clothing is worth around 100, it indicates that they are anchored to the initial price of 100.

Subsequently, researchers extended the study of anchoring bias to successive decisions such as perceived loudness of sounds played in sequence, group decision-making [5,6], evaluations of facial attractiveness and ringtone likeability [7], financial decision-making [8], reviews of books and college applications [3,4,9]. In the experiment design in these research efforts, the decision maker had to determine a decision outcome (in other words, evaluate) tasks that appeared in a sequence. Each task had a fixed set of features or attributes and the decision outcome was a function of the attribute's values. The task remained the same over time, but the values of the task's attributes were different for each task. The decision maker was affected by anchoring bias if they bypassed or shortcut through the function that maps the attribute values to the decision outcome, but, instead used a previously encountered task's decision outcome to determine the current task's decision outcome. For example, in admissions decisions, if the reviewer did not scrutinize the current applicant's credentials closely, but instead relied on a decision made for a previously seen, albeit similar (in terms of credentials) applicant, the decision was marked as influenced by anchoring bias.

These research settings are complementary to the research in this paper. The two main differences between our work and these are, first, we do not reveal the current problem's features (e.g., current book or college application under review) to the decision maker and the decision maker has to rely only on past task features and decisions from memory to make the current task's decision. Another slight distinction is that these technique use offline data that was not generated specifically for the bias studies and there was limited information about the background of the decision maker. on the other hand, the subjects in our study are people that were familiar with computer-game playing and decision-making in scenarios similar to our game.

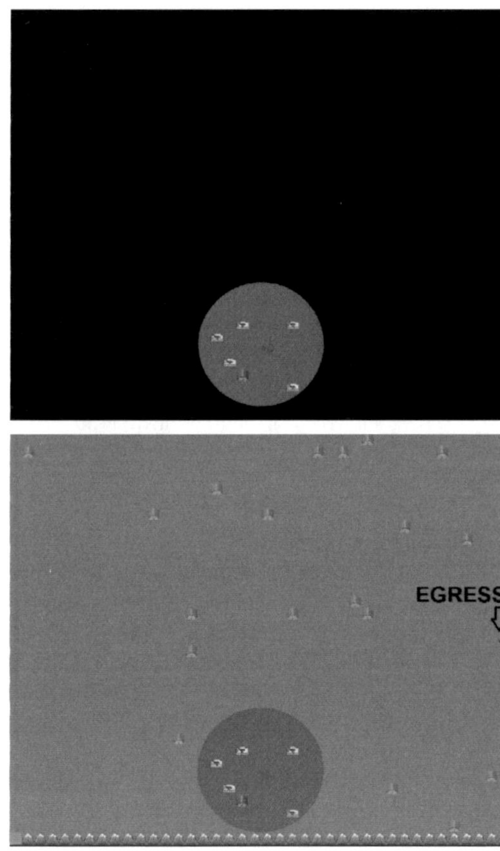

Figure 2. Top: Tankgame with viewport on; the red cluster of dots at the middle of the viewport is the player's game-piece. Bottom: Tankgame with grayed map outside viewport (for legibility).

III. METHOD FOR ANCHORING BIAS DETECTION

Recently, the concept of gamification or using computer-based games as an enabler for humans to perform learning or decision-making tasks has been extensively used in the fields of education and cognitive analysis [10]. Following this, we

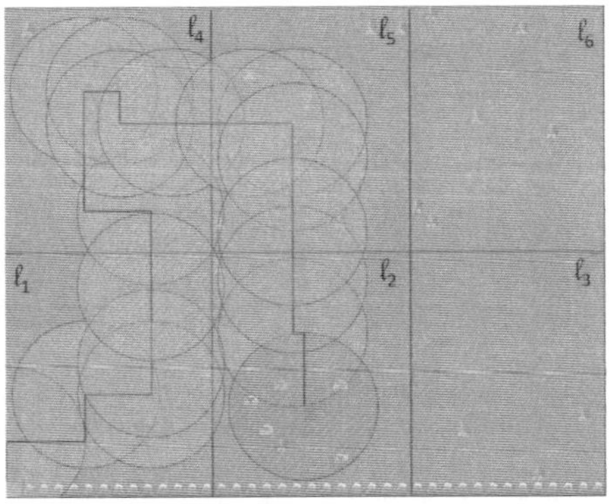

Figure 3. A sample trajectory (red curve) taken by a player. Lighter green dashed circles show the player's viewport as it moves along the trajectory. Only the current viewport was visible at any point along the trajectory.

describe a technique for detecting anchoring bias in a sequential decision making task implemented as computer-based game. In our game, a player has to move around a game-piece in a grid-based 2-D environment. At any point in the game, the player can only see a portion of the game board revealed via a circular viewport of radius rview centered around the game-piece's current location (red clusters of dots), as shown in Figure 2 (top). The environment contains objects called tanks that are placed in a cluster around a certain location in the environment. Figure 2 (bottom) shows the tanks on the game board with the region outside the viewport grayed out for legibility. A tank can be removed or cleared by the player by pressing a specific key on the game controller (e.g., keyboard space bar) when the game-piece is in the vicinity of the tank. There is also an egress at a specific location in the environment (elliptical pad on the right edge in Figure 2 (bottom)). The egress can be view only when it is in the players' viewport, but its location is known to the player from the start of the game. The player has two objectives: 1) detect and clear all the tanks in the environment, 2) after clearing all the tanks in the environment, navigate to the egress and exit the environment. Due to the limited size of the viewport, a player cannot know beforehand where the tanks are located inside the environment. Consequently, they have to search the environment by moving around the game-piece. Once the tanks are visible inside the viewport, they can move the game-piece to each tank's vicinity, clear the tanks, and finally move to the egress. The game-piece can be moved in four cardinal directions, Up, Down, Left or Right, and the game board is discretized into a grid-like environment for the purpose of tracking the game-piece's location. Figure 3 shows a trajectory of game-play (red curve) taken by a player while playing the game. Only the current viewport was visible to the player at any moment of the game; however, the figure shows the full game board for illustrative purposes.

We leverage the searching behavior of the player to study whether repeated placement of the tanks around the same location in the environment in initial iterations of the game induces the player to expect to look for the tanks at the same location in later iterations.

A. Inducing Anchoring Bias via Spatial Placement of Tasks

We partition the environment into $L = l_1, l_2, l_3, ...$ cells. The anchoring bias experiment consists of n_r game rounds. Each game round is divided into two phases:

- **Anchoring Phase**: During the anchoring phase, the game-piece is placed in cell l_1, while all tanks are placed inside a randomly selected cell, $l_i \in L - \{l_1\}$. The location of the tanks is not observable by the player. The player then plays the game n_{anc} times; the value of n_{anc} is not revealed to the player. We call each game-play a run. At the start of each run, the game is reset by placing the game-piece in l_1 and the tanks in the same cell, l_i, as in the first run.
- **Evaluation Phase**: For the evaluation phase, the game-piece is placed in l_1, while tanks are randomly placed in a cell $l_j \in L - \{l_1, l_i\}$. The player plays n_{eval} runs of the game and at the start of each run, the game-piece is placed in l_1 and tanks are placed in l_j. As before, the number of evaluation runs, n_{eval} is not revealed to the player.

At the end of each game round, the random number generator seed is randomized to prevent correlations between the random placement locations of tanks across game rounds. The player session is saved upon the completion of n_r game rounds. Overall, each player plays the game for a total of $n_r(n_{anc} + n_{eval})$ runs. Player data during each game run is collected in the form of a trajectory, $\tau = (s_0, a_0, s_1, a_1, ...)$. Here, s_i denotes the location or grid cell currently occupied by the game-piece, a_i denotes the action or direction in which the game piece was moved, and i denotes the time-step. We informally denote the time-step as the time required to move the game-piece from one grid cell to one of its adjacent grid cells. τ_{anc} and τ_{eval} denote trajectories generated during the anchoring and evaluation phases respectively.

B. Detecting Anchoring Bias

For detecting anchoring bias, we check whether, during an evaluation run, the player visited the location where the tanks were during the anchoring runs before exploring other regions of the map. Recall that the map of the game board outside the view port is not visible to the player while playing the game. So, the only reason for a player to go towards the anchoring location would be due to anchoring bias induced by the location retained in their memory during anchoring runs. To quickly determine if the player started exploring the map instead of going towards the anchoring location, we partition the map into cells, as shown in Figure 3. We then check if the evaluation trajectory of the player shows excursions into cells that that do not contain the shortest trajectory between the start and anchoring locations. A positive outcome of the latter check confirms anchoring, a negative outcome indicates no anchoring.

C. Model-based Prediction of Anchoring Bias

We further analyzed the trajectories from the anchoring runs in each game round to determine if the player had developed a propensity towards being biased by the anchor. For this, we used the model for the influence from the anchor proposed [6]. Their model parameterized the anchor's influence as a linear combination of three factors: the stimulus from the current task perception, the stimulus from the task in the previous time-step, and the outcome of the decision in the last time-step. In our setting, because we mask the current task perception, we consider that the influence of the anchor in the current time-step as a linear combination of the stimulus from the anchors stored in the memory. We consider the distance of the player moves the game-piece (that is, the length of the trajectory) up to viewing the first tank in the viewport during an anchoring run as the stimulus or attraction from that anchor. Based on this idea, we define the anchor's influence during an evaluation run as:

$$J_{eval} = \alpha + \sum_{i=1}^{n_{anc}} \beta_i J_{anc,i}$$

where α and β are constants and $J_{anc,i}$ is the influence of the ith anchor from memory and n_{anc} is the number of anchoring runs. We used linear regression with least squares [11] to solve this equation. Let m_{anc} denote the slope of the regression line. We then define the anchoring bias propensity as True if $m_{anc} < 0$ and False otherwise.

IV. Anchoring Bias User Study

The computer game for testing anchoring bias was approved by the Naval Research Laboratory Institutional Review Board and given to U.S. Navy and Marine personnel at the Naval Aerospace Medical Institute (NAMI), Pensacola, FL, USA. The game was played by 74 human players on a voluntary basis; informed consent and demographic data were collected from each player. The average age range of the players was between 21 - 23 years. Each player was given a tutorial at the start of their session that gave the objective and rules of the game, and how to move the game-piece to navigate the game-board. For all games in our experiments, the size of the game map is 40 × 32 cells and the viewport radius $r_{view} = 5$ cells. Each player played $n_r = 2$ game rounds, each with $n_{anc} = 5$ anchoring runs and $n_{eval} = 2$ evaluation runs. We collected the following data for each player:

- game-play trajectory in the form of coordinates of the cells on the game board the player moved the game-piece through,
- number of time-steps (measured in number of cells traversed by the gamepiece) to locate the first tank,
- time spent by the player in playing the game including the tutorial.

We evaluated the following Research Questions (RQs) related to anchoring bias from the players' data. The overall rationale for these RQs is to determine whether anchoring bias, if present, affects a player's future decisions and for how long, in the context of a time-extended decision-making task.

RQ1 Do subjects show anchoring bias after 5 anchoring runs?
RQ2 Does anchoring bias, if present, last more than one run?
RQ3 Does a player who shows anchoring bias during anchoring runs also show anchoring bias in evaluation run(s)?

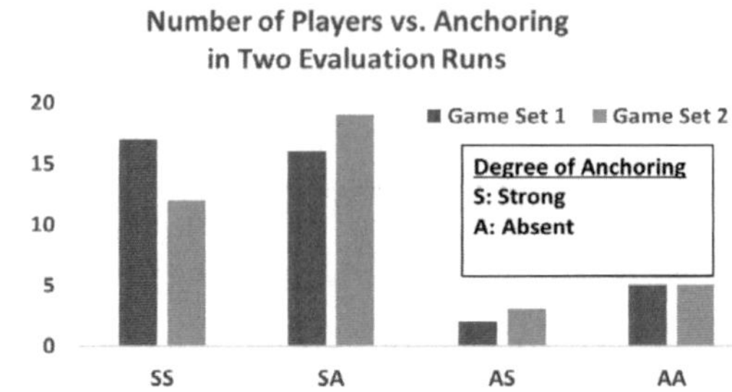

Figure 4. Bar chart showing the number of players (y-axis) that have Strong or no (Absent) anchoring (x-axis) in the two game rounds in our experiments.

A. Game-play Data Analysis

From the 74 players that played our game for 2 game rounds each, we were able to collect 148 data instances, each instance comprising $n_{anc} = 5$ anchoring runs followed by $n_{eval} = 2$ evaluation runs. These data instances were analyzed for detecting anchoring bias. While analyzing, we found that some of the data instances had to be discarded owing to an oversight in the placement of the anchor: if the location of the tanks during the evaluation run was in-between or en-route from the start location and the location of tanks during the anchoring runs, then it was not possible to determine if the player was anchored or not. We discarded 69 of the 148 data points, leaving 79 valid data points.

RQ1 We detect anchoring bias when the trajectory data from either the first or both evaluation runs meets the criteria above (Section III-B). The results are shown in Figure 4. In the figure, the x-axis labels indicate the degree of anchoring in evaluation run 1 followed by the degree of anchoring in evaluation run 2. Overall, these show a strong evidence of anchoring bias. Out of the 79 data instances, 64 data instances (roughly 81%) showed that the player had been anchored (SS and SA in Figure 4) either in both or only in the first evaluation runs. Across the two game rounds, there was very little variation (6%) in the number of subjects displaying anchoring bias. This indicates a strong propensity for anchoring bias among the subjects.

a) RQ2: We determined the number of data instances that showed strong anchoring in the first evaluation run versus those that showed strong anchoring in both evaluation runs (SA versus SS in Figure 4). We found that in 35 instances players showed that the effect of anchoring waned between the first and second evaluation runs, while the anchoring remained strong between the two evaluation runs for 29 instances. These values indicate that there is a small but non-negligible support that the effect of anchoring bias diminishes if the player gets information that contradicts the anchor.

We found that in the first game round, 16 players showed anchoring only in the first evaluation run and 17 showed anchoring in both evaluation runs. In the second game round, these numbers became 19 and 12 respectively. The decrease in strong anchoring in both evaluation runs between the first and second game rounds (from 17 to 12), and simultaneous increase in subjects that showed anchoring only in the first evaluation run (from 16 to 19) points further in the direction

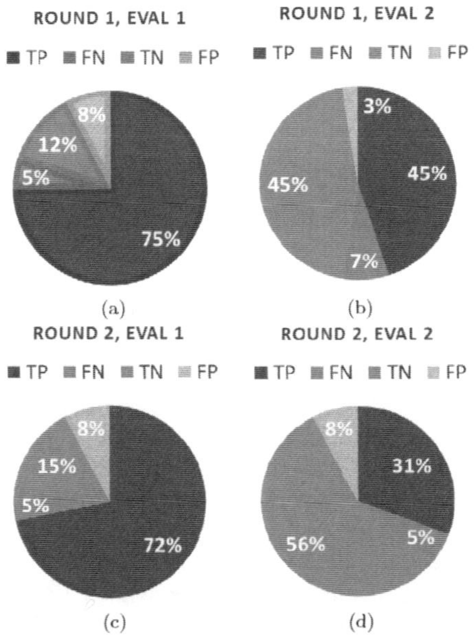

Figure 5. Effect of anchoring bias propensity during anchoring runs on decision in evaluation runs, for rounds 1 (40 trajectories) and 2 (39 trajectories).

that, as the player sees more information contradicting the anchor, the effect of anchoring diminishes. Players may have been more fatigued at the start the second round of evaluation runs, after playing 12 (5 anchoring runs in each of two game rounds plus 2 evaluations runs in first game round) of the game. Conventionally, fatigue would lead to the human brain making shortcuts via heuristics and strengthening the anchoring bias. However, in our experiments, we saw diminishing anchoring bias across game rounds. This seems to indicate that the disappointment of not finding the tanks at the anchoring location weakens the anchoring bias and motivates the player to explore in a more objective, less biased manner.

b) RQ3: The output from the bias prediction model (Section III-C) was compared with the detection criteria (Section III-B). We identified four combinations depending on the agreement between these two outputs. Figure 4 shows the results of this analysis for the two evaluation runs in each of the two rounds. We see that for the first evaluation run (Figures 4(a) and (c)), the model had an accuracy of 80% and 77% respectively in each round, in predicting whether the human would show anchoring bias. As expected, the prediction accuracy of the model diminishes considerably to 52% and 37% respectively in the two rounds (Figures 4(b) and (d)). The exposure to a different location of tanks than the anchoring runs in the first evaluation run reduced the player's reliance on the anchor to search for tank during the second evaluation run. Beyond two evaluation runs, the (binary) prediction was not relevant any more as the accuracy decreased below 50%.

Players played the two rounds of the game back-to-back without any break. We then ask the question: does the model predict if the player will get re-anchored in round 2 even if thew saw information (tank locations) contrary to the first round's anchor during the first round's evaluation runs? The answer from the game data analysis shows that the prediction model is still valid in round 2; its accuracy diminishes by only 3% for evaluation run 1 from the first to the second round. For evaluation run 2, the accuracy decreases by a larger amount of 15%. Overall, these results show that the linear regression model for anchoring bias is a reasonably reliable predictor for the decision of first evaluation after the anchor in both rounds, but not for decisions after the first evaluation. This result corresponds to the findings in other sequential decision-making applications like college admissions and book reviews in [4] where a positive decision's anchoring effect diminished as the decision maker was exposed to more information from successive decision problems that were contrary to the features of the problem in the positive decision instance. Overall, our findings of the anchoring bias prediction model indicate that a more robust prediction model would be worth investigating for longer term prediction of anchoring bias effects.

V. Lessons Learned

During our study, we observed a few relevant points related to the human subject experiments, that we summarize here.

a) Diminishing effect of anchor: For a small fraction of the players (1 out of 74 instances in round 1 and 3 out of 74 instances in round 2), we found that they initially showed influence of the anchor during the first few anchoring runs, but in subsequent anchoring runs and in the evaluation run, the anchoring effect went away and they started exploring the map instead of heading to location where the found the tanks previously. An example is shown in Figure 6 where the first two anchoring runs (left image) shows anchoring but the subsequent anchoring runs do not. This de-anchoring effect was more pronounced in round 2. Possibly the two round 1 evaluation runs reduced the reliance of the player on the anchor during round 2 even after they found it and this prompted them to start exploring again.

b) Ergonomic Factors Affecting Human Subjects: The movement of game-piece in our computer-based game was controlled by keyboard arrow keys; thus, it was limited to the four cardinal directions. This resulted in players using long horizontal or vertical tracks to explore the environment. The number of keystrokes made by players in the game was not recorded and there is a possibility that some players were trying to reduce the number of keystrokes by continuing in the same direction for longer periods. This could again have stemmed for psychological factors like motivation, interest, and engagement with the game and overall experiment.

c) Bias Intersection: Anchoring bias, as we have used the term, intersects with other types of biases. For instance, sequential bias deals with the effect of repetitive decision outcomes on the choice made in sequential, albeit not necessarily time-extended tasks. Experiential bias considers the reliance of humans on experience from past decision outcomes on the current decision-making task. It would be interesting to analyze our results with appropriate theoretical models for these other

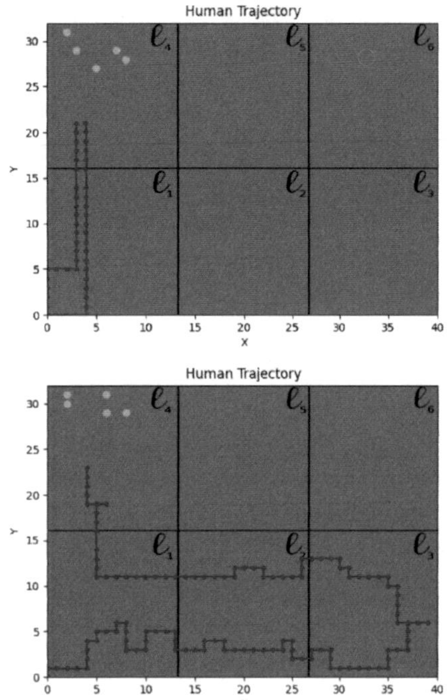

Figure 6. Trajectory of a player during round 2 anchoring runs 1 and 2 (left) and during anchoring run 3-5 (right).

biases as well to understand overlap, similarity, and divergence between these biases.

d) Underlying Cause for Bias: What causes humans to depend on anchors for making decisions? The conventionally accepted theory is the human brain is inclined to make shortcuts via heuristics [2] due to boredom, motivation, repetitiveness and other factors. In contrast, 12 and Strack's [12] selective accessibility model proposed an alternative theory that the brain made information related to the anchor more readily accessible to its decision process. The difference is subtle but consequential, as the former attributes the cause of anchoring bias to the internal working of the brain's decision-making process while the latter attributes it to the information presented to the brain's decision-making process. A deeper understanding, fortified with appropriate mathematical models for these two theories, would help with a clearer understanding of anchoring bias.

VI. Conclusion and Future Work

In this paper, we presented a human subject study for detecting anchoring bias in time-extended decision-making tasks enabled through a computer game-based technique. The principal research question we studied was that if the current task's features are not available to the decision maker, does the influence from past information anchors affect the choice made by the decision maker? The results from our human subject study showed that past anchors significantly influence immediately future decision choices. This influence diminishes as the decision maker is exposed to information contrary to the anchor. But if the same decision maker is subsequently exposed to another anchor, anchoring bias is again observed, albeit with lesser effect than the first anchor. There are several directions we plan to extend this research. These include the effect of distractions and deceptions (e.g., mobile non-playing characters, tank-like objects that aren't real tanks), the effect of task complexity (e.g, clear tanks at multiple clustered locations in a larger map), the effect of multi-level decisions (e.g., while clearing tanks, explore the houses to retrieve a hidden key that let's the player unlock the egress from the game), and the effect of presence of teammates and/or adversaries in the game, on anchoring bias. Extending the game environment as platform for detecting other types of biases is also an area of interest. More efficient, clustering-based techniques instead of the linear regression model used in this research to analyze anchoring propensity, is another direction we are exploring. Finally, we are currently working on techniques for mitigating anchoring bias via automated decision aids that use the output from our anchoring bias detection model (Section III-C) and guide the decision maker towards less-biased decisions in real-time.

Acknowledgements

The authors thank Bryan Brandt for developing a preliminary version of the tank game and the Office of Naval Research for supporting this research via the NRL Base Program.

References

[1] E. Dimara, S. Franconeri, C. Plaisant, A. Bezerianos, and P. Dragicevic. "A Task-Based Taxonomy of Cognitive Biases for Information Visualization," *IEEE Transactions on Visualization and Computer Graphics*, vol. 26, no. 2, pp. 1413–1432, 2020.

[2] A. Tversky and D. Kahneman. "Judgment under Uncertainty: Heuristics and Biases," *Science*, vol. 185, no. 4157, pp. 1124–1131, 1974.

[3] P.T. Sukumar, R. Metoyer, and S. He. "Making a Pecan Pie: Understanding and Supporting The Holistic Review Process in Admissions," in *Proceedings of the ACM Conference on Human-Computer Interaction, Volume 2 CSCW*, Article No. 169, 22 pages, 2018.

[4] J.M. Echterhoff, M. Yarmand, and J. McAuley. "AI-Moderated Decision-Making: Capturing and Balancing Anchoring Bias in Sequential Decision Tasks," in *Proceedings of the 2022 CHI Conference on Human Factors in Computing Systems*, Article No. 161, 9 pages, 2022.

[5] T. Stewart *et al.* "Group Decision Making in the Context of Anchoring Bias," *Decision Support Systems*, vol. 42, no. 1, pp. 123–134, 2006.

[6] W. Jesteadt, R.D. Luce, and D.M. Green. "Sequential Effects in Judgments of Loudness," *Journal of Experimental Psychology: Human Perception and Performance*, vol. 3, no. 1, pp. 92–104, 1977.

[7] J. Huang *et al.* "Sequential Biases on Subjective Judgments: Evidence from Face Attractiveness and Ringtone Agreeableness Judgment," *PLOS One*, vol. 13, no. 6, 2018.

[8] F. Ni, D. Arnott, and S. Gao. "The Anchoring Effect in Business Intelligence Supported Decision-Making," *Journal of Decision Systems*, vol. 28, no. 2, pp. 67–81, 2019.

[9] D.W. Vinson, R. Dale, and M.N. Jones. "Decision Contamination in the Wild: Sequential Dependencies in Online Review Ratings," *Behavior Research Methods*, vol. 51, pp. 1477–1484, 2019.

[10] M.W.B. Zhang, J.B. Ying, G. Song, and R.C.M. Ho. "A Review of Gamification Approaches in Commercial Cognitive Bias Modification Gaming Applications," *Technology and Health Care*, vol. 26, no. 6, pp. 933–944, 2018.

[11] Y. Nievergelt. "Total Least Squares: State-of-the-art Regression in Numerical Analysis," *SIAM Review*, vol. 36, no. 2, pp. 258–264, 1994.

[12] T. Mussweiler and F. Stack. "Comparing Is Believing: A Selective Accessibility Model of Judgmental Anchoring," *European Review of Social Psychology*, vol. 10, no. 1, pp. 135–167, 1999.

Geozone-Aware Unmanned Aerial Vehicles (UAV) Path Planning Using RRT* and Jellyfish-Inspired Optimization for Urban Air Mobility (UAM)

Judit Salvans Baucells
Industrial Systems Engineering and Product Design
Ghent University
Industrial Systems Engineering (ISyE), FlandersMake@Ugent
Ghent, Belgium
judit.salvansbaucells@ugent.be

Elham Fakhraian
Industrial Systems Engineering and Product Design
Ghent University
Industrial Systems Engineering (ISyE), FlandersMake@Ugent
Ghent, Belgium
elham.fakhraian@ugent.be

Ivana Semanjski
Industrial Systems Engineering and Product Design
Ghent University
Industrial Systems Engineering (ISyE), FlandersMake@Ugent
Ghent, Belgium
ivana.semanjski@ugent.be

Abstract— **The growing demand for autonomous aerial operations highlights the need for efficient and regulation-compliant trajectory planning, particularly in Urban Air Mobility (UAM) applications. This paper presents a UAV path planning framework that combines a geozone-aware Rapidly Exploring Random Tree Star (RRT*) algorithm with a jellyfish-inspired optimization technique to navigate complex airspaces while adhering to safety and regulatory constraints. The method accounts for obstacles, no-fly zones, and altitude limits, and has been tested using real-world geospatial data from Piombino, Italy. Results demonstrate the generation of smooth, efficient trajectories. By enabling scalable and adaptive drone operations, this work supports reliable urban delivery services and integration into future U-space traffic management systems.**

Keywords-Unmanned Aerial Vehicles (UAV); Unmanned Aerial System (UAS); path planning; Rapidly-Exploring Random Tree Star (RRT*); geozones; optimization; jellyfish Swarm algorithm; Urban Air Mobility (UAM).

I. Introduction

Unmanned Aerial Vehicles (UAVs) are playing an increasingly vital role in a wide range of civil applications, including logistics, surveillance, infrastructure inspection, and emergency response. Their growing presence in urban environments brings significant opportunities, but also introduces new challenges related to airspace safety, regulatory compliance, and operational efficiency [1]. To address these concerns, regulatory frameworks have been evolving rapidly. In Europe, the European Union Aviation Safety Agency (EASA) has developed a set of regulations specifically for UAV operations. A key component of this regulatory landscape is the introduction of geozones, which are "portions of airspace where drones, or to use the more official term Unmanned Aerial System (UAS), operations are facilitated, restricted, or excluded" [2]. For example, in urban areas, geozones may prohibit UAV flights over sensitive infrastructure such as airports and government buildings, and restrict altitude near densely populated zones, or define specific aerial corridors above main roads. Adherence to these geozones is mandatory and essential for maintaining safety, minimizing airspace conflicts, and enabling the scalable deployment of UAVs within the broader aviation ecosystem.

Path planning algorithms, particularly sampling-based methods such as Rapidly Exploring Random Trees Star (RRT*), have proven effective in generating feasible trajectories for UAVs in cluttered environments[3]. However, classical RRT* does not inherently account for legal or regulatory constraints. It may produce paths that are kinematically valid but violate geozone boundaries, making them unsuitable for real-world deployment. This paper introduces a geozone-aware extension of the RRT* algorithm that embeds airspace regulatory constraints directly into the path planning process. This enhancement ensures that the generated trajectories are fully compliant with operational regulations. Furthermore, the planning framework incorporates a bio-inspired optimization stage, based on jellyfish swarm behavior, to refine the resulting paths, improving smoothness, efficiency, and safety.

The proposed method is tested using real-world geospatial data from Piombino, Italy, demonstrating its potential to support reliable and scalable UAV operations in regulated urban airspaces. This work contributes to the development of advanced path planning tools essential for the future of UAM and U-space integration in Europe.

Despite its effectiveness, the proposed method relies on static geozone and obstacle data, requiring manual updates when regulations or environments change. It also focuses on single-UAV operations, without yet supporting multi-agent coordination or real-time weather adaptation.

The remainder of this paper is organized as follows: Section 2 reviews related work in UAV path planning and regulatory-aware navigation. Section 3 describes the proposed geozone-aware RRT* framework and the jellyfish-inspired optimization method. Section 4 presents the experimental setup and validation using real-world data from Piombino, Italy. Section 5 discusses the results, including trajectory quality and computational efficiency. Finally, Section 6 concludes the paper and outlines directions for future research.

II. Related Work

Path planning for UAVs has evolved significantly in recent years to meet the demands of increasingly dynamic and constrained airspace. Among various techniques and sampling-based algorithms, particularly RRT and its variant

RRT*, are widely used due to their ability to explore high-dimensional search spaces with low computational cost.

However, the classical version of this methodology has known limitations when applied to real-world operations. It does not account for dynamic constraints or airspace regulations such as altitude ceiling, restricted zones, or geozone boundaries. To address these shortcomings, researchers have proposed a range of extensions to the base algorithm.

Zhang et al. [4] , for example, introduced a potential-based RRT* approach that integrates artificial potential fields into the sampling logic, improving convergence in dense urban areas. In multi-agent scenarios, Li et al. [3] proposed a cooperative bidirectional RRT* framework using potential field heuristics to coordinate multiple UAVs while avoiding conflicts in shared airspace.

Also, hybrid methods have been developed to combine global path generation with local, real-time responsiveness. Himanshu et al. [5] presented an RRT and Velocity Obstacles (VO) structure for Unmanned Traffic Management (UTM), where initial paths are generated offline using RRT, and then refined in real time using VO to avoid dynamic conflicts. Peng et al. [6] extended this idea by incorporating B-spline smoothing to generate continuous, flyable trajectories suitable for UAVs.

In parallel, bio-inspired optimization strategies have been proven to increase effectiveness for post-processing and path selection. Wang et al. [7] proposed a Multi-Objective Jellyfish Search Algorithm (UMOJS) that integrates swarm conduct with adaptive weighting to optimize path length, smoothness, and threat avoidance. While these methods improve flexibility and robustness, they still treat regulatory constraints as a post-processing step. In contrast, our approach integrates geozones awareness directly into the path generation process.

III. METHODOLOGY

The proposed path planning framework, summarized in the workflow diagram on Figure 1, consists of two integrated stages: (1) a geozone-constrained RRT* algorithm that ensures regulation-compliant path generation from the outset, and (2) a jellyfish-inspired stage that selects the best raw trajectory based on multiple objectives and applies smoothing to improve flight stability while preserving regulatory compliance.

A. Geozone-Constrained RRT* Expansion

To ensure that all generated paths are both physically feasible and legally compliant, we extend the standard RRT* algorithm by incorporating regulatory constraints directly into the tree expansion process, ensuring both safety and regulatory compliance, which has been a growing concern in autonomous UAV operations, as highlighted in recent regulatory reviews [8]. Each candidate edge is generated against the following conditions:

- Collision avoidance with 3D environmental obstacles, such as buildings.
- Geozone compliance, ensuring that the edge does not enter prohibited or restricted airspace volumes [2], [9].
- Altitude limits, verifying that flight segments do not exceed the maximum allowable height. typically, 120 meters Above Ground Level (AGL) for civil UAVs in Europe [10], but we restrict our planner to an 80m maximum height and 10m for the minimum limit for a better match with the test scenario characteristics.

Each candidate edge is accepted only if it satisfies all physical and regulatory constraints. This decision process is formalized in equation (1):

$$isValid(e) = \begin{cases} 1, if\ e \cap O = \emptyset,\ e \cap G = \emptyset,\ h(e) \in [h, H] \\ 0, \quad otherwise \end{cases} \quad (1)$$

where e is a candidate edge, O is the set of obstacle volumes, G represents restricted geozones, and $[h, H]$ denotes the edge's altitude range.

If any of these constraints are violated, the edge is rejected from the growing tree. However, instead of passively discarding invalid branches, the planner includes adaptive behaviors aimed at overcoming persistent constraints, unlike methods such as RRT with Velocity Obstacles or spline smoothing, which handle constraints only at post-processing [5][6]. For instance, if a branch consistently encounters a building, the algorithm attempts to reroute above it, provided the new segment remains within legal altitude bounds and moves the UAV closer to its goal.

Regarding the initial and final positions, the planner does not accept arbitrary coordinates. Instead, both start and goal points are randomly selected from a set of physically realistic surfaces. Either ground-level terrain or the rooftops of volumetric structures. If any of the selected start and goal points lie within a restricted geozone, the system first attempts to descend to the nearest collision-free, permitted height. If this is not possible, it searches nearby horizontal positions until such a descent becomes feasible. The horizontal distance allowed within restricted zones during takeoff or landing is strictly limited to ensure regulatory compliance.

To promote flight realism and efficiency, the planner favors stable, horizontal trajectories, maintaining constant altitudes whenever possible. Vertical movements are permitted only when horizontal progress is obstructed. Even in such cases, the algorithm evaluates nearby altitude levels and selects the one with the least obstacle density, balancing safety and flight efficiency.

These three mechanisms, as detailed in Figure 1, operate sequentially and iteratively: constraint-aware expansion ensures initial feasibility, adaptive maneuvering handles repeated constraint conflicts, and temporal validation filters results within a time-bound planning horizon. This combination of constraint-aware expansion, adaptive maneuvering, and temporal validation ensures that all generated trajectories are not only technically feasible but also optimized for legal, safe, and practical deployment in urban airspaces.

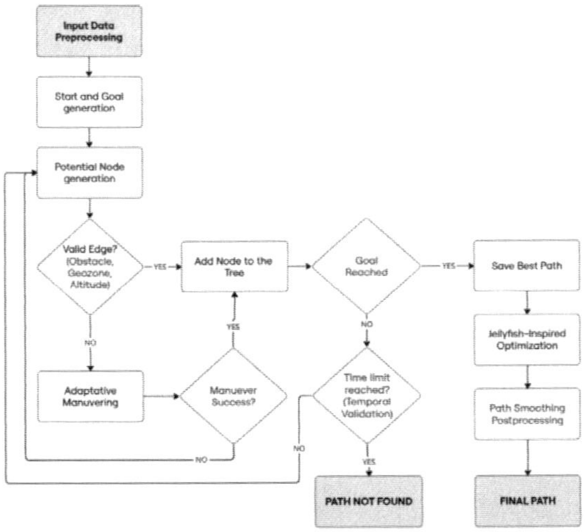

Figure 1. The algorithm's workflow.

B. *Jellyfish-Inspired Optimization*

After generating a set of 10 valid trajectories, the second stage of the framework selects the most suitable one using a lightweight, jellyfish-inspired optimization approach, which has been proven effective in balancing flight criteria [7]. The optimizer, emulating a multi-objective decision-making process, evaluates each candidate path using a composite score derived from three performance metrics:

- Path Length: Total 3D distance traveled, serving as a proxy for energy consumption and mission duration.
- Threat Cost: A cumulative penalty based on proximity to static obstacles, reflecting the overall collision risk.
- Smoothness: Quantified by the sum of angular deviations between consecutive trajectory segments, indicating flight stability and control effort.

All metrics are normalized using min-max scaling to ensure comparability. A randomly sampled weight vector $w = [w_1, w_2, w_3]$, with $\sum_{k=1}^{3} w_k = 1$, is used to compute the composite score for each path i, as presented in the equation (2).

$$Score_i = \sum_{k=1}^{3} w_k \, . \, normalized_{k.i} \tag{2}$$

This stochastic weighting strategy draws inspiration from the adaptive foraging behavior of jellyfish swarms, which adjust their movement patterns in response to environmental stimuli. By sampling different weight combinations for each run, the optimizer implicitly explores diverse trade-offs, sometimes favoring shorter paths, and at other times prioritizing safety or stability. The path with the lowest total score, computed using the randomly sampled weight vectors on all 10 initial simulations, is selected as the final trajectory. This selection mechanism is modular and can easily be extended to incorporate additional criteria, such as estimated energy usage, time-of-day restrictions, or weather-related risk.

In practice, this two-stage approach produces UAV flight paths that are balanced, regulation-compliant, and operationally efficient, making them well-suited for use in real-world UAM scenarios

IV. Case Study: UAV Delivery in Piombino, Italy

To evaluate the effectiveness and real-world applicability of the proposed path planning framework, a comprehensive case study was conducted in Piombino, Italy, as a representative mid-sized coastal city with a mix of residential, industrial, and open areas. The location provides a realistic urban environment with varied terrain, man-made obstacles, and multiple regulatory geozones, making it well-suited for testing UAM planning methods under complex conditions.

A. *Environment and Data Sources*

Terrain elevation data and official geozone definitions were obtained from authoritative sources and national geospatial databases. These datasets were integrated into a 3D simulation environment that reflects Piombino's actual topography and airspace constraints [9][11].

B. *UAV Specifications*

The UAV simulated in this study is based on the commercially available multirotor platform DJI Matrice 300 RTK, shown in Figure 2. This model was selected because of its size, weight, and flight characteristics, detailed in Table I, are suitable for typical urban applications such as parcel or medical delivery. Its specifications defined the applicable regulatory context, under EASA's Open Category A3, which imposes specific restrictions on flight altitude, proximity to people, and operational environments [10].

Also, the working temperature range aligns with local conditions in Piombino, and its maximum speed and flight time allow it to cover up to 75.9 kilometers, which is more than sufficient for the scale of the study area. While these specifications are not directly integrated into the path-planning algorithm as constraints, they serve to ground the case study in a realistic operational and regulatory context. This ensures that the mission profiles and legal framework used in the simulation reflect real-world deployments, while also supporting potential future extensions such as energy-aware planning or charging station integration.

Figure 2. DJI Matrice 300 RTK [12].

TABLE I. THE DJI MATRICE 300 RTK MAIN SPECIFICATIONS [12].

Parameter	***Value***
Max Payload	3.6 kg
Max Flight Time	55 min
Max Speed	23 m/s
Operating Temperature	-20ºC to 50ºC

C. Mission Scenarios

A total of sixteen diverse origin-destination pairs were randomly defined across the study area to ensure broad coverage of different locations, obstacle densities, and geozone configurations. Although all scenarios are set within the same urban environment, the variation in spatial layouts allows the planner to be tested under diverse conditions. The complete list of origin-destination pairs is provided in Table II. Each pair was executed 10 times per configuration to assess its robustness and consistency. Consistent success rates and stable path quality metrics (e.g., length, smoothness, and threat cost) across runs indicate the planner's reliability.

TABLE II. ORIGIN-DESTINATION PAIRS.

Nº	**Start**			**Goal**		
	Lon	Lat	Alt	Lon	Lat	Alt
A	10.5375	42.9361	30.9	10.5313	42.9310	22.7
B	10.5350	42.9307	25.2	10.5335	42.9295	0.5
C	10.5326	42.9330	27.7	10.5301	42.9320	22.9
D	10.5360	42.9308	29.5	10.5377	42.9376	20.5
E	10.5318	42.9305	0.5	10.5393	42.9363	0.5
F	10.5354	42.9356	31.4	10.5364	42.9308	25.4
G	10.5332	42.9303	32.1	10.5384	42.9339	0.5
H	10.5398	42.9298	0.5	10.5314	42.9289	34.4
I	10.5363	42.9293	21.5	10.5336	42.9349	28.4
J	10.5381	42.9345	30.6	10.5327	42.9329	0.5
K	10.5353	42.9292	0.5	10.5333	42.9320	0.5
L	10.5335	42.9289	40.9	10.5296	42.9288	26.1
M	10.5339	42.9343	0.5	10.5399	42.9261	0.5
N	10.5320	42.9301	0.5	10.5334	42.9303	32.1
O	10.5375	42.9361	30.9	10.5377	42.9296	28.1
P	10.5358	42.9369	23.3	10.5374	42.9308	25.7

V. RESULTS

To assess the performance and adaptability of the proposed UAV path planning framework, we conducted a series of experiments focusing on the impact of varying the STEP_SIZE parameter during RRT* tree expansion. This parameter determines the incremental distance between nodes and plays a critical role in balancing solution quality, computational cost, and planning success.

A. Parameter Evaluation: STEP_SIZE Impact

Four values of STEP_SIZE (4, 8, 12, and 14 meters) were tested across all origin-destination pairs. These values were selected based on early development insights: smaller steps improved the path significantly, increased execution time, while larger steps sped up computation but reduced success rates. Also, step sizes larger than 14 meters were not considered in the final evaluation because they sometimes caused the planner to miss narrow obstacles, slipping over them without proper detection due to the coarse sampling resolution. Finally, a time limit of 250 seconds was set for each run to keep computation times within practical bounds.

Table III summarizes the average performance across all metrics for each tested STEP_SIZE, based on multiple executions of each configuration. The evaluation metrics included are:

- Success Rate (%): Percentage of runs that resulted in valid, regulation-compliant paths.
- Execution Time (s): Average computation time required to generate a trajectory.
- Path Length: Total 3D distance of the trajectory.
- Threat Cost: Cumulative penalty for proximity to obstacles, indicating environmental risk.
- Smoothness: Sum of angular deviations between consecutive path segments.
- Node Count: Average number of RRT* nodes required to construct the path.

TABLE III. IMPACT OF STEP_SIZE ON PERFORMANCE.

Metric	**4**	**8**	**10**	**12**	**14**
Success Rate (%)	40.0	70.62	71.88	79.38	77.5
Execution Time (s)	68.06	45.22	43.55	24.81	25.26
Path Length	4.34*	4.02*	4.0*	4.22*	4.07*
Threat Cost	2.67*	1.32*	0.96*	0.69*	0.6*
Node Count	2.01*	2.01*	1.62*	1.71*	1.39*
Smoothness	6.15*	3.16*	2.64*	2.42*	2.03*

B. Path Smoothing and Postprocessing

RRT*- based paths, though feasible, often include abrupt angular changes or minor detours that can degrade flight stability, increase energy consumption, and challenge onboard autopilot systems, a limitation also noted in prior RRT*- based planning studies [13]. To address this, we applied a postprocessing smoothing algorithm designed to enhance path fluidity while preserving legality. The smoothing process uses a sliding window averaging filter: each waypoint is adjusted based on the average position of its immediate neighbors, effectively reducing sharp transitions. To ensure regulatory compliance, each smoothed waypoint is validated against all constraints (e.g., geozone boundaries, altitude limits, and obstacle collisions). If a violation is detected, the point is reverted to its original position.

Post-smoothing, the trajectory's smoothness metric is re-evaluated, typically revealing significant improvements with negligible changes in path length or threat exposure. This enhancement contributes to more energy-efficient and dynamically stable UAV flights. Figure 3 illustrates this process on a representative example, Experiment D, corresponding to the start and goal points listed as pair D in Table II. The raw trajectory - Figure 3(a) exhibits several unnecessary turns and sharper angles, while the smoothed version - Figure 3(b) shows a more direct and stable path towards the destination, offering more realistic and controllable flight behavior.

a)

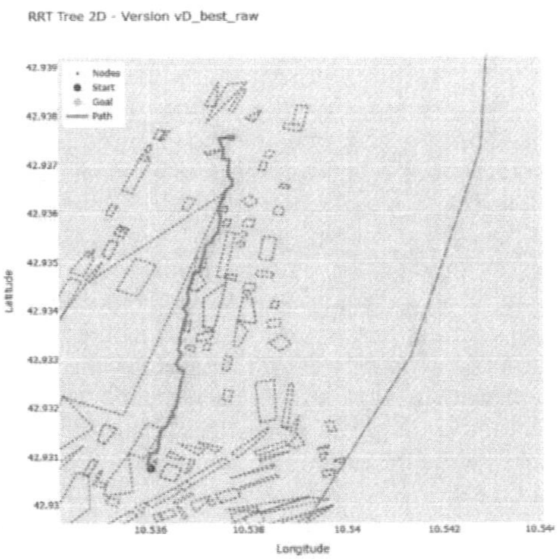

b)

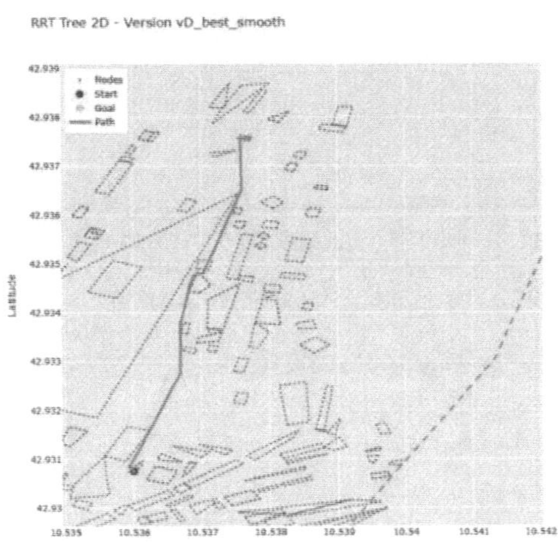

Figure 3. Trajectory Comparison between (a) initial RRT* path and (b) postprocessed trajectory.

C. Optimization Results

The jellyfish-inspired optimizer was used to select the best trajectory among 10 valid candidates for each mission scenario. Based on a composite score, combining path length, smoothness, and threat cost with randomly sampled weights, the optimizer prioritized balanced paths without additional computational cost. In all test cases, the selected trajectories already demonstrated better overall quality than the raw alternatives. After selection, a lightweight smoothing process is applied to further enhance flight realism by reducing sharp turns. This step preserved all regulatory constraints while improving the trajectory's fluidity and controllability, both assessed using the smoothness metric, based on angular deviations between path segments, which indirectly evaluates the presence of abrupt transitions.

Together, the optimization and smoothing stages significantly improved the final path quality, enabling safe, efficient, and realistic UAV operations in constrained urban environments.

D. Geozone-Aware Path Planning Result

A key objective of the proposed algorithm is to ensure that all trajectories remain fully compliant with regulatory geozone constraints. The geozone-aware RRT* planner achieves this by filtering geospatial violations during node expansion and enforcing strict exclusion of restricted volumes throughout the trajectory. The only permitted geozones entry occurs during the initial takeoff or final descent.

Figure 4(a) provides a clear example of this behavior, taken from experiment D. In this case, the UAV has the start point inside a restricted geozone and performs a vertical descent to reach a valid flight altitude before continuing horizontally toward the destination. Conversely, Figure 4(b) shows the trajectory from experiment E, where neither the start nor the goal lies within a restricted zone. And the final example is in Figure 4(c), where both the start and the goal points are inside the restricted volumes of the geozones. The comparison demonstrates the planner's adaptability to different constraints or situations.

Overall, across all scenarios, the planner successfully generated paths that respected all airspace regulations, maintaining safety and legality even in dense and constrained urban environments.

VI. Discussion

The proposed path planning methodology demonstrates a robust ability to generate compliant geozones, obstacle-free UAV trajectories across a wide variety of urban conditions. The combination of the regulation-aware RRT* expansion with the multi-objective trajectory selection and the final smoothness postprocess results in a consistent, safe, and efficient performance. Results across all 16 mission scenarios show that the algorithm can adapt to various obstacle densities and regulatory constraints.

However, the performance variations observed across different configurations suggest that some mission scenarios are inherently more complex. This is likely due to the spatial arrangement of certain origin-destination pairs, the proximity of restricted zones, or the presence of specific obstacles that hinder maneuverability. These findings highlight the importance of introducing more refined and context-aware constraints when defining operational areas.

The methodology also presents some structural limitations. It relies on static representations of geozones and environmental obstacles, requiring manual updates to reflect changes in airspace regulations or urban infrastructure.

Nonetheless, once the input data is updated, the algorithm is fully capable of recalculating optimized trajectories under new conditions without requiring internal modifications. This highlights its adaptability to different urban scenarios and regulatory environments, provided that accurate and up-to-date inputs are supplied. Moreover, as currently implemented, the system assumes a single-UAV context and does not incorporate weather conditions, which may influence practical deployment feasibility in complex environments.

a) b) c)

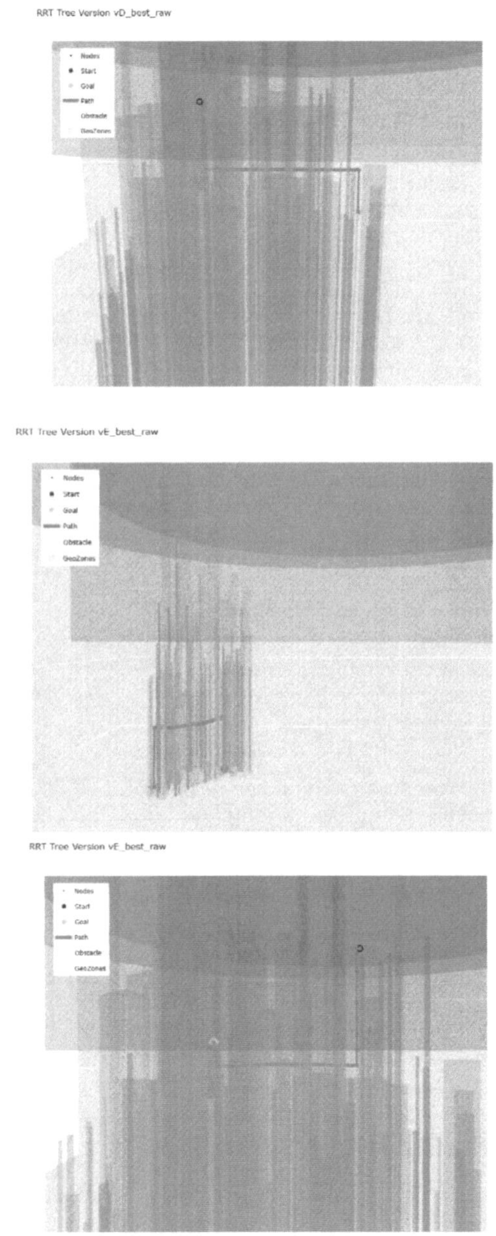

Figure 4. Trajectory Comparison between (a) example of geozone-aware vertical geozone avoidance, (b) example of a path without geozones interference, and (c) example of a path with start and goal points inside a geozone.

VII. Conclusion and Future Work

This work introduces a UAV path planning strategy that respects both physical and regulatory constraints in urban airspace. By combining a geozone-aware RRT* with a lightweight, jellyfish-inspired optimizer, the system generates safe, efficient, and regulation-compliant trajectories. Tested on real-world data, the planner delivered consistent results while maintaining low computational demand and requiring only lightweight postprocessing. Specifically, the path generation times remained within practical limits, and the postprocessing stage, focused on smoothing and basic filtering, was kept simple, without relying on heavy optimization frameworks or complex interpolation techniques.

As future work, we aim to analyze which specific areas of the urban environment systematically reduce planning success or limit trajectory feasibility. Identifying such "critical areas" could help make operational decisions, such as excluding them from permitted takeoff or landing locations or avoiding them as candidate sites for drone charging stations. This geospatial analysis would support more reliable UAV operations by guiding the placement of more infrastructure and enabling smarter regulation-aware launch and recovery strategies. In parallel, incorporating dynamic geozone updates via real-time regulatory feeds or U-space integration could further enhance the system's adaptability to temporary restrictions and evolving airspace conditions.

Another future direction involves enabling multi-UAV coordination under shared constraints, especially in scenarios like medical supply distribution or emergency evacuation. This may require a centralized coordination layer or negotiation protocols. Additionally, temporary regulations issued during events like wildfires or floods could be incorporated through real-time updates from civil authorities or firefighting services

Acknowledgment

This work was supported by the funding from the European Union's Horizon 2020 research and innovation program under grant agreement No 101007134 and Regional and community funding: Special Research Fund's project Robust and Trustworthy Smart Mobility Systems (grant number BOF/STA/202209/004).

References

[1] E. Fakhraian, I. Semanjski, S. Semanjski, and E. H. Aghezzaf, "Towards Safe and Efficient Unmanned Aircraft System Operations: Literature Review of Digital Twins' Applications and European Union Regulatory Compliance," Jul. 01, 2023, Multidisciplinary Digital Publishing Institute (MDPI). doi: 10.3390/drones7070478.

[2] European Union Aviation Safety Agency (EASA), "Geo-Zones – know where to fly your drone." Accessed: Jan. 20, 2025. [Online]. Available: https://www.easa.europa.eu/en/light/topics/geo-zones-know-where-fly-your-drone#:~:text=Geo%2Dzones%20are%20portions%20of,protect%20the%20privacy%20of%20others

[3] C. Wu, Z. Guo, J. Zhang, K. Mao, and D. Luo, "Cooperative Path Planning for Multiple UAVs Based on APF B-RRT*

Algorithm," *Drones*, vol. 9, no. 3, Mar. 2025, doi: 10.3390/drones9030177.

[4] X. Xu, F. Zhang, and Y. Zhao, "Unmanned Aerial Vehicle Path-Planning Method Based on Improved P-RRT* Algorithm," *Electronics (Switzerland)*, vol. 12, no. 22, Nov. 2023, doi: 10.3390/electronics12224576.

[5] Himanshu, J. V. Pushpangathan, and H. Kandath, "RRT and Velocity Obstacles-based motion planning for Unmanned Aircraft Systems Traffic Management (UTM)," Feb. 2023, [Online]. Available: http://arxiv.org/abs/2302.14543

[6] M. Peng and W. Meng, "Cooperative Obstacle Avoidance for Multiple UAVs Using Spline_VO Method," *Sensors*, vol. 22, no. 5, Mar. 2022, doi: 10.3390/s22051947.

[7] X. Wang, Y. Feng, J. Tang, Z. Dai, and W. Zhao, "A UAV path planning method based on the framework of multi-objective jellyfish search algorithm," *Sci Rep*, vol. 14, no. 1, Dec. 2024, doi: 10.1038/s41598-024-79323-0.

[8] E. Fakhraian, I. Semanjski, S. Semanjski, and E. H. Aghezzaf, "Towards Safe and Efficient Unmanned Aircraft System Operations: Literature Review of Digital Twins' Applications and European Union Regulatory Compliance," Jul. 01, 2023, *Multidisciplinary Digital Publishing Institute (MDPI)*. doi: 10.3390/drones7070478.

[9] d-flight, "Italian u-space platform." Accessed: Jun. 02, 2025. [Online]. Available: https://www.d-flight.it/web-app/

[10] European Union Aviation Safety Agency (EASA), "Open Category of Civil Drones." Accessed: Feb. 01, 2023. [Online]. Available: https://www.easa.europa.eu/domains/civil-drones/drones-regulatory-framework-background/open-category-civil-drones

[11] Regione Toscana, "Geoscopio." Accessed: Jun. 02, 2025. [Online]. Available: https://www.regione.toscana.it/-/geoscopio

[12] DJI, "Matrice 300 rtk specifications." Accessed: Jun. 02, 2025. [Online]. Available: https://www.dji.com/be/support/product/matrice-300

[13] H. Li, R. Jia, Z. Zheng, and M. Li, "Energy-Efficient UAV Trajectory Design and Velocity Control for Visual Coverage of Terrestrial Regions," *Drones*, vol. 9, no. 5, May 2025, doi: 10.3390/drones9050339.

International Academy, Research,
and Industry Association (IARIA)
412 Derby Way
Wilmington, DE 19810

ISBN 979-8-3313-2331-8

CURRAN ASSOCIATES INC.
proceedings.com

9 798331 323318